DATE

HOW OPERA GREW

Books by

ETHEL PEYSER and MARION BAUER

HOW MUSIC GREW

MUSIC THROUGH THE AGES

HOW OPERA GREW

PORTRAIT OF THE YOUNG MOZART

Attributed to Jean Baptiste Greuze. Reproduced by permission of the Belle Skinner
Collection of Musical Instruments, Holyoke, Massachusetts, through
the generosity of Katherine Skinner Kilborne.

HOW OPERA GREW

FROM ANCIENT GREECE
TO THE PRESENT DAY

Ethel Peyser and Marion Bauer

FOUNDED 1838

GPPS

G. P. PUTNAM'S SONS   NEW YORK

Acknowledgment is gratefully made for permission to quote from the following published works:

Essay by Erwin Stein in *Benjamin Britten: A Commentary on His Works
from a Group of Specialists,* edited by Donald Mitchell and Hans Keller.
Published by the Philosophical Library, New York.
Benjamin Britten: A Sketch of His Life and Works by Eric Walter White.
Copyright 1948, 1954 by Boosey and Hawkes, Ltd., London.
International Cyclopedia of Music and Musicians. Excerpts reprinted by
permission of Dodd, Mead and Company, publishers.
The Juilliard Review. Copyright by the Juilliard School of Music.
My Life by Richard Wagner, revised edition 1936. Published by the Tudor
Publishing Company, New York.
Menagerie in F Sharp by Hans Heinsheimer. Copyright, 1947, by H. W.
Heinsheimer. Published by Doubleday and Company, Inc., New York.
Mozart: His Character, His Work by Alfred Einstein. Copyright 1941 by
Oxford University Press, Inc.
Opera by Professor E. J. Dent. Excerpts quoted by permission of the author
and the publisher, Penguin Books, Ltd., London.
Opera News. Excerpts quoted by permission of the publisher, the Metro-
politan Opera Guild, Inc.
Wagner as Man and Artist by Ernest Newman. Published by Alfred A.
Knopf, Inc., New York.

MANUFACTURED IN THE UNITED STATES OF AMERICA

VAN REES PRESS • NEW YORK

THIS BOOK IS DEDICATED
TO
OUR MUTUAL FRIEND
CLAIRE LINGG
WHOSE INTEREST AND ASSISTANCE
HAS BEEN TO US
A CONTINUOUS STAFF AND INSPIRATION

Music expresses that which cannot be said and on which it is impossible to be silent.

VICTOR HUGO

With a straight face, opera can tell the impossible as if it were possible.

ETHEL PEYSER

Form is the external expression of inner content. . . . The most important thing is not whether the form is personal or national or full of style, not whether it corresponds to the chief contemporary trends or exists quite alone. . . . The most important consideration in the question of form is whether or not the form has grown out of inner necessity.

VASILI KANDINSKI

Translated from *"Über die Formfrage,"*
Der Blaue Reiter, Munich, 1914.

Acknowledgments

WE ARE delighted to be able to express our appreciation to the many busy people who helped us in the preparation of this book.

To Rosamond Tinayre we are deeply indebted for the many musical anecdotes which she collected and for the exquisite lines of music script which would have glorified the pages of this book were it not for the high cost of printing.

To the *Musical Quarterly* and the *Juilliard Review* we are particularly grateful for material which could not be obtained elsewhere. The kind co-operation of Boosey and Hawkes, publishers, ever ready to lend us books whenever possible and to supply us with information, is highly appreciated. Among other valuable aids to us was the *Metropolitan Opera News,* particularly Frank Merkling of its staff.

We wish to thank Professor Charles Denoe Leedy, head of the Music Department of Mount Holyoke College, South Hadley, Massachusetts, for making it possible to obtain from the college library at "off hours," and from his own collection, books of much value to us. At the same time we wish to express our thanks to the librarians of the Williston Memorial Library at Mount Holyoke College for their always gracious and intelligent assistance in our hunt for data.

Nor can we forget our ever-faithful music librarians at the Main Branch and the Music Branch of the New York Public Library for their constant help in supplying data, books, pamphlets and solution to problems over the telephone. In particular we wish to thank Gladys Chamberlain, head of the Fifty-eighth Street Music Library, and her assistant Catherine Lee Miller, ever amiable, alert and able, as well as Paul Meyer of the Drama Division of the Main Branch of the New York Public Library.

We also owe our thanks to Liljan Espenak, accomplished dancer and teacher, for data on modern schools of the dance ballet, and to Grace Bliss Stewart for constant aids.

To Professor and Mrs. Harrison Potter we wish to express our gratitude for the use of their charming apartment on the edge of the Mount Holyoke Campus where we worked during the months of two summer vacations; to Florence Foss, professor emeritus and former chairman of the Art Department of Mt. Holyoke College, for giving invaluable suggestions and advice; to Anne Hull, piano instructor at the Juilliard School of Music; and to Alix Young Maruchess, violist.

Last but not least we wish to thank those firemen of the editorial world, our assistants, without whom—well, without whom this book would never have been written: Marea Adleman, with her editorial flair; Gloria Bader, music scholar; and Anne Spreemann, meticulous, resourceful and swift; as well as Ruth Ellis, Ruth Lewis, and Rose Livant, interested pinch-hitters whenever an alarm was sounded.

E. P.
M. B.

CONTENTS

Act V. Opera Waves National Emblems

Act VI. Opera—A Bundle of the Arts

Act VII. Opera Is Led by Great Commanders

Act VIII. Opera "Goes Modern": Twentieth Century

Act IX. Opera in America from Revolutionary Days to Television

Introducing Opera

THE old cracked street organ dispensing Verdi and Donizetti to the man in the street (and to the children too) is a thing of the past. But in this day of radio, television, and phonograph recordings, opera, once the property only of royalty and nobility, is within reach of every man, woman, and child. Throughout this land the Saturday afternoon broadcasts from the stage of the Metropolitan Opera House in New York City have brought opera, the unapproachable luxury, within the experience of millions of listeners.

Here, there, and everywhere, opera-giving groups, amateur and semiprofessional, have sprung up in schools, colleges, clubs, and church communities. The "little theatre movement" has been duplicated by little opera groups that have nurtured and awakened interest in that "bundle of the arts" known as opera. Even the moving picture industry has recognized it as a vehicle for its products, and a few successful cinema showings of famous operas, such as the most recent screening of *Aïda,* have drawn crowds and perhaps wakened a curiosity.

The widespread interest in opera has aroused a desire to know more about its background and its history. There are many volumes telling the stories of the operas, but this book is designed solely to supplement such valuable books by telling the kaleidoscopic story of how opera grew throughout the ages, as simply as possible, to meet the needs of the layman or young student. Moreover, with all the opera departments that have developed in the music schools, colleges, universities, and study groups, we hope that *How Opera Grew* may be a timely contribution.

How Opera Grew covers the history of the subject from its prenatal period in Greece (800 B.C.) to Stravinsky's *The Rake's Progress* (1951) and Menotti's *The Saint of Bleecker Street* (1955). The history of opera is like the history of a nation, with its ups and downs, its advances and retrogressions, its maladies and its cures, never in a straight line but in constant zigzags, dependent on the fluctuation of social and economic change in each era.

Furthermore, *How Opera Grew* surveys all varieties of lyric stage works covering the field between the extremes of *opera seria* and American musical comedy and "grass-roots" opera.

It stresses the interrelation of the various arts which are bone and sinew of the complete opera. For that reason we have included short discussions of the libretto, song, ballet, scenery, overture, and orchestra.

The authors lay no claim to having written an exhaustive account between these covers, lest the reader be burdened with detail, and the book be too long for practical and comfortable use. Many prominent composers are not mentioned because they have not contributed significantly to the growth of opera.

New York   E. P.
June, 1955   M. B.

ACT I. Before the Beginnings of Opera

SCENE I

The Seeds of Opera Are Planted by the Ancient Greeks

THE goat might be to blame for it all! Eight hundred years before the birth of Christ, the ancient Greeks, in the worship of their god Dionysus, dressed in goat skins and danced around a little altar accompanied by pipes and perhaps lyres (small harps).

The lovely Greek country served as scenery. The space around the altar was the stage. The little altar, the wine cups, the flowers, the wreaths and other articles used in this worship were the stage "props" (or properties).

This early theater grew as the Greeks grew in their experience of beauty until their drama became a world-enriching national and religious ritual.

Three hundred years after this (500–400 B.C.), modern opera's remote grandparent was born: the Greek theater, for which the greatest plays of all time were given. They included tragedy, comedy, and satyric drama, which always presented a procession of satyrs (beings that are half man and half goat). These plays, instead of taking place around the little altar in the fields, were produced on stages in front of which was the same type of altar, in the great outdoor arenas called *amphitheaters* (from two Greek words: *amphi,* which means "around" or "on all sides," and *theatron,* "to be seen"). The most important Greek drama was called *tragoidia,* from two words meaning goat, *tragos,* and song, *odos.* So it is not difficult to trace opera, the offspring of Greek drama, back to the goat-song (and dance) and other primitive rituals. Among these is the Greek *komos,* song, or *komoidia,* the revel-song, from which we get our word *comedy.*

The Greek language held the seeds of opera. Music, the art of reasoning, and the adventure of beauty were the bases of Greek life. A child's first school was the music school. He was taught gymnastics, mathematics, public speaking, music, singing, and reading. Such training made the Greeks competent critics. All the studies went under the name of *mousike,* or music, to honor their nine Muses who were goddesses of the arts, or "Matron Saints of the Arts."

In Greek drama, a distant grandparent of opera, most important was the classic tongue of ancient Attica, a half-sung, half-spoken language. It is supposed to have sounded somewhat like the chant of the Christian Church. Instead of accenting syllables of a word, as we do, the Greeks lowered or raised the tone and pitch of the voice. Such a language is easier to put to music than Italian, French, or English. It never occurred to the ancient Greeks to separate their poetry from music. To this team they wedded dancing, so in their poetic plays it was natural for the lines to be spoken, often along with dancing and always with pipe or strings. What a pity the gramophone had not been invented to record the productions of the plays of Aeschylus, Sophocles, Euripides, Aristophanes, and many others!

Standing in line was an ancient custom. Baseball fans have copied the Greeks! Had we lived in 500 B.C., we would have been among long lines of people waiting all night at the portals of the amphitheaters for admission to the national Greek festivals which lasted several days.

As the people entered the amphitheater, they saw a great open-air arena with a stage at one end, a semicircular space in front of the stage with a little altar in the center, and around the edge of the semicircle a row of stone armchairs or seats for the influential and wealthy. From these, stretching back and upward, were row upon row of shelves for seating the audience of many hundreds. To each spectator (in Rome and probably in Greece) admitted free, the State gave a small bone tablet upon which was carved a skull and crossbones. From this ancient ticket we get our name for those admitted free to the theater—"deadheads."

The space in front of the stage was called the orchestra, from the Greek word which means *dancing.* Today the orchestra is still the portion of the theater in front of the stage. We call the seated group of instrumentalists an orchestra because its usual place is in front of the stage.

The Greeks had a treasury of dramatic legends which comprised their religious beliefs, known to us as Greek mythology. Among the countless stories loved by the poets and the people were those of the Trojan War; of brave Hector and his beloved wife, Andromache; of valiant Achilles; of the gory and tragic history of the Agamemnon family; of the most popular Eurydice and her "boy friend," Orpheus. There were also stories of Ariadne and Apollo, the adventures of the Argonauts, and the terror-laden tales of Oedipus. Be prepared to meet these heroes and heroines even in the twentieth century in such operas as those of Stravinsky, Richard Strauss, Milhaud, and others. Then, too, there were merry tales of Phoebus (Apollo) and Pan and the plays by the comic poets, such as *The Frogs, The Birds,* and *The Wasps* by Aristophanes, in which he criticized by ridicule and innuendo the habits, customs, and laws of his fellow Athenians.

The plays for these national Greek festivals were chosen by vote of a committee. The prize-winning dramatist was given honors, a laurel wreath, but no money. The government did not pay for their production, but a wealthy citizen, called a "liturgist," did. *Leitourgia* means service and was a form of taxation. The liturgist for the drama each year was called the *choregus.* He paid for, trained, fed, housed, and costumed the actors and chorus—a vast tax! For this, his name, with those of the poet and flute player, and the date were inscribed on a little *choregus* monument in the *agora,* or market place, in Athens.

In the beginning, the goat-song and dancing required no individual parts. The group acted in unison. But as the plots grew more and more complex, actors up to three were added—never more than four—although mute soldiers, pages, messengers, and others made entrances and exits.

The philosopher Aristotle laid down laws that all action must be controlled by one set of events; that it should cover approximately one day; and that the scene should conform to one general location. These rules held drama in bonds as late as the seventeenth century in France.

In addition to the actors, there was, in the early days of Greek drama (around 500 B.C.), the *choros* (chorus), another word for dance. In the half-moon space in front of the stage the *choros* explained in words and gestures the story of the drama and was a part of the action. Today we have printed librettos giving the whole story of the opera. In ancient Greece the stories were well known, and the *choros,* in a way, took the place of the libretto.

As time went on and the actors became more necessary, the *choros* lost its importance. It was, however, never like the chorus of modern days that limits itself to singing, nor was it like the old-time ballet in which the women dancers wore stiff skirts (*tutus*) resembling lamp-shades. The Greek chorus was more like the twentieth-century ballet, which, although it hardly ever speaks, describes a story in bodily motions. Dancing, to the Greeks, was poetry without words, in which the body made explanatory gestures. A Greek writer, expressing the high skill of an orator, said that "he danced with his hands." The Latin poet Ovid, in his "Art of Love," advised a young lover anxious to win a maiden to "sing if his voice was good and to dance if his arms were flexible."

All the actors wore large masks. These masks represented comic faces for comedy, tragic for tragedy, women's faces for feminine impersonations (for women did not act in the classic Greek theater); and other masks were designed so that everyone in the vast theater might know what to expect of the actors. The Greek theater has given the modern theater the mask as its symbol.

Audiences were not slow to show their reactions, and were particularly definite as to their feelings for the dramas. They demanded, with cheers or jeers, clear singing speech which could be heard to the farthest row of seats. To make this possible, the actors wore footgear (*kothurnos*) which raised them some inches from the stage floor. Allegedly great copper bowls were placed in the back of the amphitheater as sound resonators. This was the early ancestor of our loudspeaker systems.

So the Greek plays had their choruses, actors, music, poetry, and dancing. Nor were they without scenery. They used many complicated devices for changing the scenes and making the action better understood. Their best known bit of machinery was what in Latin was called *deus ex machina*—the god from the machine. This was a device for lifting above or dropping "below stage" a god (or goddess) with lines to say. When the phrase is used today, it means that somebody is "pulling the strings" or influencing a project. Other bits of scenery brought ghosts to the stage; trapdoors in the stage floor admitted gods from the underworld and the rivers. To make lightning, a plank painted with a white streak on black was shot out of a box onto the stage! (See page 290.) All of which gave ideas to the Italians, who built opera years later. The Greeks were ingenious even though they had no electricity or jet-propelled machines.

Ingenious as they were, they used very few instruments, nor did they ever think of separating poetry and music. The principal instrument was the *aulos,* which sounded like our oboe and sometimes was used in pairs, looking much like the letter "v." It was blown from the point of the "v." The number of *auloi* (plural of *aulos*) used in a performance varied, as did the small harplike lyres, the strings of which were plucked with a *plectrum* (pick) as is the mandolin.

Little has come down to us of the actual music, but we do know that in spite of their artistry and inventiveness the Greeks never sang in harmony. Everyone sang and played the *same* melody. What is known of their complicated musical system and notation has been dug out by scholars. Yet upon the ideas of the Greek modes (scales) were fashioned our early Church modes; and upon the scientific findings of men like Pythagoras, inventor of the monochord, we based the science of sound (and music). The monochord is a one-stringed instrument with a movable bridge by which, when pressed down, Pythagoras found the string could be subdivided into intervals such as octaves, fifths, fourths, thirds. (For a more detailed account of Greek music see *How Music Grew* and *Music Through the Ages* by Bauer and Peyser.)

ROME BORROWS

Rome, pre-eminent in engineering, law, and the science of war, borrowed most of her ideas for drama from Athens. It was fashionable in the Roman Empire and in other nations to do things the Athenian way. Every wealthy Roman child had a Greek tutor and studied Greek and the Greek arts.

The Roman name for actor was *histrio*. We get our word, *histrionic,* meaning theatrical, from this. The Romans were more theatrical or showy than the Greeks. Instead of philosophical and poetical drama they liked vast spectacles, garish and noisy circuses and gladiatorial contests. And what started in earliest times in Rome, their pantomime and fun-making, never developed into great drama. Their poets did not put their legends into verse comparable to that of the Greek dramatists.

The exceptions were their comic dramatists who managed to ridicule the ways of men and women, much in the manner of the opera buffa of later centuries. Among their greatest writers were Plautus (254–184 B.C.) and Terence (190–158 B.C.), whose classic Latin was for ages a model to all scholars. The works of these men were islands of joy when the Dark Ages enveloped Europe, for their plays gave the early writers for the dramatic and musical Italian stage many ideas.

Seneca, much later (3 B.C.–65 A.D.) branched out in tragedy and was a follower of the Greek Euripides. He even used the same names and plots. He used a chorus, not to help the action, but for the display of rhetoric. Horace, Rome's greatest poet, kept the playwright down to the "unities" established by Aristotle.

The Roman love of display is shown in their noisy instruments: cymbals, trumpets, rattles, drums, and castanets. They also used the *kithara,* or harp, to which the kitharoedic chant was sung.

The great value of the Roman plays was that they kept formal drama alive and satisfied the Roman Empire's thirst for processions, plays, pageants, and garish shows, which blossomed in the Middle Ages into plays that were the definite background of Italian opera.

The value of the Greek drama was that it was a basis for all Western music and drama. Opera did not spring fully developed from the head of Zeus, as did Minerva, but was the blossoming of centuries of art

SCENE II

Early Backgrounds of Opera

Music has traveled two roads: the sacred, or music of the Church; and the secular, or music of the people. These roads, occasionally merging and occasionally going their own independent ways, influenced the early history of music. Indeed without indispensable contributions from each, opera would never have entered upon the path that developed into one of the important highways of music.

The Church supplied many of the necessary ingredients, such as scales, modes, notation indicating pitch and rhythm, and rules governing the movement of parts, before music could become an art. The people supplied popular songs and dances, and the means of carrying them from town to town, from castle to castle, and from country to country.

GREGORIAN CHANT

The Church developed the stately plain song, the first great art music of Europe. This was a proselike chant, set to texts from the Bible and sung in unison in which the rhythm was dictated by the syllabic stress of the words. The chants were made up of groups of tones, supposedly based on the Greek scales or modes, and even carrying the same name, although the medieval or church modes worked quite differently. In the fourth century, St. Ambrose, Bishop of Milan, organized the chants and wrote hymns (words only) that are still used. Later St. Gregory, Pope of Rome (540–604) had them collected into what is known as the Gregorian Chant

For centuries these chants were used as single-line melodies without accompaniments; that is, they were monodic. As time went on, successful attempts were made to combine two or more melodies, and the musicians learned how to add other parts to the original plain song, developing into what was called polyphony (many-voiced music).

The first attempts at putting a second voice to the plain song may

9

sound crude to our ears for we are not accustomed to hearing a tune
sung a fifth or a fourth below the plain song melody, called the *cantus
firmus,* or fixed song. The new part was the "tenor" (from the Latin
tenere, to hold), because the singer "held" the melody around which
the other parts were sung. The high male voice is still known as the
tenor. This first style of singing in parts was called *organum* (or'ga-
num) and was used in various ways from the ninth to the twelfth
centuries.

From this innovation came richer and more complicated lines of
melody weaving in and out that developed into counterpoint, or the
practice of sounding two or more notes or strands of notes together—
not as we write chords vertically, but as we weave them horizontally.
"Counterpoint" comes from the Latin *contra,* meaning against, and
punctum, point, the early term for note: *punctus contra punctum,* or
"note against note."

But when homophony, or harmonic music, arrived, some centuries
later, this style of many-voiced polyphonic music was relegated to the
background. Two "golden ages" of music, that of Palestrina and of
Johann Sebastian Bach, were heirs of this development from plain song
as were also the first experiments in opera, which began about the time
of Palestrina's death (1594).

(All of this is discussed in more detail in *How Music Grew* and
Music Through the Ages by Marion Bauer and Ethel Peyser.)

The birth of opera was brought nearer by the development of the
Mass with its daily sections and holy-day portions, with its choral
treatment and its many moods; and by the plays based on Bible stories,
lives of saints and heroes, and on chivalry, presented sometimes in
costume in the oratories of the churches, on the steps of cathedrals, and
in town squares or in the backs of wagons in the villages.

MINSTRELS AND TROUBADOURS

Music had its enrichments, too, from secular sources in dance and
one-line songs with light instrumental accompaniments. These
stemmed from the folk and minstrels from the tenth to the fourteenth
centuries. Some of the minstrels composed their own songs and some
used the songs of others with or without changes. Some were from
the trades, many were from the nobility and royalty, and even from the
clergy. Many of the higher classes were troubadours, from Provence
in the south of France, trouvères from the north of France, and
minnesingers (singers of love) from Germany. All of them were the

poets and composers of their own songs. There were also the goliards, wandering clerics, often singers of ribald songs; and the best known of the minstrels, the *jongleurs,* who juggled and trained bears to do tricks, and assisted the troubadours. The minstrels, including a few women, also sang, danced, or did both, and carried delighting gossip and news from town to town.

The majority of the minstrels' songs were of love and of heroes as in the *chansons de geste,* the *Chanson de Roland,* the national epic of France, and of Huon de Bordeaux, the hero of Weber's opera *Oberon.* Their songs among many others were of work, of play, of spinning and weaving (*chansons de toile*), of their exploits and services (*sirventes*) to their lords.

Among other valued offices to music, the minstrels brought to unborn opera a variety of song forms, the main body of which were homophonic, with one line of music, the melody, and no interwoven melodies as in the sacred polyphonic songs. Their songs, it is surmised, were sometimes accompanied by pipes, lutes, or vielles, small portative organs, guitars and psalteries. The dances, of course, were accompanied by instruments. There were also the *alba* or *aubade* (dawn song), the *lai,* or the *virelai* which was also called the *chanson balladée,* and the rondeau. Many of the songs, stemming from the people, were humorous and gay. The minstrels added short instrumental preludes and postludes at times, and two-line *ritournelles* after each stanza, giving independence to instruments which later blossomed into such pieces as preludes and overtures. Later the ritournelles were to be played to keep the audiences amused during the intervals when the actor-singer was not on the stage. Other reminders of the minstrels are the engaging *chants-fables* one of which has come down to us with music in the charming *Aucassin et Nicolette.*

There were many famous troubadours and trouvères, such as Richard the Lion-Hearted, King of England, and his faithful Blondel de Nesle; Thibaut, King of Navarre; Bernart de Ventadorn; Colin Muset who rose from the status of jongleur to that of trouvère because of the engaging songs he composed; Adam de la Halle (c. 1240–1288) who wrote *Le Jeu de Robin et Marion,* a pastoral play recognized as the first opéra comique; and countless others.

When homophony arrived, the Church frowned on it because of its secular popularity, and the churchmen were unable to encourage its use if they wished to keep their posts. But such men as Leontin in the twelfth century and Perotin in the thirteenth, in Paris, advanced music

from their important places in the Chapel of the Holy Virgin Mary
on which site the Cathedral of Notre Dame now stands.

MOTET AND MADRIGAL

Philippe de Vitry (1291–1361) also sought to make song more
melodious. During his day the *motet* was born. This was a form of
choral music usually without accompaniment, sung to sacred texts.
Even the different parts of the Mass were composed as a string of
motets.

Song is now traveling toward its life in opera, for the madrigal and
the *frottola,* outside of the Church, are smiled upon by the clergy. The
madrigal is a part song, polyphonic in structure, usually for two or
three to eight voices, and the *frottola* is a song of stanzas harmonized
or homophonic in style, falling between the more stately (polyphonic)
madrigal and the lightest of country songs. The madrigal is a secular
counterpart of the motet, and sometimes when written to a sacred
text it brought variety to sacred polyphony.

As the madrigal developed in the sixteenth century in Italy, it
became a direct forerunner of opera, as for example in the hands of
Orazio Vecchi (c. 1550–1605) who wrote *L'Amfiparnaso,* a musical
counterpart of the *commedia dell' arte,* the comedies based somewhat
on ancient models and presented extemporaneously by strolling players.
Whether Vecchi's type of "madrigal comedy" was merely sung or
whether pantomime accompanied an offstage performance of the music,
is not known. In 1954, *L'Amfiparnaso* was presented at Tanglewood in
the Berkshires as an opera, with the five-part madrigals sung by two
groups and the action mimed with much burlesque, in the style of the
commedia dell' arte.

REVIVAL OF LEARNING AND INVENTION OF PRINTING

The momentous fifteenth century brought the fall of Constantinople
(1453) to the Turks, whom we may thank for the exodus of scholars
as refugees to Italy and other parts of Europe. These scholars brought
with them the classical learning of ancient Greece and Rome, devoured
by Western people in the fruity Renaissance or Rebirth of Learning
which led to the birth of opera in Florence at the turn of the seventeenth century. Also, through the passion for new learning and the
search for truth, this became the era of discovery and of great men.

The invention of movable type by Gutenberg (1397–1468) does not
sound operatic, but it did give wider currency to music, vocal and

instrumental, so that it was disseminated more broadly. Whereas before only the rich could read, now the poor were to have their opportunity. The first printing press of movable type was set up in the reign of Charles VII of France and forty-one years later Ottaviano dei Petrucci printed the first musical score in Venice, a book of motets. Although Venice became the music center, music was also studied and composed elsewhere.

MARTIN LUTHER AND THE CHORALE

Martin Luther's chorales came to reform church music long grown corrupt. The most lewd words in the vernacular had been sung in church along with sacred tunes and sacred texts. Sometimes popular tunes were used as *cantus firmi*. This Luther changed. The music had grown so difficult that only professionals could sing it. Luther wanted music that congregations could sing as well as the choirs, and the words were to be in the tongue of the country, not only in the language of the scholars and of the church. So Luther made up simple melodies, borrowed well known folk tunes or popular songs, adapting them to religious texts. Here again did the secular troubadours and other minstrels, with their stock of one-line melody and folk tunes, unwittingly enrich the Church, and help to create a secular art.

Luther with his vertical music loosened the clutch of polyphony by gaining favor in high places for the song and accompaniment. He helped along the independence of the instruments through their function as legitimate accompaniments.

The people now understood the words of their songs in church and in play. Soon the major and minor scales, as we still use them, became established, and through the years music gradually grew into the sublime forms as we know them.

No doubt stirred by Luther's reforms, the Church tried to purify its music, which was rapidly disintegrating. Palestrina, because of his genius, simplified and made more melodic the polyphony of old, and wrote sometimes in a lovely homophonic style. He taught composers how to mass voices effectively and did many other things so well that the era is known as "Palestrinian," and he was called "Prince of Music."

In addition to the golden age of polyphony in Italy, the work of the Burgundian, Flemish, Franco-Flemish Schools and of France helped to perfect polyphonic writing. The establishment of an accompaniment to the chorale and the development of monody (solo song) freed the instruments to "stand on their own feet." Now the song itself, although accompanied by instruments, grew in individuality and beauty.

So much for the deeds of the Church in developing song. It provided the materials to be used in opera, but the actual shove that pushed music into opera came from the people.

SCENE III

Mother Church Mothers the Theater

OUR own theater, the father of opera, stemmed as did the Greek theater from religious worship influenced by minstrels and other secular composers. The church fathers, in their wisdom, presented religious plays, for they knew that it is easier to teach by means of plays than by lectures and sermons.

The dramas given by the medieval Church were based on the May Festivals (*Maggi*), rituals or offices of the Church—Christmas (*Noël*), the Passion of Christ, the Entombment or Office of the Sepulcher, the Resurrection, and so on. These early plays had no spoken words, save occasionally when Christ spoke without music. Plain song (chant) and hymn tunes were used, and the syllables of the words furnished the rhythm.

One of the oldest of these Church plays is the drama *The Three Marys*—inspired by the Office of the Sepulcher—and has five characters: the three Marys, an angel, and a Guardian of the Sepulcher (of Christ).

Another is *The Wise and Foolish Virgins,* a liturgical or religious drama. A Latin chorus, with a sad and grave melody, opens it. Then the Archangel Gabriel, in Provençal (French) announces the coming of Christ and tells of his sufferings. Each strophe or verse ends with a refrain, of which the conclusion has the same air as the first stanza. "The Foolish Virgins" confess their sins and ask help of their sisters. They sing in Latin and their three strophes have different airs.

They end the song in Provençal: *"Dolentes! Chétives! Trop i avem dormit";* or, in English: "Unhappy ones! Sinners! We have slept too long." Their good sisters prepare the oil and tell them to trim their lamps. The strophes change melody as persons change. Finale: Christ enters and censures the Foolish Virgins—in chant, not to music.

A German fourteenth-century liturgical play is called *Die Marien- klage (Mary's Lamentation).* This is partly sung and partly spoken.

15

Besides these sacred plays were the very popular *lauds* (praises), religious poetry in the vernacular (language of the people). Among them was one giving a dialogue between the Virgin Mary and Jesus. This was followed by a lamentation of the Mother, pointing to Pilate, and was rudely broken into by the crowd with "Crucify Him! Crucify Him!"

These lauds were the parents of the elaborate *sacra rappresentazione* (sacred representations) in which gesture and music were used, but very few spoken words. The play givers did not yet know how to use words without song to help the action of a play. Occasionally, however, when Christ had to speak, it was without music. It's difficult to believe that words alone were of least importance to the sacred representations, one of the most important grandparents of opera! There were interludes of music, or *intermezzi,* between the scenes. Sometimes they were stories of warriors told in gesture and action, with musical accompaniment. Sometimes they were stories from Greece and Rome, told with dances; and sometimes they presented tilting scenes.

In the fourteenth century, the Church entertained and educated the people with such plays as *The Fall of Lucifer, Three Kings,* and *Abraham.* The trade guilds, too, gave versions of sacred stories in plays. For example, *The Deluge* was often given by the Water Carriers' Guild. This bit of gross fun tells us that Mrs. Noah did not want to embark on the ark and leave her friends on land. She suggests that Mr. Noah find himself another wife and give her a holiday. But Shem, her son, not too politely shoves her into the ark. She is so angry that she gives Noah a resounding slap in the face! Thus did early players, in their crude and elementary humor, poke fun even at Bible characters.

The religious drama, however, was in high favor, for the Passion play, known to us today, derived from the Church plays of ancient days. This dramatic story of the last week in the Saviour's life, with some music, was acted by townsmen and women usually chosen for their good characters. The most famous of the Passion plays is that of Oberammergau, Germany, given first in gratitude by those spared from the plague in 1633. It was given every ten years, with two or three exceptions, up to Hitler's time, and was revived in 1950.

Before opera dawned, the people, particularly in Italy, France, and England, reveled also in mystery, miracle, and morality plays given by Mother Church. In Italy, they had the devotional plays, like the French miracle plays, in which portions of the church services (or liturgy) were enacted. Such plays told the story of The Last Supper, of the good deeds and miracles performed by the saints, and other Bible narratives. These had an influence on the building of opera because of the blend of music, religion, story and scenery.

The mystery plays were not about crime, but related the Mystery of the Acts of the Apostles, of the Passion of Christ, of the Annunciation, of the Ascension, and so on. There was singing and the use of instruments during the processions announcing the plays when they arrived in a town, as the calliope announces a circus in our towns. Music also announced the beginning of an act. Even "dubbed in" music, like that of the modern cinema, was employed, for an angel would seem to play the harp onstage when it was actually played by someone backstage. Yet they did, sometimes, play their own harps. Among the instruments used in those days were: pipes; flutes (played across the tube, transverse, and flutes blown straight); *tabors,* little drums like tambourines without the jingles (bells); trumpets; bagpipes; organs of which the large pipes were played to represent violent storms or great occurrences, even to heralding the Devil himself. It is easy to see what these early Church activities did for opera.

In addition to the mystery play the miracle play, on the deeds of the saints and of miracles, was produced. A typical miracle story used by Jules Massenet in the nineteenth century for his opera *Le Jongleur de Notre Dame* (*The Juggler of Our Lady*) was taken from Anatole France's *Étui de nacre* (*The Mother-of-Pearl Box.*) It tells enchantingly of a poor young juggler who could do nothing but his juggling, and so felt inferior to the learned monks who had rescued him from starvation. One day to show his gratitude he juggled as best he could before the statue of Our Lady, the Mother of Jesus. She descended from her pedestal, reached out her hand, blessed him, and took him up to heaven with her, for he had done the very best he knew.

Much like the miracle play and the mystery play was the morality play, beloved by the English. The characters personified the traits of human beings with such names as Greed, Purity, etc. They always pointed morals. The best-known is *Everyman*. It has little music and its speech is mostly intoned.

These were watched by the clergy, who soon discovered that their parishioners were not as serious as they seemed to be. So they decided that they themselves would act in and produce plays. Before long the churches were full of elaborate scenery, and it was here that Mother Church actually built the foundations of the theater and opera. When the scenery outgrew the altar spaces, the plays were given on the church steps, in the market squares, on backs of carts, and in booths set up in the streets.

This great love of acting among clergy and people was seen in Italy, in the May Festivals or *Maggi* given in the countryside, with dance, song and instruments. But in the cities such as Florence and Rome, they gave the most important dramatic spectacles which influenced opera —the Sacred Representations (*Sacre Rappresentazioni*). The foremost architects, painters, musicians and poets combined to make them beautiful. They might have been advertised:

A PLAY—THE ASCENSION OF THE SAVIOUR

A BIBLICAL MIRACLE

Play by Lorenzo de' Medici
Poem by Poliziano
Scenery by Brunelleschi
Technicolor by Tintoretto
Scenery painted by Raphael and Leonardo da Vinci
Music by Alfonso della Viola

Scene: The streets of Florence are seething with people. Shops are closed and houses are locked up. Everyone is dashing hither and yon for good vantage points from which to see the sacred representation, about to begin. Little playhouses have been built on nearly every street and square. Each cardinal has his own theater with which to entertain the Pope, who is in town for the day. The principal square is a mass of white and blue, and street arches are decked in wreaths of greens and flowers. On every pillar stands a young angel singing holy chants. In the center of the Square is the tomb of Jesus, around which sleeping soldiers lie, and angels nearby guard the group. Then an angel singing the "Song of Resurrection" descends from the "sky" on a rope attached to the roof of a tent. After the song, intense silence fills the square . . . when *crack!* . . . an explosion of powder shatters the peace. The soldiers awake. Christ arises from the tomb and sings in Italian of the salvation of the world He died to save. Angels bear Him heavenward, more music is played, and the play is over. [Adapted from *Some Musicians of Former Days* by Romain Rolland. New York, Henry Holt & Co., Inc., 1915.]

This presents but a meager idea of the complicated scenery and machinery used in these early dramas, given as often in the churches as in the streets. Sometimes the Good were taken up into heaven, which was often built with doors! Sometimes the Bad were lowered beneath the stage floor. Real fire was used. One day, an actor personify-

ing "God the Father" was burned to death, and at another time a
church rocked by "thunder and lightning" was almost destroyed by
fire. But the people wanted scenery and were thrilled by fantastic stage
"props" and zoos of dramatic animals, which could have made a
twentieth-century composer envious!

It wasn't long before the people in love with these spectacles "took
over" and gave plays without religious stories. Lorenzo de' Medici, the
Magnificent of Florence, poet-musician, and patron of art and artists,
wrote many songs (*canzoni* in Italian) and dances which delighted the
people. Later, one of his plays particularly noteworthy was *St. John and
St. Paul,* in which his own son, Julian, acted. It was very much like
the Roman tragedies, which often aped the Greek drama.

Lorenzo's friend, Poliziano, started something! He wrote a play
called *Orfeo,* about the Greek demigod Orpheus, one of the most
popular young men of Greek mythology. It began the rage for "operas"
about Orpheus and Eurydice, which hasn't died yet. *Orfeo* was given in
Mantua in 1471. The scenery was built, as it would have been for the
mystery plays, by the most accomplished artists. It had the usual
musical prelude, incidental music, and solo songs, only then beginning
to be used in plays with music.

Orfeo was the last of the "sacred representations," although it was far
from sacred. Because of this, the sacred representations were soon forbidden by the Church. But another kind of play developed because of
the indomitable will of the Italians to give, act in and see plays—what
we call now classical Latin tragedy and comedy, such as those by
Plautus, Terence, and Seneca, given with music and scenery. The coming of this new kind of play brought opera a step nearer.

The people disdained the sacred stories, as we now disdain silent
motion pictures. Their desire to write independently of the Church
helped to develop opera. Isn't it a strange contradiction that the Church
gave us the plays in the beginning, and that breaking away from the
Church also helped toward the birth of opera? But what better mixture
could there have been than art works created by Holy Church and
developed by men outside of the Church?

The people and the nobles welcomed these new plays, for they were
sick unto boredom of the Bible stories and even of the mythological
Venuses and Cupids. They were, however, infatuated with the amusing
and often vulgar stories of the Latin authors whose characters were
very much like themselves. They enjoyed seeing the types of people
they knew, such as the greedy mistress, the bootlicker, the miser,

wealthy patrons, and maidens not too good to do naughty things. Yet it took a few hundred years to bring to them this type of everyday characterization, such as *La serva padrona* by Pergolesi, 1733.

People of wealth and rank attended these shows in such numbers that Hercules, Duke of Este (Ercole, Il Duce d'Este) built a theater in the fifteenth century which held five thousand people. It was under the supervision of the poet Ludovico Ariosto (1474-1533). Four of his plays were about the rascally tricks of a servant who tries to get money for his master to carry on his love affairs; a fifth is about the same servant who manages to keep his master cherished by two wives at the same time. Ariosto's *The Pretenders* is one of the sources of Shakespeare's *Comedy of Errors*. When the writer of these usually coarse comedies was adversely criticized, he would loftily say, "Well, I am only doing what the great Plautus or Terence did before me!"

From a letter to the Duke of Ferrara about Ariosto's play, *I Suppositi* (*The Pretenders*), with scenery by Raphael, we quote: "After every act there was an interlude for music for fifes, bagpipes, two cornets, viols, lutes, and a little organ with various sounds. There was a flute and a voice which gave much pleasure. A harmony of voices was also to be heard . . . the last interlude was 'Moresca' (a dance scene) which set forth the fable of the Gorgons." This use of music had nothing to do with the story of the play, and was a form of the intermezzi, or little plays between the acts of the main play. Now what was to become opera had all the elements it needed except one: dramatic dialogue—recitative—(1) to connect its songs and dances and (2) to produce continuous action.

These tragedies and comedies were given with splendor at the ducal courts and palaces by men of wealth who subsidized the artists and composers of the day. It is amusing to find, however, that Ariosto, patronized by the Duke of Ferrara, boasted that he paid for his own house. Patronage was important, for there were no theaters or public halls for concerts. Art makers had to be "patronized" until the nineteenth century, when Beethoven and Mendelssohn freed composers.

As early as the fourteenth century the Italians were enjoying the commedia dell' arte or Comedy of Art. The actors traveled all over Italy, presenting amusing plays in and out of doors. Most of the time they invented their lines as they went along. This commedia laid a foundation for a comic type of opera. The people, however, tired of its stock characters: Pantalone, the stupid shopkeeper, who was deceived by everybody, including his wife; the bragging, swashbuckling captain;

Punchinello, the hunchback with red nose; and the most famous ones who still live, Pierrot, Pierrette, and Harlequin.

Neither Punchinello nor Pierrot could stave off hard times for Italy. Rome was sacked once more, by Emperor Charles V's army, and three years later (in 1530) Florence was conquered and humbled. For many years the petty princes and kings tried to control men's minds, and the Church and the Spanish tyranny (the Inquisition) demanded obedience ..."or else"! It was a time of witch-hunting by irresponsible power-seeking men. Censorship stalked. Men like Michelangelo were accused by lesser men and jealous ones of heretical and irreligious work. The classic comedies and tragedies were condemned as immoral and were stopped.

But nothing could bind the spirit of the Italian people. They loved drama and spectacles more than we love sports and motion pictures. So they took another important step (sixteenth century) toward opera in their *dramma pastorale,* or pastoral drama—*pastor* means shepherd. These were peaceful, soothing dramas, not about saints or Greek gods but about shepherds and their loves who dwelt in Arcadia, an imagined region where Love ruled and struggle was unknown.

The people were craving for peace and release from misery, and from the struggles between petty princes and the Church, which brought them neither security nor happiness. Yet on every hand they heard of the ease and extravagance of the nobility.

The pastoral drama, with its sweetly named characters, Daphnis, Chloë, Corydon, and Amaryllis, captivated audiences. This was the last link in the chain binding words and music, which was soon to become opera.

One of the most admired writers of pastoral dramas was Torquato Tasso (1544–1595), author of *Jerusalem Delivered* (a tale of the Crusades). His *Aminta* gained high favor, too. It was set to music by Gesualdo, a seventeenth century modernist. The young Claudio Monteverdi, who was to become the foremost writer of early opera, also used Tasso texts. Another interesting pastorale, by Giovanni Guarini, was called *Pastor Fido,* the "Faithful Shepherd." The *librettos* (poetic texts) of *Aminta* and *Pastor Fido* became models for future opera writers, although many used the works of the ancient dramatists for material.

The pastoral play is a mild mixture of lyric poetry, narrative poetry, and song, rather than exciting action. Like everything else in which the people at first delighted, these *pastorales,* too, became monotonous.

Their lack of action, excitement, and timing weakened them, and they died of their own inadequacies.

We come now to an exciting point on the march of opera, for we are on the step just before opera enters. The steps are indicated in the following diagram:

FIRST OPERA HOUSE

1637

5. The Camerata—Recitative (dramatic Italy)
4. Pastoral Drama
3. Classical Comedy and Tragedy and Commedia dell' arte
2. Sacred Representations—May Festivals
1. Devotional Plays—Lauds (dramatized)

While these steps were being mounted, France, Belgium, the Netherlands, Germany, and Great Britain, particularly England, were becoming ripe in music under some of the greatest of the composers and were almost as ready for opera as Italy, its inventor.

ACT II. Opera Is Born

SCENE I

Beginnings of Opera in Florence, Italy

AFTER many trials by Italian poets and composers, the story with music had found a way to write itself down, a way to keep time, to use stage scenery, make costumes and stage machinery. It had its poets and new forms of poetry, its dramatists to write plays, and its composers to set them to music. To its stories of ancient Greece and Rome, it added religious stories of every day and of idealized mortals in the guise of shepherds and shepherdesses. It could tell in words and music a tragic, comic, heroic or fantastic tale. It used preludes to introduce its plays, interludes and intermezzi between the acts—verses or dances which later became ballets—and sometimes a curtain, usually drawn to the sides. These are all present today in opera, but in the seventeenth century, the story with music still lacked the steepest and most difficult "last step"—the one to connect the parts and make them *act*.

What was going on in Europe? France grasped the ideas of Italy and adapted them to her own special genius in polished and new verse forms in order to fulfill her passion for setting texts to music. England was reveling in her *masques* (groups of singers and dancers, costumed and masked), and in the illustrious poets who wrote for them—Ben Jonson, John Milton and others. Germany was developing her strings of folk tunes and dances into *Singspiel,* subsequently improved by Hans Sachs and his colleagues; and the composers of the Burgundian and Franco-Flemish schools, such as Guillaume de Machaut, Guillaume Dufay, Josquin Després, and many others, had been adding beauty to vocal writing.

Nevertheless, up to the sixteenth century the musical plays or dramas with music were *not* dramatic. The music, chantlike, made the jolliest or most thrilling story stately and slow. Imagine today using a church chant to tell a tale of football or of gay romance. There was need for a speed-up. After each song (usually a madrigal), the action bogged down or stopped completely. There was no way of joining the songs. Nothing

25

held action and music together. The stories set to music would not act!
Something had to be done. But what?

THE CAMERATA

With the dawn of the Renaissance or Rebirth of Learning, about forty
years before Columbus discovered America, the Italians drank deep of
the learning Eastern refugee scholars brought with them after the fall
of Constantinople. Although the Italians had known the classics, the
refugee scholars stimulated and excited a real thirst for the Greek and
Latin arts. In the beautiful palace of Count Giovanni Bardi (1534-1612)
in Florence, they formed a club called the *Camerata,* or "People of the
Chamber [or Room]." The word for "room" in Italian is *camera.*
(Our *camera* is a dark chamber wherein the image to be photographed
is captured on a film or plate.) Here are some of the best-known members of the Camerata who did what they didn't intend: created opera.

COUNT GIOVANNI BARDI	A mathematician, musician and poet, who wrote scenes for masques and inspired his fellow artists.
LAURA GUIDICCIONI	Poet, who wrote the poems for the first two operas composed for the Camerata.
VINCENZO GALILEI	Storekeeper, lute player and father of Galileo Galilei, the astronomer.
EMILIO DE' CAVALIERI	Writer of ballet and *dramma per musica,* "drama with music"; composer of *Representation of the Soul and Body.*
GIULIO CACCINI	Singer and composer of *The Combat of Apollo and the Serpent, Euridice, Il Nuove Musiche (The New Music),* a collection of songs written in monody.
OTTAVIO RINUCCINI	Poet, who wrote the poem for Peri's *Euridice,* as well as collaborating with Monteverdi later.
JACOPO PERI	Poet and the composer of *Dafne* and *Euridice,* the first recognized operas.

There must have been much discussion and even quarreling among these club members. The "old-fashioned ones" must have wanted to keep the old-time, polyphonic, slow melodies based on the Gregorian Chant and the old madrigal forms; while others must have wanted to use a newer way to make the stories more dramatic. Here are some of the questions that must have caused excitement: How can we combine music and poetry so that together they express the story? How can poetry and music be so mated that a battle story will not sound like a lullaby, or a wedding scene like a burial? How can we make an exciting story excite, and a soothing story soothe? How can we carry on a story without stopping it between the songs or the stanzas of a song? How can we make drama with music, dramatic? How can we fit the word to the music, and the music to the word—still (1955) the most difficult problem for every writer and translator of opera texts. Yes, there must have been violent arguments. But it worked out fairly well and the results were invaluable.

In passionately trying to imitate the Greek drama with its differently inflected language from the beautiful Italian, they invented song-speech or recitative (*stile parlante*), speech half sung, half declaimed, with more or less musical accompaniment. It is well they were brave enough to try the impossible, for in doing so they fell upon this device to connect song, scene and dance, which in the hands of future professionals led to the building of a new and beloved art—opera.

By degrees with the invention of recitative the composers were led to the greater use of the *one*-melody song with accompaniment (monophonic or homophonic) and this gradually banished the madrigal, the beautifully woven but undramatic polyphonic song. (So recitative, with its instrumental accompaniment, helped to establish harmony. By freeing instruments from the voice, the making of music written just for instruments, such as preludes, *ritornelles* and *sinfonie* or overtures, was furthered.)

The Camerata accomplished something, even if it was different from the Greek drama, because this connector-recitative activated both the religious drama, *oratorio;* and *dramma per musica,* or opera.

At first composers did not use the word *opera. Melodrama,* or drama with melody, was one of its names. What *we* mean by *melodrama* is an over-theatrical "thriller," usually non-musical. Yet it would not be incorrect to say that many operas are true melodramas, because of their tragic and lurid plots. The word *opera,* meaning "work," was first generally used about the end of the eighteenth century, for dramma per musica.

THE BIRTH OF ORATORIO

But before opera was actually born, and even afterward, Mother Church encouraged Philippo Neri (1515-1595), a devout priest (who later was canonized) to present his Biblical stories with music. They were given in the small chapels or *oratories* of the churches where people went to pray (*orare*—Latin "to pray"). Therefore the plays were called oratorios. St. Philippo was aided by his friend the illustrious Palestrina.

Oratorio was given sometimes in costume, using religious stories, whereas opera took its stories usually from Greek mythology. The Church did not object to the use of dancing when it helped the story. Of course these were the stately dances of the day, such as the *pavane,* the *sarabande.* The same instruments were used in the oratorio and in the dramma per musica. So Mother Church once more influenced what was to become opera, particularly in Italy, where was developed a most beautiful and smooth way of singing: *bel canto* (beautiful song).

The Church oratorio with recitative, song and scenery hastened the birth of opera. One of these oratorios was *La rappresentazione di anima e di corpo* (*The Story of the Body and of the Soul*), in which Emilio de' Cavalieri (1550-1602) made use of monody (tune and accompaniment) as early as 1600. It was little more than a string of hymnlike, one-line melodies connected by recitative, for the first time breaking away from polyphonic music. It wasn't opera in spirit; it was more like a morality play. Laura Guidiccioni, the woman member of the Camerata, wrote the words. De' Cavalieri overused declaimed speech to such an extent that it would be tiresome to us today. Yet in spite of this, he had amazingly good ideas as to what an "opera" should be like:

The instrumentation [he wrote] should change according to the emotion expressed. An overture or instrumental and vocal introduction are of good effect before the curtain rises. The *ritornello* and *sinfonia* (used as the opener or overture to the drama with music) should be played by many instruments. A ballet, or better a singing ballet, should close the performance. The actor must seek to acquire absolute perfection in his voice . . . he should sing with emotion . . . as it is written . . . he must pronounce his words distinctly . . . The performance should not exceed two hours . . . Three acts suffice and one must be careful to infuse variety, not only into the music, but also the poem and even the costumes.

Sounds modern, doesn't it?

A contemporary of de' Cavalieri was Jacopo Peri (1561–1633). He was one of the Camerata, and his opera *Dafne,* on a text by Ottavio Rinuccini (1562-1621), is called the first opera. With one-line music and accompaniment (homophonic), it tells the story of the lovely nymph Daphne, who, being pursued by Apollo, was turned into a laurel bush by Zeus, to save her from capture. Apollo, finding in his arms a bush instead of the maiden, made the laurel his favorite flower. The laurel wreath has ever since been a symbol of artistic achievement because Apollo was the God of the Arts.

Peri's *Dafne* had a chorus and a sizable orchestra and was acted in costume, of course. It made him so widely known throughout Europe that he was invited to write an opera to celebrate the wedding (1600) of Maria de' Medici of Florence and Henry IV of France. It was one of the good customs of those days to order musical works for special occasions. So Peri, with the poet Rinuccini, wrote the opera *Euridice.* This drama with music came nearer to what we call opera because it was far more melodious and less stiff than the epoch-making *Dafne.* Its orchestra contained one harpsichord, two lutes, one bass viol and three flutes. Dull as this might seem now, *Euridice* with its sad story was a popular opera in its day.

Euridice is the earliest opera of which we have the complete text. Poor *Dafne* was lost! Many Eurydices have trod the opera stages, including the most beautiful of all—Gluck's, in *Orpheus and Eurydice.* The first *Euridice* is merely a pastorale in ten scenes, all of them in shepherd-like settings, composed of dances, choruses, solos, entrances and exits of characters. You may note that Euridice's beloved husband Orfeo is not included in the title. As then, so now, glamour was ascribed to the girls! This opera begins with a prologue or introduction, in which the character Tragedy announces the subject of the story and flatters the audience—a pleasant habit! And, lest the reader grieve, let it be said that in this version Orfeo and his beloved wife are united in the end.

Another *Euridice* soon followed, written by Giulio Romano Caccini (Rome, 1546, Florence, 1618), to a poem by Rinuccini. From these Italians France learned about opera, when it was still more declamatory and more chantlike than lyrical.

In this *Euridice* by Caccini there was no overture or sinfonia. He concealed his instruments behind the scenes, as they were still menial members of *dramma per musica* and had to hide their faces! He used a harpsichord (*gravicembalo* in Italian), a bass lute (*chitarrone*), a lyre which might have had twenty-four strings and was played with a bow instead of being plucked (*lira grandi*), a *theorbo*—sometimes called a double lute, but in Italy, a large lute. These instruments propped up the recitative.

The action in *Euridice,* carried by the solo voice in recitative, was slow and steady. It was poetry little more than chanted. Caccini used mainly background music. At the end of every verse, he wrote a cadence, a "falling," or ending. These cadences became monotonous. Occasionally, there are songs or dances (a forerunner of Italian ballet) at the ends of the scenes. This early "try" at opera was monotonous and had little expression. But it was dressed in rich costumes and scenery, because of which opera has always been the "sport" of the wealthy.

Caccini's most important contribution is a collection of monodies, *Il nuove musiche* (*The New Music*), one-line melodies, the "modern" music of his era. He also started the solo song on its enticing way.

With these experiences of dramma per musica by Peri, Caccini, Cavalieri and others, its poets and composers who were cultivated amateurs, the members of the Camerata helped to create opera.

Among the steppingstones from oratorio and Signora Laura's drama to opera was the work of Giacomo Carissimi, born in 1604 near Rome, where he died in 1674. In his oratorios he developed recitative and built the church cantata so skillfully that it very shortly displaced the church madrigal. The *cantata* was a string of songs connected by a narrator, a speaker on whose words were hung story and music. Carissimi is important too because of his disciples Cesti, Alessandro Scarlatti and others, who carried on Italian opera. Unfortunately most of Carissimi's works were destroyed, or sold as rubbish—during a church squabble!

SCENE II

Opera in Venice, Rome, and Naples

PERI and the Camerata in Italy did start opera! But these pioneers stuck too closely to the first lifeless patterns. While Peri in his dramma per musica had excellent taste and used recitative, this new connection device was still flavorless and dull. Peri, Cavalieri, and Caccini presented the *favola,* the popular name at first for opera. It was delicate and charming, but it needed humanizing, warmth, variety and action in order to express feeling.

When *favola* or opera was coming into being in Italy, each city or province or group of cities was presided over by a nobleman who had won in battle, or inherited, the throne of a sumptuous court. These noblemen were often art lovers, men like the Gonzaga of Mantua, the Barberini of Rome, the Este of Milan and others—in places north, east, south and west. They ruled with bejeweled hands and daggered belts. But many encouraged music and the other arts, until, and even after, the drama left their spectacular courts for theater buildings. Over the dukes, marquises and duchesses hovered the Popes who, often members of these families, were determined to keep the treasures, lands and art makers for themselves.

This was the stage upon which entered Claudio Monteverdi (1567–1643), the first "genius" among opera writers, "a modern when he wrote and modern to this day" (Marion Bauer and Ethel Peyser in *Music Through the Ages*). As a composer, he used all that was known in music and illumined it.

He was born in Cremona, the home of the unexcelled string instrument-makers, Stradivarius, Guarneri, the Amati, and others. Monteverdi's father was an eminent surgeon. Claudio went to school, to the university, and studied polyphonic music with the great master of his day, Marc Antonio Ingegneri, composer and choirmaster of the Cremona Cathedral. Even as a young man, Monteverdi showed a flair for the dramatic, and for breaking rules almost before he had digested

31

them. Let us be grateful that his willfulness helped the growth of opera.

At twenty, Monteverdi showed amazing feeling for dramatic utterance in a book of madrigals (1587). He used chord sequences and rhythms that expressed atmosphere and emotion. A critic of his time, a monk from Bologna, Giovanni Maria Artusi (1550–1613), abused him, however. This holy man wrote a most scathing bit in his *Imperfections of Modern Music,* accusing Monteverdi of breaking "natural laws." He said, "Though I am glad to hear of a new manner of composition, it would be more edifying to find in these madrigals reasonable *passagi,* but these kinds of air castles ... deserve the severest reproof.... Behold, for instance, the rough and uncouth ..." etc., etc.

This kind of criticism still is used against men who compose in new ways, who do not break the laws of nature but stretch the expressiveness of music to the ire of people to whom it is unfamiliar. Had not Monteverdi written as he felt, opera would have lagged far behind in the march of music.

Because Monteverdi's madrigals combined the best traits of polyphony with those of monody, he was often given credit for originating this "modern style." He was one of the first to compose the dramatic madrigal, or the salon piece, Chamber Cantata (*Cantata da camera*), in which a short story or drama was recited by one person in verse with instrumental accompaniment. This is one of many reasons why he has been called "The Father of Opera."

His madrigals were excellent "publicity," for they attracted the patron of patrons, Vincenzo Gonzaga, Duke of Mantua. His dukedom had cherished the poet Petrarch, lover of Laura; Palestrina, "The Prince of Music"; Tasso, the writer of *Jerusalem Delivered* and many classical tragedies and comedies; Rubens, the magnificent painter-diplomat; and many others.

When Vincenzo Gonzaga traveled over Europe, he took with him a retinue to provide him with entertainment. Among these scenemakers, poets and musicians was Monteverdi. In the course of his travels with the Duke, Monteverdi witnessed pageants, celebrations, battles and their din in the war between Austria and the Turks, and profited from his contacts with composers and poets in France and Flanders, a home of song.

He brought the secular and religious madrigal to supreme beauty, but the contribution which won him singular renown was dramma per musica, which he picked up where the Camerata had left off. So, in his early forties, he experimented with the *favola*. In his attempts to write expressive music, he was really the first to tie together the story, the song, the instrument, action and scenery by using both monody and polyphony with a much more pleasing and richer recitative. One of the new devices, many of which he had helped to invent, was the *basso continuo,* or figured bass, an accompaniment that soon developed into what is called *concertante,* or instrumental style. Without this invention, opera would have had no foundation on which to grow.

Another device introduced by the Camerata was the solo song, known as monody, which later expanded into the operatic aria. Monteverdi added expressiveness to the melody that had become the important line.

Instrumental sections took on greater importance as introductory overtures or *sinfonie* (not to be confused with our use of the word *symphony*); *ritornelli* or little instrumental interludes; and *intermezzi* or more extended interludes.

While in Flanders with Duke Vincenzo, he must have heard the French *chanson* (song), and may even have come in contact with Jean Antoine Baïf, founder of the French Academy of Music and Poetry. This Academy stressed the mating of words and music, a practice in which Monteverdi became supreme, making song and recitative more potent and smooth-flowing.

Monteverdi's *Orfeo,* written in 1607, with libretto by Rinuccini, was far better than Peri's *Euridice,* even as his *Arianna* outrivaled Peri's *Dafne.* In *Orfeo,* Monteverdi, contrary to Peri, stressed the music as an interpreter of the poetry. This has remained ever since a mark of Italian opera. He struck a nice balance between song and story. His *Orfeo* has a prologue and five acts. In the prologue the nymphs and shepherds rejoice over the marriage of Orfeo and Euridice—soon to be parted by Euridice's death from the bite of a serpent. In this tragic, grief-laden story with a happy ending which, however, had never been used before, he expressed human feeling in strong contrast to the more rigid Florentine opera.

For the opening of *Orfeo* he wrote a *toccata* (a touch piece—one for instruments, not voices). It had flourishes of trumpets repeated three times. Then he had a prologue which also started with a *ritornello* or *sinfonia* (instrumental piece). The same theme appears throughout to typify Orfeo, in somewhat the way the motifs (or "calling cards") typify characters or special things, much later, in operas by Scarlatti, Wagner, Puccini, Massenet, and others.

In *Orfeo,* as to some extent in Arianna, Monteverdi is the first and direct ancestor of Hector Berlioz (nineteenth century), who painted emotion and character with instruments. But Monteverdi used only thirty or forty instruments, whereas Berlioz was notorious for the occasional use of an orchestra of exaggerated size. The following is the orchestra Monteverdi used in *Orfeo.* The similarity of names does not mean that these instruments sounded like ours. (*History of Orchestration* by Adam Carse.)

Two *gravicembali* (harpsichords or spinets)
Two *contrabassi de viola* (double basses)
One *arpa doppia* (double-string harp)
Two *violini piccoli alla francese* (treble violins in the French style)
Ten *viole de braccia* (arm violas, discant or tenor violas)
Two *chitarroni* (bass or archlutes)
Two *organi di legno* (organs with wooden pipes)
Three *bassi da gamba* (bass viola, *viola da gamba*)
Four *tromboni* (trombones: altos, tenors, and bass, softer than the modern trombone)
One *regale* (small portable organ)
Two *cornetti* (old, hornlike wind instruments, not like our cornets, with cup-shaped mouthpiece, wooden tube straight or curved, with finger holes. This was hard on the lips and went out of use in 1600 in favor of the violins, which carried the treble—usually the tune)
One *flautina alla vigesima seconda* (flute at the twenty-second, equivalent to three octaves)
One *clarino con trombe sordine* (of the clarinet family, but sounds like a trumpet, eight feet long, in C)
and
Three trumpet mutes (soft-playing trumpets)

So skillful was Monteverdi in putting heart into instrumental and voice music that Duke Gonzaga, his patron, asked him to write an opera to celebrate the marriage of his son, Ferdinando, to Princess Margherita of Savoy. He wanted to express all the furore, pomp, and magnificence to impress the Medici, his rivals in Florence. For this splurge, Gonzaga ordered Monteverdi to double the size of the orchestra and to train it himself! This request depressed Monteverdi, as he was overworked and deeply grieved by the recent death of his beloved wife. But nevertheless he was called back to Mantua from Cremona to complete *Arianna* with Alessandro Striggio, librettist. It was performed in 1608 for the Gonzaga before nearly six thousand persons and was a great success. This effort, added to his grief and fatigue, almost caused his death. He wrote *Arianna* in the *stile parlante,* or recitative style. The last straw was set in place when a relative of the Duke asked Monteverdi to put some comic relief into *Arianna,* the tragic tale of Ariadne and Theseus. Like it or not, he had to do it, so he called in Rinuccini, who had collaborated with Peri, to put in the humor. They inserted the ballet, in the French decorated manner, *Il Ballo dell' Ingrate* (*The Prudes' Ball*). It was presented elegantly, in the French style (*ballet de cour*), with a single theme or tune varied and in different meters. It was more than sumptuous, with "super" scenery, regal satins and silks, a rolling sea, vaulted heavens, and an ocean reef. The most garishly arrayed gods and goddesses ascended and descended in "glorious sheen."

But nothing, said a contemporary reporter, was more moving than Arianna's lament, *"Lasciatemi morire"* ("Abandoned I Die"). It was the most celebrated composition of the early seventeenth century. Yet, according to custom, Monteverdi set this song, because of its popularity and its moving quality, as a five-part madrigal, also as a religious chorus, *"Pianta della Madonna"* ("Tears of the Madonna"). The Lament, poignantly moving, was sung at that time in many forms, in cottages and castles throughout Europe. Later (1642) it became a popular song, mushily named *"Maggio fiorita"* ("Flowers of May").

Unfortunately, *Arianna,* like Peri's *Dafne,* is another lost maiden of opera. The only thing that remains is her Lament.

This song has lived because it is human and touching. Monteverdi believed that to make opera satisfying, its subject should be people and their feelings—not just winds, skies, rains, windmills, and other impersonal elements. People's sorrows, hates, and loves appeal to audiences, and he believed that *Arianna* had been a success because it stressed human grief, not because of the elaborate scenery or even the poem. How right he was! This is one of his most valuable contributions to the growth of opera.

After the successful production of *Arianna* and the marriage of the son of Gonzaga, Monteverdi was unhappy and yearned to leave Mantua. This he did after the death of Vincenzo I, but not of his own free will. He was dismissed by the very man for whom he had written *Arianna!*

In 1613 he received the much-desired call to the impressive St. Mark's Church in Venice as "Director of Music to the Most Serene Republic of Venice." Serene? Indeed! On the contrary, it was continually in the midst of battle, feud, disease, and famine! Yet here, for the first time, Monteverdi knew economic freedom and peace of mind.

Men from all nations went to Venice to study and to teach, to enjoy beauty and to revel in the most sophisticated and "modern" art forms. The painting, sculpture, and architecture were, and are still, incredibly beautiful.

THE VENETIAN SCHOOL

Toward the end of his life, Monteverdi became the center of Venetian opera. In 1630 there was a great plague. At the time he pledged that were he spared, he would go on a holy pilgrimage. Instead, he took holy orders and wrote beautiful sacred music! Jacopo Peri died of the plague in 1633, but Monteverdi, spared, wrote more operas.

Before Monteverdi was appointed Director of St. Mark's, Venice had become a vital music center, known as the "Venetian School." While Venice became an important influence in the growth of opera, the first men, recognized as having founded a school, were not opera writers, but did much to develop instrumental music, an indispensable factor in opera.

Adrian Willaert, founder of this school, was born in Flanders between 1480 and 1490 and went to St. Mark's as choirmaster in 1527. He began his studies in law in Paris, but soon took up music with Jean Mouton, a pupil of the treasured Josquin Després. Through Willaert the Franco-Netherlandish and the Italian influences were blended in what was to become known as the Venetian School. He wrote secular and sacred music. He was not only Director of Music but a teacher of counterpoint at St. Mark's for thirty-five years. The Italians, therefore, were excellently trained in the technique of the North. Even the superb work of Palestrina was influenced by Willaert, whose three contributions, according to Dr. Gustave Reese in his *Music of the Renaissance,* were:

1. Establishment of Franco-Netherland technique as part of the musical language of church music in Italy.

2. The development of choral antiphony—or one choir answering the other. St. Mark's had two organs which Willaert used to the richer expression of music in the church.

3. The cultivation of a "modern style," emphasizing faultless declamation of the text.

Willaert was followed in Venice by his distinguished pupil Cypriano de Rore (1516-65), the last of the Netherlanders in Italy. Then came another pupil, Gioseffo Zarlino (1517-90), whose treatises were more distinguished than his compositions. Others in Venice were Claudio Merulo (1533-1602), an organist at St. Mark's, and the two Gabrieli, Andrea (1520-86) and Giovanni (1557-1612). These men, about the last of the great composers of the Venetian School before Monteverdi, though not interested in opera, together with the Roman Frescobaldi (1583-1643), so furthered the growth of instrumental music, that their impetus to composition reached to the opera writers following them in Venice.

In Venice Monteverdi found the freedom to write and to compose almost without censorship in musically congenial surroundings which fed his imagination and fired his creativeness. Except for some religious music, some madrigals, and his last two operas, all he wrote there, however, has perished!

Monteverdi added many new things to music in the manner of his writing and the vitalizing of the orchestra, as well as new ways of expressing emotions. Having seen a battle between the Turks and the Austrians, he knew that the sounds of war could not be caressing music. He expressed emotions other than the soft ones of love, grief and laughter. In his cantata *"Il combattimento di Tancredi e Clorinda"* ("The Combat of Tancred and Clorinda," 1624), from the epic *Jerusalem Delivered,* by Tasso, he for the first time purposely portrayed in his orchestra the strong emotions of the fury of combat in the duel between the crusader Tancred and his beloved Clorinda, the Saracen maiden disguised as a man. He also used a new way of expressing the stress of emotion, *stile concitato* (excited style), in what we call *tremolo*. This was first heard in *Arianna*. It is a swift repetition of one tone, or the holding of a tone on the violin by the rapid alternation of down and up bow strokes. In singing, it is a wavy tone used for emotional effect. In this, he was a forerunner of Verdi.

THE FIRST OPERA HOUSES

Like Verdi, Monteverdi wrote his very best works after he was sixty-five. At seventy he adjusted himself to new conditions—the coming of opera on a commercial plane in public theaters, instead of in the halls of the nobility.

As early as 1565, Andrea Palladio had designed a wooden structure in which to present plays. The first of these was built in Vicenza,

Italy, and many architects copied it. Yet before Monteverdi's time, throughout Italy, plays or dramas with music were not given in theaters but in churches, palaces, private homes, tents, improvised shedlike buildings, on streets and on public squares or wagons.

The building of the first public theater—the San Cassiano in Venice (1637)—for the presentation of opera six years before Monteverdi's death, was of almost as much importance to opera as the music.

It was "no picnic" witnessing opera at the San Cassiano. Great credit should be showered on Venetian opera-lovers, whose endurance was tested sorely for the sake of music. The theater was badly ventilated. There were no beautiful windows and hangings as in the halls of the nobles, nor fresh air as in the outdoor carnivals. The theater was dirty, the audience sat on crowded benches, and for boxes or loges, unknown then, rickety wooden seats were placed on steps.

The first opera given in the San Cassiano was *Andromeda* by Francesco Manelli, in which both he and his wife sang. Four years later, in 1641, Monteverdi's *Il ritorno d'Ulisse in patria* (*The Return of Ulysses to His Country*) was presented there, and in the following year, *L'incoronazione di Poppea* (*The Coronation of Poppea*) was given at another opera house, SS. Giovanni e Paolo (St. John and St. Paul). These two works that still remain to us were advances on his earlier Mantuan operas. *Il ritorno* was on a text by Giacomo Badoaro. Giovanni Busenello wrote that of *L'incoronazione,* which was considered Monteverdi's most important work. He composed it at seventy-four years of age! He made it tragic, he made it sumptuous like ancient Rome, and he made it dramatic.

In his advanced age, again like Verdi, he proved to be one of the greatest dramatists in opera. In *The Coronation of Poppea* Monteverdi gave up Greek gods and legendary shepherds for exciting stories about real people. This was an innovation of the librettist—historic opera— and it set a new pattern for Italian opera. The composer used music, as well as the poem, to carry out the meaning of this story. With recitative and tuneful songs, he stimulated other composers to employ tune and accompaniment (homophonic) songs instead of keeping to the polyphonic madrigal.

Monteverdi suffered so greatly from rheumatism that at times he was crippled and almost blind. Nevertheless, he started to write operas and a book on music, *Melodia,* never completed, to show that music can mirror life. In 1643 he obtained a leave of absence from St. Mark's for a sentimental journey to Cremona and Mantua, during which he became ill and was brought back to Venice, where he passed away on November 29.

But Claudio Monteverdi will never die, for he did ever-living things for his beloved music. He made the first attempt at building the orchestra into a group of mutually assisting instruments that helped balance each other in tone and volume. Before his day, instruments had been used willy-nilly. No one seemed to know or care whether the lute was drowned out by the bass viol or whether the trumpet drowned out the *gravicembalo,* or indeed, whether a trumpet pictured Pluto, the God of the Underworld, or a delicate maiden like Dafne. But Monteverdi used the soft viol and the quaint and plaintive woodwinds to paint in musical tones the shepherdesses or tender maidens and their sweet songs of love. He used drums and flutes and trombones to paint the fury of battle or storm or struggle. He made experiments in painting with music—and in expressing heart quality.

With him instruments began to live for themselves rather than just to prop up the voice. Their days of slavery to song were almost over! Now they were emancipated and had a life of their own.

He gave to the stringed instruments, this man of three hundred years ago, a new importance, and to the orchestra a new vitality, tenderness, and usefulness.

A pupil of Monteverdi who threatened to rival his master was Francesco Cavalli, born Pier Francesco Caletti-Bruni (1602–76), who took the name of his patron, Cavalli, as was the custom of his day. From 1639 to 1645, with the exception of Monteverdi's *Il ritorno d'Ulisse in patria,* all of the operas produced at San Cassiano were by Cavalli. So great was his fame that his operas, written according to Monteverdi's teachings, were produced in many Italian and European cities, including Paris. His best opera illustrating Venetian style is *Giasone (Jason),* about Medea, Jason and the Golden Fleece.

Like Monteverdi, he had a strong dramatic sense, colorful orchestration, and attractive harmonic language, as well as a decided feeling for rhythm and clever delineation of moods. He added a quicker second section in triple time to his first, majestic eight-measure section in duple time, thus emphasizing the importance of the prelude, or overture. As did Roman composers, he recognized the value of the chorus more than had other Venetians. Cavalli used the aria, with no fixed schedule as was later the mode, but as the story dictated, never sacrificing drama to form as was the case with the later baroque composers.

As the theater San Cassiano was a success, many wealthy men in Venice saw their opportunity to make money, and began to build theaters for the presentation of concerts and musical dramas. Opera for the first time was not dependent on the nobility—the patron—but put itself into the hands of the people—the customers, who *paid* for their seats. This stimulated more people to see opera and more composers to create it. In Venice alone, seventeen theaters were opened between 1637 and 1679!

European centers caught the opera fever from Florence, Venice, and Rome. Paris had a severe case of opera-itis, so it called in an Italian "doctor" from Venice—Francesco Cavalli, the first so-called "popular" opera writer. After the death of his teacher, Monteverdi, he was the leading musician in Venice, and was called hither and yon.

He was asked to produce his opera, *Xerxes,* for the marriage festivities of Louis XIV in France (1660). Before this time, France had imported operas by Peri and not composed her own. Yet she had to her credit many good composers of song and her much-adored ballet. Cavalli's music was delightfully tuneful, rhythmic, with a nice use of instruments. He wrote forty-one operas, church music, and, as he was a superb organist, was awarded a post at St. Mark's. His *Giasone* (1667) was so well known that it was parodied ten years later in Florence. Nevertheless, after Cavalli left France, France decided to have "no more Italian opera."

OPERA IN ROME

Rome was the connecting link between opera in Florence, the birthplace of recitative in the Camerata, and opera in Venice, which supplied the solo aria. Rome taught composers much about the chorus. This was natural, for the Holy City abounded in church singing schools and choirs of distinction. Soon the chorus became a characteristic feature of Roman opera and a definite pattern for all opera.

To Rome, Emilio de' Cavalieri (1550–1602) of the Camerata, famous for his dramma per musica, "Representation of the Soul and Body" had gone in 1600, and taken with him ideas on monody, recitative, scenery, and general points on dramaturgy.

There dramatic performances were given in vast private auditoriums like, for example, the Palace of the Barberini, who were great nobles as well as princes of the Church. This hall held three thousand people. Steffano Landi's opera, *Sant' Alessio* (*St. Alexis*), opened it in 1632. It was said that this was the first opera whose action was concerned with the ideas and thoughts (or *inner* life) of a human being, St. Alexis of the fifth century. In this, Landi used choruses at the end of each act, and the part of St. Alexis was sung by a tenor *castrato,* as was Orfeo in Monteverdi's opera. A castrato was a singer on whom an operation had been performed to keep the voice from changing so that it would remain in the female range. Although *castrati* were not looked upon with favor by opera lovers, they were necessary for many years to come because the Roman Church would not permit women on the stage, and opera needed women characters, even if portrayed by men.

Landi was the first to write dramma per musica with some farcical situations based on the amusing happenings of everyday life. His orchestra was one of the first to use modern violins, not viols. After Landi, the next man to advance opera was Luigi Rossi (1598–1653). His *Le Mariage d'Orphée et Euridice* (*The Marriage of Orpheus and Eurydice*), presented in Paris after his death, was the first opera given under the patronage of Cardinal Mazarin of France for the people as well as the nobility. Including the people was an innovation. The Cardinal, with all his faults, did much to establish French opera. Even though *Orphée* was a hodge-podge and dull in plot, nevertheless, it was presented with all the pomp and splendor of the French court, and served as another invasion of Italian opera into France. Francesco Buti wrote the text.

The music had the grace and style that characterized also Carissimi and Cesti of the seventeenth century.

Luigi Rossi wrote only one other opera, *Il Palazzo Incantato* (*The Enchanted Palace*), and gained favor for his many cantatas. His operas showed the baroque tendency in a feeling for form.

COMIC OPERA

There had been little of comedy in opera up to this time. Commedia dell' arte purveyed most of the comic element in dramatic entertainment, as did some of the madrigal comedies of Vecchi and Banchieri; some comic scenes (pastoral in feeling) in Landi's "Death of Orpheus"; and a few other instances—such as are found in *Sant' Alessio*. But the first real comic opera, with a libretto by Giulio Rospigliosi, who later became Pope Clement IX, was *Chi soffre, speri* (*Who Suffers, may hope*) with music by Vergilio Mazzocchi and Marco Marazzoli. As Rospigliosi was a friend of the Barberini, the first performance was given in their palace in 1739. "Among those present" were John Milton and Cardinal Mazarin.

Although it dealt with characters of contemporary Italian life, it still maintained gay features of the commedia dell' arte. The dialogue was more modern in type than was the monody of the Camerata, and later was called *recitativo secco* (dry recitative), because it had few chords to back it up but was sprightly, unevenly accented musical speech, delightfully adapted to the humor of the text and to the unique features of the Italian language.

As a separate form, this *commedia musicale* can be said to have been the foundation of the enjoyably persistent coming opera buffa.

Roman opera, whose road was difficult because of the papal inclination towards religiously slanted music, had the spirit to start comic opera, which was to have its full flowering in the eighteenth century.

SECOND GENERATION OF VENETIAN COMPOSERS

While Rome was carrying forward its particular development in dramatic music, the second generation of Venetian opera writers began notably with the Franciscan monk, Marc'Antonio Cesti (1623-1669), who, contrary to his predecessors, made the singer more important than the music. With his church cantatas, oratorios, and operas, the day of the disturbing virtuoso had dawned. Cesti was born in Arezzo, studied under Carissimi in Rome, and held a high position in Florence. He traveled abroad in France, Germany, and Austria.

He started the art of singing on its often too insistent way. Had Cesti preserved Monteverdi's superb balance between song and instrument, singers would not have throttled opera later. He abandoned the woven song (polyphony) and introduced humor, and transferred the church cantata to the opera stage. From now on, for many years, sometimes the composer, and *always the singer,* not the poet, nor the poetry, are to be the most important elements in Italian opera. Only fragments of his operas have come down to us, and some lovely songs.

Cesti's best known operas—of the one hundred he is said to have written—are *Orontea* (Venice, 1649), *La Dori* (Florence, 1661), and *Il pomo d'oro* (*The Golden Apple,* 1667). His work is more delicate than Cavalli's, often more tender. With Cesti the separation between aria and recitative becomes wider and deeper; the aria and not the recitative becomes more emphasized; and he centers the attention on lyrical song, with arias of display which forsehadow the vocal fireworks ahead.

Cesti's arias are rather short, but of many kinds, composed with much care. Along with nobility of expression he uses crisp and spar-

kling rhythm, as well as martial rhythm; *buffo* (comedy) arias, as well
as serious arias in the da capo form with the repeat or return (ritornello) between the first and second part and again at the end. He
engages his audiences with his variety!

Indeed, the opera writers of Venice followed the Roman innovation
and to gather large audiences introduced comic plots as well as comic
intermezzi; some sort of comic relief was demanded by the new
public paying admission to the opera houses.

Allesandro Stradella (c. 1645-81), an opera writer of Venice, adopted
Cesti's style in four operas, which became an international mode. His
and other such operas were given in opera theaters in Florence, Rome,
Bologna, Modena, and elsewhere in the next ten years. Besides four
operas, Stradella wrote 200 cantatas and other dramatic works, full of
charm and melodic originality. He became a forerunner of Scarlatti and
the Neapolitan School of the eighteenth century. Among Stradella's
operas is *Tiepolo.*

Friedrich von Flotow, composer of *Martha,* wrote an opera, *Stradella,*
on this man's dramatic life and violent death.

Venetian opera became popular because of its exceptional composers
and because it pandered to the tastes of the multitude, not only in
comic innovations but in extravagant scenery—"machines flying in
air" and numerous changes of scene.

Other valued, late seventeenth-century opera writers were Giovanni
Legrenzi, Carlo Pallavicino, and Antonio Lotti, among others. The
orchestra began to assume a very important role. The mood of most
operas was the comic, save in the case of Legrenzi. The aria was king.

OPERA IN NAPLES—

ALESSANDRO SCARLATTI AND THE CLASSIC MANNER

Neapolitan opera was personified by Alessandro Scarlatti (1659-1725),
who came on the Baroque scene at a most interesting time. He realized
that lyric drama had become a favorite entertainment of both the
"people" and the peers.

He inherited much from the opera writers of Florence, Venice and
Rome. He had knowledge of the sumptuous ballet-opera of Lully in
France. And although English opera perished with Purcell, and German
opera, in its collision with Italian, became Italianate, these national operas
and their writers could not but interest Scarlatti. He worked only in the

homophonic style as developed in Venice and demanded by a public
that adored tuneful song and brilliant execution.

Scarlatti, born in Sicily, besides contributing to the growth of opera,
sired the greater Scarlatti, Domenico, who laid the basis for the school
of piano music with his masterly harpsichord music. The father was
often called "The Serious Scarlatti." Like Cesti, he was a pupil of
Carissimi.

Alessandro's greatest talents were in the lyric theater. He did, however, write some church music when necessary.

Scarlatti lived in Venice during some of the many papal upheavals.
Although Venice was supplied with theaters, she was throttled by the
prohibitive decrees of Pope Innocent XI, who succeeded Urban VII of
the opera-minded Barberini family. So at this time it was difficult to
"put over" a spirited story. Opera has suffered this way through the ages.

But Scarlatti became attached to the household of Queen Christina
of Sweden, who was then living in Rome (1680–1684). Here he could
write as he wished. His second opera, for the queen, was probably *Il
Pompeo* (1683), the only one extant from this engagement. The
librettist was Niccolò.

Happily for opera, Scarlatti's sister so schemed that he was invited to
Naples, which was then in the hands of the Spanish. Being twice favored
by patrons in Naples, he inevitably created the Neapolitan school of
opera, where a traveling company of players had given Monteverdi's
Coronation of Poppea in 1654 and had awakened the appetite for lyric
drama. The Spanish theater and its humor had already invaded the
Neapolitan stage, and was getting a little out of control. As is seen
throughout the career of opera, whenever things get too bad something
happens as a cure, even though another malady may soon set in!

Apostolo Zeno, poet and librettist, trying to make opera more dignified and less worldly than it was in Venice and less "peppy" than
in Naples, made it into something stiff even though it had quality. So
Scarlatti, always a conformer, conformed, and put his lovely music to
Zeno's stilted texts.

Too much conformity is bad for art, and his work soon deteriorated.
At times, for example, he surrendered to the fashion of lugging in arias
written only to show off the singer's skills. Yet never has the art of
bel canto reached such a height of cultivation and beauty as in the time
when the songs or arias did so much to adorn, even if they often
blocked the action. Naples, however, became famous for its music while
Scarlatti's operas held the stage.

At the turn of the century, 1702–1703, Scarlatti did his best work at the Court of Prince Ferdinand III in Florence, while still yearning in vain to be taken on as its permanent composer. E. J. Dent says: "Of what... he was capable... may be seen in the opera *'Mitridate Eupatore'* ...Venice (1707) ...a remarkable example of the Classical manner at its grandest." The libretto is unusual, as it depends entirely on its political interest. There are no love scenes, but the devotion of the heroine for her brother is expressed with a passionate sincerity far better than anything Scarlatti had written before. " 'O Mitridate mio' "— the recitative—Dent says, "has hardly been surpassed in dignity by J. S. Bach." This is followed by the magnificent aria, *"Cara Tomba"* ("Blessed Tomb").

In 1703 Scarlatti left for Rome, where he became the assistant, and later chief, choirmaster at the Church of Santa Maria Maggiore, and choirmaster to the household of Cardinal Ottoboni. But in 1709 he resigned his posts and went back to Naples. There he taught at two conservatories. Among the students were Johann Adolph Hasse of Germany and Nicolo Logroscino, a writer of comic opera, who also introduced the beloved group songs—duets, trios, quartets, sextets—into Italian opera.

Professor Edward J. Dent in his *Alessandro Scarlatti, His Life and Works,* quotes from a letter of Scarlatti about his opera, *Lucio Manlio:* " 'I have always aimed in composing for the theatre to make the opening act like a child which takes its first steps uncertainly; the second is a youth that walks erect and sure; the third should be like a young man, swift, bold of undertaking and successful in all that he undertakes. This I have done in *Lucio Manlio.'* " This opera has been lost but completes the number of eighty-eight dramatic works Scarlatti composed in less than twenty-three years!

Although Scarlatti's music was free and expressive, sweet and charming, and some consider him to be the musical ancestor of Mozart, it has little appeal for us today, in spite of his 693 works in various forms. Fifty operas of this master craftsman exist but are not heard.

He died in Naples on October 24, 1725, and was buried in the Church of Monte Santo. He is the most important of the early group of men who used the monodic style, based on our scales.

At Scarlatti's height, opera became more tuneful, lighter, simpler, save in its spectacular arias in which the singer could display his skills and tyrannize over the composer.

WHAT SCARLATTI ACCOMPLISHED

In this Baroque period, opera was anchored to a string of arias. The solo song, Caccini's innovation, was king. No longer was there argument as to which was the more important, recitative or solo. Opera now had the spectacular aria which departed from the polyphonic style, based on strands of beautiful music woven together.

Opera crystallized, through Scarlatti's efforts, around the *da capo* aria, a development of the earlier Roman composers. This aria is made of three divisions or sections: A-B-A, known as ternary form. The words *da capo* mean "from the beginning." At the end of the second part of the song is usually written *da capo al segno,* which tells the performer to repeat from the beginning of the song and to continue to the sign. In these arias, Scarlatti often used the minor mode to express sadness. Like Shakespeare's Cleopatra, they have "infinite variety." There are many kinds and their names tell exactly what they mean to express. The Neapolitan composers, principally Scarlatti, were responsible for establishing these forms of the aria which tended to create the standard Italian opera:

1. The *aria cantabile,* a quiet flowing melody expressing gentle moods and allowing much latitude to improvise.

2. The *aria di portamento,* of more strongly marked and dignified rhythm, symmetrical in form and having a wide range between the softest tones and the loudest.

3. The *aria di bravura* or *d'agilità,* with much display of technical skill (or fireworks).

4. The *aria di mezzo carattere* (aria of half-way character), between the gentler *cantabile* and the stronger *portamento.*

5. The *aria d'imitazione,* in which the voice and the instruments compete with each other in imitating the sounds of nature.

6. The *aria all' unisono,* in which the voice and the accompaniment carry the same melody.

7. The *aria parlante* (in speaking style), declamatory in character; as it became more intense it was called *aria agitato,* or *aria strepito,* or *aria infuriata.*

8. The *aria concitato,* with elaborate instrumental accompaniment.

9. The *aria senza accompagnamento,* the unaccompanied aria, seldom used.

Then there is also the *cavatina,* which differs from all the other arias in that it has no second part.

The aria in its many forms so queened it over the opera that were an opera presented in another theater than the one in which it was first given, any composer on the spot could insert an aria, whether carrying out the plot or not. Indeed, opera plots bothered no one! The interloper, moreover, would make it as ornate as the singer demanded. This created a tedium which led to the subsequent reforms of Gluck and Wagner. These writers, as had the Camerata, wanted opera to act, not to stand still, so they abandoned the opera form that had become merely a succession of crystallized *arie da capo,* which amounted to many repetitions of the same form in the same act and choked the story. They were hostile to the da capo aria and used melody without repetitions to further the action. Imagine a good detective story set to music, and just before it gets to the most exciting point, someone enters to sing a song about birdies in the trees (just to show off his or her voice) and repeats the first part of his story all over again!

In addition to the aria in the Classic opera of Scarlatti, there is the *arioso,* which is usually a flowing melody when it is not the connective tissue or recitative, or when the recitative glides into a sort of melodious section not quite aria and not quite recitative.

Another important innovation of Scarlatti the Serious is his overture. Until this time an overture or sinfonia was an instrumental opening piece in any mood, with no particular form. Scarlatti's overture had form. It had three contrasting parts, A-B-C. The first part is fast and usually gay (no doubt to attract interest); the second part is slow and song-like (no doubt to soothe); and the third part is fast and often robustious (no doubt to wake up the listener for the first act which is to follow). Not only was this an excellent opener for an opera but, with the aria, was one of the roots from which came our sonata form. Scarlatti's overture is known as the *Italian overture.*

In addition to the aria da capo and the Italian overture, we can credit Scarlatti with the accompanied recitative; that is, the recitative with more supporting music; and the "ensemble of perplexity," a song shared by three or four characters all shouting their inability to resolve a terrific dilemma.

Scarlatti's opera became known as the Classic, out of which developed a system of rigid rules. For example, only the three principal tenors and sopranos were permitted to sing the arias and sometimes only the star singers. This often created indescribable jealousies which even led to physical violence. No baritone, no alto, no basso could have arias without a struggle. If that rule had not been broken later, we would have been cheated out of the basso songs of Amonasro in *Aida,* Méphistofélès in Gounod's *Faust;* the great arias for basso in Mussorgsky's *Boris Godounov,* and many others.

Vain and egotistical singers prevented the composers from writing many chorus numbers. Indeed, they only permitted one at the finale! They demanded trilly, frilly showpieces for themselves, arias chosen for vocal gymnastics. Of course, the trapeze work in the high voices was passionately demanded by the audiences, and the orchestra soon began to be nothing but a stepchild.

Classic opera had five or more acts and much scenery with arias, choruses, and vocal ensembles, all strictly prescribed.

As early as the 17th century, plots began to be monotonously alike. People, including the composers, were bored. They battled as to whether the aria or the recitative was the more important way of carrying on the story, or whether the singer or the composer was in command. The struggle continued for years, and came to a climax with Handel.

That opera stiffened wasn't Scarlatti's fault. The fault was among the younger composers who copied the poorer or probably the more popular of Scarlatti's operas rather than his best. So one hundred years after the invention of opera, it is ready for a "house cleaning."

If Scarlatti didn't stiffen opera, he, among other things, did build so-called Classic opera, equipped with homophony, the Italian aria, the da capo aria, accompanied recitative, balanced melodic phrases, development of themes into broader tunes.

LA SERVA PADRONA—ONCE MORE

One of the additions that had been put into drama-with-music some time even before Monteverdi's day, during it and long afterward, was the use of little pieces sung or danced between the acts of the dramas with music, and later called opera. These were the intermezzi or Between Pieces, which had a definitely refreshing influence on the growth of opera. Fancy seeing *Pop-Eye the Sailor Man* given between the acts of *Faust!* But scene-shifting took a long time in those days, and something had to be done to hold the audiences until the next act. Furthermore, there was no curtain until the final act, if then. But these Between Pieces did not seem so unrelated to the opera itself in the early days, for there wasn't much variety between the intermezzi and the pomp and stateliness of the drama itself, until in 1733 along came the little gay intermezzo, *"La serva padrona"* ("The Mistress Maid") given with Scarlatti's *Prigionieri Fortunato.* This intermezzo was so light and amusing that it became the foundation of a new kind of opera ... *opera buffa* in Italian, *opéra bouffe* and *opéra comique* in French, comic or comedy opera in English.

The inventor of this new kind of opera was Giovanni Battista Draghi Pergolesi, who was born in Jesi, Italy, in 1710. His father was a cobbler, as was Hans Sachs. During his twenty-six years Pergolesi, who died of tuberculosis in Pozzuoli (1736), brought fresh air to opera. He was devoted to the lyric theater and seemed to have been born with the genius for writing sharply dramatic music that gave itself to humor and lampooning.

He composed several operas, only a few of which succeeded, writing for the theater in Naples with little success. Then he wrote a *Stabat Mater* and two exceptional Masses which made him famous.

But what survives among his operas is *La serva padrona.* In this he showed command of nimble wit, his ability to match humorous music to humorous text, and a dangerous skill at musical lampooning which had cost him many engagements throughout his short life. *La serva padrona* still holds our stage and is riotously funny even in English.

Comic dramas were not new to opera even when *La serva padrona* took Paris by storm, but it established the feasibility of the basso song and the Italian *canzonetta,* a folk type of song used later in French opera and in Mozart opera to further the dramatic story (See *"Deh vieni alla finestra"* from Mozart's *Don Giovanni*).

Pergolesi uses *recitativo secco* to hasten speech, which must tumble off the tongue. When he employs repetition of idea or words it seems comical, not useless nor arbitrary. Indeed, *La serva padrona* has such swift pace that the music and text seem like natural twins. There are only three performers, a soprano and a basso, and one character who doesn't either speak or sing!

SCENE III

Beginnings of French Opera

ALTHOUGH France learned much from Italian opera, her opera had its own romantic and delightful background. The trouvères and troubadours influenced the making of the French song, or *chanson,* the monodic (one-line) and secular song so useful to Lully when he founded the French lyric stage (opera and ballet). Another delightful part of the background of French opera is the string of trouvère songs and dances put together in the pastoral comedy, *Le Jeu de Robin et de Marion* by Adam de la Halle. Usually claimed as the first comic opera, it was first performed at the French court of Naples in 1275 or 1285. De la Halle was one of the "great handicapped" who made good, for he was a hunchback, yet a minstrel to one of the French courts. This "opera," the musical *pastourelles* (pastorals), and the song-plays and dances given at fairs all over the country bred the love and desire for lyric expression in the French way, which is based on the careful matching of word to song and instrument. Opera in France also has in its background the dance in *ballade, ballata,* or *ballet,* accompanied by song, and the *vaudeville* named after the drinking songs of the mid-fifteenth century. They were sung in the little valleys (*vaux*) of Normandy near Vire and called at first *vaux de Vire,* which did not take long to become *voix de ville,* or "voices of the city." That's where our entirely different vaudeville gets its name!

Pierre de Ronsard and other poet-musicians, members of a club called the "Pleiades," had experimented with verse-making, in forms such as the sonnet, a poem of fourteen lines. One of the club's members was Jean Antoine Baïf, who, with some other eminent poets and musicians, had formed the French Academy of Music and Poetry in 1570. The object of this club was to write music that would express poetry, and follow its meter. It was in great part through its efforts that music finally became "measured" (written with time signals).

So while the Florentine Camerata was developing opera, the French were arranging songs for single voices with instruments, and attending to that very important part of opera—the keeping time and verse forms, with emphasis on the verbal expression, and the meticulous fitting of text to the music—the permanent germ of French opera through the ages.

All this varied background, combined with the religious plays of the fourteenth, fifteenth, and sixteenth centuries, is the woven texture on which the opera of the French was appliquéd or based after they banished Italian importations of dramma per musica.

LULLY'S OPERAS

One of the most amusing things in the history of opera is that, with all French antagonism to Italian importations, characteristic French opera was founded by an Italian! His name was Jean Baptiste Lully; in Italian, spelled Lulli.

Lully (1632–87) was born in Florence twelve years after the Pilgrims landed near Plymouth Rock, one year before Peri of the Camerata died, and six years before the Grand Monarch, or the "Sun King," *Le Roi Soleil,* Louis XIV of France, was born.

Opera, with its libretto writers, singers, designers, ballet masters, and composers, had come from Italy to all the courts of Europe. Instead of using "who dunnit" stories for librettos to help the people forget their troubles, composers used stories about Pompey, Caesar, the realms of Venus and Orpheus, and every opera writer, particularly in France, had to cater to the exploits and glory of their monarch and his followers. Every opera began with a eulogy of the king, and long speeches lugged in about love and the glories of his reign or of visiting princes.

Lully's own life was like an opera, so incredible was it with "good and bad fairies" serving his will in the fantastic seventeenth century! As a poor boy he taught himself to play the guitar and soon joined a group of traveling players. During carnival time in Florence when the people, in fancy costumes, sang and danced in the streets, the Duke of Guise, a French noble, heard Lully sing. He asked him to go back to France with him to become kitchen boy in the household of Mademoiselle Montpensier, Duchess of Orleans, and cousin of King Louis XIV. It is thought by some, however, that he held a higher post. Lully soon won his way by clever handling of Mademoiselle, of himself, and of the whole household.

After a courtier taught him to play the violin, however, he became Mademoiselle's orchestra leader and eventually one of the most brilliant violinists in France. Soon, Cousin Louis (then fourteen years old) thought that Cousin Anne (Montpensier) had too brilliant a household, and he took young, amusing, and companionable Lully away from her.

From this time on, Lully rose higher and higher in the brilliant court. He held every job imaginable, such as Instrumental Composer to the King, with a "fat salary"; Composer of the King's Chamber Music, with another "fat salary"; Music Master to the Royal Family, with yet another "fat salary"; Master of the Violins, with still more salary —and was able, besides, to become a real estate magnate. He even became the King's Secretary, a post never before attained by any but a peer of the realm.

He was the devoted slave, entertainer and flatterer of King Louis, glamour boy of France from 1643 to 1715. Sometimes it is hard to tell whether Lully's music or his flattery pleased the King the more. Whichever it was, Lully became almost the most important man in France: czar of music—when lo! something happened that didn't please him too much. Robert Cambert's *La pastorale en musique,* with words by Pierre Perrin (the "first" French musical comedy, 1659), was given at the court with such success that they later obtained (1669) a patent to "establish the *Académie Royale de Musique* for the giving of representations with music in the French language, after the manner of those in Italy." This made Lully furious, particularly the phrase, "after the manner of those in *Italy."*

Pomone, by Cambert and Perrin, which opened (1671) in the theater of the Palais Royal, forerunner of the Paris Opéra, was enthusiastically received. This, of course, was intolerable to Lully. Their second opera was never given, for it failed under suspicious circumstances. Lully seized his chance to wangle the "patent" from Perrin, and obtained exclusive right from the King to organize and produce French opera in Paris. He founded what is now called the Grand Opéra (Académie Royale de Musique et de la Danse), opening it in 1672 with his own heroic pastoral, *Les fêtes de l'amour et de Bacchus (The Festivals of Love and Bacchus).* In 1673 Lully obtained a stranglehold on drama with music, for by a decree every other theater was forbidden to employ more than two singers and six violinists—hence there could be no pageantry or opera in any but his!

Following the alleged statement of the King, *"Je suis l'État"* ("I am the State"), was it any wonder that Lully, the tyrant and czar of music, said cleverly: *"L'Opéra, c'est moi"* ("I am Opera")? It was true, for he browbeat his staff, struck the singers and behaved like the musical totalitarian he was!

Of course, Lully was an unusual fellow, a magnificent coach, a delightful dancer, yet a homely man. He was the best violinist and conductor in the kingdom. Beyond all, he was a superb organizer and manager. He was often kindly, more often cruel, tricky, crafty, and always the tyrant. Suave, courtly and grasping, he maintained his position with the King, in spite of Cardinal Mazarin, the Prime Minister.

Mazarin, the Italian, had brought to France two operas of the Venetian Francesco Cavalli, one of which was performed at Louis XIV's wedding. Mazarin, no doubt, made it difficult for Lully to suit the French King and the French court.

But Lully studied Italian opera, and started French opera on its graceful, romantic, elegant, glamorous way with his own *Psyche* (1671), an opera, someone said, "without recitative" but with the ballet beloved by the French. It was tragicomic—sadness and gladness mixed. Soon he was clever enough to add the required recitative.

So Lully did not jump into writing French opera without thinking. He took into consideration that the French had liked before his day their strings of little songs and stories put to music, called *vaux de Vire*. He knew, too, that they loved their miracle plays. He understood their love for *Le jeu de Robin et de Marion*. He remembered that the French did not like Peri's *Euridice* because of its use of plain song, which they found dull and uninteresting. He realized, above all, their passion for *les ballets de cour* (court ballets).

These ballets were composed of dances, with some connected speech, and were acted with song, vast scenery, elaborate costumes and pantomime. But they were excellent flatterers of nobles and glamour carriers and, as such, the perfect foundation of an opera for monarchs.

At first Lully followed the custom of letting the dancers compose the airs, and the composers the orchestration. All the while he absorbed the effects produced and, loathing Italian opera, cleverly invented an opera of grace, limpid beauty, and courtly fitness—his *ballet opéra*.

He was the first to make an art of the composition of a ballet. It was an easier job for him than for his predecessors, for by this time homophony, and not polyphony alone, was used for secular music and drama. Lully's own invention, the "dance of (or with) expression" in the ballet developed into French opera. His comedy ballet consisted of:

1. Scenes in recitative.
2. Pantomime.
3. Interludes and ever-increasing incidental music (instrumental).
4. Elaborate scenery and costuming.
5. Vocal dialogues.

Some of the dialogue was spoken because the most important thing in the making of French opera was the facile language. He knew it was nimbler, more shining, and more flexible than Italian. He knew it could not be used with music the same way as Italian or any other language. You need only pronounce *fenêtre* (French), *finestra* (Italian), and *window* to realize how very different the vowel sounds are and the matching of them to music must be. Furthermore, although many in love with Italian opera thought that the French language could not be used in recitative, Lully proved that it could. He threw out much of the vocal gymnastics, long runs and trills in highest registers, called *coloratura* (or highly colored), and beloved by the Italians. He used coloratura only on the words that he thought needed brilliance, such as the word *brilliant* itself.

His use of recitative was more musical than that of the Italians. His chief object was to express the sentiment of the word, and when the feeling of his sentence became intense, his recitative itself glided into melody. He would work for days to fit the word to the music, and the music to the word.

From Lully's time on, French opera stresses the word and the sentiment, while the Italian stresses song and melody. The French in their theaters, ever since, demand the clearest, cleanest kind of diction, and the perfect pronunciation of every word.

Not unnaturally, this gilded age of Louis XIV in France, where words were of highest importance, was rich in French poets such as Racine; Molière, the writer of dramatic comedies; La Fontaine, whose fables are well known; and Pierre Corneille, the maker of great dramas. Lully took the classic dramas of his time as models for texts. He used a number of librettists (including himself), but Philippe Quinault lasted through twenty operas and two ballets because he did what he was told. Lully would have him rewrite a scene twenty times if necessary! And often the scene had been examined and considered perfect by the wise men of the French Academy.

Lully's early stage works were comedy ballets. One of the first things he gave was a ballet called *Xerxes,* from the opera of Cavalli, which was performed in Versailles at Cardinal Mazarin's invitation.

Lully wrote nineteen court ballets; among these were the *Ballet des arts (Ballet of the Arts,* 1663) and *Ballet de Venus,* 1665. These subjects demanded elaborate settings and glittering costumes. Besides these, he wrote twelve comedy ballets, less ponderous and occasionally slightly humorous ballets, nine of which were to texts by the dramatist Molière. One of these was *Le Bourgeois Gentilhomme (The Would-Be Gentleman,* 1670), which Richard Strauss used over two hundred years later.

As none of Lully's operas are heard today, the titles of two are sufficient: *Acis et Galathée* (1686), and *Armide et Roland* (1685). His *Cadmus et Hermione* was the first singable, or lyric, French musical tragedy and was performed in 1673.

In keeping with the French plays which French opera followed carefully, Lully used five acts. He usually had but one stage set in each act instead of many, as found in the Italian opera. Sometimes he set a scene in the underworld for effect, and then miraculously delivered the heroes by the intervention of a spirit, which was brought to the stage by a *deus ex machina,* invented by the early Greeks. Indeed, he was a far greater dramatist and showman than composer.

Lully emphasized the orchestra, rather than the singers, as was done in Italy. He forced the voice-proud singers of the musical spectacles to have respect for it. He conducted from the harpsichord, as was the custom until the early nineteenth century. He coached singers, instrumental players, stage hands, and even built some of the elaborate scenery himself. This one-man direction contributed to the grace, elegance, and beauty of all his productions.

Again in his dislike for everything Italian, this Italian-Frenchman invented his own overture, known as the French overture. Scarlatti's overture was three-part; Lully's was two-part—probably suggested by many of the exquisite French songs (*chansons*), also in two parts. Usually the first section of Lully's overture is slow and majestic, and is repeated; the second part (or section) is lively and written in fugal (polyphonic) style, or in counterpoint like a fugue. The second part is also repeated and may end in a short bit of the first section, somewhat broadened out, slowed down, and stately in feeling.

How is it that although his operas held the stage for a hundred years after his death, they are rarely if ever heard today? One reason was the lack of humor. They are written, moreover, about things which hold no interest for us today. Too much ballet pageantry slows up action. Even little scene-changing slows up the meager action. The spectacle is emphasized at the expense of the story.

But Romain Rolland, the French man of letters, says Lully's greatness was in his being not a poet-musician, but a musician-*architect*. The operas before Lully's time were neither well proportioned, balanced nor shaped, Lully's were so well designed that no one part outweighed the other. So the architect Lully had to be on the spot to carry out his ideas. Without him they lose the breath of life. His operas, always elegant, were designed to divert and tickle the eye, ear and the patron's *amour-propre* (self-esteem). Lully was a greater diplomat than he was dramatist or composer. Were he living today, he could have organized the UN with one hand and a United States of Europe with the other!

He gave France an opera entirely her own. Although the Lully opera fell into deep ruts of bad habits, later it pulled itself out onto the open road when France again ruled the opera world.

Not long before death actually came to Lully, he fell ill and thought he was about to die. So he decided to do a bit of last-minute cheating. He sent for his father-confessor to absolve him from his sins. The priest refused unless Lully would destroy the manuscript of *Achille and Polyxene* (or it may have been some other opera), based, so the priest believed, on a wicked story. Acting his part beautifully, Lully gave the manuscript to the confessor with sighs of deep regret. The priest burned it in the fireplace. Later, however, Lully was visited by a friend who shouted, "Baptiste! Were you fool enough to burn your wonderful opera?"

"Be calm, dear friend," Lully replied with a wicked smile. "I have another very good copy!"

His death, however, came in a strange way. One day while beating time with his baton (as he conducted the *Te Deum* written for the recovery of the "Sun King" from an illness), he accidentally thumped his foot. The heavy baton cut him, and blood poisoning set in. Lully died in 1687 at fifty-five, renowned, wealthy, feared, and the father of six children.

JEAN-PHILIPPE RAMEAU

In spite of Lully's greatness, France presented another, Jean-Philippe Rameau (1683-1764), still considered to be her most important composer of French blood. He was the first of his time to be interested in the grammar or the science of music (harmony), as well as its composition and performance. He was honest and hard-working and, although sweet and kindly, was always in the thick of warring musicians.

He came of a musical family and had been a very talented child. As a small boy, Rameau was trained by his father as an organist. Like little Franz Peter Schubert (1797–1828), most of his time in school was spent jotting down music instead of paying attention to his teacher's commands. And Rameau had another bad habit; he used to sing so loud that he drowned out all the other voices.

When little more than a boy (1702), after composing and playing violin in touring orchestras, he became organist in the cathedral at Clermont-Ferrand. He grew bored with his work, and was anxious to get away for further study, as he was not satisfied with the pieces he had already composed for the harpsichord (*clavecin* in French). So anxious was he to learn more that he began purposely to make mistakes while playing the organ when the congregation was singing in the cathedral and when he played solos. He did this, hoping he would be asked to leave. And he was! But this story has a happy ending. For, many years later, he returned to the same post, much honored and, better still, much loved.

He did learn more and began to write operas. Soon, of course, Rameau yearned to be admitted, because of his operas, to the French Opéra or to the French Académie, but then, as always, the French were more insistent upon a good libretto than upon good music. He wrote to the blind poet, Houder de Lamotte, in 1727 and asked him to write a lyric tragedy. Rameau wrote naïvely that he was no novice and that he knew how to write without the marks of labor or, in other words, he had mastered the great "art of concealing his art." The poet refused his request, but later Rameau was assisted by other willing poets for his prodigious output of more than thirty operas. Rameau was fifty years old when the first of these, *Hippolytus and Aracie,* (1733) was written. After that he wrote many ballets, opera ballets, instrumental works, and operas which unfortunately belong to the "never heards."

Hippolytus and Aracie wasn't very popular because, as in every country during any period of time, there are always the old-fashioned ones struggling to keep everything the way it used to be. In this case, the Lullyists, or lovers of Lully's French operas, hissed Rameau's work. They said that Rameau used queer chords. He probably did, but his

music, not Lully's, is still studied by musicians who want to understand the foundations of French music. His *Traité de l'harmonie*
(*Harmony Treatise*) was used for many years by music students all
over the world. Rameau set forth for the first time certain chord relations and so helped the progress of music.

Rameau, nevertheless, conquered French hearts with an opera about
the Greek twins, *Castor and Pollux,* with a libretto by Pierre Bernard,
skillful and somewhat dramatic (1737). In this "he struck a . . . balance between the simple and the sumptuous," says Kathleen O'Donnell
Hoover, in her engaging *Makers of Opera.*

He used an overture very much like Lully's, but with Scarlatti's
"bill-of-fare" idea. That is, he expanded and used bits of the opera in
the overture. This procedure was copied by other composers later on.

THE WAR OF THE BUFFOONS

It would be pleasant if we could leave Rameau, after his success with
Castor and Pollux, to enjoy his new popularity. But something was
about to happen to spoil the comfort and fame he deserved at court,
something to help opera along its march, a musical war was coming!

Yes, the music-loving public was stirred by "The War of the Buffoons"! Troupes of Italians had been coming to France for years with
musical plays. In 1752 a band arrived with a graceful, humorous,
sparkling and natural little opera by G. B. Pergolesi, called *La serva
padrona* (*The Mistress Maid*), about ordinary people, not shepherds,
gods or heroes. It was amusing, melodious, with crackling dialogue;
a swift-moving little play that is still heard with delight. It had neither
stately and interrupting dances nor choruses.

Some were charmed by it. Some hated it. The music world was
divided into two factions—those who were for Lully's and Rameau's
French operas—and those who wanted every opera to be like Pergolesi's
La serva padrona. Even the court was divided into two camps. The
Queen was for Italian opera, the King was for the French. Poor
Rameau! First, he was hated because the people loved Lully; second,
they thought he was too modern; and now, because he didn't write in
the style of Pergolesi, he was called an "old fogey."

Rameau, of course, was anti-Pergolesi. This threw him to the side
of the Lullyists, his former enemies, who had maintained that his music
was "queer"! So musicians, like politicians, have "strange bedfellows."
But stranger yet, it is said that Rameau later in life tried to write like
Pergolesi.

No doubt Rameau was wise enough to know that opera needed a new draught of air and that the criticisms were reasonable. Everything was cut and dried. At this time the people, as well as the critics, were getting tired of prescription-made operas, with stories about remote characters. The exact number of songs was prescribed for sopranos and tenors; songs were rarely given to a basso; choruses were few, even in Rameau's operas; when the singer finished his song, he had to leave the stage.

PHILOSOPHER AS CRITIC

Jean Jacques Rousseau, critic, philosopher and musician, lover of the gayer, more tuneful, less serious Neapolitan opera, took up arms against poor Rameau. He wrote *Le Devin du village* (*The Village Sooth-sayer,* 1752) to show what a simpler opera could be. He lambasted the opera of his day, saying:

The actresses are almost in convulsions, forcing loud cries from their lungs, with their hands clenched against their breasts, their heads thrown back, their countenances inflamed, their veins swollen, their bodies heaving. It is difficult to know if the eye or the ear is the more disagreeably affected. Their efforts cause as much suffering to those who look at them as their singing does to those who listen to them; and what is really inconceivable is that this shrieking is almost the only thing applauded by the audience. By the clapping of hands, one would take them for deaf people, who were so delighted now and again to catch a few piercing sounds that they wished the actors to redouble their efforts.

Rousseau liked the natural comic opera of Naples, where singing "comedians" rather than "singers" acted the pieces. It is interesting to see that in the new musical dramas today singing factors are demanded.

Another critic of Rameau's day said: "The actors generally speak in maxims and proverbs, and sing madrigal after madrigal. When each has sung two or three couplets, the scene is ended, and the dancing begins anew—if it did not, we should die of boredom." The madrigal died hard. It was still able to block the action of opera!

The "War of the Buffoons" may have interfered with Rameau's career, but for the good of limbering up the heavy, lumbering opera, we should rejoice. Composers all over the world took hold of Pergolesi's snappy ideas which helped to make opera international, and so did away with many formal national peculiarities. But, best of all, the audiences were saved from boredom, and opera-writing was rescued from decay.

The French soon frowned on the Italian troupes that gave opera buffa akin to *La serva padrona*. Taking the hint from Pergolesi, they began to use their own *Le jeu de Robin et de Marion* as the basis of French opéra bouffe; and a most enticing kind of opera, opéra comique.

In spite of the "War of the Buffoons" and the deserved harsh criticism, opera was strengthened by Jean-Philippe Rameau because of his more effective and more expressive orchestra; more piquant or spicy rhythms; ingenious and new tone combinations (harmonies); and bolder modulations, or the traveling from one key or scale to another, the result of his scientific studies.

Anyone following Lully would have had a hard road in France. Yet Rameau was a link between Lully and Gluck, whose first opera was given in Italy four years after Rameau's successful *Castor and Pollux*.

Rameau's ballet was more showy and less a part of the opera's action than Lully's. This would have hurt Lully's sense of operatic architecture, although Lully did not mind inserting all kinds of tiresome, lifeless songs, dances and recitatives. But now elements of Italian opera were creeping in, such as the aria da capo; the use of Italian backgrounds in scenes of ballet and opera; the exaggerated athletic vocal music and other things.

RAMEAU'S CONTRIBUTIONS

Rameau gave more attention to improving the expressiveness of both orchestra and chorus than Lully. Although he developed Lully's art of declamation, he added more songs, which made his operas more enjoyable.

Musical grammarian that he was, he did much experimentation with overtures, and his "symphonies," or instrumental pieces, were meant to describe things happening on the stage. Whereas Lully could describe beautiful pathos and soft sentiment, Rameau was the first of the early French composers to use the orchestra descriptively: to picture storms, offstage battles, disasters, heavy seas, winds, and the sounds of animals. This he carried into his pieces for the *clavecin* in such titles as "The Whirlwind," "The Call of the Bird," "The Hen," etc. He suggested emotion and events in the many dances of his time. Some of these, as well as Lully's, were the basis of the *suite,* a collection

of dances in contrasting speeds and rhythms, which became one of
the important instrumental forms.

Rameau's orchestra usually consisted of about forty-seven instruments: two flutes, four oboes, five bassoons, one trumpet. The rest
were strings, some percussion, horns, subsequently the clarinet, and
occasionally the musette (similar to a bagpipe). He gave each instrument a distinct part of its own, which made for more life and color.

In spite of the demanding soloists' opposition, Rameau developed
the chorus, and his melodies were so charming that they were copied
in Italy and Germany.

It might be asked why Rameau didn't reach Lully's dizzy heights.
For one reason he was not particular enough about his libretto. He
even boasted that any composer could put anything to music, saying:
"I could set the *Holland Gazette* to music." But he fell into a pit, for
sometimes the words were not well chosen, so the music turned out
to be artificial. Rameau, however, wrote beautifully when the situation
was tragic, but was prone to drag out his scenes when the text was
dull. Furthermore, the "War of the Buffoons" and the new opera buffa
detracted from his glory. Another reason, too, that Rameau's music
is not heard more often is that he was the last of the great composers
of his era. It was the fault of Father Time. A new art, a new attack,
a new handling of music and drama was being born.

Jean-Philippe Rameau, however, won the people's love, and was
deeply mourned as France's greatest composer when he died in 1764,
just before he was to have been elevated to the nobility, and after he
had become (1745) Composer of the King's Chamber Music, one of
the dozen posts formerly held by Lully.

With Rameau ending an era, France was well started in the arts
of opera. After she had expelled the Italian traveling companies from
whom she learned the value of the comique and its everyday romance,
she forged ahead quite conscious of the supremacy of Italian opera in
Europe.

SCENE IV

Beginnings of Opera in Germany

THE FOLK SINGSPIEL

LIKE other European countries before the birth of opera, Germany had her sacred plays, akin to the miracle, mystery, morality and pastorals, or the characteristic plays of the French, Italian and English, as well as her popular plays with instrumental music, dancing and songs.

The folk *Singspiel,* or song-play, the German secular play with music, was popular from the thirteenth century well into the sixteenth. It was somewhat like, and stemmed from, the French *vaudevilles.* It was not opera, for it had no recitative to connect the songs, and the actors spoke and joked without any musical accompaniment. Nevertheless, the Singspiel influenced opera in Germany and even in England.

The early Singspiel became a bit "rough," but the cobbler composer-poet and one of the most eminent Meistersinger, Hans Sachs of Nuremberg (1494–1576), is said to have helped to reform it by showing in his own compositions what could be done.

MARTIN LUTHER'S SPUR TO MUSIC

In addition to the Singspiel, the Germans had been fortunate in having Martin Luther's first hymnbook, published in 1524, for it spurred the writing of song with melody and accompaniment (monody), released music from the older forms of plain song and Gregorian Chant, and permitted a freer and a more distinctive use of instruments —so dear to the German musical mind and heart.

HEINRICH SCHÜTZ AND THE BAROQUE ERA

Some years after the death of Hans Sachs, news of *Dafne* by Peri and Rinuccini (librettist) reached Germany. The ruler of Saxony, a virtual King Cole, although he did not "call for his fiddlers three," did summon Heinrich Schütz (1585–1672), Germany's most expert composer of oratorio, cantata, and opera before Johann Sebastian Bach, and asked him to put to music a German translation of Rinuccini's poem *Dafne*. When completed, it was performed in 1627 for the wedding of Princess Louise of Saxony. So the first attempt at Italian opera was celebrated as the first of the German operas. Strange to say, again the music of this *Dafne* was lost. With *Dafne* and other Italian operas, the Italian invasion was on.

It may be surprising to learn that Heinrich Schütz was called the "Father of German Music," when we have usually considered Bach in that role. But when you hear the heart-warming compositions of Schütz and realize that he was born a century before Bach, the title is understandable. J. S. Bach, one of the greatest Germans, did not open an era, but closed one.

The period known as the Baroque followed the Renaissance. It started about the middle of the sixteenth century with Claudio Monteverdi as one of the initiators of this musical style. The name is supposed to have come from a pearl of irregular shape that was used at the time for decoration and was called in Portuguese *barrocco*. The style denotes greater freedom and irregularity in the European arts which followed the serenity and disciplines of the Renaissance. It is distinguished by the youthful energy of its composers (and, indeed, men in all the other arts) in striving for forms to express deeper feeling, color, and contrast. In opera it developed fantasy, elaborate plot, dramatic effects, and magnificent scenery. Its worst faults were overexaggeration, overornamentation, and incongruities of style. These characteristics are found not only in music, but in architecture, painting, sculpture, and literature. The Trevi Fountain in Rome may be cited as a typical example of Baroque art.

This Baroque Period has often been belittled. But an era needs no apology which gave us, in music alone, the works of Palestrina, Orlando di Lasso, Monteverdi, the Scarlattis, Schütz, Keiser, Lully, Rameau, Purcell, Bach, and Handel, to name a few. Nor should an age be frowned upon which gave us the vocal compositions: oratorio, cantata, opera, aria de capo, passion music, and other elaborate and profound choral works; and instrumental forms such as the overture, the suite, the early sonata, the *concerto grosso*. Furthermore, instruments themselves were miraculously improved, and the violin, in all its nobility, was born. Indeed, this Baroque Period gave so much to music and especially to opera that later it inspired Gluck, Mozart, Beethoven, and Weber to cut new paths.

FIRST OPERAS IN GERMANY

Every little German court of peer or king had its Italian opera, while the "people" clung to their amusing and substantial Singspiel, for the Singspiel influenced and stimulated the German kind of opera as did nothing else. It also kept alive the dance, which was banned by the Church in formal operas. As French was the court language— French opera, too, invaded Germany. Native poets translated Italian and French stories and works into German. In Leipzig the opera fever was so widespread that even Johann Sebastian Bach was influenced by it and wrote two very amusing cantatas, *Phoebus and Pan* and the satirical and more original *Coffee Cantata* (*"Schweigt stille, plaudert nicht"*—"Be Still and Complain Not"). In the former, new musical methods were lampooned—quite the reverse of what Richard Wagner was to do many years later in *Die Meistersinger,* when he upheld the *new* and ridiculed the *old* (see page 314). In the latter, the drinking of the new beverage, coffee, caused comic and romantic complications. Bach evidently, like the Venetians and Neapolitans, relished humor in drama. He understood, furthermore, as well as opera writers, the use of dramatic processes, seen in such works as *"The Passion According to St. Matthew"* and *"The Passion According to St. John,"* which are more dramatic than many operas.

The first so-called German operas (then known as *Singspiele*) were tinged with more Italian and French traits than German, and were more like the dramma per musica, the pastorales and French dances. The Singspiel made use of the popular coloratura singing, with its flighty trills and high tones, held so long that the singer seemed often to be on the verge of exploding! Recitative was also made use of, but not too skillfully.

Even in the Italian-French, and often English-tinged, operas, the Germans showed their love of instruments by giving them special attention and discriminating use.

Among those writing internationally flavored "operas" was Sigmund Theophilus Staden (1607–1655), whose opera *Seelewig,* (*Eternal Soul*) was a pastoral drama mixed with highly moral sentiments like the old morality play. This is what was called a "school drama," for it was the kind given by students of German schools and was supposed to preach as well as to entertain. In our day, too, the school and university are presenting opera fitted to their capacity and resources.

But try as he would, Staden did not have the knack of writing recitative, so his string of many-versed songs, somewhat in the English ballad-play fashion, just didn't "act," and his so-called opera, *Seelewig,* is nothing more nor less than a Singspiel with frills.

SECOND OPERA HOUSE IN EUROPE

For years Italianate and "Frenchified" operas were given in the small courts of noblemen in Dresden, Bonn, Düsseldorf, and other German cities, until the Free City of Hamburg, not ruled by the French-Italian speaking people of the nobles' courts, built a theater in 1678 to give what they then called German opera. It was the second theater to be built in Europe, the San Cassiano in Venice having been the first. (It is interesting to remember that at this time the American Colonies called music played on instruments artificial, or man-made, therefore ungodly and to be banned.)

The first German work given in the new Hamburg opera house was written by Johann Theile (1646–1724), a pupil of Schütz. It had to have an undeniably religious theme and title to "get by" the censors, and Theile did himself proud with his! Its name is *Adam und Eva, oder Der erschaffene, gefallene, und wieder aufgerichtete Mensch, Die Geburt Christi (Adam and Eve, or the Created, Fallen, and Resurrected Man, the Birth of Christ),* produced in 1681.

The title of this opera sounded like an oratorio fresh from church. It did so purposely in order to placate the clergy and prove to the censors that opera was not frivolous. In England, too, at this time, the composers had to pick their secular way just as carefully. Nevertheless, these trial spins along the early operatic roads gave composers practice.

KEISER, IMPORTANT OPERA COMPOSER

One of the most important Hamburgians at this time was Reinhard Keiser (1674–1739). His works followed many other good experiments in German opera which had songs *(Lieder)*, dignity, good rhythm, fine melody, less dry recitative, duets, more choruses, ballets, and better orchestras than the Italian operas. He could write in the bantering style of the Neapolitan and in the vein of the English ballad-opera.

Keiser joined the qualities of the elegance of the French dignified song with the melody of the Italians. He wrote opera with a light and charming, Mozart-like touch, and with the lovely lubrication of folk music—the ever-living basis of all national music. He united the best of the Italian and the French with the German ideas and skills, with emphasis on the orchestra. Yet, he, in the manner of his day, presented all his songs in Italian, and all the recitative in German. The arias were sung with much *bravura* (decoration and force) in Italian while translations were given in German to the audiences!

The first entirely German opera in German was awaiting Mozart, the Miraculous, in the eighteenth century, for frankly, German opera did not march independently of French and Italian elements until around the end of the eighteenth and beginning of the nineteenth centuries. Before then it was but an imitation or compound of alien national operas.

In Keiser we see the sturdy qualities that were to make German opera pre-eminent. It was unfortunate that he had to use the silly libretti of his time, especially in his *Prince Jodelet*. His best works were *Octavia* and *Croesus*. His efforts helped to establish opera in German for the Germans. Indeed, his songs were so delightful and so well bulwarked by the orchestra that Johann Mattheson called him an "Emperor of Song." Yet, with the compositions of George Philipp Telemann, Mattheson, and Handel, the Hamburg opera ceased to exist in 1735, and Italian opera "took over" until late in the eighteenth century.

J. J. FUX

Coming between Keiser and Handel was Johann Josef Fux, an Austrian (1660–1741), who was carried to his own elaborately staged, outdoor opera, *Costanza e Fortezza* (*Constancy and Fortitude*), on a litter because he was suffering from gout. The performance took five hours, including an elaborate ballet. This performance celebrated a royal birthday, and had all the marks of splendor in a theater seating four thousand. Imagine the vast and elaborate scenery! Imagine a thousand candles and hanging lamps! Fux used the dramatic German style, in which the orchestra was given importance with some ornamental or florid passages. He employed an aria somewhat like Scarlatti's—but with less florid passages. Three *castrati* sang in the production. His ballet was written by another composer. Recently Smith College gave a performance of this *Costanza e Fortezza,* its first revival since its première in 1723.

SCENE V

Beginnings of Opera in England

ENGLAND, unlike Germany, France, Italy and the other European nations, has not given the world a developed opera of her own.

GOLDEN AGE OF MADRIGALS

As background for great opera, England had had her Golden Age of Madrigals and had grown as beautiful a crop as ever exercised the vocal chords of men, women, and children; her writers such as Shakespeare, Marlowe, Dryden, Milton, and others; and she had the examples of writers of youthful opera, such as Lully and Rameau in France; Monteverdi, Scarlatti, Pergolesi in Italy; and Staden, Keiser, and Hasse in Germany.

England also had as beautiful a treasury of masques, glees and catches (rounds with jokes and puns introduced) as could be found on the continent of Europe which could have formed the bases of an opera school. Besides, she had a music-loving people and lively dramatic folk music. The English had always loved the masque, which began as court entertainment. The nobility dressed in elaborate costumes and masked themselves at their grand balls. These were extravagant entertainments with pantomime, instrumental music, singing and dancing, and every kind of scenic effect and costume. Among the best texts were those by their poets, Ben Jonson, Beaumont and Fletcher and John Milton. Shakespeare's *Tempest* and Milton's *Comus* were put to music. The mask itself, first used in Greece and then in Italy, traveled to all the European countries. It is easy to see why, for even now we enjoy masking at balls and at carnival times because we can "let ourselves go" when no one knows who we are!

About this time, the theater stage became framed in what we call the proscenium arch, and the people sat in front of it. In Shakespeare's theater on the other hand, the stage folk had acted in a sort of arena, and the people and audience sat above and around it. This is now called the "arena theatre," and seems to be straggling back into the twentieth century. After Charles I lost his head, and after the Civil War, Cromwell was in command. He banned opera and theater as wicked (1649). In spite of him, however, "drolls" (rather vulgar farces) crept in at fairs and village shows. These, with the masques and some plays, given religious names to fool the censor, kept drama alive in England in spite of their being often very shocking!

Among the polite ones were the first so-called English opera, *The Siege of Rhodes,* given in 1656. The music was by Henry Lawes, who was probably helped by Matthew Locke, both writers of excelling airs and madrigals. Inigo Jones, one of the world's great architects, designed the scenery. Sir William D'Avenant wrote the book. The story, based on the capture of Rhodes from the Knights of St. John, was only a background for the romantic and imaginary episodes which seemed aimed at encouraging the noblest love. It had to have a moral to "get by" the censor while Oliver Cromwell ruled. *The Siege of Rhodes* was in five acts (*entries, fyts,* or *fitts,* as they called them in those days). Indeed, at this time many plays with music were given in private homes and advertised as "lectures"! In order, furthermore, to sound unlike wicked opera, they put a chorus at the end of each act, and only one song in the whole "opera." All the rest was recitative. The music of the many collaborators has been lost.

PURCELL

Other operas followed but none of the composers' attempts, even when collaborating with as accomplished poets as John Dryden (1631–1700), can be compared with the work of Henry Purcell (1658–1695).

Little is known about Purcell except that he wrote music with great ease and lovely melody. He was about two years old when Prince Charles was restored to the throne (1660) as King Charles II. With music and the revived theater going full blast, no one had to pretend to give a serious or moral lecture or an oratorio when he produced a play with or without music. It was the most amusing, brilliant, and the "naughtiest" period of English drama. Among the dramatists, whose plays, however, never reached the grandeur and beauty of Shakespeare, was William Congreve (1670–1729). They wrote wittily about people, but did not actually paint character. The Restoration writers parodied historic and heroic drama, and had a good time with the people and events of their day.

When Henry Purcell was six years old, he became one of the pupils, called "Children," of the Chapel Royal, where the lucky boys learned to play, sing, read music at sight, and studied Latin. He learned later to play the lute, and to build and tune organs as well as play on them. He also became expert on the violin, which was just being perfected in Cremona, Italy. Henry had just begun to write pieces to celebrate birthdays and other events, like Mozart a century later. Indeed, in many ways, he was like Mozart, even to an early death in his thirties.

At twelve, he wrote a merry piece celebrating the birthday of Charles II, the gay King. It was not written for the voice, but for one instrument alone. In Purcell's time, we see the emancipation of instruments, which were now to be independent of the voice after all the years of acting as accompaniments in serious music.

Purcell was best known for his incidental music to plays, which most poets, with the exception of Shakespeare, have liked. Purcell, besides, wrote music in nearly all forms, for the church as well as secular cantatas and fantasias.

He was the first Englishman to write pieces for instruments called *sonatas*—meaning in Italian "sound pieces," to distinguish them from "voice pieces." So much of the music had been written for the voice, that the word *sonata* had no reference to the form the sonata was to take later under Haydn, Mozart, and Beethoven.

Purcell is best known today for his charming songs and for one opera in particular—*Dido and Aeneas*.

Although his operas were not what we call opera today, they were more like it than any of the old masques had been, with their more or less continuous action and clear-cut story. But the plots and stories and dances in operas of Purcell's time such as *Dido and Aeneas* have scant interest for opera lovers of today. They are too "old-fashioned" and slow moving. Whatever he wrote in the way of incidental music and opera, however, showed that had he lived longer than thirty-seven years, he might have given England a distinctive type or school of opera. The music in England had more reserve, akin to the Flemish, rather than the glamour of the Italian composers.

Yet he profited by the advice and teaching of Pelham Humphrey, who knew Lully's secrets and brought many a good idea from France to make English opera less stodgy and dull. Charles II was sick of the stately counterpoint of the court. So, when Purcell was a lad of fourteen, he imported Robert Cambert in 1672 after his Lully-made failure in France. Henry, too, probably learned much from Cambert, who became Master of the Music to the Court.

Among others who had a definite influence on Purcell was John Blow, a writer of songs, masques and attempts at opera. He had been educated in Italy and passed on inspiration to Purcell. He did much, it is said, to divorce English opera from the Italian. Because Purcell was able to catch an idea and write very rapidly, he was often called upon for music for spectacles and large public shows. *Dido and Aeneas* (1680), written for a girls' school, "was one of the most original expressions of genius in all opera," said Gustav Holst. Mozart was the greatest prodigy—but he was reared on opera and other music. In England there was not any opera tradition. "Yet," continues Holst in *The Heritage of Music,* "he wrote the only perfect English opera ever written. . . . Probably the English language has never been set so perfectly either before or since." Maybe Humphrey, seeing the care Lully gave to the mating of words with music, had been careful in his instructions to young Henry. *Dido and Aeneas* is in rhymed verse. Professor Dent says that it ". . . hovers between singing and declamation." Its plot moves in a continued line, and is quite convincing and dramatic.

Yet *Dido and Aeneas* is more like a masque ballet than an opera. Purcell used dances the way Lully used them, and music like the cantatas of Monteverdi. This turned out to be charming, not a musical hash. No other writer in England, not even he, followed it up by operas in this same style. Instead, much incidental music was composed for plays—graceful and tuneful, but contributing little to the march of opera.

Purcell used a kind of decorated recitative, not quite as dry (independent of accompaniment) as the Italian. He used overtures (much like the French); melodious songs, often with the loveliness of folk tunes; duets, solos and ensembles. Purcell thought, with other composers, that although opera was a story to be sung with proper "action," it was mainly scenery, "machines," dance and lights.

His other two operas, *King Arthur* and *Fairy Queen,* with his sweet melody and his own kind of recitative or declamation, are more like English masques. Indeed, Purcell has a sense of action or drama in everything he wrote for the stage, and he does not stiffen his story with the da capo aria or other Italian embroideries. But his subjects and plots do not interest modern audiences.

His use of instruments, particularly the horn, was engaging and lovely. "Come If You Dare" from *King Arthur* illustrates this. Often he wasted beautiful music on poor poetry. He did not have the taste shown by the French in their choice of texts.

Purcell was the first non-Italian to use Italian words such as *largo,* meaning slow; *allegro,* fast; *presto,* very fast; and all the rest. (Today, we are going back to directions in English for playing works by American and English composers.)

Unfortunately, most of Purcell's works are in huge books, or tomes, which Harvey Grace, in the New Cyclopedia of Music and Musicians calls "Tombs," because they hold buried music he thinks should be dug out.

With Purcell's death in 1695 the development of English grand opera ceased. England never excelled in opera again, until possibly in the twentieth century, but often outshone other nations in the operetta, both romantic and humorous.

Purcell began and ended a period of English opera seria. England embarks now on the march of opera with light opera of a delightful type, the ballad opera, and with France and Germany keeps her eyes and more particularly her ears, open to a time of innovation and Italian opera.

Purcell achieved fame, probably with fewer known works than almost any other composer.

BALLAD OPERA

The English invented a charming kind of opera which suited them very well. It is ballad opera and descended from their beloved masques. It was inexpensive to produce, and beyond all, was a democratic method of bringing operatic performances to the people. It was not fancy or "fanciful" in any way. The scenery was simple. The songs were simpler. And the story was simplest.

It was decidedly a democratic kind of opera, spoken drama, with musical numbers set to tunes that were already familiar to the audience. So anybody could go out of the opera house whistling or humming its tunes. (In 1949 it was said that Stalin rebuked composers because, as they left the theater, people could not whistle or sing tunes from the music they had heard.)

Ballad opera was not popular in the undemocratic countries of Europe, where it made no difference to the higher-up whether the masses enjoyed opera or not.

THE BEGGAR'S OPERA

The most amusing and most important of the ballad operas of the eighteenth century was *The Beggar's Opera,* first given in 1728. It was a satirical (see page 77) revue, containing a string of sixty-nine familiar airs, by masters of satire, which the English have always been.

SCENE VI

Handel, Creator of Vast Canvases

AT THE Hamburg opera, glorified by Keiser and commanded by Mattheson, we can thank a button for having saved the life of a colossus in music, George Frederick Handel (born in Halle, Germany, 1685; died in London, England, 1759). We can thank the button for Handel's *Largo, Messiah,* and many other glorious works, for it splintered the sword wielded by Mattheson in a duel between him and Handel. Nevertheless they became such great friends that Mattheson wrote a biography of Handel. It would be difficult to overestimate Handel's influence on the opera writers and composers who came after him; what he *did* for opera was more important than are his operas.

Fortunately, his genius for music overrode his father's determination to make him a lawyer, so little George Frederick learned to play the harpsichord, the organ, and the violin. The violin, at eighteen, got him into Hamburg, where he played "second fiddle" in the orchestra and sometimes conducted when Mattheson was singing on stage. Mattheson's triple ability to sing, conduct, and compose led to the duel, because Handel, so enamored with conducting while his friend was singing in his own opera, refused to relinquish the baton when Mattheson returned to the pit.

Handel, who could be as sweet as saccharine, had a violent temper; he was sometimes obstreperous and always as unpredictable as a volcano.

His invaluable experience at Hamburg led to his first opera, *Almira,* after only two years. *Almira* was a pronounced success. The text was a mixture of Italian and German. His next venture, *Nerone* (*Nero, or Love Obtained Through Blood and Murder*), was a failure. The audience did not take to it as it did to *Almira,* and the Keiser regime, because of jealousies and intrigues, was nearing its end.

Hamburg had served to convince Handel that opera was his destiny and that in Italy he could study it at first hand. During the years from 1706 to 1710 he visited many cities in Italy, where he was called *il caro Sassone* (the dear Saxon). In Rome there was no opera at the time, but he heard magnificent church music which nourished him later in perfecting the oratorio. Also, he won fame for his harpsichord and organ playing. There he met Alessandro and Domenico Scarlatti, and Arcangelo Corelli, who wrote surpassingly well for the violin. He was also admitted to an exclusive circle, the Arcadians, which met at the palace of Cardinal Ottoboni. For this group Handel wrote two oratorios, *La Resurrezione* and *Trionfo del Tempo* (*The Triumph of Time*). In Rome he began *Roderigo,* his first opera to an Italian text, which had a successful première in Florence in 1707. He visited Venice, the opera capital of the world, and Naples, where he profited by hearing Spanish as well as Italian music.

HANDEL IN ITALY

In Italy he learned the best of Italian opera habits, as in Germany he had the German. He heard French opera during those years and acquired the artistic foundation essential to developing his technique.

Cardinal Grimani, whose family owned an opera house in Venice, was the author of the libretto to Handel's opera, *Agrippina,* which was performed in 1709 and 1710.

He also met in Rome a composer and bishop, Agostino Steffani, who was *Kapellmeister* (conductor) at the court of Hanover, Germany. In Venice he had met Prince Ernst Augustus of Hanover at the time *Agrippina* was performed. Owing to the Prince's enthusiasm, Handel was invited back to Germany, and Steffani relinquished his post to him. An historian said that he had "walked in the steps of Steffani, but his feet were larger"!

He was barely established in Hanover when he was invited to England, where he went for a brief stay in 1710. Before returning, he had produced a successful opera, *Rinaldo,* and had paved his way to a career in London that was to last the rest of his life. *Rinaldo* was based on a text adapted by an Italian, Giacomo Rossi, from a famous classic, Torquato Tasso's *Gerusalemme liberata* (*Jerusalem Delivered*). Practically overnight, Handel won both the aristocracy and the people with the beautiful melodies, many of which, including *"Lascia ch'io pianga"* ("Let me weep"), still find a welcome place on recital programs.

LONDON ADOPTS HANDEL

But Destiny was playing queer tricks! He lost his heart to London, and after a short time in Hanover, received another leave of absence from the Prince "for a reasonable time." Handel forgot all about the "reasonable time"; he forgot all about his promise to return. But if Mahomet did not go to the mountain, the mountain went to Mahomet, and, following the death of Queen Anne (1714), the Hanoverian Prince was called to the English throne as George I.

Not only did the King forgive Handel's disobedience, but obviously he, with a German's love of music, was overjoyed to have a genius from his fatherland at his beck and call. The monarch, delighted with Handel's opera *Amadizi,* in 1715 made him music master to the princesses with a substantial annual pension.

Handel anglicized his name to George Frederick Handel from the German Georg Friedrich Händel. He became a British citizen and had more influence on English music than any native composer since Purcell. Here was a German in England, writing and producing Italian opera. Yet, in spite of almost fifty years spent on British soil, he never learned to speak English without a heavy German accent.

He was not only composer, but also impresario and conductor. He composed about thirty-six operas for London; among the chief ones were *Radamisto* (1720), *Ottone* (1723), *Giulio Cesare* and *Tamerlano* (1724), *Rodelinda* (1725), *Admeto* (1727), *Orlando Furioso* (1733), *Alcina* (1735), *Serse* (1738), and *Deidamia* (1741).

The Royal Academy of Music opened its doors in 1720 with unprecedented success during its first season. From April until June, *Radamisto* registered one of the greatest triumphs of Handel's opera career. He was riding high as undisputed czar of music in London.

Unfortunately, however, with the second season, a second composer was introduced, the Roman Giovanni Battista Bononcini, who, although less talented, proved to be a serious rival to Handel. London society was divided into factions, as one writer expressed it:

> Some say, compared to Bononcini,
> That Mynherr Handel's but a ninny;
> Others aver that he to Handel
> Is scarcely fit to hold a candle.
> Strange all this difference should be
> 'Twixt Tweedledum and Tweedledee.

HANDEL VERSUS SINGERS

Handel brought to London the two *castrati* Seresino and Farinelli, whose careers were sensational. Also, the day had dawned for the prima donna, who actually became "first lady" when Handel engaged the famous soprano, Francesca Cussoni (1700–1770). His troubles began when he added a rival soprano, Faustina Bordoni. In an opera by Bononcini, Cussoni and Bordoni, on one occasion, did a hair-pulling and face-scratching scene which won them the title of "fighting cats." They were the models for a play by Colley Cibber, *The Rival Queens*.

Handel was no angel, and was difficult to get along with, although he could also be charming, affable, and full of humor. But he met his equal in Cussoni, who was accustomed to domineer over composers. One day she refused to sing an aria the way Handel wanted it. Handel was no Casper Milquetoast! As she began to scream and gesticulate, he carried the struggling rebel to a window and said, "Madam, you will sing the aria as I have written it, or I will throw you out of this window!" She sang it as written.

Cussoni's attitude was not unusual, but Handel's was, for composers were bullied by singers and had a fiendish time with them up to and through the time of Rossini. Sometimes a singer would insert passages in an aria the composer was glad he had never thought of, and for which the orchestra was unprepared. Imagine the consternation of the producers and orchestra during these unending cadenzas!

OPERA STIFFENS

The singers demanded the kind of song they wished and would not let composers depart from the following prescription: principal male singer must be a soprano; second male singer must be a soprano or a contralto; third male singer must be a tenor; fourth male singer must be a basso; there must be three women's rôles among them—a prima donna who must be a high soprano, and two others. Each main character had a certain number of songs in a dictated and particular style. The secondary characters were only allowed two songs. At the end of each song, the singer had to leave the stage. This was a rigid rule made by the poet librettists Zeno and Metastasio, for they contended that the emotional situation must end with the song. The finale and explanations and the happy ending were given in the driest kind of recitative, with the least accompaniment. (This made the *scena—*

whether recitative or melody—dull and stiff.) There was occasionally a chorus at the end, and the finale closed with a dance.

No wonder opera became set! No wonder people wearied of it! No wonder critics were praying for a new kind of opera that should be less serious and weighty, more interesting, more surprising! Composers would have found exciting and surprising enough plots had they made stories out of the tyrannical antics of the singers! Jealousy stirred the pots of discord. Each singer demanded the best part. None wanted anyone else to be on the stage longer than himself. No one permitted another to sing a better or more important part than his. Sparkling, ornate passages with long-held high tones were eagerly sought. Woe betide the composer who gave more high tones to one songbird than to another, even though the libretto demanded them.

In performance, the notated score and what was sung were two different affairs. The notation was a mere skeleton of what actually was heard, for custom permitted the singer to fill in the outline with ornamentation (trills, runs, turns, roulades, etc.) which he extemporized or, better still, wrote out to suit himself. True, the singer was trained in composition as no vocalist is today. Sometimes the elaboration consisted of a few additional notes to a given melody; but sometimes the changes were spectacular and disrupting to the original musical idea. Vocal elaborations approached the virtuosity of the cadenzas in violin concertos, and one wonders how vocal chords stood all the demands made upon them. This is true particularly of the cadenzas Farinelli composed. Unfortunately, the singers had become so pampered and spoiled by wealthy patrons that the composers had to bow, for the most part, to their wishes. Because of the restrictions put upon composers by the singers, opera became more stereotyped and repetitious, and the audiences found it more boring.

Handel, however, might have succeeded in creating an English school of opera, but for the coming of John Gay's roisterous piece, *The Beggar's Opera,* which dislodged formal opera and made audiences crave merry plots about everyday people rather than highly polished and serious stories out of the past.

THE BEGGAR'S OPERA

THE first performance of *The Beggar's Opera* took place on January 29, 1728, and had a run of more than two months. The librettist was John Gay and the English folk tunes, popular French airs, and tunes from works by the composers Purcell, Bononcini, Carey, and Handel, were compiled and arranged by Dr. Johann Christopher Pepusch, who, like Handel, was a German living in London. The work satirized Italian opera and the political and social conditions of the day, even going so far as to caricature the Prime Minister, Sir Robert Walpole.

The vitality of this ballad opera, which became the model for many more of its kind, is apparent in the fact that it has never died, but is subject to revisions and revivals to the present day.

HANDEL OPERA ON THE WANE

The Royal Academy of Music went bankrupt in 1728, two years after Handel had become a British subject and was appointed Composer to the Court and to the Chapel Royal. But in 1727 George I had died, and George II ascended the throne. He continued Handel's pension and Handel taught the young princesses and wrote four coronation anthems that brought him more fame.

Unwilling to admit the defeat of serious opera, Handel again opened the Royal Academy with Heidegger, the Swiss manager, with whom he had worked before. But now he had to contend not only with artistic failures but with social and political issues as well. Seresino and Farinelli went over to a rival company, the Opera of Nobility, that opened in 1733. London, which had ceased to support Handel's company, now was called upon to patronize two. Handel's rivals were the Italian composers Porpora and Hasse, the German-Italian who had married one of Handel's "songbirds," Bordoni. An anti-German faction arose among the nobility, headed by the Prince of Wales, which backed the brilliant but brief new opera venture. In 1734, Handel became the opera director of the newly built Covent Garden Theatre.

When he could no longer meet the onslaught of his antagonists in the Opera of Nobility, he turned to the middle classes with whom a new interest in choral music was rapidly becoming a tradition. His interest in oratorio, however, was not an admission that opera as opera was a failure, or that he could not meet the requirements.

In spite of his own failing fortune, he devoted himself to a charitable "Society for the Support of Decayed Musicians"; had won praise for two settings of Dryden, *Alexander's Feast* and *Ode to St. Cecilia,* and solaced himself by writing his *Concerti Grossi.* Characteristic of the extremities of Handel's ups and downs, he was threatened with imprisonment for debts and at the same time was honored by having his statue in marble set up in Vauxhall Gardens where his works were frequently played.

Not long before, he had been invited to Oxford to receive an honorary degree of Doctor of Music, which, however, he is supposed to have turned down when he heard it would cost 100 pounds! A biographer, Newman Flower, says that his arrival in Oxford might have "been the triumphant entry of a king. The town was overcrowded; even accommodations at the hostels ran out and people slept in the streets." The event was celebrated with a whole week's offerings of his oratorios: *Esther, Deborah,* the Utrecht *Te Deum, Acis and Galatea* and *Athali,* written specially for the occasion. The difference between opera and oratorio was largely a matter of staging and costuming, and in oratorios more choruses were used than in opera. Even the distinction in subject matter was not definitive, for the works produced at Oxford as oratorios included secular as well as Biblical subjects.

In 1737, Handel had a complete physical breakdown, a stroke of apoplexy from which he recovered sufficiently to produce more operas. The following year he wrote *Serse (Xerxes)*, his only comic opera, which has nothing to do with the ancient Persian king and isn't very comic to modern ears. But it brings us the familiar Largo, one of his best known and best loved melodies. Although we hear it most frequently in its organ version, in the opera it is the opening tenor aria, *"Ombra mai fu"* ("Never was there a shadow"), a song of thanksgiving to a plane tree for its gracious shade.

By 1741, Handel's opera ventures were over. The public, tired of serious opera in Italian or German, gave its support wholeheartedly to the more down-to-earth, comic, satiric, ballad operas in English that followed the coming of John Gay. So Handel, bankrupt and almost blind, turned to oratorio that was to bring him the lasting renown which he had looked for from his operas.

ORATORIOS

Handel did not turn from opera to writing his greatest and best-loved *Messiah*, in 1741, without having had years of experience in the oratorio field. In 1733, he had had the week of performances at Oxford. Among these were *Esther*, with words by Alexander Pope and John Arbuthnot after Racine, and *Acis and Galatea*, on a text, amusingly enough, by his later arrival John Gay. Both were written about 1720, when Handel was private chapel master to the Duke of Chandos in which capacity he wrote twelve sacred works known as the Chandos Anthems. *Esther*, although written by a German, was the first English oratorio, and, like many of his oratorios, was taken from the Old

Testament. Both were called masques and were probably presented in costume with scenery. They differed from opera principally in the importance given to the chorus. Bukofzer divides the oratorios of Handel into three classes: "the choral opera, the choral cantata, and the choral drama." He says too that "the oratorios share with the opera such external features as the division into three acts and the conventional types of aria." Naturally the "choral operas are those bearing the closest resemblance to opera." Because of their subject matter and form, they could be called English opera. In style they are comparable to the Italian operas of the Viennese court, which are notable for their choruses. Handel's oratorios were models of eloquent moving choruses, crystal clear instrumental music, and musically effective solos. With the power of an eloquent orator, he depicted character and many sides of the same character in broadly flowing and facile song and instrumental line. His melodic treatment both in oratorio and opera was a spur to composers of his time and a joy to his listeners, even to the present day.

Before the *Messiah,* he had written, besides the Oxford presentations, *Saul* and *Israel in Egypt* (both in 1738), the Dryden choral cantatas and John Milton's *L'Allegro, il Penseroso ed il Moderato* (1740).

MESSIAH

Messiah belongs to none of the three types, and stands alone as a work of genius, loved by musicians and laymen alike. It differs from all of his other oratorios in embodying a deeply religious spirit, whereas the others are not primarily ecclesiastical in character, "but are rather concerned with whole nations, in their relation to the divine laws, with events of national, even world-wide importance; they glorify...the ethical dignity of heroic and just action; they specify the validity of God's moral law..." So Hugo Leichtentritt wrote in the International Cyclopedia of Music and Musicians.

In such categories belong *Samson* and *Semele,* from which come the familiar arias "Where'er You Walk" and "Sleep, Why Dost Thou Leave Me?"; and *Joseph* (1743); *Belshazzar* and *Hercules* (1744); *Judas Maccabaeus* (1746); *Solomon and Susanna* (1748); *Theodora* and *Alceste* (1749); *Jephtha* (1751); and finally *The Triumph of Time and Truth,* a revision of his Italian oratorio written in Rome (1757), and others. An amazing list in view of the fact that he became blind while composing *Jephtha* and had to work with the assistance of his friend, John Christopher Schmidt, who had acted as his copyist and business manager for fifty years.

The text of *Messiah* was put together by Charles Jennens from Bible verses and is notable for its universal religious appeal. Its entire composing occupied Handel from August 22 to September 14—an incredible feat! The first performance took place in Dublin, Ireland, in April, 1742. It was heard in London the following March. So deeply affected was George II by the justly famous "Hallelujah" chorus, that instinctively he rose to his feet, the audience of necessity following the sovereign's lead. Thus was initiated a custom that is followed to this day.

In 1748, the King commissioned Handel to write appropriate music to celebrate the signing of the Peace of Aix-la-Chapelle. His contribution was the "Fireworks Music." This composition Handel played a month later for a benefit concert for one of his pet charities, the Foundling Asylum. He was made governor of the institution and donated a new organ. He opened the hospital with a performance of *Messiah* in 1750, from which many people were turned away. The proceeds of an annual performance he gave to the Foundling Asylum.

He died on April 14, 1759, and was buried in Westminster Abbey, where a monument was erected in his honor.

"Handel's long career," says Herbert F. Peyser, in the Foreword of his short pamphlet *George Frideric Handel,* "resembles a gigantic tapestry, so bewilderingly crowded with detail, so filled with turmoil and vicissitude, with vast achievements, extremes of good and ill fortune, and unending comings and goings..." "The supreme master of florid pomp," Peyser calls him, "...a composer of exquisitely delicate colorations and sensuous style, not to say a largely unsuspected master of many subtle intricacies of rhythm."

ACT III. Opera Changes Its Colors—Classicism

SCENE I

Gluck Would Cure Opera of Stiffness

BEHIND Gluck loom men who contributed to opera. Lully built ballet opera out of the French ballet, and made the love of spectacle and reverence for the word the basis for his librettos. Jean-Philippe Rameau brought Lullyism to its height. He developed opera ballet, loosened up the use of choruses and freed the orchestra from slavery to the voices. To Scarlatti and those of the Neapolitan school of opera who came after him was left the making of bel canto, the Italian overture, and the aria da capo. These Neapolitans had been forced to employ the unnatural stories and stale librettos which few could use well save a Pergolesi.

Gluck was the center of a group who desired to reduce the stiffness which had developed in libretto and ballet. Like Columbus, who did what he didn't intend, and like the Camerata, too, Gluck in giving his own works a shot of reform, opened up an unsuspected and new path for opera. "His historic significance lay, not so much in the new ideas— but in his ability to bring them to tangible embodiment in works so beautiful and powerful as to arrest the attention of the musical world." (Waldo Selden Pratt in *The History of Music*.)

Christoph Willibald Gluck (1714–87), the son of a gamekeeper, was born in Erasbach near Nuremberg, in Germany. His family had little money, so Christoph's early schooling was scant. He roamed the forests in which his father worked for a peer. In spite of little education, however, in 1756 Pope Benedict XV made him Ritter (Knight) von Gluck, a title of which he was proud.

His output was tremendous: 107 operas, including ballets and cantatas, 92 of which were produced in Italy and 8 in London. At seventy-three he died of a paralytic stroke after a short illness.

While still a child, his family moved to Vienna, where the gamekeeper-father was employed by Prince Lobkowitz, who became Gluck's most appreciative patron.

Gluck was exposed to music wherever his father worked. At eighteen he entered Prague University, after having had a public school education and after spending some time in a Jesuit school. The school, run by the Society of Jesus of the Catholic Church, gave him his first real interest in beautiful music. In 1732 he began to study the violin, the cello, and the harpsichord, and four years later he had to think of earning his living. He was kept busy singing in churches, giving lessons, concerts, and playing in orchestras. When he was twenty-two, Prince Lobkowitz took him to Vienna as his private musician. Lobkowitz was one of the good patrons.

As luck would have it, in Vienna Christoph met another prince: Prince Melzi of Milan, who took him into his own home.

In Italy, Gluck met a famous teacher, Giovanni Battista Sammarco, with whom he studied four years (1737–41), from whom he was graduated to the stage with his first opera, *Artaserse* (*Artaxerxes*) containing all the conventional devices of the popular librettist, Metastasio. Italy became the first grade in the school of composition for Christoph. He wrote several more operas in Italy, became popular, and was invited to many European cities. Probably because he became satiated after hearing so much Italian opera, the seeds of reform were implanted in him. As yet, however, he did nothing to make opera very different from the popular operatic diet, and so for this reason, no doubt, his work, *Ipernestra* (1741) became famous.

When he went again to London with his friend, Lobkowitz, he gave two operas that were not successful. Yet, by a stroke of luck, he met Handel, then on the crest of the musical wave in England. Although Handel was hot-tempered and said of Gluck that "he doesn't know as much counterpoint as Walse, my cook," the two hotheads became excellent friends. Gluck learned much from Handel about singing, and writing for the chorus and for instruments, and gave many concerts with the older genius.

By 1748 Gluck settled in Vienna, but he did not stop traveling. After his return to Vienna in 1750 from a trip to Prague, he married Marianne Pergin.

On his way to London, he stopped in Paris, where he watched French opera closely. He heard Rousseau's compositions, learned what he could of writing for chorus and ballet, and tried to attain the French skill at recitative. He was anxious to learn how to make the text of importance and how to match the words to the music, which Claude Debussy, in our time, said, "Gluck has done with the heavy hand."

Yet, for his time, and as a foreigner, he did his task well. He spent so much time in France thereafter that people began to think of him as a French composer. Indeed, this German never wrote an opera using a German text. He always used French or Italian.

In 1752 Gluck went back to Italy and became so popular that he was called "the divine Bohemian." Soon we find this world traveler back in Vienna, where he taught the child Marie Antoinette, later the unfortunate Queen of France. It is said that she used to laugh prettily at Gluck when his wig fell off as he became excited or angry while conducting.

By now he had been honored by the Austrian Court and became *Kapellmeister* to the Court Theatre in 1754, after having written an opera for the Empress Maria Theresa's birthday.

The first glimmer of the reforms that made him one of the four or five great opera writers of history can be seen in his *Il Re pastore* (*The Shepherd King,* 1756).

While he was at the Viennese court, because of the Seven Years' War, too many elaborate serious operas could not be produced. Therefore he had to revive some of the French *opéras comiques*, which he did skillfully and successfully. It was sound training for him, for we find him even writing *opéra comique*, one of which, *L'Ivrogne corrigé* (*The Reformed Tippler,* 1761), was quite successful. This is very different from Gluck's masterpieces, but in writing them he had the opportunity of limbering up his style and absorbing some methods of French dialogue and declamation.

Another instance of Gluck's versatility was in the ballet *Don Juan* (1761), which later gave Mozart the idea for his opera *Don Giovanni.* Gluck was versatile enough to take the advice of a friend and base the action of his ballet on dramatic lines rather than on the skills of the dancers. This idea had just been published by Noverre, the ballet reformer.

GLUCK MEETS CALZABIGI

Now Gluck entered the part of his career which is of the greatest importance on the path of opera. He had the good fortune to meet (1761) Ranieri de' Calzabigi who not only helped him to help opera, but won him everlasting fame. Calzabigi was an excellent poet, librettist, adventurer, libertine, diplomat, with definite ideas about drama with music. In his forty-eighth year, with *Orfeo ed Euridice* (*Orpheus and Eurydice*), the first Gluck opera for which Calzabigi wrote the libretto, Gluck began to step out of the old-fashioned frame.

It is a high spot along the march of opera and more nearly approaches the Greek pattern longed for by the Camerata than any seventeenth-century opera. It was given in Vienna in 1762. Today it is still melodious and delightful. Although it is like stately "marble statues miraculously endowed with life," nevertheless, it overthrew many opera customs.

It must have seemed at that time somewhat like the *Pelléas et Mélisande* of Debussy seemed to early twentieth-century audiences. A puzzle! Gluck's is a French opera in Italian; it follows Lully and Rameau somewhat in its style of many choruses and ballets, but he makes the chorus a character in the plot and uses the ballets more as part of the action rather than just showpieces or divertisements. For example, when Orfeo descends into Hades, he has first to pass the Furies before he can get to the Valley of the Blessed to find his beloved Euridice, and the Furies, as the chorus, really "act up" musically, and order their dog, Cerberus, to tear him to pieces. But this demigod, Orfeo, son of Apollo and the Muse, Calliope, charms the Furies with his music, and he is allowed to go on to the Valley of the Blessed, where is heard music of a gentler kind.

The opera was written for a contralto (Orfeo). Later it was rewritten for a tenor, but now it is sung by a contralto. It seems strange today to hear impassioned love songs like "I Have Lost My Eurydice" sung by a woman. This song, however, is one of the most beautiful ever written. One lovely recitative, "What Pure Light," sung by Orfeo upon reaching the Valley of the Blessed, is answered by the chorus, "Sweet Singer, You Are Welcome."

In this first opera in the newer style, it is interesting that its story should have been the same as that of the first extant opera of the Camerata, the *Euridice* of Peri.

Gluck is economical in his use of only three singers in this: Orfeo, Euridice, and Amor (Cupid). It has three acts, as in Italian opera, and not five, as in the French style in which it is cast; and it is much shorter than the usual eighteenth-century opera. It is far more like Peri and Monteverdi than like the composer's immediate predecessors, Rameau and Lully. His economy in singers may have been for financial reasons, but probably because singers were such nuisances and hindrances to composers at that time.

Originally *Orfeo* was written in Italian, but when it was given in

Paris, French was used, and Gluck gave the role to a tenor. The famous Pauline Viardot García created the role in Vienna, and played it 150 times "in a row." A toned-down declamation made a happier marriage with the instruments. The audiences from now on must interest themselves not only in vocal stunts but in story and action, combined with music, as well.

Gluck's heroic stories had noble, simple, and often very "catchy" melodies. Among the songs are "I Have Lost My Euridice" from *Orfeo;* and the minuet from his noble *Alceste (Alcestis)*, and its still popular aria sung by Alceste at the end of the first act, *"Divinités du Styx"* ("Divinities of the Styx"). *Alceste* begins with a tragic overture, which leads into the magnificent opening chorus.

Besides the *Orfeo* libretto, Calzabigi wrote *Alceste* (1767) and *Paride et Elena (Paris and Helen,* 1770). *Alceste* has been given often, although *Paris and Helen* is seldom performed even though it has only three characters—those of the title and Cupid. It is, notwithstanding, very beautiful, and is a forerunner of romantic and more emotional opera.

In *Alceste,* in his fifty-third year, Gluck stepped out and stayed out of the old-fashioned Metastasian frame and wrote a monumental work which was the first totally tragic opera, matching in somberness the drama *Alcestis* of Euripides, from which he took his libretto. In his preface to the opera, he said in part: "I seek to put music to the true purpose, that is, to support the poem, and thus to strengthen the expression of the feelings and the interest of the situation without interrupting the action ... in short, I have striven to abolish all those bad habits which sound reasoning and good taste have been struggling against in vain for so long." As far as it was within his power, Gluck did this and many other things mentioned in his long preface.

"Beauty enters with the overture, called an 'intrada' by Gluck, presumably because it leads without a break into the scene. It is the first truly tragic introduction to an opera.... This piece in D minor is the ancestor of an illustrious line from the Overture to *Don Giovanni* to the 'Tragic Overture' of Brahms." So said Alfred Einstein in his *Gluck.* Ernest Newman, too, said that it was "a notable triumph of dramatic expression..."

With all Gluck's skill the opera *Alceste* was a little too somber at first for the Parisians, although later it "took hold."

Up to now all the experimental operas were not particularly markmaking. But Gluck's *Iphigénie en Aulide,* produced under the auspices

of his former pupil Marie Antoinette in Paris (1774), was very successful. François du Roullet (1772) adapted it from a poem of Racine's.
Gluck wanted to fit the poem and music to the language and to the
nationality of the characters, a procedure still being attempted. French
productions in Paris of *Orfeo* and *Alceste* followed this, and they, too,
became successes. These, with *Iphigénie,* caused a sensation.

GLUCK WINS CONTEST

As with love, the course of success does not always run smooth. Paris
soon became a battleground! Great and famous men took sides—for
and against—Gluck and a composer named Nicola Piccinni (1728–
1800). Jean Jacques Rousseau (see below) was on the side of Gluck,
while others preferred Piccinni. Finally, it was decided to test the
composers' abilities by giving them both the same story on which to
base an opera. This was hard on them, for they were friends. The
subject was *Iphigénie en Tauride* (*Iphigenia in Tauris*), another part
of the story of Agamemnon and the Trojan War, in which Iphigenia
was to be sacrificed for the good of the Greek fleet.

Gluck won the contest in 1779. Piccinni never bore him a grudge.
Indeed, at Gluck's death, he arranged a concert in his memory. Thereafter, Piccinni lived to please the French people with light opera. "The
heroine of one of them, *La Buona Figliola,* (Rome, 1760), has given her
name to a railway station outside Rome—Cecchina. Other operatic
railway stations are Swiss Cottage (London), after Adolph Adam's *Le
Châlet* (called in England *The Swiss Cottage*) and *Szep Ilona* (Budapest), named after *La Belle Hélène* (Offenbach)." (Edward J. Dent in
Opera.)

A FORERUNNER OF ROMANTIC OPERA

Strange as it may seem, among the operas of Gluck that are rarely
given, *Armide* has seemed most modern to audiences of the nineteenth
and twentieth centuries. The libretto was written by Lully's librettist,
Philippe Quinault, after an episode from Tasso's *Jerusalem Delivered,*
as was Handel's opera, *Rinaldo. Armide,* given at the Opéra in Paris
in 1777, tells of a crusading knight who strays into the magic garden of
the enchantress Armide near Damascus. The writers saw this presented
by the Metropolitan Opera Company in New York in 1910, with a
cast which included Olive Fremstad as Armide, Louise Homer, Enrico
Caruso, Pasquale Amato, Alma Gluck, and others. Arturo Toscanini,
at that time a staff conductor at the Metropolitan, directed.

Armide, a forerunner of romantic opera, however, had little success, even though Gluck introduced into the orchestra the imitation of singing birds and purling brooks. Perchance the use of the dance in *Armide* gave a germ of an idea to Wagner for Kundry and the Flower Maidens in *Parsifal.*

<h3 style="text-align:center">GLUCK WATCHES OTHERS</h3>

Gluck always had a watchful ear and an alert eye. Although a contemporary of his, Niccolò Jommelli, a famous member of the Neapolitan school of opera (1714–74), was criticized for emphasizing the orchestra at the expense of the singing, Gluck thought Jommelli "had something" and profited by his good sense. He also learned from Johann Christian Bach, "the London Bach"—who made choruses important and reduced vocal fireworks—to emphasize the plot.

Gluck also watched Alessandro Scarlatti, Johann Adolf Hasse, and Nicola Porpora (1686–1766 or '67). Porpora wrote many operas, but is best known as an eminent "singing teacher, who kept the singer Caffarelli working five years on one page of *vocalises* (vocal exercises without words) and made him the greatest vocal technician of his time." (Oscar Thompson's International Cyclopedia of Music and Musicians.)

Hasse's importance to Gluck was in his mastery of melody and song form, but more important, in Hasse's work, Gluck had examples of the inefficiency of the outworn Metastasian libretto (See Act VI).

Gluck profited also from Tomasso Traetta (1727–79) by noting his beautiful melody and his complex scenes on a grand scale. Traetta might have been greater had he had a surer dramatic sense. Yet Jommelli, Hasse, and Traetta, although among his rivals, helped Gluck more than they knew, and his greatest rival, Nicola Piccinni, spurred him on to one of his best operas, *Iphigénie en Tauride.* That's the way to take one's rivals—improve on their methods!

<h3 style="text-align:center">OPERA'S REFORMATION</h3>

With Calzabigi's collaboration, Gluck advanced opera and has been called not the Father of German Opera or French, or Italian, but the Father of Modern Opera. This is because Gluck injected his own ideas into the opera fashions of Italy, France, and Germany, from which he adapted their best elements for his own use.

With Gluck, the orchestra began to get its place in the sun. Now it not only reflects the story's mood but can offer discussion and contradictions. Donald Grout points out in his *A Short History of Opera* that Gluck was the first composer to use an orchestral device (reiterated sixteenth notes on one tone) to denote the mental state of a character who may declare that he feels calm, when actually he is in reasonable fear for his crime. Wagner may be in debt to Gluck for this device, out of which he made a system. But the difference between Wagner's orchestra and Gluck's is obvious in the opening of the first scene of the first act of Wagner's *Die Walküre,* with the storm as background, and Gluck's agitated background music in the scene with the Furies. How much more exciting Wagner's music is! Yet Gluck did open the path for Wagner.

Gluck was among the first to use the cymbals and timpani. After Gluck, of course, composers kept making the orchestra richer to heighten effect and expression.

SONG

Song with Gluck becomes more a part of the story, not the interrupter of the opera's action, as was and is the aria da capo, which Gluck abandoned in his "reform." Song, with Gluck, is *meant* to develop the character, and transform him from a puppet into a human being. He abandoned the athletic and interrupting cadenza, written to show off the skill of the singer. The singers are now forced to consider the opera, not only their vanities. Indeed, some critics maintain that aside from some of his new ideas, this reform was the most valuable thing Gluck did for opera.

Gluck made opera an art in itself, not just a costume concert and a vocal gymnasium. Although the operas of Handel and other eighteenth-century composers are seldom given today, Gluck's *Orfeo, Armide,* and parts of the two *Iphigenias* and *Alcestis* get occasional performances.

Gluck was the first real reformer, after the Camerata, of dramma per musica. Others had improved it, or added something new. Gluck made the recitative more musical by making the stream of sound continuous through the use of strings and the harpsichord. He made his overture a preview of the ideas in the opera, as well as a partial bill-of-fare of the melodies, instead of using the formalized three-part Italian, or two-part French overture. The overture to *Iphigénie en Aulide* is fascinating and one of the world's greatest.

GREEK FEELING

One critic said in Gluck's time, when listening to *Iphigenia in Tauris*: "When I am at 'Iphigenia,' I forget I am at the opera. I seem to be hearing a Greek tragedy." So with *Orfeo* and his other operas in the new style, Gluck recaptured, with the help of Calzabigi, more of the Greek feeling than the Camerata could possibly have done.

INFLUENCE OF GLUCK

Gluck felt the need for limbering up the arthritic opera of his day. He realized the need for some kind of reformation. He, however, advocated reforms more than he embraced them. Few including himself could use his ideas; even Mozart was little influenced, for what Gluck made pontifical, stately, and remote, Mozart made brisk, human, and contemporary.

Withal Gluck earned the name of pathfinder. In fact, he did much for a far later period of opera writers. For example, much that Wagner did, which he considered his own invention, was first conceived by Gluck. Berlioz too, was a Gluck worshiper.

NICOLA PICCINNI

Nicola Piccinni, loser to Gluck in the contest, gave the orchestra a more independent music. The orchestra begins increasingly now to be able to stand alone without being hitched to a song or just being connecting tissue.

Piccinni's most important opera was *Didon,* a melodious and lovely composition. His librettist, Goldoni, the founder of modern Italian comedy and drama, wrote many librettos.

JEAN JACQUES ROUSSEAU

One of the first Frenchmen (1712–78) to write an opera on an everyday subject was Jean Jacques Rousseau. He was philosopher, critic, novelist, and clever, untaught, amateur musician, who took it upon himself to criticize and try to reform opera. He is author of the famous tract, *Le Contrât social* (*Social Contract*), and other books, as well as scathing articles against Rameau's kind of opera, which he considered pompous, dull, and outdated. His own opera *Le Devin du village* (*The Village Soothsayer,* 1752), was not very unlike the song plays with spoken dialogue and the vaudevilles that were loved in France in earlier days. Yet it was also a bit like Mozart's youthful effort, *Bastien et Bastienne,* which took ideas from Rousseau's opera. It was almost opéra comique. Presented twenty-one years after Pergolesi's *La serva padrona,* it held the stage for sixty years! Yet it is never given today, and its plot is not found even in opera-story books.

Nevertheless, *The Village Soothsayer* gave encouragement to the writing of light operas in the comic vein, hampered so long by the strictures of the arch-librettists Metastasio and Zeno, and their plot factories. It gave stimulus to the more democratic, less elaborate operas which lampooned the upper classes, pedestaled the everyday folk, and became the voice of the people.

SCENE II

Mozart the Miraculous

THE CLASSICAL PERIOD—OR THE PERIOD OF FORM

DURING the seventeenth century many interesting things happened to music. The major and minor scales came into use following the church modes. Opera, with its recitative and aria and accompaniment, was born in Florence, Italy. Chord music (harmony) came to bless the world in addition to its mother, counterpoint—or *woven music;* French opera was born and bore fruit. Instruments were much improved and instrumental music gained some independence from the voice. It was the period in which instrumental music also freed itself from Church music and contrapuntal music (polyphony).

The Classical Period was established in the eighteenth century. Bach glorified the fugue. His sons gave intimations of the German art song (*Lieder*) and the beginnings of the sonata and sonata form, the father of the symphony, the concerto and the quartet. At this time too, the giants—Haydn, Mozart and Beethoven—perfected the sonata and the symphony, and Gluck and Mozart brought opera to a pinnacle of beauty. All this inspired the next group of writers (Romanticists) to add to established musical forms, human and personal feeling.

Opera buffa had separated itself from opera seria and just needed the finishing touches of Mozart and Rossini. Besides, it bestowed upon its divorced member, opera seria, the beauties of the duet, trio, quartet, finales and other concerted numbers.

Now orchestral music became of greater importance to composers; Germany entered as an orchestral power, superseding Italy, the land of song, which had been in command for two centuries; soloists or virtuosi, violinists, singers, organists and harpsichordists became powerful. The scene of opera shifted to Vienna, the Italianated, and to Paris, the coveted.

Gluck, who wrote classical tragedy, and Handel, who painted vast historic canvases, leave the field to the greatest of them all: Wolfgang

Amadeus Mozart—the writer of (among other forms) what he called *dramma giocosa* (gay opera) with intimations of the Romantic Opera which was to come.

WOLFGANG AMADEUS MOZART, NAÏVE PLUNGER (1756–91)

Wolfgang Amadeus Mozart, born in the little city of Salzburg, was gay, charming, full of life, and to this day his delighting music paints such a picture of him.

In spite of his mystifying precocity, prematurely heavy travel as a child, his struggle for mere existence, the cruel treatment of jealous men and his death at thirty-five, he wrote hundreds of musical works in all forms, excelling in each, throwing over, in bubbling and naïve energy and with supernatural skill, several of the procedures of Gluck and his followers. Many of Mozart's forty-one symphonies are played and replayed, as well as many of his enchanting divertisements like *Eine Kleine Nachtmusik;* a few of his more than twenty operas; his church music, songs, many concertos and much chamber music. But here the interest is in what he meant to opera.

MOZART'S PRECOCITY

Mozart was one of those rarest of miracles—a prodigy who actually became a miracle man. Although following Gluck the theorist, he was not interested in reforming opera but wrote to carry out his own ideas. From childhood he was endowed with a sense of "good theater" (of dramatic effects). This is shown in his first two operas *Bastien et Bastienne* (1768), with a libretto by Friedrich Wilhelm Weiskern (1710–1768) on a story used by Rousseau in his opera *The Soothsayer;* and *La finta semplice* (*The Simple Deceiver,* 1768), for which Goldoni, the popular Italian, wrote the libretto. It was much like the plots for the old commedia dell' arte which Goldoni was trying, withal, to kill. Mozart soon changed his librettist. Here the boy of twelve displays a gift for contrast of mood, a sense of fitting word to music and an engaging talent for sweet sounds and charming plot. Not yet, of course, has his ability developed as a character painter in music.

To tell the amazing and breathtaking story of young Mozart's life would be to duplicate the multitudinous books about the greatest musical genius and the most amazing child that ever lived. He was writing small symphonies at four and had composed other dramatic pieces before *Bastien et Bastienne*. At eleven he was composer, concert master and leader of an orchestra for the Archbishop of Salzburg.

At fourteen he earned the Order of the Golden Spur which Gluck also had received from the Pope. This authorized both of them to use the title *Ritter,* or Knight. Mozart, contrary to Gluck, never used the title, but his father did in its Italian form of *Cavaliere,* when he was trying to get posts for his son.

At fourteen he was made a member of the Bologna Philharmonic Society, after passing a musical test with almost mystical glory. Furthermore, in Rome after he had listened to Gregorio's *Miserere* in the Sistine Chapel he wrote down the nine parts and two choruses from memory! This almost earned him excommunication from the Church, for the sacred Mass was not to be removed from the holy precincts, and how could he have had a manuscript of it in his possession had he not copied it from the score?

In his fourteenth year he produced his third opera, *Mithridates, King of Pontus* (1770) while he was studying with Padre Martini. It was presented twenty times with great success in Milan and the young Mozart conducted.

From a little child of five to a boy of seventeen, he made a series of long and arduous tours throughout Europe. Whether sick or well, tired or rested, he and his sister were pulled about and prodded by their overambitious father, Leopold. These travels which may have shortened Mozart's life never gave him any post he deserved, but did give him ideas. Particularly did he pick up knowledge in Italy of opera buffa, which he so magically improved that he wrote the three greatest works in that form probably ever penned.

His next opera was for the inauguration of Hieronymus von Colloredo as Archbishop of Salzburg. The opera *Il Sogno di Scipio (The Dream of Scipio,* 1776) was but a prelude to Mozart's leaving the tyrant who slapped him, made him eat with the servants and, as was the custom, dressed him in servant's livery.

THE OPERAS OF MOZART

Every opera that Mozart wrote was produced. The tragedy was that there was no copyright or system of royalties and everyone save the composer made money out of them.

Mozart when writing for the Emperor of Austria, Joseph II, received (translated into our money) about $360 a year; and when with the tyrannical Archbishop, approximately $230 a year! The highest price he ever received for an opera, his immortal *Don Giovanni,* was only $225; while Richard Strauss, although no Mozart, received for a new opera a guarantee of ten performances at $1,000 each, and a further guarantee of royalties afterwards. What a thousand dollars would have meant to Wolfgang Amadeus Mozart!

The Mozarts' notebook of travel would please a tourist agent today. Nearly every big city on the Continent called him, where he either concertized or presented his operas. With no railroads, no motorcars, airplanes or motor buses, travel was hard work. How Wolfgang would have loved an airplane!

By seventeen, Mozart had lost his standing as a prodigy. He was no longer judged as a circus performer, as he had been in his childhood when Vienna turned out with more excitement than it would have shown for Barnum and Bailey's Jumbo the Elephant. Now, he was much feared by lesser men, such as Antonio Salieri, court musician of Vienna, who felt the sting of his genius. In 1772, Mozart's *Lucio Silla* was given in Milan. It was successful. While there, his father, Leopold, became ill, but not too ill to beg at the court of Tuscany for a post for his son, which was not forthcoming.

Both said good-by to Italy forever.

Leopold was equally unsuccessful when he applied for a court post for Wolfgang in Vienna, in spite of the blandishments of Empress Maria Theresa. Undaunted, however, the young man, at that time, wrote six string quartets which still live in the hearts of musical people. Next we see them in Munich, where he wrote (1774) *La finta giardiniera* (*The Faithless Gardener*). Its text was probably written by Calzabigi, Gluck's librettist. In this Mozart had not yet struck his stride. He shows, however, an amazing self-confidence in taking a story, already familiar in Rome as an opera. But he used it so refreshingly that it was accepted as if it were something new. Fancy a composer today having the courage to write another score to Strauss's *Der Rosenkavalier!* Yet, this is an example of Mozart's genius, his superb confidence and delightful naïveté. *The Faithless Gardener* is a charming piece, made up of buffa and "heavy" elements—almost tragedy! This combination was magnificently set forth in his greatest opera buffa, *Don Giovanni,* thirteen years later.

During a Paris visit, in 1778, he met Johann Christian Bach (1735–1782), son of Sebastian, from whom Mozart had learned much in the past about song writing, and now received cheer and encouragement.

From Paris, Wolfgang went to Mannheim where he heard the clarinet, not yet generally used, in the orchestra. It became his favorite instrument and he composed so skillfully for it that he is considered to be the founder of the clarinet (playing) school.

The second result of the Mannheim visit was his meeting (1782) with a cousin of Carl Maria von Weber, Constanze Weber, whom he married later. His life with her was fruitful in work but was cast in poverty. The boy needed affection and care, and maybe it was a good thing for him to marry as he did. Who can tell? Sometimes so poor were they that, without fuel, they danced in their small attic room to keep warm. Perhaps Constanze was a poor manager, for when they had money they spent it and without it they suffered.

It was not until 1781 that Mozart's first important opera was produced—*Idomeneo, Rè di Creta* (*Idomeneus, King of Crete*). It is exciting and dramatic. Mozart includes a shipwreck, with people on the shore anxiously looking on, and he uses the chorus as an active character. From now Mozart begins to advance opera.

The story is like Jephtha's daughter, in the Bible, but dressed in Greek mythological clothes. The libretto was not too good, for he had an obstinate librettist, Giambattista Varesco, who did not like Mozart's passion to "make things brief" for dramatic impact, and resisted his frequent warnings, "It is too long."

This was always Mozart's favorite opera. It is rarely given today, but the recordings are lovely. The Julliard School presented this work in 1955.

In the year that Mozart married Constanze (1782), Emperor Joseph II asked him for a *German* opera. So Mozart composed the blithe *Die Entführung aus dem Serail* (*The Abduction from the Seraglio* [or *Harem*], 1782). After hearing it for the first time, Joseph said that it was too good for Vienna, but that there were "too many notes, dear Mozart," to which the young man replied, "Only the required number of notes, my Emperor." Its debut was at the National Theatre in Vienna.

This gay and "wacky" Singspiel (in three acts) had its background in some bits from an opera that Mozart was intending to call *Zaïde,* which he never finished, but whose name the critics used, at first, as the name for *The Abduction from the Seraglio.* It has Italian high-flown song and sweet airs and is captivating.

A "FIRST" IN GERMAN

The Abduction was epoch-making. Its book was written by Gottlieb Stephanie, the younger. Goethe said it was so good that it spoiled everything in the way of texts for any other opera. Evidently Goethe relished a merry tale. It is about a Turkish Pasha, a speaking character. Not an old-time Singspiel, although related to it, it is a song and dance concoction with spoken dialogue, an operetta with amusing antics, and costumed in Turkish exaggerations. Mozart could not only make a funny story funny, but could give a serious story, as in life, amusing moments.

The Abduction from the Seraglio was first given at the National Theatre in Vienna in 1782, and first saw the New York public at the German Opera House in New York in 1862, in German. English versions have been produced in recent years in New York, under the aegis of Vladimir Rosing at the New York City Center.

In this work, a collection of little masterpieces in a delicious musical fricassee, Mozart first comes to his brisk, Mozartean self. He doesn't use any of the buffa finales (ensembles: choruses and dances), just for end-pieces, but inaugurates ensemble singing in opera to carry out the story. No character stands around like a singing machine. What he or she says is part of the action. In addition, he gives in less to the vagaries and demands of the singers than either he or others had before. Now he seems occupied with character painting rather than his singers. His rogue is not a stock character from opera buffa or commedia dell' arte, but a "devil of a rogue," dangerous and spiteful. Now he is warming up for the extraordinary *Don Giovanni* to come.

Der Schauspieldirektor (*The Impresario,* 1786), which Mozart wrote with Emmanuel Schikaneder, must have given him an easy time, because he included many of his own pieces not previously used. The story is simple. Herr Buff engages a troupe of singers for his theater. A fine spat follows as to who is to be the prima donna. The tenor restores harmony. A surprise ending: having a tenor of *his* day establishing peace! *Der Schauspieldirektor* has an overture and some excellent numbers. (It dates from two months before *The Marriage of Figaro.*) It was revived by Thomas Scherman (1955) in concert form in New York.

THE THREE GREATEST OPERA BUFFE

Mozart during his travels in Italy saw and heard the regulation opera buffa. He evidently felt that this kind of opera painted people much more as they are than did the trumped-up set of characters in serious opera. Burlesque he must have felt was nearer to his contemporaries than gods and heroes.

The greatest opera buffe that have ever been written are: *Le Nozze di Figaro* (*The Marriage of Figaro,* 1786); *Don Giovanni,* 1787, which he called a dramma giocoso (a gay drama); *Così fan tutte, ossia La scuola degli amanti* (*So Are They All,* or *The School of Lovers,* 1790), and Rossini's *The Barber of Seville;* Mozart's tuneful, brilliant, amusing and sometimes even tragic opera buffe are entirely different from each other, even though their librettos were written by the same man, the extraordinary Abbé Lorenzo da Ponte.

When *The Marriage of Figaro* (in two acts) was first written, much romanticizing was done about it. The society into which Mozart–da Ponte's *Figaro* was dropped was not far wrong when it wondered whether this was a social or a revolutionary tract. It was revolutionary, a most amazingly dramatic opera buffa, cast as a comedy about the gentleman of leisure and his servant with better brains than he had. Somewhat the same servant versus master had been used in the old Latin comedies but not in opera until Mozart and Abbé Lorenzo da Ponte "magicked it."

In *The Marriage of Figaro,* Mozart plunged into what many might have thought tempestuous seas. The plot and da Ponte's libretto were taken blithely and written more blithely on what was originally a revolutionary story by Pierre Augustin Caron de Beaumarchais, born a commoner in a dangerous time, shortly before the Revolution in France. Beaumarchais was familiar with, and had chafed under, the woes visited upon the common people by the peers and nobles of the realm. Therefore, he wrote two plays: *The Barber of Seville* used later by Rossini, and its sequel used here by Mozart. We see the same Barber elevated to better thinking and scheming than the Count he serves. Mozart had had experience in the home of the Archbishop of Salzburg, and well knew the social unbalance between masters and servants. In *Figaro* he knew how to lampoon it! Indeed, Beaumarchais' *The Marriage of Figaro* contains a jocularly served germ of pre-Revolution in France. Beaumarchais may have sought to be a Figaro himself! Born poor, in spite of underground and above-ground political intrigues and dramas, he became wealthy. Finally *de* was added to his name and the nobles patronized the entertaining plays that helped them later to lose their heads to the guillotine. In spite of it all, so popular were the play and the opera (*The Marriage of Figaro*) that mobs gathered to hear them.

Nevertheless, Beaumarchais became familiar with short sojourns in prison! He transported guns for the French Revolution from Holland,

and had supplied America with arms for her Revolution twenty years before. This debt was only recently paid to the family of de Beaumarchais!

The Marriage of Figaro, a comedy in music (more important than opera buffa), is one of the examples in opera of speed, brevity and crackling wit, combining in music to make the most fascinatingly glowing work of art. Da Ponte himself commented on the trouble they took to achieve short and pithy expressions.

The motto *E pluribus unum,* "One out of many," typifies Mozart's best operas, particularly this one. It is a unit of scintillant arias, a few tiny choruses, recitatives, ensembles, with a treasure of a self-important little march at the end of the third act. The overture is not one of the bill-of-fare type, with bits of the opera to follow it, but gives the spirit of briskness that characterizes the action of this rollicking four-act play, and as Alfred Einstein says, "Mozart has added to the world's understanding of people and to its lightness of Spirit." And again "...that the first of the two great finales exhibits a mastery of the counterpoint of characterization and of the expression of feeling, such as has been equaled by few and surpassed by none. Here seven people sing and each is characterized!"

Boris Goldovski writes delightfully in *Opera News,* February 6, 1950:

> This finale seems to foreshadow the whole trend of *operatic development* which took place in the Nineteenth Century, and reached its peak with Wagner, who finally did away completely with separate musical numbers and substituted instead a continuous, flowing musical line.
>
> But Wagner only carried forward what Mozart had begun in this *Figaro* finale. Here is the beginning of music drama, years before Wagner was born. In this finale are *eight musical numbers* welded into one.
>
> The finale is the famous closet scene (Act II)—a now-you-see-it, now-you-don't scene! Fascinating, amusing!...We have moved without a break in its musical and dramatic development....During that time from the first moment to the fall of the curtain, we have not only heard a glorious finale, without an equal in all opera; we have also witnessed—years ahead of its time—the birth of *music drama.* (By permission of the publishers, the Metropolitan Opera Guild, New York.)

Figaro is indeed one of the art works ahead of its time, yet miraculously popular at once. Although known to be a play with revolutionary and anti-royal sentiments, it appealed to all classes—and still is as brisk as a rabbit in sparkling dew!

It was far from simple for Mozart and da Ponte to make an Italian buffa out of Beaumarchais' French play in five acts, *Le Mariage de Figaro*. Italian comedies were usually in two acts. *Figaro* is in four long acts, which always seem too short. Although they used many of the stock characters of the commedia dell' arte, they introduced new characters: the gardener and the Countess. Susanna is the mainspring of the action in Mozart's opera, whereas later, in Rossini's *The Barber of Seville* (1816), Figaro the barber is the storm center. Figaro was the comic servant who transferred the author's ideas to the audience as did Harlequin in the old commedia dell' arte.

Mozart and da Ponte had a difficult time, no doubt, making their finales and their songs come at the dramatic moments. Furthermore, they must have had no little trouble to make this play pass the censor. In countries where the language is known the story unfolds with much "naughtiness," so much so that it was at one time *verboten* in Vienna and *defendu* in Paris! But it won't hurt people today—even though they be Italian scholars. Nor will it hurt anyone in the spritely English translations of Ruth and Thomas Martin, of George Meade, and of Marion Farquhar.

Although Mozart in his day was considered to know nothing about writing for the voice, every singer today thinks himself of no account if he doesn't get a chance to sing his superb melodies, which so richly endow *The Marriage of Figaro*. One of the melodious songs is Cherubino's *"Non so più cosa son, cosa faccio"* ("Oh, What Feelings Now Possess Me"). Any authoritative book of the stories of the operas will contain the titles of the principal songs.

Figaro was given at the Burgtheater, Vienna, in 1786. There is some question when it came to America. It seems that it was renamed *The Follies of the Day* and is said to have been given in New York as early as 1799. Notwithstanding, it was advertised by the Park Theatre in 1824 as "first time in America." It was popular in New York in English versions throughout the first half of the nineteenth century. The New York Academy of Music gave it in 1858 in Italian, and the German Opera House in German in 1862. The Metropolitan included it in its repertory, in Italian, in 1894, with a glorious cast: Lillian Nordica, Emma Eames and Edouard de Rezské. Rudolph Bing has included it in the repertory (1954) with new settings.

Figaro had been very successful in Prague. The enthusiasm about Mozart was such that in order to get a hearing, musicians enticed audiences by playing pieces by Mozart as bait! *Don Giovanni* was commissioned there (1787) when Mozart's *Prague Symphony* was played. Then he went back to Vienna, where he met Beethoven.

So Mozart and da Ponte "connived together" again, and wrote *Il Dissoluto punito, ossia Il Don Giovanni (Don Juan, or The Rake Punished,* in two acts), in their brand-new version of a very old subject, *The Stone Guest* by Giovanni Bertati. As it was the custom of the day to take over other composers' ideas, da Ponte was not so honest as not to steal some of Bertati's thunder. But our "unheavenly" twins made something so much greater out of Don Giovanni, the dissolute cavalier of the opera, that there is no comparison with any other. The opera is a tragedy and buffoonery. No one can classify it. It is the story of a gay, lustful gentleman of leisure, with his comical manservant (Leporello), who bore the brunt of his master's misdeeds. Leporello was a magnificent partner, and their love affairs with the ladies were not only funny but often ridiculous, a delectable habit of Mozart's in all his operatic love contests.

Don Giovanni, when he first appears in literature, was a Spanish "cavalier," Don Juan. Many, including Molière, used the story of the stone man (statue) descending to a feast.

It was considered shocking and was banned in both Paris and Vienna, so that Mozart and da Ponte had only their courage and self-assurance to give this social satire (on love and idleness) an airing as an opera buffa with tragedy.

THE BASSO IS ACKNOWLEDGED

One of the things that Mozart did for opera was to show how beautiful and how important a basso can be. Leporello (basso) was given some of the loveliest songs, in an era when the tenors and sopranos demanded all the glory. In Act I, Leporello sings of his troubles, *"Notte e giorno faticar"* ("Never a Rest by Day or Night"). When he pretends to console but really discourages a lady who loves the Don, he sings the magnificent song *"Madamina! il catalogo"* ("Dear Lady, the Catalog"), which lists two thousand sixty-five ladyloves the Don has had in every nation in Europe! If there is exaggeration on Leporello's part, there is economy of power in the wondrous music. Probably the best-known of all the Don's songs is *"Là ci darem la mano"* ("Your Hand in Mine, Dearest").

At the end of Act II, one of the great masterpieces of opera with sense and nonsense is heard, for here the gaieties and wizardries charm with the well-known minuet. Three orchestras on the stage take it up at the same time, the minuet, a rustic quadrille in double time, and a waltz in triple time, plus the tuning up of some of the instruments, added as a joke by Mozart! All this goes on while the orchestra meanwhile is also accompanying the singers! The audience is entranced, hardly realizing Mozart's musical feat.

In the second act, the song that all tenors yearn to sing is Don Ottavio's *"Il mio tesoro intanti"* ("Fly Then, My Love Entreating"), a test of tenors in classic song.

In the last act, the stone guest, the murdered father of the heroine, enters at the Don's invitation and frightens the boasting Don, who at last is seen descending from his pedestal of braggadocio into the depths of Hell. Before this happens Don Giovanni entertains his guests with music and a quotation from Mozart's own opera, *Figaro*: *"Non più andrai"* ("Play No More the Part of a Lover"). Quoting one's own works was then a habit of composers.

The overture picks out and reproduces the Banquet Scene where the grim white statue enters. This is followed by a swift or allegro section, picturing the impulsive, rollicking Don. The overture paints the character of the opera and continues into the first act. It is thus linked with Leporello's complaint that he never rests night or day. It is said that Mozart wrote this overture in three hours, plied with food and drink by his wife!

Everyone agrees that it is one of the greatest masterworks. In it Mozart weds the comic and the tragic in human nature to the music of the theater with the skill of the divinely gifted. It has been argued that the opera is this, that or the other: a tragedy, a comedy, or the first of the romantic operas.

Don Giovanni was first performed at the National Theatre, Prague, in 1787; the first performance in New York was in the original Italian at the Park Theatre in 1826, with the great Garcìa's Company, including his daughter, Maria Malibran. In 1883, it was given at the Metropolitan.

COSÌ FAN TUTTE, OSSIA SCUOLA DEGLI AMANTI

Unlike Gluck, who used mythological or Biblical heroes, Mozart loved the people of his time. Their foibles attracted him. His *Così fan tutte* is the story of a wager between two young men and a friend; the latter held that their fiancées would favor other men when they went away. On this, Mozart builds some of the funniest and most rollicking situations ever written into an opera. With all the fun, the dramatic balance is kept. Nothing gets out of hand; the characters, the music and the plot connive with perfect unity.

Così fan tutte was considered so shocking in its own day that many other librettos were written to the score, to replace da Ponte's, but none was adequate.

Some say that this libretto was unfit for Mozart's music, but we disagree. Mozart used an amusing typical story of his day and clothed it dramatically and wittily. The music may not be quite as "catchy" as the music for his other operas, but it is effective and highly entertaining. In style it stems almost directly from the old opera buffa, such as *La serva padrona*.

The opera begins with a scintillant overture, which uses a theme from the end of the opera, where Don Alphonso (the friend), to placate the two young men, sings the song *"Così fan tutte"* ("So Are They All"), meaning that all women are inconstant. Among the few songs which are recorded are: Despina's *"In uomini, in soldati"* ("In Lovers and in Soldiers for Constancy You Look") and Fiordiligi's dramatic *"Per picta, ben mio perdona"* ("Oh, My Lover, Forgive My Madness").

Così fan tutte was first performed at the Burgtheater, Vienna, in 1780. It came to America as late as 1922, at the Metropolitan Opera House.

LA CLEMENZA DI TITO

The Clemency of Tito, Mozart's last opera, was written ten years after *Idomeneo,* and was his second opera seria (1791). The Queen of Bohemia called it "German rubbish." It was written for the coronation of Leopold II of Bohemia (Prague). It did not catch on at first. At that time there was no repertory system. The people demanded new operas as we do new movies and new plays. There is some beautiful music in *Clemenza,* which has now been well recorded. It was the first of the Mozart operas to reach London.

FIRST GRAND OPERA IN GERMAN

At the time of Mozart, operas in Europe for the most part were given in Italian or French. Gluck never wrote an opera with a German text. Mozart's grand opera, *Die Zauberflöte* (*The Magic Flute*), was the first in German, and is also the greatest Singspiel of all.

The text was by Emanuel Schikaneder, an actor, who ran a theater (*Theater auf der Wieden*) in a suburb of Vienna. The story goes that Schikaneder needed a play for himself and his troupe, so he, recognizing the genius of Mozart and knowing his financial need, practically forced him to write the music. But it is possible that Schikaneder was authorized to offer this commission to Mozart as both were members of the Masonic Order which had a strong following in eighteenth-century Austria.

The Grandmaster of Freemasonry is supposed frequently to have helped Mozart financially and to have encouraged him when everything went wrong. Mozart seemed lighthearted and easygoing, was pleasant and affable, but with all his love of fun, he was deeply sensitive, profoundly religious, and he reflected the undercurrent of melancholy so characteristic of his age.

Where did the material for *The Magic Flute* come from? Did Schikaneder really write it? Did Mozart take a hand in shaping it to his needs? Is it based on Freemasonry? Has it political undercurrents? Can its symbolism be interpreted by "just everyday folks"? The answer to many of these queries is "yes."

Some people find the libretto complex and incomprehensible; others think it is profoundly philosophical and symbolic; others find it pure comedy. Mozart did not seek to write a "magic" opera; but he did so in more ways than one, for *The Magic Flute* has gathered praise wherever it has been heard since it was completed (1791). It still holds magic for its listeners.

That Schikaneder was actually responsible for the libretto seems unquestionable. In the first place, his troupe presented fairy tale plays in Oriental settings, "with improvised dialogue, gross farcical episodes, spectacular scenic effects, and tableaux with live animals, the whole spiced with allusions to current events and personalities," writes Donald Jay Grout in his *Short History of Opera*. Many of these features are to be found in *The Magic Flute*. Its vulgarities of speech and childish words would seem to be Schikaneder's, as he wrote the part of Papageno for himself in a comic opera with plenty of "gags."

Possibly as Mozart became engrossed in writing the score, he may have added mystic and serious elements that turned the Singspiel into grand opera. As brother-Masons, they may deliberately have used the symbology of Freemasonry, especially if they wished to pay tribute to Ignaz von Born the Grandmaster, an influential aristocrat of Vienna. The scene is mythical Egypt and the librettist made use of the Egyptian-like mysteries of trial by water and fire, as well as suggesting other Masonic rituals.

With this Schikaneder combined material from a fairy tale by Wieland called *Lulu oder die Zauberflöte* (*Lulu or the Magic Flute*). Papageno and Papagena resemble characters from another opera for which Schikaneder wrote the libretto. The complex story is all wrapped up in fantasy, fun, caprice, mystery, intrigue and nobility. The music is often simple, folklike, and childlike in its buffoonery. For instance, the glee of Papageno and Papagena when they sing "Pa-Pa-Pa! Pa-Papagena!", "Pa-Pa-Pa! Pa-Papageno!" is in the manner of a musical pop-gun. This is Mozartean hilarity, a wonderful thing in a composer!

The Magic Flute is a marvelous bundle of opera buffa, opera seria, idealism, mythology, mysticism, grandeur, morality, wit, and down-to-earth good sense. In a few words, it is a fairy tale about Pamina, the daughter of the Queen of the Night, who has been abducted by Sarastro, the High Priest of Isis. A prince, Tamino, arrives from distant lands and the mother sees in him her daughter's possible rescuer. Papageno, a bird-catcher, half-bird, half-human, is to accompany Tamino on his quest. Tamino is presented with a magic flute to protect him in every difficult situation. Papageno is given a set of magic bells, the Egyptian *sistrum*. Before Tamino wins Pamina he has to go through the tests of silence and fearlessness which in the Egyptian rites are initiations through fire and water. Papageno succeeds, with the help of his magic bells, in driving away Monostatos, a treacherous Moor, chosen to watch over Pamina. Tamino playing on the magic flute passes successfully through the trials, winning Pamina as his bride.

We offer the following as a possible interpretation: The Queen of the Night rules over a realm of darkness, that is, ignorance, superstition, and fear. Sarastro is light: the mind, enlightenment, learning, science, wisdom, kindliness and justice. Through experience and powers of resisting evil (which at the opening of the opera attacks him as a serpent from which he is saved), Tamino represents the highest spiritual attainment to be reached by man. Pamina shares this attainment through her purity and goodness. Papageno, a prototype of Pan, represents physical man who looks for nothing more than physical comforts and his mate, Papagena. Monostatos is the lower animal element in man, criminal in intent and action. The flute is much more than a fairy tale implement of magic. It represents faith in a Divine Power.

THE OVERTURE TO THE MAGIC FLUTE

The overture opens with three great chords, the only music taken from the opera. They are supposed to mirror the mystery and splendor of the Egyptian temple ritual. Mozart's reverence for Masonry is reflected throughout the seemingly fantastic plot. Besides the somber chords the overture has a swift-moving and marvelous fugue. Indeed the opera is a Mozartean mixture in orchestra and song of the lilting and somber. Mozart uses a bell for the first time (it is supposed) in opera, to paint a fairylike atmosphere.

SONGS

Two of the best arias in *The Magic Flute,* "O, Isis and Osiris" and "Within This Hallowed Dwelling," are given to Sarastro (High Priest), a deep *basso.* The Queen of the Night sings a vengeance song so high in register that every soprano yearns to sing it, whether she can or not. Most cannot! On the other hand, some of the quaintest, folklike tunes of German mold, such as "A Fowler Bold in Me You See," are given to Papageno, a fantastic creature, a braggart, who claims he knows all about catching birds and that once he killed a serpent (the one that attacked Tamino) which in truth he did not do.

The Magic Flute had its first performance at the Theater auf der Wieden, Vienna, 1791, about two months before Mozart's death. America saw it first at the Park Theatre in New York in 1833, in English. The work was presented at the Academy of Music in New York, 1859, in Italian, and it was given at the German Opera House, New York, in an unexpurgated German version, in 1862. The Metropolitan Opera House presented it in Italian in 1900. It was given with a new English translation by Ruth and Thomas Martin at the Metropolitan in the season 1941–1942.

It has been said so often that the era in which he lived was responsible for Mozart's bubbling, scintillating, lighthearted music and fun-making. But this is not so. He lived in one of the most turbulent periods of the Western world. The times did not make Mozart. He was one of God's believable and incontestable miracles.

What was it, then, that gives Mozart so important a place in opera? First of all, he added German orchestral skill to the Italian melodic skill, really started grand opera in *Figaro,* and made a vital, vibrant pattern for German or any other opera.

Mozart was not a revolutionist in the way Gluck thought himself to be. Gluck had a philosophy and a set of set things to be done, as he stated in his preface to *Alceste* (see page 89). Supernaturally endowed with genius and a blithe spirit, Mozart enlarged opera and clothed the text in iridescent streams of bubbling music, but always consistent with the dramatic purpose of his story. He never subordinated the text to the music. The naïve Mozart, with unfailing instinct for action, excitement, humor and climax, went ahead and wrote with two things in mind—the story *and* the music—and made the orchestra a part of the plot, without seams, smooth and logical. He cut through difficulties and tradition with a musical gallantry entirely his own.

USE OF VOICE AND ARIA

Contrary to the opinion of the time, Mozart was a master at writing for the voice. He wrote the overused aria in his own way and it became more dramatic in all its parts—even the so-called *scena,* its dramatic portion. His aria kept the current of the action flowing rather than damming it. He carried out his plan of fitting the aria to the singer and went to all lengths to do so, for he said, "...I like an aria to fit a singer as perfectly as a well-made suit of clothes." Whereas he often did conform to the singers' demands, he never betrayed his own sense of "rightness." In so doing his vitalized arias gave impetus to the growth of opera. They also paved the way for the instrumental concerto, for contrary to general opinion, the developed aria was the father of the concerto for instruments.

His recitative is as varied as the flowers in the field and equally beautiful, colorful and refreshing. He excelled in melody and his operas still sparkle, thrill and entertain with more success than in his own day and far more successfully than most twentieth-century operas. Among ten favorite operas recorded in a radio poll in 1948, three of them were Mozart's.

THE REQUIEM

While on his deathbed, Mozart believed that someone had poisoned him. Some say he thought it was his jealous rival at court, Antonio Salieri. Others say Mozart thought it was his despised patron, Archbishop Hieronymus of Salzburg. This, however, was not true. The cause of his death is a moot question. It may have been Bright's disease or typhoid fever exaggerated by his depleted condition from overexertion since childhood. He was dying as he was trying to finish his Requiem Mass (*Mass for the Dead*), which had been ordered in a mysterious way by a mysterious patron. He kept saying that he was writing his own requiem. And so it proved to be. His friend Franz Sussmayr had to finish it for him.

While he was ill, his incomparable *Don Giovanni* was being given at the opera house in Salzburg. Of course he could hear it in his mind's ear. But think of it—had there been radio at that time, he could have had the satisfaction of going to his last, indeed, his *first* rest, to the accompaniment of his own gloriously buoyant music.

IN AN UNKNOWN GRAVE

Mozart was buried in 1791 on a day so stormy that few people, not even his wife, who was ill, could go to the cemetery. No one knows where he is buried. One of the tragedies of this fruitful young life is that while he was on his deathbed he was offered the only job that had any permanency or financial security to it—the Director of Music at St. Stephen's Church in Salzburg.

There is no doubt that Mozart, with Shakespeare and Leonardo da Vinci, was one of the greatest givers of beauty to mankind.

UNBELIEVABLE!

1. Yet, about 1800, the "Friends of Prussia" reported in a German newspaper that they heard a composition (church music) of Mozart, about which was said: "It is devil's music, and all that is missing are the salvos of cannon to complete the Inferno. The instruments produced a veritable pandemonium. The music is said to be educational." This speaks for itself.

2. Another Mozart opera, *Don Pedro's Return,* has been added to the already astounding list. This is a synthetic opera put together from many scripts. It was given (1953) by the "Lemonade" Opera in New York City. It is in two acts and the music is supposed to have been written at about the period of *The Abduction from the Seraglio* and *The Marriage of Figaro.* Some of the music was taken from two operatic fragments, *Lo sposo deluso* (*The Deceived Husband*) and *L'Oca del Cairo* (*The Goose of Cairo*), yet it is all of one consistent piece.

SCENE III

Beethoven's *Fidelio*—Bridge Between Mozart and Weber

LIFE FORGES HIGH PRINCIPLES

Ludwig van Beethoven, writer of nine world-gripping symphonies; thirty-two unexcelled piano sonatas; ten violin sonatas; chamber music the world has never bettered; masses, overtures and songs; but only one opera, was born into a world of revolution and unrest, the era of *Sturm und Drang* ("storm and stress"). His father, Johann, was a drunken court musician, and as weak a man as Ludwig was strong. He beat the boy, forced him from bed at night to practice, thinking to make him an infant prodigy like Mozart.

Some think that Beethoven's life at home made him conscious of the wretched condition of men and women throughout the world. Whatever it was, he showed very early signs of independent thinking, in his life and work. He believed in the aristocracy of brains, not in the aristocracy of money or birth; that a man should write as he feels, not according to certain prescriptions. This is why he became the bridge between the Classic era when composers were interested in *how* they wrote (form) and the Romantic in which they were interested in *what* they expressed (personal feelings).

IN SPITE OF TURMOIL

Ludwig van Beethoven (1770-1827) lived during the height of the French Revolution, during Napoleon's European campaigns, and during the founding of the "suspect" American republic. He lived in turmoil; for the better part of his life in Vienna, he was within earshot of battle. During Rousseau's and even in Mozart's day, liberty was a theory, but in Beethoven's day it was getting some trials. It was difficult to live honestly in Europe if one believed in republican

112

methods. Indeed, Beethoven believed deeply in liberty, both in state matters and religion. To be a liberal in his day was almost heretical! Yet Beethoven went about among aristocrats and nobles, and although he was never diplomatic enough to cloak his opinions, he never flinched from his beliefs.

PARENTAGE

Beethoven was born in Bonn. He came from lowly and poor parents. His grandfather had emigrated from Holland. This is why the Dutch *van* in his name and not the German *von* is correct.

He was fortunate in the choice of his mother! She was a professional cook, a noble soul, and he loved her dearly as she loved him. After her death he was burdened with poverty, overwork, and the care of two younger brothers. He left Bonn for Europe's greatest music center, Vienna, where in spite of artistic recognition, aristocratic patronage, and success, his life was unhappy because of his deafness and unfortunate love affairs. Yet in his short 57 years, he was a man of unflagging courage and stubborn will.

A QUEER URGE

What induced this man, with little dramatic experience, to want to write an opera? Because he wanted the financial security, which he believed Viennese opera writers were achieving.

This man, who thought that justice and liberty were man's highest goals, yearned to write an opera but said that he could not find a libretto worthy of his music. Indeed, he thought that Mozart's libretto for *Don Giovanni* was immoral!

FIDELIO

When Beethoven heard of the play *Leonore,* by Jean Nicholas Bouilly, which was the rage in Paris, he thought that after his long search he finally had a plot sufficiently moral to fit his music. The plot was Spanish, although Bouilly was a French revolutionist who fed the story from his own bitter experience. Joseph Sonnleithner translated it, but made a poor libretto.

Frankly, Beethoven, without being considered a great composer of opera, wrote a great opera *Fidelio, oder Die Ehelich Liebe (Fidelio, or Conjugal Love)* fifteen years before Weber wrote his romantic opera *Der Freischütz.* In it he tells a story of the supreme love of the frail Leonore for her husband, Florestan, to rescue whom she braves all dangers. Disguised as a man, she finds the jail where he is imprisoned and wrests him, at the point of a pistol, from his jailer. The rescue in the final act is one of the most exciting and poignant bits in all opera.

At first it had three acts. After a few very drastic revisions, it came down to two acts with many good changes, but still leaving the first act "slow" and confused. Beethoven worked like a beaver to write his score and there are dozens of sketches for each song in his notebooks.

Beethoven was in heart and mind a symphonic writer with deep spiritual power. He did not have the pictorial sense of character nor the dramatic sense for incident, yet he did what he could with the Bouilly mixture of climax, commonplaces and rescue story. He was glad to write an opera based on the liberation of "the trapped," concluding with a majestic rescue. The final revision became more than the usual "rescue" opera, a popular plot after the Revolution. It became a spur to romantic opera, both in France and Germany.

Beethoven wrote four overtures to *Fidelio* (see page 276). Other parts of the opera he wrote eighteen times before he was satisfied. It was his custom to write until a measure or piece suited him, but never to alter a note after he once considered it finished. He didn't develop it completely in his own mind before sitting down to write, as Mozart is supposed to have done. The music in *Fidelio* is as carefully made as is all his music. In some spots it is more oratorio than opera, but it eventually leads to the finale where love triumphs over greed, freedom over captivity, with the operation of Justice. It is a sincere expression of idealism.

The characters in *Fidelio* are somewhat in the manner of stock characters of the old commedia dell' arte, comic opera, opéra bouffe and buffa. There is to be found the very wicked man who gets his well-deserved punishment; the very good man who is rewarded; the noble wife who suffers and is united with her husband; and even the manservant and maidservant, or the "girl friend," and above all, the triumph of love and justice. The great fault with this opera, *Fidelio,* is that Beethoven is so anxious for freedom, justice, goodness and love to triumph that in this Pollyanna effort with a bad libretto he cannot always be dramatic, and the action lags. He neglects drama for morality. He forgets the drama for great musical beauty and his profound loyalty to his convictions. Even Wagner with all his preachments did not err so much in this respect.

Fidelio was given in Vienna on November 20, 1805, one week after Napoleon's army occupied the city. Many aristocrats had fled while the others feared to leave their homes. *Fidelio* ran exactly three days! Soldiers of France attended the opera. They disliked the German version of Bouilly's play that they had enjoyed in France. They are not to be blamed, for the libretto was poor. It is thought that Beethoven would not have used the Sonnleithner libretto had he not been preoccupied with a love affair with Countess Josephine von Deyn. Although he was a staunch republican, his friendships were mostly among the aristocracy.

Before and during the growing pains of *Fidelio* he was also writing and thinking out his immortal scores: the *Eroica Symphony,* the *Waldstein* and *Appassionata* sonatas, and the *Fifth Symphony,* among others.

This opera about the devoted wife was unpopular because it was too long. It is still not popular but is not heard often enough. Beethoven accomplished musical beauties by expert and ingenious departures from the usual to an almost divine intenseness. Indeed, it has some music so superb that the words seem to be interlopers—for example, the quartet between Marcelline, Leonore, Rocco and Jaquino, and Florestan's superlatively touching song in the last act, as well as the duet between Florestan and Leonore. One of the finest songs ever written for a woman's voice (and some say that Beethoven couldn't write for the voice!) is the one which begins *"Abscheulicher, wo eilst du hin"* (*"Oh Monster, Whither Dost Thou Hasten?"*) which Leonore sings after she hears the dastardly plot to kill Florestan.

Beethoven was bothered greatly because he had to make the orchestra an almost secondary feature in opera. He found opera a very difficult task. And when this one opera was being rehearsed, he complained that they did not follow his dynamics, or his marks of interpretation.

Yet Beethoven, after the difficulties of creating *Fidelio,* tried constantly to get orders for other operas, and engaged librettists and writers to help him find suitable stories.

It is obvious that Beethoven had planned other operas, because of overtures and other compositions bearing the names of *Coriolanus, Egmont* and the ballet *Prometheus.* Moreover, he had previously started an opera called the *Vestal Fire* by Schikaneder, which he did not finish, but some of which he used in *Fidelio.*

According to many Beethoven is the god of music. He conquered deafness by hearing music in his mind's ear. Added to his deafness, which increased as he grew older, his last years were made more unhappy by family law suits and his relations with a nephew from whom, unfortunately, Beethoven demanded more affection than the nephew had it in his power to give. It was a tragedy of misunderstandings on both sides, a tragedy of a noble man, a gruff egotist, and a gay young blade trying to "hit it off."

Beethoven was a noble soul, but not a gentle one. He was often uncouth and fiery. He pooh-poohed money, but craved wealth. He hated men but loved mankind. He was a paradox, at times elated and at times desperately unhappy. Nevertheless, his was a glowing, constant fire whose heat flared highest to redress wrong. He never neglected his work and he rarely gave pain or discouragement to anyone purposely. He said of himself that he always tried, from childhood, to grasp the thoughts of better and wiser men of every era. With all his peculiarities he made many and good friends among the illustrious and high-born. During the last years of his life the famous men who gathered together for the Congress of Vienna (1814–15) paid court to him.

The dedications on his works show that, for the most part, he wrote not for gain, but out of admiration and love. Strange as it may seem, many of these people such as the Counts von Waldstein and Rasoumowsky, who were men of wealth and fame, are known to the world today only because of the dedications to them by the poor, clumsy, often savage Beethoven—who broke the back of patronage to composers because he could truckle to no man.

Specifically, he liberated music from "rococo" elegance to a realization of power, simplicity, mysticism, reality, force and tenderness. He made music conform to the internal feeling, as well as the external, as Sir Hubert Parry said, and we add, to the eternal. His earlier bridging or departure from the classic forms to the romantic can be seen in "The Moonlight Sonata" (slow movement) when compared with sonatas before it. He was able to change the mood within a set piece. This gave music a new vitality, a new purpose, and new functions. It helped opera. Beethoven used old forms in his own fiery and expansive way, and above all, Beethoven's miracles made them welcome even in his own time!

The result of the mass of Beethoven's work is that he made music titanic, tumultuous, exalted and ethereal. He could express eternity and the elemental struggles of humanity, and he could almost write a whole drama in four notes, as for example, the opening of the *Fifth Symphony,* as fresh today as the day it was written. The result of his opera, *Fidelio,* was that the overthrow of past form and formulas, in spite of his symphonic use of the orchestra, made composers take notice, and in Robert Haven Schauffler's words, "freed music" from many operatic "musts." He didn't paint pictures in music. He expressed the qualities of the human soul. Today, with visualization by camera, cinema, and television, Ludwig van Beethoven can be a reminder of forgotten ways and byways of the imagination and spirit.

At an early age, he began to name his piano pieces by special names, such as "Bagatelle" instead of using one of the formal names of the classic era, like toccata, sonata, and others. This, of course, made the way easier for the Romantic musical poets such as Schubert and especially Schumann, who named his pieces with descriptive titles, as had been done long before by the French composers for the clavecin (harpsichord).

So Beethoven, by stressing in music human feeling and destiny, built the musical bridge of freedom from the classic age of form, or fixed patterns, to the romantic age of more liberty, self-expression, and more freedom of thought, action and structure.

Beethoven died in 1827, in the midst of a titanic thunderstorm. How fitting!

ACT IV. Romantic Opera—Revolution and the Individual

PRELUDE

Opinion, Feeling, and Choice Affect Forms

THE Romantic Period was the product of revolts and revolutions at the end of the eighteenth century and their culmination in the American Revolution in the Colonies of the New World and the French Revolution. At the same time Italy was forming itself into one nation, the period called the *Risorgimento*. These changes were the result of man's thinking about himself in relation to himself, his country, and to other men. It was the outcome of his weighing his inmost thoughts and believing that he and every man had his own needs and qualifications. Jean Jacques Rousseau said, "I am different from all men I have seen. If I am not better, at least I am different."

Romanticism, then, is a word that is applied to the new music, poetry and painting, spanning the late eighteenth and early nineteenth centuries. During this time, the standardization of human traits and characteristics went somewhat out of fashion, and men and women took on a new dignity and ceased to be mere cogs in the machines of Church and State. Above all, this was the time when men and women began to fight to begin to think.

The Romantic composers (nineteenth century) added the super-natural and nature to human nature. Indeed, Rousseau had advocated a "back to nature" movement. Nature, now, affects and is a part of the moods of human beings, not just "happenstance," or for scenic effect, or for comic effect, or for decoration. In Romantic opera, for example, the music of the storm heard in Wagner's *Die Walküre,* the mighty roll of the River Rhine in *Das Rheingold,* the cave magics of Weber's *Der Freischütz* not only match the mood of man, but intensify it even to the supernatural. Wagner went further in his *Der Ring des Nibelungen (Ring of the Nibelungs),* for he identified man with the supernatural and even with the mythology of the Northlands.

The Romantic Period was the time of breaking away from forms and models which were the chief characteristics of the Classical Period, when music was dominated by sonata form. In the Classical Period, law was ruler and it was only an exception, like Beethoven, who broke the order. He was the musical bridge between the Classical and Romantic periods. Romanticism in poetry, painting, and in music became more personal.

This romanticism is seen in the works of such men of letters as Honoré de Balzac, writer of the personal and romantic histories of characters he either saw or invented. Another is Victor Hugo, who wrote the tragic stories, *Les Misérables* and *Notre Dame de Paris*. And, marking the very earliest intimates of the age, was Jean Jacques Rousseau, author of *Contrat social* (*The Social Contract*), who boldly took up questions of the rights of man, upon which, later, the Assembly of France modeled some of its revolutionary doctrine.

Among the foremost composers of the Romantic Period were: Weber, Rossini, Schubert, Schumann, Chopin, Liszt, Berlioz, and Mendelssohn, who was part Classicist and part Romanticist.

Among the painters who more or less followed the romantic line were Jean François Millet and Jean Baptiste Camille Corot of France; in England those primarily of the so-called Pre-Raphaelite Brotherhood, such as William Morris, William Holman-Hunt, John Everett Millais, Dante Gabriel Rossetti, Edward Burne-Jones, and G. F. Watts. These men influenced for a time in the Victorian era the thinking on art and literature. Keats' influence upon them was great, and the Arthurian legends were of much inspiration. It was a rich dawning, this Romantic Period; greater in the plastic art and poetry of England than in its music. Throughout its history the plastic arts have naturally affected, more or less, the décor of opera.

In spite of Lully, Rameau and Gluck, opera had become stiff in Italy, flat in France, monotonous in Germany. This condition continued up to the time of Mozart, the arch-writer of gay and lilting drama, with the exception of pieces like Pergolesi's *La serva padrona* and Gay's *The Beggar's Opera*. Pergolesi, first, and Mozart, second, showed what opera could become.

Opera, working so diligently to perfect itself, had become a vocal athletic field by Handel's time, the early eighteenth century, in which singers contended for honors in doing vocal hop-skips, jumps and runs. The recitative, with little accompaniment, called *secco* or dry, and it *was* dry, carried the action of the hackneyed plots unsatisfactorily. Opera had grown so dull that listeners played cards and visited each other in their boxes, or sauntered out in the lobbies of the opera houses. (In fact, it was difficult to stop this practice even in the early Wagnerian days.) They returned to their seats only when they knew that an aria was to be sung by their pet singer or a ballet was to be seen. The arias were the usual da capo type, which in themselves were beginning to clog the action, reducing opera to a music prescription, rather than a refreshing draught. The soprano, not the music, stunts, not melody, were the "whole show."

A bit of new life was injected into opera when writers first tried to carry plot and action into the songs, duets and choruses, and even into the ballets, instead of just into the recitative. This is probably one of the most important moments in the growth of opera. But as there is always some fly in the ointment, something else began to block its beauty. This was the practice of repeating over and over again the same phrase, the same sentence, the same words, in a single song, or chorus, or duet, even in the supremely gifted Mozart.

It was particularly out of place in a duet and provoked laughter from the "man in the street." Some languages could bear this practice better than others. Yet, in any language, to hear a tenor crying, "Do you love me, do you love me, do you love me?" never sounds "normal," for if he really wanted to know, he should have waited for an answer! Of course this stops the action. It is one of the things that Wagner attacked later. This repetition might have come about in the Classical Period because of the popularity of symphonic music, purposely built on a kind of repetition in the development of themes.

Now opera lifts itself into the Romantic Period and out of some of its classical formalities, but it falls again into other faults which even today have not been eradicated.

THE BATTLE OF HERNANI

As often with new ideas, this romanticism had to engage in skirmishes to get a foothold. Again Paris became a battleground. Again the revolt against artificial and frozen forms took place. In the drama, it came to a head when Victor Hugo's play *Hernani* was given (1830). This play, later adapted by Verdi for his opera *Ernani,* opened up new and romantic paths to George Sand, Alexandre Dumas, and others. The conservatives, those who liked the old, were pitted against the liberals, wanting the new. Théophile Gautier, a romantic writer, had a scarlet satin vest made, which hooked up the back, so that it would not be torn off him by the struggling conservatives, when

Hernani was first given in Paris! The young radicals, poets, dramatists and composers formed a most "vocal" clacque (an organized group of paid or unpaid listeners whose duty it is either to applaud or hiss the performance or a performer). The scrambles and fights were so many that the forty-five performances of *Hernani* were called the "Battles of *Hernani*" (*les "Batailles d'Hernani"*).

Charles X (soon to abdicate and flee from Paris) received a petition to stop the performance, but the play went on with some changes. To read it today is to marvel at what the conservatives could find to fight about!

From now on, opera marches in more flavorful patterns to when, in national dress, it again begins to make new ruts, to be trampled out by Wagner, the greatest romanticist of them all, and later by men in the twentieth century.

SCENE I

The French and the New Spirit—Cherubini, Czar of Music in Paris

THE French, ready pioneers in the arts, remembered the time when the Italian troupe of *La serva padrona* had come to France. After they had used this sort of musical story too long, their own French comedies grew so Italian that the authorities finally dismissed the Italian troupes from France.

OPÉRA. COMIQUE

Then the composers took over the lighter kind of opera by writing their beloved and traditional vaudevilles, first played at city and country fairs. These had given birth to opéra bouffe, or comic opera, but soon developed into the more graceful, delightful and ingratiating opéra comique. They had, however, a stiff rival in the performances of the *Théâtre des Italiens* in Paris. But the intellectually thrifty French profited even from what they didn't like.

At first, the operas classed under opéra comique were *comique,* as the French would say. But today, opéra comique doesn't have to be comic—in fact, it can range from serious to tragic. For example, Massenet's *Manon* is an opéra comique although it tells a tragic tale. An opera is called comique only because it uses some spoken words and is usually simpler to mount than grand opera. In Lully's time, many a serious opera had to be given in the theater called the Opéra Comique because Czar Lully's pet restrictions kept them out of the Paris opera house if for any reason he wished to bar them. The use of spoken words was one of the restrictions.

"RESCUE" OPERA

Romantic indeed was "rescue" opera, a psychological and historical residue of the French Revolution. For example, King Richard in Grétry's *Richard, the Lion-Hearted* was rescued by the troubadour Blondel de Nesle, whom the King heard singing their favorite song while passing his prison. Beethoven, too, in Germany, using a French story, succumbed to the rescue plot in his only opera, *Fidelio*.

GRAND OPERA

The French also went in for elaborate opera in the grand style. They even returned to Rome and Greece for plots, such as the story of Medea, used by Cherubini. Grand opera is to opéra comique, comic opera, and light opera, what an ocean liner is to a yacht.

Grand opera is usually very elaborate and expensive to produce. Compared with opéra bouffe it is more concerned with orchestral effects. According to its plot and music, grand opera becomes romantic, "rescue," or lyric.

LYRIC OPERA

The operas of the early nineteenth century in France have won the name of "lyric." All operas are lyric, if they are intrinsically singable. It is a throwback to the Greeks, who never used poetry unless to the accompaniment of the lyre or the *aulos,* an oboelike instrument. But, as opera grew up, lyric opera became the kind that falls between the prettiness and jaunty simplicity of comic opera and the formality of the more elaborate grand opera. It is more personal. It usually deals with the woes and joys of a person or persons, not of a god, of a nation, or of a political movement. Nor can lyric opera be a series of amusing and grotesque situations. *Die Götterdämmerung* is not a lyric opera because it is a story about the fall of the dynasty of the gods; is about heroes, dwarfs, and giants, with scenery, spanning Heaven (Valhalla) and Earth, on an epic, not a personal, scale. Lyric opera is usually sentimental, romantic and glamorous. It has the melody and vitality, glint and liveliness of opéra comique. It has, too, the tenderness, flavor, and occasionally even the grandeur of grand opera without being as ornate. The writers of lyric opera were essentially romanticists, and consciously or unconsciously their works are based on the Mozartean spirit. The Théâtre Lyrique in Paris was founded for these works and did a lovely thing for the growth of opera, as well as for composers and opera lovers.

Paris was Queen of Opera when lyric opera was at its height. Meyerbeer was the Czar of Music; Richard Wagner was storming the musical front for admission; and Hector Berlioz was writing operas that were never appreciated. Charles Gounod (1818-93), Ambroise Thomas (1811-96), and Georges Bizet (1838-1875) were writing their enchanting operas, while Camille Saint-Saëns, composing in all forms, made a hit with his exotic *Samson and Delilah*. César Franck (of Belgian birth), although he wrote two not too successful operas, emphasized, in France, her taste for beauty and form in whatever she produced.

WAGNERIAN INFLUENCE

Although no one succeeded in writing Wagnerian operas, nearly all of the composers were accused of imitating him, including Verdi in Italy and Massenet in France. Some of those who hated Wagner made the accusation as a crushing criticism; those who loved him, as highest praise. Some of the best writers at first hated Wagner, then adopted his style, then freed themselves and went their own ways. Nevertheless, the composers after Wagner did attempt, with more or less success, his continuous flow of music, some form of his fixed idea (*idée fixe*), which he called *Leitmotif,* his enriched orchestral combinations and new chord sequences.

From the nineteenth century, after Berlioz' hard days, the French rule French music—no more alien czars like Lully, Cherubini, and Meyerbeer. France is French, and happily has stayed so.

Among the lyric operas is a string of very interesting *mademoiselles, señoritas,* and *fräuleins,* whose names are the titles of the operas. They have become famous women. *Mignon* (of Ambroise Thomas); *Carmen* (of Bizet); *Manon* (of Massenet); *Thaïs,* too (a most intriguing character); and Marguerite, although her name was left out of the title of Gounod's *Faust,* should have been so honored for what she had to endure.

The romantic age would have been unromantic had there not been grand opera, with its stress on the heroic and the epic. For example, Verdi's *Simon Boccanegra,* with the vast halls of the doge's palace and expansive gesturings, seems to encompass the whole stage and could never be made "to act" on a small stage. Cherubini's *Lodoïska;* Meyerbeer's *Les Huguenots;* Berlioz' *Les Troyens* (*The Trojans*), and Wagner's *Lohengrin* (or any number of his operas), with spacious themes, grandiloquent music, and scenery of magnificence contain the elements of grand opera. This type came to its richest point in the middle of the nineteenth century, and seems to have remained in the minds of most people as the definition of all opera.

But, as the French Revolution had stirred politics to the boiling point, its vapors still spread over the European arts. It made French opera more and more exciting, until grand opera itself became melodrama, or melodramatic, resulting in Italian *verismo*. All kinds of hairbreadth escapes; the reappearance of lost children; gypsies, robbers, pirates; and finally, murder, rape, and suicide; every imaginable thrillmaker—as in our "Western" and gangster movies—was used for alarms and shivers. Opera can gloss over the most inconsistent happenings much better than any radio "soap opera" or Western movie.

OPERA VARIETIES

From now on, and in every country, the forms opera takes become freer and quite difficult to classify. They take any shape the composer fancies. But the dramatic differences are matters of pace and subject.

1. COMEDY tells an amusing story, more probable than improbable.
2. FARCE tells an amusing story, more rapid in action than comedy, and more impossible than possible.
3. DRAMA tells a serious story, more or less mirroring real life.
4. GRAND OPERA is a drama, often with heroic and epic plots (tales of heroes, nations, and national or religious movements) put to music, and staged on a grand scale and with more stress on the orchestra than on vocal calisthenics, but with no spoken words. *Faust,* when rid of spoken words, became, in the revised version, grand opera. *Carmen,* though tragic, is still opéra comique when presented in its original version with spoken words.
5. OPÉRA COMIQUE tells a story, tragic or comic, with music and some spoken words, instead of just song and recitative, and is usually more personal than epic.
6. MELODRAMA today means a different thing from what it used to mean, when it was just drama with music, *melos*—melody. Today it is a serious story, with everything exaggerated beyond reasonableness; very exciting, and without intention of being anything but thrilling or tragic—in a word, sensational.

CHERUBINI, CZAR OF MUSIC IN PARIS

Luigi Cherubini (1760–1842) was the second Italian czar of French music, and one of the cleverest composers of elaborate, or grand, opera, as well as of church music. Paul Henry Lang calls him "the last great Italian master of classical instrumental music." He spent fifty-four of his eighty-two years in Paris. His life spanned that of Beethoven and Schubert, Weber and Schumann. While they dominated German music, he ruled French music with an iron hand, as head of musical Paris and of the Paris Conservatory. Although an alien, he wouldn't permit an alien to study at the Conservatory, not even the Hungarian Franz Liszt, who became a composer, conductor, and probably the world's greatest pianist.

On the other hand, Cherubini encouraged French opera and did much to make France the opera center of the world for many years. At first he wrote sacred works of quality. After a visit to London he wrote an opera which failed. A few years later (1791), a second, *Lodoïska,* succeeded. In it he invented a new dramatic style, a bridge between the classic and romantic. He introduced new and richer orchestral writing, more forceful choruses and ensembles. This influenced French grand opera. Men like Méhul and Grétry followed his lead. His *Medea* (1797) is grand opera of definite beauty. His most important was *Les Deux Journées* (1800), a typical rescue opera. This was very popular in Germany and in Vienna, where it was called *Der Wasserträger,* so that now for some reason it is called *The Water Carrier,* even though *The Two Days* would seem to be a more exact translation. This opera had a definite influence on Beethoven's *Fidelio.*

Cherubini's operas are not given today, probably because of the slow pace and the virus "monotony," which keep many operas on shelves instead of on our stages. Yet his *Medea,* although in the Gluck manner, had a definite effect on Carl Maria von Weber, the first to write German romantic opera in German.

Cherubini was a strict taskmaster at the Conservatory. Yet the students knew he was able and that they could learn much from his methods of writing, brilliant orchestral effects, rich harmony, expert transitions from one musical phrase to another, and his effective modulation into different keys, which created a music of richer colors.

His music was calm, yet had power enough to carry the frightful tragedy of *Medea.* He never overstepped good taste. This endeared him to the French, particularly in the era of and after the Revolution, when nerves were taut and people sought opera as a means of distraction. He made the ensemble numbers more forceful and showed the coming composers the effect of more intense dramatic effects.

But when Boieldieu and Auber came upon the scene, the severe but learned composer lost his hold on the French imagination, save in his religious music, and he has since been little played. Mendelssohn, the great reviver and appreciator of other men's work, brought *The Water Carrier,* the effective *Mass in C* and one of Cherubini's requiems to Germany. Incidentally, Mendelssohn was one of the foreign lads to whom Cherubini refused admission to the Conservatory!

SCENE II

The Italians "On Stage"—
Rossini, Bellini, Donizetti, and Others

GLUCK and Mozart had greatly advanced the growth of opera. Now it held the imagination of all nations. In Paris all the roads joined. Italians, Germans, and English were as thick as leaves on the ground in autumn. The English took notice of French opera and profited. The Germans loved the French operas and stories and translated many of them into German (cf. Beethoven's *Fidelio*). Although Italians kept their "birthmarks," many arrived at Parisian productions and acclaim.

DOMENICO CIMAROSA

With his *Il matrimonio segreto* (*The Secret Marriage*), a comic opera still enjoyed, Domenico Cimarosa (1749–1801), the musical bridge between Mozart and Rossini, almost approached Mozart in airiness, tunefulness, and swift action.

Domenico was born near Naples and was among the Western composers whom Catherine II of Russia invited to St. Petersburg. One of his teachers was Piccinni, friendly rival of Gluck. At the court in Vienna, where *The Secret Marriage* was written, Cimarosa succeeded Salieri, who had been the foe of Mozart.

Cimarosa was imprisoned and condemned to death in 1799 in Naples for sympathizing with the French revolutionists. Later he was pardoned. But, heartbroken, he went from St. Petersburg to Venice to die, leaving his opera *Artemesia* unfinished. Comedy opera, opéra comique, and buffa were Cimarosa's main gifts, but he wrote opera seria full worthy of a place on the opera stage. He was astonishingly talented in his use of the orchestra and so furthered the growth of opera.

PAISIELLO—BRILLIANT FUN-MAKER

A contemporary of Cimarosa, Giovanni Paisiello (1740–1816), could parody and make brilliant fun in music of anything. Imitating serious men like Gluck, he wrote, apart from ballets and religious music, operas such as *I Socrate immaginario* (*The Man Who Thought He Was Socrates,* 1773). His *La molinari* (*The Maid of the Mill*) and *Nina* were charming.

He is often like Mozart. His *Barber of Seville* was popular until Rossini presented his version (1816) which covered the operatic world with a "lather" of excitement. Among Paisiello's operas was another *La serva padrona* (1769). He became so famous that he, like Cimarosa, was invited to Russia.

His parody awoke other composers—maybe even Richard Strauss and Wagner—to its potentialities in opera.

SPONTINI AND HISTORICAL OPERA

Gasparo Spontini (1774–1851), born a peasant, in Majolati, Italy, is known for writing the first historical operas of modern times. He was an admirer of Mozart and used many of Gluck's ideas.

Historical operas had begun with Monteverdi, and Handel had used vast historical subjects, too. Spontini profited by everything in the past and became an example for Meyerbeer, Halévy, and even for Wagner and Verdi. Few of his operas are heard now, but in 1925 his *La Vestale* (*The Vestal Virgin*) was revived at the Metropolitan for Rosa Ponselle. *La Vestale,* in three acts, foreshadows the brilliant and glamorous effects in future operas. The scene is in architecturally magnificent and magnetic ancient Rome, most fitting for grandest of opera.

Napoleon gave Spontini a prize for *La Vestale.* The judges were the composers Méhul, Gossec, and Grétry. Had Spontini, Handel and Wagner lived today they could have made imposing documentary films and films of adventure.

GIOACCHINO ROSSINI

Gioacchino Rossini (1792–1868) was born in Pesaro, on the Adriatic, in Italy, and to quote our own words from *Music Through the Ages:* "A master of the trivial, he made the trivial masterful."

During his life there was hardly a village or town in Italy where opera wasn't given. Italian life centered around the opera house. To the people of fashion, the opera was an important salon. The boxes or loges became reception "stalls" throughout the evenings. To those who didn't sit in the loges, opera was a sort of club where they gathered to talk, to use the gaming tables, and to rejoice in their favorite singers and dancers. That opera was whittled down to the stature of the audiences is well illustrated in the spots composed for those using the theater, where they could smoke, drink, and eat sherbets (*sorbetti*). The aria, called *sorbetto,* attests to the practicality of composers of these days.

Rossini's mother had been a buffa singer in a traveling opera troupe, in the orchestra of which his father was a trumpeter. After some musical instruction in Bologna, Rossini was given a private teacher and later traveled with his parents as a singer and an accompanist. Like Weber, he gathered en route much experience for his future work. He was sent to the *Liceo* (Conservatory) in Bologna (1807), where he studied the cello. Not liking school, he left the Liceo and studied by himself. When he was eighteen, he brought out in Venice a one-act opera buffa, *La cambiale di matrimonia (The Marriage Contract),* and when he was twenty, he was given commissions for five light operas!

Rossini was blessed with native wit and dash, a genius for melody, a unique dramatic flair, and he bubbled over with glee like a Pergolesi or a Mozart. Once he was asked to write an opera for a soprano whose only good note was a B flat. He limited her to B flat and let the accompaniment carry the melody! This was for the opera, *Ciro in Babilonia (Cyrus in Babylon),* presented in 1812.

In 1813 Rossini scored his first real success in *Tancredi,* on Tasso's play. Scarcely a year passed that he did not write one or more operas, until his *Guillaume Tell (William Tell)* was produced in Paris in 1829. With his *L'Italiana in Algeri (The Italian Lady in Algiers),* the people in Venice were subjugated. And his *Elizabetta, Regina d'Inghilterra (Elizabeth, Queen of England,* 1815), a great success, was better than his other Italian operas.

THE BARBER OF SEVILLE

Soon after *Torvaldo e Dorliska* (1815), had been poorly received, the manager of the Argentine Theatre gave him Beaumarchais' play, *Le barbier de Seville, ou la precaution inutile (The Barber of Seville, or Useless Precaution).* This story had been used by Paisiello and others. Mozart had used Beaumarchais' play about the same barber, *Le*

Mariage de Figaro, for his opera, *The Marriage of Figaro.* Rossini had self-confidence, and he also had the wisdom to recognize Cesare Sterbini as a genius, and asked him to write the book. Rossini was somewhat apprehensive because Paisiello's opera had been much liked, so he wrote to tell Paisiello. Paisiello didn't seem to care very much then, even though he was smarting from the sensation caused by Rossini's *Elizabetta.* But he banked on the failure of *Torvaldo e Dorliska* and hoped for the worst!

No sensible person would have believed that anyone could approach the brilliancy and sparkle of Mozart's *Figaro.* Yet it is difficult to say which *is* the better. (We "give the palm" to Mozart!) But Rossini's opera ranks with Mozart's as one of the two great buffa operas. When someone compared the versions, Rossini said, "Mozart is the angel of music...who would dare touch him without committing sacrilege!" Yet Rossini has grace, fun, sparkle, and occasionally even the elegance of Mozart, if not his tenderness.

The first appearance of *The Barber of Seville* (1816) in Rome was fabulous. In spite of the fact that Rossini showed the letter received from Paisiello and the one he sent to all mutual friends about his intention to write *The Barber,* the rumor spread that Rossini was doing a traitorous thing.

Rossini, as composer, was to preside over the orchestra, at the piano, for the first three performances, as was the custom of the time. At the first performance everything went wrong. "Hot-headed enemies" were backstage and in front. By a peculiar oversight the guitar, which was to accompany Almaviva, was not tuned, and Manuel García (who played Count Almaviva) had to tune it on the stage. This brought laughter from the house. Then a string broke. More whistling! Someone said that all the whistlers in Italy were present! Then when Rosina, sung by the popular Madame Giorgi-Righetti, appeared on the balcony, there was a tremendous burst of laughter and whistling because her first words were: "Continue, my dear, do always so." It seemed that doom was forecast, but Rosina shortly after sang *"Una voce poco fa"* ("A Little Voice I Heard Just Now") and saved the moment, but not the day. Applause has followed the singing of this aria ever since. When Adelina Patti once sang it to Rossini in Paris, in his usual "don't care" way, he said, "A very pretty song! Whose is it?"

Rossini left the theater after the disastrous première with as much nonchalance as if the opera had been by someone else. His friends, however, were concerned and rushed to his lodging only to find him fast asleep.

This *Barber of Seville* is one of the notable first-night failures of operas which have become famous in the operatic repertory; another was *Tannhäuser* (Paris, 1861).

Before the second performance of *The Barber of Seville* Rossini borrowed from his older operas to bolster the new one. Instead of the Spanish song, of which the trickery of the broken string had forced García to make a mess, Rossini substituted the lovely cavatina, *"Ecco ridente il cielo"* ("Lo, Smiles the Morning in the Sky"), from his own *Aureliano in Palmira (Aurelian in Palmyra)*. This had seen much service, for it had also been in his *Ciro in Babilonia*.

Here we witness the elasticity of music—the same music painting utterly different things. For example, this song had been given to a Persian king in Nebuchadnezzar's ancient capital; then to a Roman emperor in the Syrian desert as an address to Isis; and to a lovesick Spanish count, Almaviva, in Seville in the seventeenth century, as an amorous serenade. It was often pointed out by writers of Rossini's day as the first example "of modulation into the minor key, later so frequently used by this master and his crowd of imitators." (Gustave Kobbé in the early version of the *Complete Opera Book*).

So we see Rossini, for the second night of his opera, cutting out everything that had been laughed at or disliked, and it went much better. It began to catch the people's fancy, and after a later performance, Rossini was carried in triumph through the streets. Result: the Paisiello version of *The Barber* was soon abandoned as dull.

It is said that Rossini took only thirteen, fourteen, or twenty days to write this opera—without its revisions. This feat is debatable. It is also said that when Donizetti, as a young man of nineteen, was told that Rossini had composed the opera in thirteen, he replied, "Why not? He's so lazy!"

With the carelessness of a man who could "knock off" forty-six operas, among other things, in thirty-seven years, Rossini is said to have lost the original overture to *The Barber of Seville*. The present one has little relationship to the rollicking Barber, the flirtatious Rosina, and the romantic Almaviva, and is one of two used for three other operas, among which was his *Elizabeth, Queen of England*. This kind of economy was customary before Verdi's time. This overture, however, is tuneful and delightful—so why should anyone care?

Owing probably to the "laziness" of Rossini, who didn't bother to write another and original overture to the opera, he did not trouble to write the trio which he intended to have in the Music-Lesson Scene in the second act. He let his prima donna sing what she wanted to sing, and forgot the trio! The directions in the libretto are: "Rosina sings an air, ad libitum, for the occasion." And all through the years every singer has sung what she wished. For example, Adelina Patti used a song, "The Burst of Laughter," from Auber's *Manon Lescaut,* which was loved as is Massenet's *Manon* today. She also sang "Il Baccio" ("The Kiss"—"Arditi Waltz"). Some have sung "Sicilian Vespers" from Verdi's opera of the same name; Amelita Galli-Curci used the "Vengeance Air" from *The Magic Flute,* and "The Last Rose of Summer," which now seems to be the stock interpolation.

Only in opera could an untaught girl taking music lessons sing superbly (sometimes!) what would take years and years for an accomplished prima donna to master. Although the opera was written in 1816, later, modern songs and songs from before 1816 are introduced in this scene without a thought from the audience or critics of their inappropriateness. Brilliant and athletic coloratura is still meat for the masses, and the classes—and opera's most delightful quality is the congruity of its incongruity. Opera with a straight face can express the impossible as if it were possible.

The Barber of Seville has been changed in many ways and in many places. Whereas Rosina's part was originally for contralto, it is now soprano. Rossini loved the contralto register because of its warmth. This helped to break the stranglehold of the soprano—an advance indeed.

"On Tuesday, November 22, 1825, Manual García, the elder, issued the preliminary announcement of his season of Italian opera at the Park Theatre, New York. The printers appear to have had a struggle with the Italian titles of operas and names of Italian composers. For the *Evening Post* announced that: 'The opera of H. Barbiora di Seviglia by Rosina, is now in rehearsal and will be given as soon as possible.' " (From *The Complete Opera Book* by Gustave Kobbé.) It was the first opera in Italian given in New York.

The first cast was be-García-ed, for Father (Manuel) García was Almaviva; Mother García was Berta; the seventeen-year-old daughter, Maria García (later Madame Malibran) was Rosina; and the son, Manuel García Jr., was Figaro! This company was imported from Italy by Dominick Lynch, a wealthy wine dealer and amateur musician.

While it would take too long to list all the songs in this captivating opera buffa, don't forget the charming trio sung by the Count, Rosina, and Figaro, as the first two decide to elope: "Zitti, zitti, piano" ("Softly, Softly, and in Silence"). It is said to have been borrowed from Haydn's *Seasons.*

The Barber of Seville was given at the Metropolitan Opera House in 1883, with Marcella Sembrich as Rosina. Since then, Nellie Melba, Luisa Tetrazzini, Frieda Hempel, Amelita Galli-Curci, Maria Barrientos, and Lily Pons are among the famous Rosinas. But the greatest of them all was Adelina Patti. Of all the Figaros, great as they have been, Charles Gilibert was such a one as Beaumarchais, or even Molière, would have embraced, thought Pitts Sanborn, one time music critic for the New York *World-Telegram.*

Rossini wrote many songs to be delivered at breakneck speed and to ascend into the highest registers. One of his famous speedy songs, the baritone's delight, is *"Largo al factotum della città"* ("Room for the City's Factotum"), and if you have heard it in English, you will remember the "Figaro here, Figaro there," and the rest of the tumultuous lyric.

Up to very recently, the only complete opera of Rossini's produced has been this same *Barber of Seville,* but we hear several of the (instrumental) overtures: *L'Italiana in Algeri* (1913); *La gazza ladra (The Thieving Magpie,* 1817); *La Cenerentola (Cinderella,* 1817); and *Guillaume Tell (William Tell,* 1829). It is a strange trick of fate that a composer who wrote chiefly for singers and loved singing and knew the voice well lives on chiefly as a composer of instrumental forewords to his operas. Lately, however, there have been two revivals: (1) *Cenerentola* (Cinderella), beautifully given at the Center Theatre in New York during the 1950's and (2) in May, 1955, *La Pietra del Paragona* as *The Touchstone,* by the Julius Hartt Musical Foundation, in Hartford, Connecticut, under the directorship of Dr. Moshe Paranov. *The Touchstone* was first produced at La Scala in Milan in 1812. Rossini was twenty when he completed this charming opera with the slightest of plots. Skill, indeed! At present there seems to be promise of more Rossini operas.

BEETHOVEN AND ROSSINI

In 1822, after marrying Isabella Colbran, the Spanish prima donna, Rossini spent happy and successful years in Vienna, where he met Beethoven, who told him that he'd better stick to opera buffa and not attempt opera seria. It might have been better had he taken Beethoven's advice, for later, Rossini was very disappointed in the reception given by the Venetians to his carefully written opera *Semiramide*. This was in two acts, with book by Gaetano Rossi, based on Voltaire's tragedy *Semiramis*. It was first given at the Teatro Fenice in Venice, 1823, and at the Haymarket, London, in 1824.

Next he went to London, where he had a marvelous time for five months, and left with seven thousand pounds (from George IV). He then went to France and became the manager of Théâtre des Italiens in Paris. He soon became Composer to the King (Charles X) and then Inspector General of Singing in France, yet no czar, like his Italian predecessors. Here he gave some successful revisions of his own operas.

SEMIRAMIDE

As with many queens, "Queen Semiramis" of Babylon has passed from the stage. It is thought, however, that if there were alive today an Adelina Patti (soprano) to sing the title role, or a Sofia Scalchi (contralto) to sing the part of Arsaces, it could be revived. This is another opera, like Gluck's *Orpheus,* where a woman takes the part of a man, Arsaces, the Commander of the Assyrian Army. In the first act, the brilliant aria for the Queen (soprano), *"Bel raggio lusinghier"* ("Bright Ray of Hope"), has kept this opera with its overture on the recording lists.

The first performance in America was probably in New Orleans in 1837. New York's first glimpse was in 1845 at Palmo's Opera House, with Giulia Grisi (mezzo soprano). Four performances were given during 1894 and 1895 at the Metropolitan Opera House, with Nellie Melba (soprano), Scalchi (contralto), and Edouard de Reszke (basso).

In 1829, Rossini gave *Guillaume Tell* with a magnificent cast. It was adapted by Étienne Jouy and Hippolyte Bis from Schiller's popular play, *Wilhelm Tell,* about the Swiss patriot. This was not only written on a French libretto, but it was done in the grand style (grand opera). So the melody is less embellished, and the instrumental score more carefully developed than was customary with the Italians.

After melting down *William Tell* from five acts to three, the management carried the reduction process, one act at a time, down to a curtain raiser, or only an accompaniment to the ballet. This was certainly adding insult to injury! "I hope you won't be annoyed," said the director of the opera to him one day, "but tonight we play the second act of *Tell*," to which Rossini replied, "The whole of it?"

This kind of opera was not Rossini's *métier* (best line of work).

This is probably the reason why the only part of it now given is its "sure-fire" overture. It is so exciting that it is used as the signature of the radio and television serial, *The Lone Ranger*. Poor Rossini! To this he would undoubtedly have said, lackadaisically, "What more?"

William Tell was first produced in New York at the Park Theatre in 1845 in French; then in Italian in 1855, and in German (1866) at the Academy of Music; and its première at the Metropolitan Opera House took place in German in 1884.

MALADIES

At thirty-seven, Rossini retired, worn and nervous, and wrote no more operas. Besides, the revolution of 1830 invalidated his contract (as Inspector General of Singing) with Charles X. It is presumed that his neuroses might have been brought on by the ill fate of *William Tell,* the rising tide of Meyerbeer's popularity, and the general delight in flamboyant and glamorous grand opera. At any rate, he suffered nearly twenty years from chronic melancholia, while living in Bologna and Florence.

In 1855 he emerged from semi-invalidism and returned to Paris (Passy). There he gave himself over to frivolities and held his famous Saturday-evening salons, where he did clever stunts with music and became known for his wit and brilliancy. Among others who attended the evenings in Passy (suburb of Paris) with the wit and genius were: Auber, Ambroise Thomas, Saint-Saens, Verdi, Gounod, Liszt, Adelina Patti, and Anton Rubinstein, besides men of the world of letters and painting.

In 1864 he emerged further and wrote his *Petite Messe solennelle* (*Small Solemn Mass*) and in accordance with his usual seeming irreverence, he dedicated it to Madame La Comtesse Pillet-Will, in whose home it was first given. He called it a "little Mass" although it was far larger than any other. He appended to it two letters which, if one does not realize that they express real feeling for the Deity, one might call flippant, as one reads: "Who would believe it? Among Thy disciples there are some who are capable of singing wrong notes . . . all mine will sing accurately and *con amore* Thy praises, as well as this little composition, which is, alas, the last mortal sin of my old age." He also attached to the *Little Mass* another letter from which we quote: "Dear God:...Have I for once written real sacred music or merely damned bad music? I was born for opera buffa as Thou knowest... So blessed be Thou, and grant me paradise."

When Meyerbeer, among others, was at the Pillet-Will's home to hear the first presentation of the *Little Mass,* he rushed up to Rossini and shouted, "See! In two months he has created a whole world! He is the Jupiter of our time and holds us all in the hollow of his hand." That was something for "Czar" Meyerbeer to admit.

A STRANGE PHENOMENON

Rossini is an example of a successful opera composer suddenly stopping his dramatic career when but half through his life. He died in Ruelle, Italy, at the age of seventy-six, known as the "Swan of Pesaro." In addition to his operas, he left six string quartets, and the two Masses, *Stabat Mater* (1832-41) and the *Messa Solenne* (1820), besides the *Petite Messe.*

HIS CONTRIBUTIONS

Rossini advanced opera advantageously by reducing the use of *recitativo secco,* or dry recitative, which even Mozart used frequently. Instead of putting the action into the recitative, Rossini frequently used a dramatic recital of the text and *scena* leading up to his vocal numbers with the accompaniment of rich instrumentation, even to the full orchestra. Others had used this device but not as often or as successfully as this master of stage effects. His accompanied recitative seems most normal to an opera-goer today, but it was a step forward—in beauty, in continuity, and action. Although Rossini was no reformer, this contribution must not be overlooked, for the smallest new departure for opera, which was in a traditional plaster cast, was something!

For example, some of the traditions that gripped opera were: An opera had to have three acts, despite its subject; the first act must end with a humorous ballet, the second with a tragic one; and it must last five hours, or even more. There must be three singers, each must have five important arias and three less important ones. The arias must appear at specific places, and the length, spirit and variety was decided upon more often by the singers than by the composers. These songs and their quality depended on what the singers could do in the way of embellishment, runs, trills, and all other coloratura athletics.

In Rossini's *Elizabeth, Queen of England,* he, the composer, was actually permitted to write the coloratura part for Isabella Colbran. This was unusual because the singer normally demanded coloratura, specifically in the cadenzas, to show off the voice and give the audience good reason to applaud. Rossini often managed to foil a singer in these exploits when they were utterly incompatible with the plot or score.

He said much about the ruination (by overdoing) of bel canto, the beautiful smooth Italian singing. Yet he himself was guilty of providing singers with vocal athletics, in spite of which he wrote some of the most beautiful songs, if often tricky, in opera repertory.

Furthermore, he had great skill in concerted pieces (choruses and ensembles), and his work, although ornate and sometimes seemingly trivial, has force and beauty. He had the grasp of a man of the theater, and the insight of a man of music. Although he feared the ascendancy of Meyerbeer, he certainly gave him and others encouragement. Technique was of vast importance to him, and although his methods in general did not advance grand opera (see Wagner, etc.), the tendency today is to return to the Rossini manner of opera buffa. It can be said that Rossini brought opera buffa to its height, after which it had to decline.

BELLINI, THE INDEPENDENT

Vincenzo Bellini (1801–35) of Catania, Sicily, had too much good taste and sincerity to build his operas of fireworks. Dying at the age of thirty-four, he left eleven operas, of which only three are given: *La sonnambula* (*The Sleepwalker*); *I Puritani* (*The Puritans*); and *Norma*.

Bellini had a superb sense of the elegant in melody. His music was graceful, and had he lived longer, he might have ranked with the greatest. He showed in *The Sleepwalker* that he had as much interest in simple words and fitting them to the music as had the French. This was something to be envied by the Italian composers of his day, when vocal calisthenics were the rage.

La sonnambula, in two acts, with book by Giuseppe Felice Romani, was first produced at the Teatro Carcano, Milan, in 1831. It was then given in Paris and London and reached New York in an English version at the Park Theatre in 1835, and in Italian, at Palmo's Opera House, in 1844. It was frequently sung by the sopranos Etelka Gerster and Adelina Patti at the Academy of Music. The Metropolitan produced it in 1905.

This opera is Italian indeed, as are the others of Bellini, for they give too much attention to lovely melody and to singing, and too little to the orchestra. The story appeals to people's sympathies because of undeserved penalties suffered by Amina, owing to her unfortunate habit of sleepwalking. Its dramatic climax and Amina's sleepwalking scene, with the song, "Ah, Scarce I Could Believe How Soon My Blossoms Would Wither," is followed by the triumphant greeting of Elvino, her lover, with "Mingle Not an Earthly Sorrow," for many seasons a coveted bit of "show-off" for tenors.

I Puritani (*The Puritans*), in keeping with the delight of the French in political and historical opera, has a story based on the wars between the soldiers of Cromwell and the followers of Charles I. In three acts, with a poor book by Count Carlo Pepoli, it is rarely given today.

It had its first performance at the Théâtre des Italiens in Paris, in 1835. It opened the new Manhattan Opera House (sad to say, nonexistent today) in 1906, and it was revived at the Metropolitan Opera House in 1917.

It had some delightful songs and opens with a thin but pleasant overture. Elvira, the heroine, has been sung by Luisa Tetrazzini, and the Spanish soprano Maria Barrientos.

SLOW COLORATURA

Probably one of the most difficult to sing well is the song with slow coloratura. Such singing has to be butter-smooth and the tone sustained between each note and phrase. There can be no slurring or sliding or cheating. Bellini's *Norma* is lovely with slow coloratura. It takes a most expert singer!

In this lyric tragedy in two acts, Norma, a Vestal Virgin (priestess), having broken her vows of celibacy and chastity by taking a Roman lover, brought down vengeance on him and upon herself after he deserted her. They are united in death on a funeral pyre, to the basso aria, with a soldier's chorus, *"O del Tebro"* ("Haughty Roman").

The soprano aria, *"Casta diva che in argant,"* ("Chaste Goddess, May Thy Silver Ray"), is without doubt one of the most superb and taxing songs in the Italian repertory, or even in the international opera repertory of the nineteenth century. Its slow and long-flowing phrases and its exquisite melody have endeared it to audiences, and all sopranos crave the part of Norma as every actress yearns to play Juliet. This is followed by *"Ah! bello a me retorno"* ("Beloved, Return to Me"), which contrasts with the measured beauty of *"Casta diva."* Another familiar number is the opening march and chorus of the Druids: *"Dell' aura tua profetica"* ("With Thy Prophetic Oracle"). It is said that Bellini wrote the "Warrior Chorus" to express his longings to get rid of the Austrians, who were then ruling Italy and weren't expelled until 1870.

One of the writers of this book, when witnessing a dress rehearsal at the Metropolitan Opera House of *Norma* (title role sung by Rosa Ponselle), was interrupted by a famous basso sitting in front of her, who said, during the song, "This is too good for human beings." Ponselle sang it with such beauty that his ardor was easy to share. The recordings of this romantic story of ancient Druid life in Britain during the Roman occupation are enchanting.

The book of *Norma* by Giuseppe Felice Romani, is based on a story by Alexandre Soumet and Louis Belmontet. Its first performance was in Milan, at La Scala, in 1831. It was introduced to New York in 1841 in an English version at the Park Theatre, and revived in 1927 at the Metropolitan Opera House. This cast included Rosa Ponselle in the title role, with Marion Telva (contralto) as Adalgisa, Giacomo Lauri-Volpi (tenor) as Pollione, and Ezio Pinza (basso) as Oroveso, Priest of the Druids.

DONIZETTI

Among the composers who carried on the coloratura gymnastics of Rossini was Gaetano Donizetti (1797–1848), writer of more than sixty operas. He was far more accomplished in the handling of his orchestra and in the use of varied harmonies than Bellini and was even more dramatic. He had a rare gift for the romantic love song and could express his delight in glitter and pyrotechnics in such pieces as the "Mad Scene" of *Lucia di Lammermoor* (*Lucy of Lammermoor*), the opera based on Sir Walter Scott's story *The Bride of Lammermoor*.

Donizetti, beside writing grand opera, satisfied audiences after the French Revolution (1789–95) in his enduring comic operas: *La Fille du regiment* (*The Daughter of the Regiment*); the fascinating *L'Elisir d'amore* (*The Elixir of Love*); and the flashing *Don Pasquale*. Unfortunately, he worked so hard in many forms of music and as a staff member of the Naples Conservatory, and traveled so much, that at fifty-one, a brain malady caused his death. He was born in Bergamo, Italy, and died there.

Composers and audiences enjoyed his brilliant operas and his amusing ones, but like many of his and Rossini's followers, Donizetti preferred glitter to control. Again, as in Handel's time, people went to opera only to hear the singers "show off." It wasn't the music that attracted them, but those who could fly to the highest vocal summit and "hang by" trills the longest.

L'Elisir d'amore, with a book by Felice Romani, is an opera buffa in two acts, a most romantic and fantastic story about a favorite topic in opera—mixed-up love potions. One of the famous songs from *L'Elisir* is the tenor aria, *"Una furtiva lagrima"* ("One Furtive Tear").

This is one of Donizetti's most delighting scores in comic vein and full of grace and charm. His accompaniments are far less monotonous than are many in the operas of his day. It is rumored that it was produced at the Teatro della Canobbiana, Milan (1832), fourteen days after it was ordered. The American première was in 1838 in English at the Park Theatre, New York, and there was another production at the Metropolitan in 1904.

THE WICKEDEST OF LADIES

As a drama lover, it is only natural that Donizetti, living in the time of romantic opera, would write one about the so-called wickedest of ladies, Lucrezia Borgia. She is reputed to have accomplished what even the most experienced chemists today cannot do: make poisons work a week or two "after taking"! One can't help feeling sorry for the lady's reputation.

Lucrezia Borgia has a prologue and two acts, on a libretto by Felice Romani, based on the book by Victor Hugo. It is rarely given today in spite of its striking songs. There is a lovely prologue, a trio and the drinking song in Act I, *"Il segreto per esser felice"* ("The Secret of Happiness").

It was first produced at La Scala in Milan in 1833 and introduced to New York at Palmo's Opera House in 1844, several months after its première in New Orleans. The only performance at the Metropolitan took place in 1904 with Enrico Caruso in the cast.

THE MAD WOMAN OF LAMMERMOOR

It is always interesting when an Italian uses a plot from a British or Scottish story. But, contrary to the opinions about the lack of warmth of feeling among the people of these British Isles, some of the great romances were born there, even when their dim and distant origins were somewhere else. *The Bride of Lammermoor* made grist for this accomplished miller of glittering romance in music.

The story of the opera, *Lucia di Lammermoor,* follows the book rather closely. It is considered by many to be Donizetti's best, yet it is often ridiculed for its vocal athletics. Despite all criticism, Donizetti has woven a score of lovely colors, interesting choruses and ensembles, excitement and thrills, and in many ways it is on the top flight of the dramatic in Italian opera.

Lucia is in three acts, with book by Salvatore Cammarano, who wrote also for Verdi. It was first produced at the Teatro San Carlo, Naples, in 1835. The Scottish lady made her bow in New York at Niblo's Garden, 1843, and as the second opera given at the Metropolitan Opera House in 1883 with Marcella Sembrich in the title role. It is still used for expert coloratura singers today, on the Metropolitan Opera House stage with Lily Pons.

The opera swings from the sentimental to the tragic. The sextet is one of the most extraordinary and exciting bit of character- and feeling-painting in spite of the florid and altitudinous coloratura. Within the six voices, Lucia's soars through the mass of sound in the character of the poor, sweet, "sinned against" soul.

The "Mad Scene" of the third act has a background of the wedding guests in joyous mood in the great hall of Lammermoor Castle, with dance music issuing from an adjoining room. Lucia has now lost her reason, and Donizetti shows his skill in putting over character in coloratura—a sort of vocal Technicolor. Her first song is sung as she brandishes a sword, after she has killed Arthur, the man she has been tricked into marrying. She sings that she has killed her husband; then, as she goes on, she shows with pathos (in coloratura) her state of mind and heart. In this scene, so renowned, the soprano singing this role must be able in tone and gesture to hold a mood of dramatic intensity probably without equal. The voice stays in the high register a perilously long time. The voice itself must be absolutely true, for often it has to follow or agree with the lacy flights of the flutes.

FLUTE AND BASSOON

Donizetti's use of the flute was brave, for in his day it was a much-derided instrument. A popular riddle at the time was, "What is worse than a flute?" and the answer was, "Two flutes." This is just another case of the excellent use of instruments that Donizetti practiced—the flute and the harp in *Lucia,* and the bassoons in the introduction to "One Furtive Tear" in *The Elixir of Love.* At this point it is encouraging and important to find an increased interest in the orchestra in Italian opera, which culminated with Verdi and his followers.

Besides Donizetti's contribution to orchestral effects, particularly in

Lucia, he shows himself, as is suggested, a painter of character. Another poignant song of Lucia's is the legend of the fountain, *"Regnava nel silenzio"* ("Silence over All Was Reigning"). It is in typical Italian style, yet skillfully depicts in dreamy melody, with extremely brilliant passages, the sweetness and the gentleness of Lucia.

The pity of it is that the role has been so overplayed and badly sung that people call it an "old war horse," whereas a study of Donizetti's work, particularly *Lucia,* would help many opera writers today.

La Fille du regiment (*The Daughter of the Regiment*) is sparkling opéra comique (in two acts) of the most feathery and romantic type, wherein Marie, the daughter of the regiment, rises from poverty to riches and returns again to poverty in order to keep the lover she adores. Besides, it is full of fun, of color, and of marching songs, for Marie is the regimental *vivandière,* a sutler, or licensed trader to an army. The soprano who sings the heroine has to dress up in a fancy military uniform and learn to play the drum. This is, of course, very "cute" when a Lily Pons sings it.

The "Rataplan Chorus" a famous spot in the opera, is sung by the Grenadiers. Again you see the love of the people for the military in opera in the heroine's song in the first act, *"Apparvi all' luce, sul campo guerrier"* ("I First Saw the Light in the Camp [of my brave grenadiers]"). The opera ends in a salute to France. This is drama.

The book is by Marquis Saint-Georges and Bayard and the first performance of the opera was in 1840 in Paris at the Opéra Comique. America heard it in New Orleans in 1843. The "Met" gave it in 1903. Marie was a favorite role of the Swedish Jenny Lind, the German Henriette Sontag, and the Italian Adelina Patti, all of whom sang it in New York. Giuseppe De Luca, Charles Gilibert, and Antonio Scotti (baritones) enjoyed singing the role of Sulpice. This opera has had little airing because of the difficulty of getting a complete cast of sufficiently skilled singers.

When *Don Pasquale* was presented to its first cast, it was received coldly by both singers and orchestra. When the rehearsal was over, it is said that Donizetti commented to his friend and publisher who was present, "Let them alone. They know nothing about it. I know what's the matter." Back at his lodgings, the composer rummaged through a lot of papers and brought out a song. "This is what *Don Pasquale* needs," said he. It was the *"Com'e gentil"* ("The Serenade"), sung by the tenor to the accompaniment of an offstage lute. There have been few more popular songs in all opera.

The other songs carry out the fun in the graceful, glinting manner of excellent and melodious, well orchestrated opera buffa. *Don Pasquale* tells the story of the outwitting of an old, wealthy, amorous bachelor by his nephew and the girl both want to marry.

The opera is in three acts, with book written by the composer, after Cammarano's *Ser Marc'Antonio,* and was first performed at the Théâtre des Italiens, Paris, 1843. New York saw it first in 1846, at the Park Theatre, where it was presented in English. Marcella Sembrich was the Metropolitan's first Norina.

Among the other engaging operas by Donizetti which have been heard occasionally in America is *La Favorita* (*The Favorite Lady*), first produced at the Grand Opéra in Paris in 1840, in New York at the Park Theatre in 1845, and at the Metropolitan in 1895.

Another opera rarely given is *Linda di Chamounix,* a melodrama in three acts, first produced at the Kärnthnerthor Theater, Vienna, in 1842, with book by Gaetano Rossi. It was given at the Metropolitan Opera House in 1890, with Adelina Patti as Linda.

Why isn't the one-act *Il campanello di notte* (*The Night Bell*) ever given? What waltz tunes!

Rossini, Bellini and Donizetti have made a garland of music that has charmed and delighted audiences, even if opera censors have seen their shortcomings, and few geniuses have improved on their methods.

SCENE III

The French "On Stage"—
Gossec, Boieldieu, Auber, Meyerbeer, and Others

FRANCE, though often indulging in understatement during the Revolution, delighted in display, and this was given in plenty by such men as Gossec, Méhul, Cherubini and many others. Cherubini, indeed, is a potent influence.

The hundreds of romantic opera writers in Italy, Germany, France and England wrote one or more kinds of operas: opéra comique, lyric, seria (grand) and light opera. It isn't often easy to place the composers in these categories. For example, Cherubini wrote *Medea,* an opera seria, and *The Water Carrier,* an opéra comique. Wagner wrote music dramas and a comic opera, and Verdi many grand operas and a comic opera.

It is impossible to classify the composers chronologically. In fact relatively few can be mentioned. Therefore, the country of origin, as well as the comparative importance of the operas, are the bases of the following brief accounts.

GOSSEC, A MAN OF IMPORTANCE

One of the judges who gave Spontini his prize for *La Vestale* was François Joseph Gossec (1734-1829), composer, organizer, and officer of the Royal School of Singing, which later became the Paris Conservatory of Music. It has graduated composers ever since. Gossec also organized and conducted *Les Concerts Spirituels* (Sacred Concerts) to supply entertainment on Sundays when opera was not permitted. He excelled as the first symphony writer in France, and he also wrote charming opéras comiques, among which was *Les Pêcheurs* (*The Fishermen*). His interest in instrumental music made opera more effective. It is said that as a young man, after he had taken care of the cows, he went home and played on a fiddle that he had made out of a *sabot* (wooden shoe of peasants).

OPÉRA COMIQUE BECOMES SERIOUS

The second of the judges who awarded the prize to Spontini for his opera *La Vestale* was Etienne-Nicolas Méhul (1763–1817). Méhul's mother was a cook, as had been Beethoven's. Gluck advised Méhul to write opera. He took this advice, and with twenty-five operas became famous. He is known for his beautifully written *Joseph* (1807), in which there were spoken words. This was the first time that a serious opera became *opéra comique*. After that composers could compose as they wished. In *Joseph,* a Biblical subject, Méhul showed originality of expression. Although in sober vein, it was not dull, for he had the ability to be serious, amusing and tender. With French skill, Méhul was successful in uniting the word or text to the music of his operas. At first he wrote three operas just for practice!

OPÉRA COMIQUE ESTABLISHED

Forced to become a headwaiter to support his family, Pierre Alexandre Monsigny (1729–1817) established the French School of opéra comique by using the best characteristics of both the Italian and French brands. Among his operas, *Les Aveux indiscrètes* (*Indiscreet Confessions*) won him fame in 1759, and in 1769 his best work, *Le Deserteur,* appeared.

THE BIRTH OF "RESCUE" OPERA

The third of the composers responsible for awarding Spontini a prize for *La Vestale* was André Grétry, born in Belgium (1741–1813). He tamed opéra bouffe into the gentler and more charming opéra comique and made it popular in France.

Richard the Lion-Hearted (1784) was the most popular of his fifty operas. The story was based on the legend of the rescue of Richard of England by the troubadour knight Blondel. Grétry, of course, made clever use of the troubadour song which gave Blondel the clue to the whereabouts of Richard. Grétry knew enough to keep it very French, very romantic and very oldtimey. It is the first important rescue opera, which later became a bore because of its over-frequent appearance.

The rescue opera idealized the peasants and made honesty and virtue always pay. The Grétry opera quoted most on records and on the air today is the one-act *La Rosière republicaine* (freely translated, *The*

Ceremony of the Rose, 1793). In this he was the first to picture a church "on stage" in France. It was possible to do this then because the French Revolution had freed men to write and think as they wished—almost. Church scenes on the English stage had been possible since the time of Shakespeare. Grétry's *Tableau parlant* (*Living Picture,* 1769) is a bit of extremely good comedy.

His ideas were followed by composers who made much better use of them than he did. From Grétry's time on there was little opera that could be called strictly French, strictly Italian, strictly German, or strictly English, for people moved about more and more, and composers learned from one another.

FRANÇOIS BOIELDIEU

One of the most popular writers of opéra comique after Grétry was François Adrien Boieldieu (1775–1834), born in Rouen, France, a most dramatic little city with magnificent churches and buildings. In it is the spot of black memory on which Joan of Arc was burned at the stake, a fitting birthplace for a writer of *dramatic* music.

Boieldieu and Auber were the musical atom bombs which blew up Cherubini's czarship over the French.

Boieldieu's *La Dame blanche* (*The White Lady*), with libretto by Eugène Scribe, was given with great success in 1825. The story is one of buried treasure, not hidden in the ground, or in the sea, but in a statue of The White Lady. Treasure hunting was a popular theme, for it was not many years (1701) since the adventures of Captain Kidd and the privateers had made exciting gossip and gangster yarns. *The White Lady* was such a popular girl that she appeared one thousand times in forty years! Quite a record. Yet—now it is never played.

With his *Le Calife de Bagdad* (1800) and other works, Boieldieu held the scene in France even against Rossini's popular comic operas. It is said that after his great success with *The Caliph of Bagdad,* Cherubini met him and accosted the happy young man with, "Unhappy one, are you not ashamed of such an undeserved success?" Boieldieu answered with modesty that he would like to have future instruction.

AUBER, THE PRINCE OF OPÉRA COMIQUE

If stories of gangsters are favorites today, so were they in the eighteenth and nineteenth centuries. The opera writers used stories of bandits which they dressed up with singing and fine scenery. So, Daniel François Esprit Auber (1782–1871), born in beauteous Normandy, near the landing places of our troops in the Second World War, produced a bandit opera in his tuneful *Fra Diavolo* (*Brother Devil* or *The Bandit Chief*). You notice it has an Italian name! Perhaps Auber didn't want to make a bandit out of a Frenchman! Eugène Scribe wrote the libretto.

Fra Diavolo, in three acts, probably the first gangster opera ever given in New York, appeared at the Park Theatre, in 1833, three years after it was produced in Paris. It was very popular in New York in the middle of the nineteenth century. Its overture is one of the most colorful, catchy in tune and lively in instrumentation. One of the best tunes (in the overture) is the "Soldiers' Chorus" of the first act. It is a story of a fabulous Italian bandit who by clever disguises eluded the FBI of the time. In a modern version this would be well received by audiences today.

Among his other *opéras comiques* are *Les Diamants de la couronne* (*The Crown Diamonds,* 1841) and *Le Domino noir* (*The Black Domino,* 1837). With Auber, French opéra comique took a new turn. The librettos became less fanciful and romantic, and more grown-up. Yet, more noisy, and strange to say, more spectacular and more Italian —they lean towards impending *Verismo* (see Scene VII).

Auber's most famous grand opera was *Masaniello* or *La Muette de Portici* (*The Dumb Girl of Portici,* 1828), in five acts, written two years before *Fra Diavolo.* When given in Brussels in 1830, it is said to have touched off a rebellion which ended in the separation of Belgium and Holland. The story itself is based on the historic uprising of the people of Naples against the Viceroy. It is full of revolutionary atmosphere.

A MODEL IS CAST FOR GRAND OPERA

Masaniello is about a dumb girl, Fenella. She is usually the ballerina, an original idea for an opera. But if she cannot speak, she can jump. For, at the finale she jumps from a royal balcony in Portici, a town between Naples and Mt.Vesuvius, into the lava flowing from Vesuvius in eruption! With the German Meyerbeer's *Robert the Devil* and the Italian Rossini's *William Tell,* it became one of three pillars or foundations of French grand opera. It is supposed that Rossini influenced Auber. So Auber not only earned the name of Prince of Opéra Comique, but helped to set up a model for grand opera.

He was a sensitive man and could never conduct an opera of his own, nor attend rehearsals. One day, it is said, he went to hear Rossini's

William Tell. Suddenly, he heard the cello in an unexpected theme. His eyes bulged from their sockets, his ears rang, and he dashed out. In the lobby he found that he had been listening to his own *La Muette de Portici* and not to *William Tell!* The director had thought to compliment the great man by "putting on" his own opera!

In the third act, Auber uses, in excerpt form, one of his early masses in the celebrated prayer, *"Nume del Ciel"* ("Divinity in Heaven"). All the music is delightful, and it is excellent grand opera, which even Wagner praised for its vigor, originality, and broad dramatic treatment.

HÉROLD

Unlike Boieldieu and Auber, Louis Joseph Hérold (1791-1833), born in Paris, did not use Scribe as a librettist. But like Auber, Hérold's best-known opera, *Zampa, (The Marble Betrothed,* 1831), is about an Italian bandit. The opera, popular in its day, is not heard now, save its melodious and galloping overture, almost as popular as Rossini's *William Tell.* It is one of the many overtures that has lost its opera.

Hérold wrote *Le Pré aux clercs (The Field of Honor,* 1832) which is never heard. When first born, it was as popular as *La Dame blanche* and it lived up to Hérold's paramount idea, in which rhythm was most important. He leaned somewhat toward vocal athletics and coloratura, as did Rossini, yet Hérold's songs were among the loveliest.

JACQUES HALÉVY

Jacques François Fromental Élie Halévy (1799-1862) was another Paris Conservatory boy. He won the *Prix de Rome* at seventeen, and the *Grand Prix* at twenty. He wrote operas, ballets and other things, but is famous above all for *La Juive (The Jewess),* which has held the stage more firmly than many other operas of his day. It is set in the fifteenth century, and is picturesque in plot. It is said to have a "jinx" with opera singers, and this idea was perpetuated when Enrico Caruso became ill while taking part in it and never recovered.

La Juive, in five acts, has a book by Eugène Scribe. It was given first at the Opéra in Paris in 1836. America greeted it first in New Orleans, in 1844, with the Parisian cast, and in 1846 it was produced in New York City at the Park Theatre. It was first given at the Metropolitan in 1885 with Materna as Rachel. It was revived in 1919 for Rosa Ponselle with Caruso in the cast.

GIACOMO MEYERBEER

Giacomo Meyerbeer (1791–1864), born in Germany, whose life spanned the years after the Revolution in Paris and the Civil War in America, was a genius and a trickster. He came of a cultivated Jewish family of bankers, always ready to encourage the arts and artists of their native land. He, like Jacques Offenbach, became an imported luxury in Paris. As a German in France, he wrote French opera, after having written like an Italian in Italy before he reached Paris. His musical progenitors were Spontini, Auber and Rossini. Meyerbeer had an international heritage.

The boy at nine became one of the best pianists in Berlin, under the tutelage of Muzio Clementi (1752–1832), the composer-pianist-publisher and piano manufacturer. Later, he studied with Abbé Vogler, who also taught Carl Maria von Weber. From Vogler, Weber absorbed German folklore and a passionate patriotism. Meyerbeer was not so inoculated. Weber was the Germanophile, and Meyerbeer, a cosmopolite.

Meyerbeer, born Jakob Liebmann Beer, changed his name because a relative who left him money had exacted a promise from him to do so. Then, always a clever caterer to circumstance, he changed his first name and became *Giacomo* Meyerbeer, in the hope of more recognition in the Italian opera world.

Around 1812 his early successes in Germany won him the position of Court Composer to the Grand Duke at Darmstadt. Soon a local success, a comic opera, led him to the music center, Vienna. He wasn't too successful there, and at the suggestion of Salieri (who might or might not have wished him out of the way, as he had Mozart) went to Venice (1814) to study the needs of the voice.

In Venice, Meyerbeer met Rossini, and wrote seven brilliantly successful operas in the Italian style. Weber protested against his lack of patriotism for German music. Soon Meyerbeer went to Paris (1826) where he wrote French music!

Naturally, his great desire was to be famous. He would often resort to musical tricks and stunts for popularity, but his skill in writing for the orchestra takes him far from the charlatan class. His full orchestration bothered the producers lest they could not adequately present his opera with the means at hand. Indeed, they frequently had to add instruments. In this orchestral interest he was fundamentally a German and an innovator.

ROMANTIC GRAND OPERA

Meyerbeer added a new dimension to drama and music in his magnificent historic, if sometimes overdramatic or theatrical, opera. In *Les Huguenots* he wrote the first romantic grand opera more effective than Spontini's, Cherubini's, or Rossini's, with ballet music such as never yet had been achieved in Paris.

The French still wanted spectacles on a large scale, and Meyerbeer obliged. Instead of writing about simple love affairs and parlor romances, or everyday opéra bouffe, he wrote heavy grand opera, with settings in great palaces, dealing with historical incidents (*Les Huguenots*) and unusual places and people (*L'Africaine*). He added a dash of the eerie in his first opera on Parisian soil, *Robert le Diable* (*Robert the Devil*), which was sensationally successful. It was given in America for the first time at the Park Theatre, 1834, in English.

Although *Les Huguenots,* Meyerbeer's most successful opera, bows to *The Prophet* and *The African Maid* in excellence, it has logic, drama and a very interesting emphasis on individual characters. It is in five acts, with book by Scribe and Deschamps. Meyerbeer's intense sense of the dramatic is seen throughout all his operas. For example, one scene of *Les Huguenots,* the "Benediction of the Swords," he enlarged because of its theatricality, and insisted furthermore that Deschamps write a love duet in Act IV. Here is an example of the librettist bowing to the will of the composer.

It was first given at the Grand Opéra, in Paris, in 1836. Its first performance in America was in New Orleans in 1839, and in the original French in New York, at the Park Theatre, in 1845. Its première at the Metropolitan was in the opera house's initial season, 1883–84.

THE HUGUENOTS

The Huguenots centers on St. Bartholomew's Eve in 1572, in France, when a command was given to massacre all Protestants. The story is told with grandeur and picturesqueness in music and scene, and involves a stormy love affair between a Huguenot and a Roman Catholic. Military bands, great halls of the nobles, and rousing, magnificent music made this opera popular. It was given in New York until a few years ago, but seems to have been crowded out by Wagner, Mozart and modern Italian opera. It may have faded from our stage because there are not enough singers trained in the "grand manner" to take the seven important roles. During the era of *Les nuits de sept étoiles*

(Nights of Seven Stars), seven great singers under Maurice Grau's management at the Metropolitan, this was possible. This was a typical cast: Lillian Nordica as Valentine; Sofia Scalchi as Urbain; Nellie Melba as Marguerite de Valois; Jean de Reszke as Raoul; Pol Plançon as Contede St. Bris; Victor Maurel as Conte de Nevers; and Edouard de Reszke as Marcel.

The Luther hymn, *"Ein feste Burg ist unser Gott"* ("A Mighty Fortress Is Our God"), is predominant in the brief overture which opens the act, with its sonorous chorus of banqueters in the palace.

Meyerbeer spent many years in the preparation of his next two and greatest works, *The Prophet* and *The African Maid*. During this period he became Kapellmeister to the King of Prussia in Berlin, and also wrote *Das Feldlager in Schlesien (An Army Camp in Silesia, 1844)*. In this opera Jenny Lind made her debut in Prussia. Here Meyerbeer conducted operas for his overlord, among them Weber's *Euryanthe,* and Wagner's *Rienzi* and *The Flying Dutchman*. When Wagner went to Paris, Meyerbeer was hateful to him, and it cannot be wondered why Wagner called him a "pick-pocket," for in Meyerbeer Wagner found his match in (to put it mildly) strategy!

The Prophet is particularly interesting. It is in five acts, with book by Eugène Scribe and its first performance at the Opéra, Paris, was in 1849. It tells the story of the capture of Münster, in Holland, under John of Leyden, around 1534. It is a tale of another religious struggle, in which, this time, the Protestants do the murderous work. Evidently, Meyerbeer wanted to be impartial. The American première took place in 1850, in New Orleans, and the opera reached the Metropolitan in New York in 1884.

Meyerbeer is notable for his effective climaxes. It is not to be wondered that he held the stage for so many years.

In *Dinorah* or *Le Pardon de Ploermel* (*The Ploermel Pardon* [or *Pilgrimage*]), Meyerbeer wrote a fantastic pastoral opera in three acts with libretto by Jules Barbier and Michel Carré. Ploermel is one of the towns in Brittany where the people make annual religious pilgrimages to receive pardon for their sins. The only thing we hear now from the opera is the sparkling "Shadow Song," for soprano, sung to her own shadow by the half-crazed Dinorah. Thrilling as this song and the overture are, they cannot bring the opera to life.

Dinorah was first performed at the Opéra Comique, Paris, in 1859; arrived in America in New Orleans in 1861; and made its debut in Italian, at the Metropolitan in 1892.

Meyerbeer worked many long difficult years to write what he and everybody else has called his best opera—*L'Africaine*. Unfortunately, he died in the midst of its preparation for production. He had worked so hard in Paris that his health became seriously impaired. With all his faults, he was a meticulous editor and spent his strength before, during, and after work on an opera.

The African Maid, in five acts, with book by Scribe, was first given in Paris, at the Opéra, in 1865. Seven months after its première, an Italian version was presented at the New York Academy of Music. It was given at the Metropolitan in 1888, and Ponselle sang in its revival in 1923.

Meyerbeer thought that the music for this score would give him immortality. It lacks, however, transcendant inspiration, and the scenery is too elaborate. Among the songs heard too seldom are: *"Adieu, mon doux rivage"* ("Farewell, Beloved Shores"). This has a charming accompaniment by flute and oboe. The fourth act is richly furnished with song. In it is one of the most beautiful and ecstatic love songs in the realm of opera.

MEYERBEER, ARBITER

He wrote seventeen operas, but brilliant as he was, he was greater as the manager of the Paris Opéra. Meyerbeer was a diplomat, and he was clever. He directed and conducted opera in Germany and Paris. Accounts of composers of his day show that their struggles to obtain recognition depended on him. As absolute czar of music, he was hated by Hector Berlioz and Richard Wagner, who tried to gain recognition from this musical egoist. In a private letter (1847), Wagner wrote:

I am on a pleasant footing with Meyerbeer, and have every reason to value him as a kind and amiable man. But if I attempt to express all that is repellent in the incoherency and empty striving after outward effect in the operatic music of the day, I arrive at the conception "Meyerbeer."

MEYERBEER'S CONTRIBUTION

To be sure, Meyerbeer inherited his ideas from Spontini and others, but he made historical opera popular although he was not the first to write it. He showed how to work up to an exciting climax in story and music, and knew the limitations and powers of the voice, and how to write for it. He knew the orchestra so well that he could stretch it to express his ideas. He combined flowing Italian melody and French rhythm with expert use of the woodwinds and brasses. These soon came into their own and reached the height of expressiveness in the work of another German—Richard Wagner.

Meyerbeer skillfully satisfied the national tastes of the countries in which he worked. Probably his operas, overpopular in his own day, have lost their position in our theaters because he did not have a deep inner conviction about anything musical. Inner conviction is the saving spiritual chemical that preserves an art work through posterity. Yet with all his shortcomings, he was an important stimulus to music drama in the growth of opera.

SCENE IV

Berlioz—Intimations of the Twentieth Century

HECTOR BERLIOZ was even more fantastic than some of his music! He looked upon himself as the hero of his own life story and suffered with and for himself. He came into the world at Côte-Saint-André, near Grenoble, France, in 1803, during a turbulent era after the French Revolution. He lived until 1869 in his adored Paris, and died a few years after the American Civil War, when France was still a problem to herself on the eve of the Franco-Prussian War.

His father, a doctor, gave Hector his education, and a good one it was, with the exception that the boy missed the experience of being thrown with other boys of his own age. Dr. Berlioz wanted his son to be a surgeon and sent him to Paris for his medical training. Although he adored music, he dutifully went to medical college (1822). Repelled by the filth and the stench of the dissecting room, he ran away from the sights that sickened him, but he remained a medical student for about a year to please his father.

During this period of enforced medical study, Berlioz fanatically engulfed himself in all the music he possibly could hear. François Habeneck was director of the newly built opera house; the famous vocal teacher, García, was training a new group of future opera stars; and French comic opera was putting up a fight against the invading Italians headed by Rossini.

Berlioz was not as much interested in Rossini's rule and the new social class that made him their idol as he was in his own ideal, Gluck, whose works he had discovered in La Côte. He reveled in performances of that master's *Armide, Orfeo, Alceste, Iphigénie en Aulide* and *Iphigénie en Touride,* and operas by Gluckists such as Salieri, Méhul and Spontini. In fact *Iphigénie en Touride* was an overpowering experience to him in which the orchestra was first revealed as a forceful medium of expressing dramatic music. Doubtless these performances led Hector to the decision that medicine was not for him, but that music was!

Finally his father realized that Hector was not meant for a medical career. Yet in his attempt to discipline his son, who had made the unforgivable mistake of wanting to be a professional musician, he often cut off his allowance, and threatened to disinherit him, and made things extremely difficult for the young man who had been accustomed to leading the social life in Paris of a well-connected youth.

From childhood Hector was "music mad." A blank piece of music paper early aroused his imagination to the point of his having exclaimed, "What an orchestral work one could write on that!" In his untutored, romantic fashion, he determined to become a composer. He learned to play on the flute and the guitar—not very substantial background on which to build a musical career. The Berlioz home did not even possess that newfangled instrument, the pianoforte. Yet Father Berlioz had encouraged the making of music in the home, a sort of a chamber-music group that played arrangements of popular music of the day, some of which Hector had made, and he even sent to another town for a music teacher.

Before he became a student at the Conservatoire, Hector discovered that he might go to the library to study his beloved Gluck scores. He came into conflict with the school's director, Cherubini, because he broke rules heedlessly, and helped himself to all the privileges to which he was not entitled, such as entering by doors forbidden to students, and taking scores home to study. He was in constant conflict with "Czar" Cherubini, who once chased the boy around the tables in an effort to get him out of the building, probably after hours. Finally Hector succeeded in being admitted to the Conservatoire as a student, but he found that he was not only inimical to Cherubini, but he could not tolerate the old-fashioned methods of teaching harmony and orchestration. He was already determined to leave the Classic for the Romantic, particularly in instrumental music which he saw as a means of dramatic expression—that is, program music.

The strongest influence in the building of his career was his teacher, Jean-François Lesueur, who found in Berlioz a willing disciple for his own romantic ideals. And regardless of his prejudices, Berlioz had to go through the discipline of the strict classical training in counterpoint and kindred branches at the Conservatory.

One of the first things he composed was a Mass given in 1825 at the Church of St. Roch. Although it was a success and Hector was encouraged, he realized that it needed revising, and he was not disturbed when many, who did not understand his music, ridiculed it. The performance ran him into debt, which made his father, when informed of it, cut off Hector's allowance.

Berlioz now had to make his living. He ushered in theaters, and sang in a chorus, both of which were good experience for him. He became an essayist and a diarist, and broke into print with an article against a well-known critic who dared to criticize Berlioz' idol Gluck. For years he was to support himself as a music critic on the *Journal des Débats* and other papers.

In these early years, Berlioz was already interested in writing opera, and was collaborating with his friend Humbert Ferrand, first in a cantata, *Heroic Scene: The Greek Revolution,* and then in his first work for stage, *Les Francs-Juges,* based on the history of the secret Vehmic Courts of medieval Germany. He also failed in his first trial for the *Prix de Rome.*

In order to win the *Grand Prix de Rome,* awarded by the Conservatory to its gifted composers, Berlioz with persistence re-entered the competition until finally in 1830 he was awarded the much coveted national prize for his cantata, *La Mort de Sardanapole (The Death of Sardanapolus).* It must be admitted that Cherubini tried to prevent his entering each year. By the time he was twenty-five, he had shown that he was someone to consider. He had already written the first version of his *Symphonie fantastique.* So he went to Rome, and although he had yearned to go, soon craved even more to return to his beloved Paris.

He brought back from Italy a sequel to his *Symphonie fantastique,* and by brilliant journalistic work, made himself prominent in musical circles. His symphony *Harold in Italy* (1834) is one of his loveliest compositions. Here can be seen his uncanny skill in orchestration and his superb use of individual instruments to paint an idea. A dissonant reiterated note, in one movement, echoes the remoteness and loneliness of a mountain scene even more poignantly than Wagner's stark, cold and elaborate music that pictures the rocky, arid opening scene in the third act of *Tristan und Isolde.*

At another time, Berlioz, discouraged and disconsolate because of poverty and failures, was saved from suicide by Chopin and Schumann who followed him to the brink of a river.

His was a long and hard struggle for recognition. He tried to storm the walls of Paris, behind which Meyerbeer and Offenbach were entrenched, and which Wagner also was trying to break through. Although known and admired all over Europe, Berlioz was still unable to get a production in his beloved Paris, because he would not write the kind of music popular at that time. He and Wagner were of a different caliber from Meyerbeer. They would not pander to public taste as did Meyerbeer.

"COLOSSAL" EFFECTS

He went on writing his kind of music, and was considered "strange" by the Parisian public. His orchestras were sometimes huge, comprising, as in his Requiem, 190 instruments and 210 voices, with timpani and brass choirs added in the section, *"Tuba Mirum,"* with chorus masters and assistant conductors, one for the woodwinds and one for the percussion, all taking their cues from Hector, the conductor-in-chief. Berlioz boasted that when his Requiem (*La Grande Messe des Morts*) was played in 1837, and 16 kettledrums were used instead of the usual three or four, a man was carried out of the theater in a fit!

BERLIOZ, INNOVATOR

Berlioz, the innovator, hated Wagner because he too was an innovator. Sad to relate, this man who had so hard a time to produce his own works, did all he could to keep Wagner's *Tannhäuser* out of Paris. Somewhat like German composers, Berlioz interested himself in orchestration; yet as a Frenchman, he never slighted or undervalued a text. His gift to opera was the unifying of the different elements or parts in drama with music, the crown and glory of the music of the Romantic Period.

THE IDÉE FIXE

The *Symphonie fantastique* (*Fantastic Symphony*, 1830–31) is somewhat autobiographical, but as such must not be taken too literally. It was written as the result of his thwarted but mad passion for the Irish actress Harriet (Henrietta) Smithson, with whom at the time he had not even spoken. In the music he gave free rein to his bitterness and grief. And handsome music it is! Later (1833) they married and lived miserably ever after!

This symphony is a candid expression, said Berlioz, of "a young musician of unhealthy, sensitive nature endowed with vivid imagination." He used the *idée fixe*—a theme or short tune repeated again and again in the *Symphonie fantastique* to picture various moods and activities. Sometimes his idée fixe is symbolic, sometimes it is descriptive. He used orchestral effects rarely thought possible before him. He pictured horror, the supernatural, love, pathos, terror, pettiness, burlesque, satire, all woven into a fabric of good storytelling in music. That the mind of the Young Artist in the plot is drug-distorted is also well expressed—a new departure and a link between Beethoven's and Wagner's vast "objectivity" or ability to express ideas in music outside of one's own personality—"a revolution in the whole concept of instrumental music," writes John N. Burk, "comparable only to the *Eroica* [Beethoven] itself." He continues: "For it should be borne in mind that symphonic music by the year 1830 had never departed from strictly classical proprieties. The waltz had never risen above the ballroom level. Beethoven had been dead but a few years and the *Pastoral Symphony* and the *Leonore* overtures were still the last word in descriptive music. Even opera with its fondness for eery subjects had produced nothing more graphic than the Wolf's Glen scene from *Der Freischütz* —musical cold shivers that Berlioz had heard at the Opéra and absorbed with every fiber in his being. Wagner was still an unknown student of seventeen with all of his achievement still ahead of him. Liszt was not to invent the 'Symphonic Poem' for nearly twenty years. That composer's cackling Mephistopheles, various phases of the *Dies Irae,* Till on the scaffold—these and a dozen other colorful high spots in music are direct descendants of the *Fantastique*." (Boston Symphony Orchestra Program Notes, 1954, No. 1.)

Berlioz uses each instrument as a separate voice and, more than his predecessors, he reveals the possibilities of the woodwinds. Often he was interested only in effects. But he could turn charming phrases such as in the "Dance of the Sylphs" or the "Will-of-the-Wisps" in *Damnation of Faust* or be very august as in the "Rakocsy March," which he orchestrated for the same work.

Berlioz was fascinated by the *Faust* story of Goethe, on which he based his dramatic cantata, *La Damnation de Faust* (1846). Wagner, Gounod, Liszt and Boito were also drawn to Goethe. Berlioz, with his fermenting passions and romantic flair, said of it, "When I liberate it (*Faust*) I will terrify the musical world." Had he let loose all his powers and his dynamic instrumentation, it might have been like an atomic bomb exploded in a musical atmosphere. It was not, however, so formidable, for the performance of the first eight scenes when given, according to one writer, was one of Berlioz' "most distinguished failures." Nevertheless, today it is highly valued, for in it he proves his ability to charm and satisfy. The composer called it a *legende-dramatique* (a dramatic legend).

La Damnation de Faust, based on Gérard de Nerval's French translation of Goethe's drama, was prepared by Berlioz with the assistance of A. Gaudonnière. It was first given as an *opéra de concert,* or a cantata, at the Opéra Comique, in December, 1846. Leopold Damrosch introduced it to an American audience, in New York, as a cantata in February, 1880. Its first stage version was in Monte Carlo in February, 1893, as adapted by R. Gunsbourg. The Metropolitan presented it as an opera in 1906. It is still played as an opera in Paris. It was not heard in its entirety in concert form until 1934, when Serge Koussevitzky, conductor of the Boston Symphony Orchestra, gave it. Twenty years later, his successor, Charles Munch, gave it as part of a Berlioz cycle at Tanglewood, Lenox, Massachusetts. In 1955, in March, it was presented by the Boston Symphony Orchestra in New York under Mr. Munch.

BERLIOZ' TRIPS ABROAD

Berlioz and Wagner introduced an important new profession in the musical field—that of conducting. Naturally, musicians before them had conducted in concert halls and opera houses, but the task of conducting Wagner's huge scores and Berlioz', especially *Les Troyens* (*The Trojans*) had taken on new proportions. The leader no longer sat at an instrument, a harpsichord, or stood with violin in hand, alternately playing and directing. As early as 1820, Spohr had conducted, standing with back to the audience, with an improvised paper baton in his hand; and François Habeneck (1781–1849), a director of the Paris *Concerts du Conservatoire* (a series of concerts at the Conservatory), had long conducted his men as our leaders of symphony concerts do today.

Berlioz was the first conductor to make extended tours throughout Europe, in many German cities, London, Brussels, Vienna, St. Petersburg, and Italy. He gave concerts including works by Gluck, Mozart, Beethoven and Weber, as well as his own compositions. He was easily the "man of the hour," having success wherever he went. He and Liszt were crusaders for the new music.

LISZT HELPS OPERA TO GROW

Although Franz Liszt was not a writer of opera, he did much to help establish it in Germany. He was engaged by the Grand Duke Charles

Alexander of Weimar, the city of Goethe and Schiller. The Duke wished to re-establish his court as a center of culture, with Liszt as conductor and musical director. Liszt's productions of operas old and new were formidable. He befriended Wagner and Berlioz, giving premières to their operas including Berlioz' *Benvenuto Cellini,* Schubert's, Schumann's, Meyerbeer's, Halévy's operas, and also those of Rossini, Bellini, and Donizetti, Cherubini, Spontini, Cornelius, as well as revivals of Gluck and Mozart, also Weber. Besides all this he directed symphony concerts which may well be regarded as the foundation of our modern orchestral concerts. Liszt belongs with Wagner and Berlioz as having established the calling of the virtuoso-conductor.

BERLIOZ AS MUSICAL MISSIONARY

For twenty-five years Berlioz regarded himself as a missionary-composer chosen to spread the gospel of drama in music. He saw in his mission a modern "revolution" to follow Gluck in "dramatizing the orchestra" and Beethoven in establishing instrumental forms. He regarded the Italian and French opera composers as old-fashioned. He disapproved of the way the composer had had to cater to the whims of the singer—"the singer who changes his part, interrupts with encores, draws attention to himself as more important than his art." Berlioz also stated in one of his books, *À Travers Champs* (*Across the Fields*), to what degree he thought music could be expressive. "It may render joy, sadness, gravity, playfulness; it will show a striking difference between the joy of a pastoral people and that of a warlike nation, between the grief of a queen and a village girl.... But if it wishes to go beyond this immense circle, music will have to have recourse to speech, whether sung, recited, or read. Thus the overture to *Alceste* [Gluck] will foretell scenes of desolation and tenderness but it will never impart either the object of this tenderness or the cause of the desolation."

A better explanation of "program music" would be hard to find. And this was Berlioz' creed. As Barzun states it: "Berlioz' conviction rested on three postulates about the nature of his art: 1. That modern music was a new and independent art. 2. That music possessed intrinsic significance, which he called 'expressiveness.' 3. That music could not be judged by pre-established scholastic rules, but only...through experience by ear..." (*Berlioz and the Romantic Century, Philosophy of a Musical Mission,* Vol. I, pp. 415–31).

OPERAS OF BERLIOZ

Since Berlioz has written symphonic works that are heard, and operas which are not, it is important for the modern opera lover to know the composer's symphonic works in order to realize his value to all music. Today Berlioz is becoming more and more appreciated. The operas, however, demonstrate his powers of innovation, and it may not be long before these, too, appear in our theaters.

He wrote four operas: *Lélio, ou le Retour à la Vie* (*Lélio, or the Return to Life,* 1830); *Benvenuto Cellini* (1838, Paris); *Les Troyens* (*The Trojans,* 1863, Paris); and the comic opera *Beatrice and Benedict* (1862, Baden; 1863, Weimar). Of these we occasionally hear the *Benvenuto Cellini* overture and the tuneful "The Roman Carnival," which is supposed to be played before Act II of the Cellini opera.

He always seemed more interested in the symphonic aspect of opera, which was a German ideal, than in the Italian concept of opera as song.

LÉLIO

Lélio, or the Return to Life, although a stage work, is not an opera. It was a sequel to the *Fantastic Symphony* and Berlioz called it a *melologue.* It was made up of six works dating from 1827 to 1829. In order to connect these various numbers, Berlioz introduces an imaginary musician who recites and acts in view of the audience, before each unrelated section that is performed by hidden soloists, chorus and orchestra.

BENVENUTO CELLINI

The first real opera, therefore, was *Benvenuto Cellini.* The libretto, a story of the rollicking, murderous, charming scamp, the superlative goldsmith and artist of the sixteenth century, was by Léon de Wailly and Jules Barbier. Its sources were picked out by Berlioz from the Cellini *Mémoires* and a short story, "Salvator Rosa," by E. T. A. Hoffmann. In 1834 the libretto was turned down by the management of the Opéra Comique. Berlioz had great trials and tribulations in rehearsing and producing the opera, and, because of annoying delays, its première did not take place at the Grand Opéra until September 12 and 14. Theophile Gautier, writer and critic, predicted that the work would influence the future of music for good or evil, and the name was caricatured as "*Mal*venuto Cellini" (*Ben* meaning good and *Mal,* bad).

Franz Liszt, who remained a devoted friend to Berlioz as he was also to Wagner, had the text translated into German by Riccius and presented it at Weimar in March, 1852. Again with a new translation by Peter Cornelius, himself an opera composer, it was given in Weimar in a revised version in February, 1856. In spite of Berlioz' popularity as a symphony conductor, in London in 1853 it registered a failure. It was believed that its failure was due to a cabal led by Sir Michael Costa, director of Covent Garden, who was interested only in Italian opera. *Benvenuto Cellini* had to be translated into Italian to be performed at Covent Garden!

A revival of *Benvenuto Cellini* took place in Paris in 1915, with Felix Weingartner conducting six performances. And before this, it was played many times in Germany from 1880 to the First World War. In the 1930's it was included in a Glasgow Berlioz cycle and it had a performance on the Paris radio. To our knowledge it has never been staged in America.

LES TROYENS

The Trojans in six acts (1856–59), proved Berlioz to be a descendant of the writers of elaborate, heroic and fantastic operas: Lully, who wrote extravagant ballet opera; Rameau, who followed Lully's formal style; Gluck, who followed the French ideals, and some of his own, with *Orpheus and Eurydice;* Mozart, who enters this list because of the mysticism in *The Magic Flute;* Spontini, who wrote *La Vestale,* an elaborate historic opera; Rossini, whose *William Tell* gives a romantic and exciting story of the Swiss hero, Tell.

The Trojans had a peculiar fate. Those who admire it say it equals Wagner's *Ring,* and that it is the masterpiece of France's "greatest composer." Those who dislike it, think it tiresome and pompous.

The libretto, written by Berlioz, is based on Virgil's *Aeneid.* As it was too long to be performed in one session (six and one-half hours), it was divided into two parts: *La Prise de Troie* (*The Capture of Troy*) and *Les Troyens à Carthage* (*The Trojans at Carthage*). The first part, in three acts, is the story of the warnings of the prophetess Cassandra, and of the wooden horse which tricked the Trojans and made it possible for the Greeks to capture Troy. The second part, in five acts and a prologue, is the story of the love affair of the wandering Aeneas and Dido, Queen of Carthage, and ends with the departure of Aeneas and the suicide of the deserted Dido.

The opera has large choral and ballet scenes; the most beautiful of all may be the Hunt Scene ballet, which has recently been revived as orchestral music and is most effective. The music itself is fascinating. It is frequently heard on the air as recorded by Sir Thomas Beecham.

Berlioz resists the Italian splurge of song and instead is restrained and majestic—to suit his epic story. He, as a true French composer, fits with fidelity the music to the text.

The second part, *Les Troyens à Carthage,* was inadequately staged in Paris (1863); the first part was not performed at the Opéra until 1899. The first performance of the entire work (both parts) took place at Karlsruhe, Germany, in 1890, and a condensed version was given in 1921 at the Paris Opéra. Few other performances have taken place.

The Oxford Opera Club in 1950 gave a telescoped edition (in French) of *Les Troyens.* The critics agreed that the music was superb and that in some parts it reminded the listeners of Mozart and even of Handel. This in spite of Berlioz's dislike of the past (particularly Bach) and his wanting only to be himself. He was himself and so freed music to be itself. In March, 1955, Boris Goldovsky produced it in Boston, cutting the two sections, *La Prise de Troie* and *Les Troyens à Carthage,* enough to fit into one evening's performance.

In *Les Troyens* as in *Benvenuto Cellini,* Berlioz was consciously trying experiments in opera form. He definitely broke away from opera tradition, especially Italian. Barzun writes that he carried forward "the Berlioz principle, . . . of choosing musical situations and linking them by the shortest path of recitative."

L'ENFANCE DU CHRIST

The 1850's were eventful years in Berlioz' career. He had won recognition throughout Europe, and he wrote significant scores. Between composing, filling his post as critic, traveling, conducting and correcting proofs of works that were being published, taking care of a sick wife, and guiding the career of a son, Berlioz was overworked and hard-driven.

Early in the decade he wrote one of his most beautiful scores, *L'Enfance du Christ (The Childhood of Christ).* After hearing it how could anyone question Berlioz' genius! It is not an opera, but it has been mounted with scenery and stage action.

First he wrote *La Fuite en Egypte (The Flight into Egypt).* It was presented late in 1853 in Leipzig and in Paris, and he met with immediate success with the "Shepherd's Chorus." Berlioz played a joke on his critics by misrepresenting it as a work by a Pierre Ducré, an unknown composer of the seventeenth century. It was praised for its simple melody, of which some said "Berlioz never could have written a thing like this." And the wonder grew that he had written it! *The Flight* became the second part of the trilogy *L'Enfance du Christ,* for all of which Berlioz wrote the libretto including "Herod's Dream" and "Arrival at Saïs." This is an example of the way he worked, in combining three apparently unrelated episodes, giving them unity through his treatment of the music. Berlioz himself was surprised at the acclaim it received. Probably audiences had not expected him to exercise such artistic restraint; to show such reverence and depth of feeling for a religious subject, or such a sense of drama in handling an oratorio; perhaps they were surprised at his literary skill and mastery of the art of counterpoint. One of the unexplained things is why it ever dropped out of sight and hearing for so long. It has lately been revived and presented annually by Thomas Scherman and the Little Orchestra Society in New York.

In 1854, Peter Cornelius, who had made the second German translation of *Benvenuto Cellini,* published an article in Berlin about Berlioz where for the first time the slogan of the "Three B's" is introduced. We have always thought of the "Three B's" as Bach, Beethoven and Brahms as Hans von Bülow named them. But Barzun points out that the original "Three B's" as named in the Cornelius article were Bach, Beethoven and Berlioz(!) for whom he sounds "a small fanfare for his favorite modern master, for the proud and daring hero, Hector..."

DOMESTIC PROBLEMS

On March 3, 1854, Harriet Smithson Berlioz died. Barzun quoted a letter from Hector's writings, *Au milieu du Chemin (In the Middle of the Road,* 1853–56) "... we could neither live together nor leave each other and we have endured this torture for ten years past. We each suffered so much at each other's hands." And Berlioz also wrote, of "her great qualities, her cruel demands, her injustice, and then her genius and her woes.... She made me understand Shakespeare and the dramatic art. She suffered penury with me; she never hesitated when we had to risk our savings for a musical undertaking. Yet contrariwise, she always opposed my leaving Paris.... If I had not taken decisive steps I should still be virtually unknown in Europe. And her jealousy, without cause, which ended by altering my whole life..."

Harriet's jealousy later was proved not without cause. A beautiful soprano, Marie Recio, who sang badly and inartistically, attracted his attention and attached herself to him. He allowed her to appear as soloist in his concerts on tour and he asked opportunities for her to be heard in opera. She first sang in his concerts in Belgium in 1842. Although he finally refused to have her sing with him, he never freed himself from her, although she made his life complicated and miserable. Finally in September, 1854, they were married. She died eight years later, and her Spanish mother, who was always devoted to Berlioz, took care of his home and of him during those last years of ill health and subsequent death, March 8, 1869. He outlived by two years his thirty-three-year-old son, Louis, who was in the Navy. Between father and son there was a strong bond of understanding and affection.

BEATRICE AND BENEDICT

Shakespeare had always been a source of inspiration to Berlioz, so when he received a commission to write a comic opera for Baden-Baden, he turned to *Much Ado About Nothing*. Although he based his ideas on French comic opera, he introduced many innovations and worked with much skill and a freshness that was hardly expected in the last opera he was to write.

The Shakespearean comedy was the basis of his own libretto using the two principle characters, Beatrice and Benedict, and inventing another couple, but with names, Hero and Claudio, that appear in the play. Another comic character, a Kapellmeister, Somaronie (which means "Donkey") was Berlioz' own invention.

In the dialogue, Berlioz quoted freely from Shakespeare. Barzun relates that the French critics at Baden-Baden wrote "that Berlioz' sense of humor in dialogue was often crude, not up to the original music, and they quoted as proof passages from the book which turned out to be direct translations from Shakespeare."

SOME CONTRIBUTIONS OF BERLIOZ

In his operas, his dramatic symphonic poems and his unique oratorio *L'Enfance du Christ,* Berlioz stretched the scope of the orchestra and the nice use of individual instruments. In fact, his book on orchestration (re-edited in 1905 by Richard Strauss), is still an authority. He uses instruments as a painter uses the brush and color. Even though he won the reputation, however falsely, of being devoted to noise and din, he had the skill to produce new effects and nuance, as well as noise. (Nuance means differences in shadings of color and sound—dynamics.) He had a way of combining the trombone with the piccolo, for example, and did much to popularize the new instrument built by Adolphe Sax, called the saxophone. Berlioz was the first to put sponges in the bells of brass instruments and bags over the horns, as our jazz players used often to cover them with their hats; and was the first to string up cymbals to strike with sticks rather than against one another. He emphasized the beauties of the viola, especially, as a solo instrument; and made crooks in natural horns to get chromatics (sharps, flats and naturals). He did this for a greater range of color in music. These are but a few of his innovations which helped develop not only the orchestra but the jazz band which did not exist at the time.

He lived to see himself honored and appreciated in Germany, England and elsewhere. He was made an officer of the Paris Conservatory, but never did he achieve a professorship because it remained too conservative.

BERLIOZ VS. ...

Sometimes people compare Berlioz with Wagner because of what they both did with the orchestra. Whether one likes Berlioz, or whether one doesn't, he wrote some poignant love music in *Les Troyens,* and rich chords in *Romeo and Juliet* very like the opening of Wagner's *Tristan und Isolde* before Wagner had written his uncontestedly superior and more beautiful love music.

Romain Rolland in his essay on Berlioz in *Musicians of Today* made a comparison between the two. Wagner, he commented, "is the pinnacle and the close of one evolution of art. Berlioz began a new art; and one finds in it all the daring and gracious ardor of youth. The iron laws which bound the art of Wagner are not to be found in Berlioz' early works, which give one the illusion of perfect freedom."

Robert Schumann extolled Berlioz after he had heard the *Fantastic Symphony*: "Talents of the second order satisfy us when they master the traditional form; we approve of those of the first order when they enlarge it. Genius alone may act in freedom.... We do not know in what respect the earlier form may be considered superior to the later one in variety and unity of treatment, but we wish we possessed the magnificent imagination necessary to the composing of either one." This from Schumann! (Robert Schumann, *On Music and Musicians.* Edited by Conrad Wolfe.)

Schumann found Berlioz' harmony "distinguished by a sturdiness and concision of a kind which we find—though certainly more complexly—in Beethoven.... Yet from time to time one does meet flat and common harmonies, or defective ones—at least such as that the old rules forbid, some of which, however, sound magnificently; unclean or vague ones, or some that sound badly, tormented and distorted.... Berlioz, however, constitutes a special case. Let someone attempt to change or improve any passage,... and see how insipid the improvements will appear!"

Rolland also claimed that Berlioz' music was suited to the spirit of the common people, recently raised to sovereignty, and the young democracy. The French historian Taine's definition of a romantic artist applies to him: "The plebeian of a new race, richly gifted, and filled with aspirations, who, having attained for the first time the world's heights, noisily displays the ferment of his mind and heart."

That Berlioz is a bone of contention between two camps of musical criticism is true. Some think him vulgar and noisy, while others think of him even today as a "coming" composer. But all know that he freed, carved out and expanded the orchestra to do valiant things; that he helped pave a smoother road for Liszt, Wagner, and Strauss—and other innovators—and was himself an innovator along many paths in opera.

THE MEMOIRS

From 1848 to 1865, Berlioz was at work on the autobiographical account of his life, his works and opinions—*Memoirs*—that has been the source book, in spite of its exaggerations, of every biographer and essayist who has written about him. It should be read by everyone interested in Berlioz or any other romantic figure. He said in his unique revelation of himself, "The dominant qualities of my music are passionate expression, internal fire, rhythmic animation and unexpected change." He was right.

Berlioz finished his *Memoirs* with a quotation from Shakespeare which he is said to have quoted when he was dying:

> Life's but a walking shadow, a poor player
> That struts and frets his hour upon the stage
> And then is heard no more; it is a tale
> Told by an idiot, full of sound and fury
> Signifying nothing.

SCENE V

From Offenbach ("Orpheus of Paris") to Bizet, Gounod, and Thomas

AMONG "mass" producers, Jacques Offenbach (1819–80) heads the list. A few of his ninety operas, given today, are enjoyed even more than when they were originally produced, in the days of the promenaders and languishers on the boulevards of Paris, in the reign of Napoleon II. Offenbach, whose operas were popular when neither Wagner nor Berlioz could get hearings in Paris, was a German Jew from Cologne, more Parisian than the Parisians and quite a fop! His clothes were more coloratura than the songs of Italian opera. Many a tale is told of his multi-colored costumes and gaudy umbrellas. Nevertheless, he wrote opéra comique and operettas of the most engaging, graceful and swift-gliding variety, becoming dignity with amusing libretti.

Offenbach left patterns for many a writer of opéra comique and light opera in all corners of the world. He combined a unique gift of melody with an inexhaustible glinting wit and humor. He was able to bring from the past the gaiety of French opéra bouffe, the vitality of the Italian opera buffa, and apply to it his own special brand of wit which made it delightful and not boisterous, with an appeal to the mature, as well as to the inexperienced, listener.

The most familiar among Offenbach's light operas now are: *Orphée aux Enfers* (*Orpheus in Hades*) with its alluring and vivid overture; *La Belle Hélène; La Vie Parisienne* (*Parisian Life*); and *The Grand Duchess of Gerolstein.*

The most popular of all his operas, however, though more in the grand than in the comic vein, is *Les Contes d'Hoffmann* (*The Tales of Hoffmann,* 1881), produced after Offenbach's death, and classified as opéra comique because of its speaking parts.

It was given almost every year at the Metropolitan Opera House after its first appearance there in 1907. It is made up of fantastic and romantic episodes, rather than a continuous story, with a prologue, three acts and an epilogue. The book is by Jules Barbier and Michel Carré (librettists of Gounod's *Faust* and *Romeo and Juliet*), based on the popular *Tales* by E. T. A. Hoffmann. In the first act, Olympia's "Doll Song" is one of the bits of caviar. It requires a soprano of athletic agility. In this opera there is found the Poet, the Necromancer, the love motif, the weird music that accompanies Dr. Mirakel (play on the word *miracle*), an evil genius, and many more fantastic elements. In spite of all this colorful fantasy, the public seems to like best the famous boat song, barcarole—*"Belle Nuit"* ("Night of Love"), which is sung to the swaying of the boat on a canal in Venice.

FÉLICIEN DAVID—INNOVATOR

Félicien David (1810–76), admirer of Berlioz, wrote the symphonic poem *The Desert* and the operas, *Pearl of Brazil* and *Lalla Rookh*, which were given at the Opéra Comique. With these he introduced to Western music a new feeling in opera—the exotic-alien features, often strange and highly flavored in melody, rhythm, customs, costumes, and scenery. Many profited by the color and warmth created by the unusual or exotic. It was from David that Bizet learned to use colorful or un-French rhythms in his *Carmen*; as did Délibes in *Lakmé*.

Now we come to the Latin ladies and gentlemen—superbly presented, clad in the garment of the accomplished singer with the glamour of grand opera and the fascination of sensational biography.

A FATALLY GAY SEÑORITA

One of the most notorious women in opera is Carmen, the cigarette girl. She fooled the men who loved her and fought and tricked all who got in her way. Finally, after four glittering, electrifying acts, this Spanish Carmen goes to her death, stabbed by her discarded lover, Don José.

The creator of this hotheaded, unscrupulous beauty was the novelist Prosper Mérimée. Georges Bizet (1835–75) was the the only man to whom Carmen was faithful, for she made him everlastingly famous as a composer of opera.

Carmen, an opéra comique in four acts with a tragic ending, had its première at the Opéra Comique in Paris in 1875. It seemed on the first night the opera was given that Carmen, true to her character, was to be untrue even to her composer, for she was poorly received, and Bizet was heartbroken! After forty-seven performances in 1875, and three in 1876, the opera was withdrawn and not given again until 1883. It became a universal favorite and is still the most popular of all operas, including Gounod's *Faust*.

Carmen paid her first visit to the United States at the Academy of Music in 1878. Since then, opera singers have made their fame in the role, particularly Emma Calvé (whose name is almost synonymous with the Vixen) who sang the role fifteen times in one season at the Metropolitan.

Many consider *Carmen* the perfect opera because of its supermelodious score, its thrilling and exotic story, fascinating and varied scenes, swift action, and its superior libretto by Henri Meilhac and Ludovic Halévy.

SONGS THAT HAUNT

The story of *Carmen* is placed in Spain and fascinating Spanish rhythms are used in such songs as "The Habañera" (an alluring kind of dance originating in Havana, Cuba). Carmen sings *"L'amour est un oiseau rebelle"* ("Love Is a Rebellious Bird") to fascinate Don José, Lieutenant of the Guards; and again, in a Spanish rhythmic song, a *seguidilla—"Sur les ramparts de Seville"* ("Near the Walls of Seville")— she beguiles him once more.

Every note of this score is melodious, clear, simple, direct, and masterfully orchestrated, whether delicately or heavily scored. The "Toreador Song" for popularity is not excelled. It was not, however, included in *Carmen* at first. Bizet was asked to change the original march for a less pompous one. He did so. At first, the baritone Giuseppe Del Puente wouldn't sing it. He exclaimed, "Why, it's for a chorus man!" and Bizet himself said to the conductor, M. Lamoureux, "Ah, they wish something cheap, well—here it is." The moral of this is—who knows what is good in music!

"The Smugglers' March" is another bit of brilliant orchestration suggesting furtiveness and villainies. The whole libretto is full of glittering loveliness with its singable songs and marches, its enchanting ballet in the French style, from Bizet's own *L'Arlésienne* Suite.

The critics at first didn't like *Carmen*. They called it Wagnerian. That was the easy adverse criticism showered on music in Bizet's day. Bizet did use bits of melodies (such as the so-called "Fate" theme) over again, and rhythms, and rich orchestrations, but not in the least like Wagner. Besides, *Carmen* had all the things the French liked, and

Wagner despised, such as arias, choruses, recitative, spoken words, repeated verses, and ballet.

REALISM AND MELODY

Bizet, however, in Carmen wrote a realistic, tragic opéra comique, vital, captivating, with not one note wasted. It was so exactly to the point of the story and so realistic that people were scandalized. But the "most unkindest cut of all" to Bizet must have been the criticism that his opera was untuneful!

CARMEN JONES—1948

So many operas and compositions have been tagged as untuneful in one era, only to have this criticism completely reversed in another. Indeed, so tuneful is *Carmen* that *Carmen Jones,* a popular Negro operetta, was written around Bizet's music.

During the season of 1949–50, *Les Ballets de Paris* created a new sensation with the many-faceted *Carmen,* in a choreographic version this time, by Roland Petit. So when you hear new music today called "untuneful," remember *Carmen, Lohengrin,* some Schubert songs and many other beautiful compositions. Time makes the seemingly untuneful, tuneful.

Bizet's skill in orchestration and in the use of the exotic is most evident. Flutes in combination with other instruments are like a Bizet autograph, as heard in the lovely *L'Arlésienne* Suite (*The Woman of Arles*), written as incidental music to Alphonse Daudet's play, and in the operas: *Les pêcheurs de perles* (*The Pearl Fishers*) and *La jolie fille de Perth* (The Fair Maid of Perth).

Bizet's health had never been good. He died at the age of forty, at Bougival, near Paris, on the day that *Carmen* was making its twenty-third appearance.

THE SOPRANO'S PET

Pity the calisthenic soprano (the coloratura who dotes on gymnastic trills and runs), for not too much honor among "highbrows" had been paid to the athletic powers of singers' throats since Wagner burst upon the nineteenth century. But a boon to coloratura singers did appear in the popular *Lakmé* (1836–1891) by the composer Léo Delibes (1836–91). The soprano part is very difficult because the singer must sing extremely high tones with (vocal) leaps, hops and skips. The "Bell Song" is particularly tricky and is desired by all coloratura sopranos, for if ever a soprano with skill can "ring the bell" it is with this song! The ballets in this opera are garish, entertaining, rhythmic, and in approved French style of its day.

Lakmé, which is in three acts, with book by Edmond Goudinet and Philippe Gille, was first produced in Paris at the Opéra Comique in 1883, reaching America in an English version at the Academy of Music in New York in 1886. Its première at the Metropolitan in Italian took place in 1890. Today when sung at all it is in French. It has had a few revivals in late years for Lily Pons.

Delibes also wrote several other operas, among which is the tuneful *Les Filles de Cadiz (The Daughters of Cadiz).* He was always light, charming, ever elegant and never profound—a nice pattern-setter for others.

True to the French love of ballet and elegance, Delibes showed his melodic gift in the engaging ballets of *La Source, Coppélia,* and *Sylvia.* The "Pizzicato" from the latter, arranged for the piano, is often heard. Besides these, he wrote twenty comic operas and other more serious works.

CHARLES GOUNOD

A most unfortunate maiden by the name of Marguérite interested Charles Gounod (1818–93). He broke all records for popularity in French opera with *Faust,* in which she plays a star part.

Of Gounod's eleven operas, only three live in public favor. *Faust* had two thousand performances in seventy-five years. A feat, when you think that opera composers ever since his day have to be satisfied with one or two performances a year. Furthermore, some fifty countries have given it, and it is sung in about thirty languages.

Why is it that *Faust* is so popular? First of all, it has constantly melodious music. Secondly, it has a spectacular as well as a touching story. The excellent libretto, by Jules Barbier and Michel Carré, was suggested by the Gretchen story in Goethe's *Faust.* Thirdly, the opera abounds in vivid and "acting" scenery. Gounod is a master in joining harmony and feeling with music and scene. Every song says something to carry the story onward and depict feelings. Fourthly, the many singable songs are well divided among the characters.

Another and fifth reason for the popularity of *Faust* is its ballets, waltzes, its rousing "Soldiers' Chorus" loved by the French and that last chorus, *"Anges purs! Anges radieux!"* ("Angels Pure, Angels

Radiant") when Marguérite, forgiven, is taken up into Heaven. Above all, there isn't a dull moment even in its conventional arias.

One scene, "Walpurgis Night," was omitted in 1917 by the Metropolitan Opera Company. It was put back in 1950. The music is somewhat commonplace. It was written ten years after the opera was given its first production in 1859 at the Théâtre Lyrique, Paris.

In this opera Gounod tells the tragic story of Marguérite, who has a passionate love affair, suffers for it and is forgiven. It is lavish in alluring songs of love and scorn, such as the popular "Jewel Song," "The King of Thule," and Méphistophélès' "Serenade" to Marguérite. This parodies a lover's song and enjoins a maid not to believe her lover until he puts the ring on her finger. Near the end of the verses, Méphistophélès laughs long and derisively. His other famous song is "The Golden Calf," in which he scornfully proclaims that gold alone is the object of men's worship.

Faust was first given as an opéra comique with some spoken words in spite of its heavy and tragic story. Later, however, to make it into grand opera, recitative was substituted for spoken words. If the leopard cannot change its spots, opera can change its category. Like a Shakespeare play, this opera has shifted its scenes and its ballets; dropped one or two of each and still remains an acting, vivid, living drama.

It is believed that the American première was in Philadelphia in 1863, but it is certain that it was selected to open the Metropolitan Opera House in October, 1883. Since then it has often been the "opener."

Roméo et Juliette is another lyric opera, in five acts, by Gounod. The librettists of *Faust,* Barbier and Carré, based it on Shakespeare's play. In contrast to the popular *Faust,* it is rarely heard in America, except for the perilously difficult and fascinating "Waltz Song" for coloratura soprano.

Gounod's *Mireille (Mirella)* is lovely and is occasionally produced. This opera, in five acts, with book by Michel Carré, was first given at the Théâtre Lyrique, Paris, (1864). In 1880, the Emma Abbott Opera Company produced the opera in English, in Chicago, under the title of *Lovers' Pilgrimage.* The Metropolitan gave the opera in French in 1919.

Gounod also composed the operas *Sappho* and *The Queen of Sheba,* and other works for the theater.

GOUNOD KEPT OPERA FRENCH

During the ten years before the Franco-Prussian War (1860–70), Gounod kept French opera French, and away from too much Italian and German influence. He gave a new inspiration to purely French music. *Faust* falls between the lighter opéra comique and the pompous Meyerbeer operas, with which the French were rapidly becoming sated. Although French, he employed the Italian aria form with skill and had a superlatively well developed sense of melody. He used all his gifts with refined taste.

GOUNOD THE RELIGIOUS

At first Gounod had intended to study for the priesthood, but finally realized that his vocation was music. After he had finished writing his operas, however, he gave himself to writing church music and noble oratorios. In his study was a pipe organ and the daylight entered through stained glass windows.

Gounod as a boy of five won a Fine Arts Medal for engraving. He was an excellent organist and was called "Abbé." One of the most popular things he wrote was his *"Ave Maria,"* a melody he set to Johann Sebastian Bach's First Prelude from *The Well-Tempered Clavichord.* Here two religious men commune across the centuries in a hymn that will endure. "Back to Gounod" was the slogan of many who wished to preserve a characteristically French melodic line.

MIGNON OR THE LOST AND FOUND

Another of the famous young women of lyric opera is Mignon. Her fate was much happier than Marguerite's. Both were creations of Goethe. This work, in three acts, was composed by Ambroise Thomas (pronounced Toe-mah') (1811–96), with book by Gounod's librettists, Michel Carré and Jules Barbier. It was first given in Paris at the Opéra Comique in 1866.

It's the romantic history of a young girl, Mignon, who is captured by gypsies and is finally restored to her father. This happens after much excitement and even a conflagration on the stage; all softened by delightful dancing and singing. It is the old substitute for the detective story of today, in which the "long lost" and forlorn child becomes the noble heiress. This form might also be considered in the light of a late "rescue" opera.

THE MUSIC IS MUSICAL

The music is so beguiling and its simple plot such excellent diet for the tired listener that it haunts him. It is gentle, insinuating, well arranged, with a skillful use of the orchestra. It is beautifully costumed and the scenery and songs are fascinating. The bill-of-fare overture carries some of the opera's loveliest tunes.

Coloratura sopranos adore the song, "I am Fair Titania," while the double chorus at the same time follows its own rhythms in a dance as a polonaise (a stately dance coming originally from Poland). This again satisfies the French love of the ballet. Some of the best-known songs are: "Knowest Thou The Land Where The Orange Blooms," (". . . Lemon Blooms" in Goethe's *Wilhelm Meister* and *"Connais-tu le pays . . ."* in the original French) and the gavotte sung by the tenor, *"Me voici dans son boudoir"* ("Here I Am in Her Boudoir").

America first saw and heard *Mignon* in Italian, at the New York Academy of Music, in 1871. Its première at the Metropolitan Opera House took place in 1883.

Thomas also wrote *Hamlet,* an opera based on Shakespeare's play. The story, however, is reduced to absurdity in the opera. The only thing heard from it now is "The Drinking Song," beloved by baritones. The music is simple, well arranged, tuneful, charming and well orchestrated.

SCENE VI

The Germans "On Stage"— Weber and Others

THE literature and the music of Germany in the Romantic Period were closely related. Both mirrored the intensely national as well as the personal. The romantic writers expressed nature as it reflected their own feelings, unlike the matter-of-fact Greeks, who were interested in nature and not in themselves. Any romantic is more interested in himself and his feelings (subjective) than in any other subject (objective).

Among the literary men having great influence on the Romantic movement was Friedrich von Schlegel (1772-1829), who with his sentimental novel, *Lucinde,* tried to express the most intimate personal emotions in words. (His brother, August Wilhelm, made a translation of Shakespeare's works so amazing that some think it is better than the original!) Ludwig Tieck (1773-1853) also took part in the early Romantic march.

Then there was the very popular Ernst Theodor Amadeus (or E. T. A.) Hoffmann (1776-1822), whose tales of madness, horror and the supernatural added the last ingredient to the Romantic brew. Three of his weird stories were used by Jacques Offenbach in his *Tales of Hoffmann.*

Johann Gottfried Herder (1744-1803), a philosopher, poet, and critic, was part of the pre-Romantic "storm and stress period" (*Sturm und Drang,* 1765-90), which was named after a drama by F. M. von Klinger written in 1776, the year our Declaration of Independence was signed. The period was ushered in by Rousseau and other "rebels."

It was the Swooning Age, when ladies swooned and boasted of their delicate health. The English couldn't "take" this German Romantic movement, and, says Sir William Hadow (1859-1937): "We did not want Schumann in England. The more serious of our musicians swore by the 'classics' and felt that the utmost limits of audacity had been reached by Spohr and Mendelssohn. . . . To most of us its [the German Romantic school's] language was a sealed book, its methods alien, its works incomprehensible. . . . There was no need for us to trouble our heads with a new composer, who wasted his time on 'poetic meanings' and 'inward voices' and other things which we could not understand." This certainly gives an idea of the contrast between the feeling in the German period of Romantic music and that of the English, and may account for the lack of great operas in England.

ROMANTIC OPERA

Romantic opera had its beginnings in Beethoven. Its pillars were in the operas of Weber who opened the broad highway of romanticism that led to Wagner. Wagner was the culmination of the use of elaborate German (Teutonic) folklore, German love ideals and mysticism, in operas which bound together all of the arts. Richard Strauss, who died in 1954, may be considered the last of the romantic opera composers of Germany.

CARL MARIA VON WEBER—FAIRY-TALE MAN—ROMANTICIST

All we hear of Weber's eight operas are the overtures to three: *Der Freischütz, Euryanthe* and *Oberon*. Yet this man established German Romantic opera and laid foundations for Wagner and Debussy. Mozart had started German opera with his supernal *Magic Flute*, and Weber with *Der Freischütz*—romantic, with Teutonic folklore mystically mixed with peasant life. "Gluck, Mozart and Scarlatti tried to free opera, but Weber was fortunate to live in an era of better instruments and more personal freedom." (*Music Through the Ages*, by Bauer and Peyser.)

Carl Maria von Weber (1786–1826), although he showed musical talent, was not an infant prodigy. One day a teacher, who was trying to make a musician of him in a hurry, became so exasperated that he struck the little boy with a fiddle stick, saying, "Whatever else they will make of you, Carl, it will not be a musician!" Yet he excelled in instrumental compositions, for example, "The Invitation to the Dance"; and became a brilliant pianist and a splendid conductor. So you never can tell!

It must have been hard for talented children to be born shortly after Mozart, for every parent yearned to have another Mozart in the family. It must have been particularly hard for Carl, for Constanze Weber, the wife of Mozart, was father Weber's cousin. It can easily be imagined how Mozart was held up as an example to this small boy!

Carl was born in Eutin (pronounced Oy-teen) near Lübeck, on December 18, 1786, and he lived during the excitement and terror of the Napoleonic Wars in Europe, and the glamorous upstart's downfall. Carl, born with hip disease, was always lame and delicate.

Yet he had an exciting childhood, for with his theatrical parents he roamed the country acting, singing and playing in castles and dilapidated small theaters, or in any place in which they could make a little money. Indeed, they lived like gypsies. Yet, the experience of performing and seeing plays and watching his father and mother act, sing and compose, was a rich one for the child. Furthermore, spending his time so much in public he learned how to meet people. He developed into one of the most charming personalities in Europe. In this case, being born of poor and working parents was an asset.

A story is told of Weber's charm. Someone told him that a man was standing outside in a thunderstorm waiting to catch a glimpse of him. In his ingratiating way he went to the door. "I've just learned," said he, "that you like my music and want to see me. I won't allow those people who like me to get soaked while waiting to see me, but as for my enemies, they'll take care themselves that it doesn't happen." The man was very shy, could hardly speak, but Weber, learning that it had taken him two days to come, invited him to dinner. And among the things he said to him was: ". . . I never forget that all my talents are from On High."

Michael, brother of Josef Haydn, was Carl's first teacher, who was delighted with the boy's exceptional ability at the piano. While in Vienna, Carl had another teacher, Abbé Vogler, who taught him German stories and legends which he used well later. At fourteen, Carl wrote his first opera, a Singspiel, and when fifteen he wrote a more developed Singspiel, a comic opera, *Peter Schmoll and His Neighbors*. By eighteen, Weber was so skilled that he conducted the Breslau Orchestra and had made himself most popular with the Germans by composing patriotic songs. At twenty-one he became the secretary to the Duke of Würtemburg, and under his patronage fell into bad company and drifted into financial scrapes. But he still had time to read and compose.

Before long, in trying to pull his father out of a financial difficulty, he got himself into such a scrape that he was banished by the King.

Later, happily, he was cleared of all blame, settled down in Frankfurt and wrote the opera *Silvanus* (1810).

From now on, he traveled and became the director of the theater in Prague, where he gained popularity and charmed the populace with his national songs. In order to get singers for his concerts, he left Prague for a visit to Vienna, where he met his future wife, Caroline Brandt. It wasn't long after this that the King of Saxony asked him to reorganize the opera in Dresden.

DER FREISCHÜTZ

Little did people know that he was about to stun the musical world! For in spite of jealousies and misery, he composed *Der Freischütz* (1820) in three acts. In English, it might be called *The Man with the Magic Bullets* or *The Free Shooter*. The libretto was by Johann Friedrich Kind. The first performance was at the Schauspielhaus in Berlin in 1821. The first London performance was in 1824 at the English Opera House and was called *The Seventh Bullet*. It was played in English in New York in 1825, a year after its American première in Philadelphia.

It was given in French in 1827 and in the original German at Palmo's Opera House in 1842 or '45. In 1850 it was given in Italian.

When it was produced in England, recitative was used for the spoken word. With *Der Freischütz*, von Weber was more popular than Rossini, Spontini and other top-notch Italians. In Berlin alone, five hundred performances of *Der Freischütz* took place before 1884!

A NEW PATH IN THE GROWTH OF OPERA

With this opera he dared to change operatic fashion. For the first time a serious opera in German combined the simple life of peasants with magic and folklore. Every element of German folk style was present, but, above all, emphasis was on the orchestral rather than on the vocal side of opera. After *The Magic Flute*, with which Mozart rose to unparalleled heights, Weber was the precursor of German romantic opera with *Der Freischütz*. Thus he cleared the way for other men to leave the Classical road and strike out in nature-interpretation, fantasy, folklore, realism, heart quality, imagination and color instead of Italian display and vocal gymnastics. Germany is now permanently established in the growth of opera.

In Weber's diary, after conducting a performance in Vienna, March 7, 1822, he says: "Conducted *Der Freischütz*. Greater enthusiasm there cannot be, and I tremble to think of the future, for it is scarcely possible to rise higher than this. To God alone the praise!" (Grove's *Dictionary of Music and Musicians*.)

The story of *Der Freischütz* is about a young ranger one of whose seven bullets is cursed. He lives in a Bohemian village in the seventeenth century. This opera was loved for its village atmosphere and is essentially German.

Der Freischütz is full of weird and beautiful music. The overture is one of the loveliest ever written and is the bill-of-fare kind. It hangs together and demonstrates Weber's gift for writing particularly well for woodwinds.

Der Freischütz is a landmark in the long path of opera, because:

1. Weber threw away Italian musical tricks.
2. He used the German language.
3. He used folklore.
4. He combined folklore with the simple, natural life of the peasants.
5. He used sympathy and heart quality with imagination, color and excitement.
6. He widened the path of opera and paved the way for the romantic opera writers and musical poets.
7. He achieved greater orchestral and vocal teamwork than his predecessors.

Even though Weber threw away Italian musical tricks, he learned the taste of the Viennese in opera from Rossini while he was in Vienna.

FRENCH ROMANCE MAKES GERMAN OPERA

In *Euryanthe* (1823) Weber tried to raise or lower, as you will, Romantic opera to the glamour of the old court operas. He used no spoken words, as he had in the original version of *Der Freischütz*. The story is a mixture of a *Lohengrin* and a Shakespearean *Cymbeline,* and is from a thirteenth-century romantic French tale of the history of Gérard de Névers and the beautiful and virtuous Euryanthe.

The libretto by Helmind von Chézy is one of the most confused tales ever told in music—a truly poor libretto. Yet the music is superb, the orchestration exhilarating and more delightful than any of the singing. The overture is strongly reminiscent of Beethoven. There is a scene of jealousy which reminds one of (and is doubtless a direct ancestor of) the jealous furies of Ortrud in *Lohengrin*.

Euryanthe had its debut at the Kärnthnerthor Theater (Vienna) in 1823. Some say that the first performance in America was given at Wallach's Theatre in New York in 1863; but at the Metropolitan it was performed in 1887, with Lilli Lehmann (soprano) singing the stellar role.

With Weber times had changed, for the singers were no longer the commanders of opera that they had been. When he might have given great moments to the singers, he gave them to the orchestra. Weber had a strong sense of writing for the theater. Although his genius was for the momentary climax and applause spots, yet the music and story do better teamwork than they had done up to his time except for Mozart. *Euryanthe,* although not a success at first, with *Der Freischütz,* which was a success, gave Wagner and Debussy inspiration to go on with the kind of orchestral and vocal coordination that Weber so gloriously began.

OBERON, HIS SWAN SONG

An opera, ordered by Charles Kemble, manager of Covent Garden Opera in London, turned out to be *Oberon* or *The Elf King's Oath.* It was given first in England at Covent Garden in 1826 and had thirty-one performances the first season. It is much like a Singspiel, with strings of beautiful musical pieces connected by spoken words. The libretto in three acts is by James Robinson Planché from an old French romance, *Huon de Bordeaux,* as adapted by the German poet Wieland and translated into English by Sotheby. Later, Weber's adored Hector Berlioz put it into French. So we see the phenomenon of the man using French romance and yet establishing German Romantic opera. Nothing is impossible to genius! Besides, Weber liked the libretto, but made many changes. He wrote in his diary concerning his criticism of it: "The cut of an English opera is certainly very different from a German one; the English is more a drama with songs." (Louise Middleton in Grove's *Dictionary of Music and Musicians.*) To be sure, his librettist, Planché, who cared more for scenery than for music, might have wrecked the opera had it not been that *Oberon* carries the most beautiful music that Weber ever wrote. Here again the overture contains some of the loveliest samples of its opera. One is carried into fairyland with its instrumental felicities.

Oberon was first heard in New York City at the Park Theatre in 1828. In 1918, it was sung at the Metropolitan. Gustav Mahler made a German edition, and Artur Bodansky arranged the recitatives.

In London Weber worked so hard on the production of *Oberon* that he became very ill. The excitement and the celebration were too much for him, suffering as he was from tuberculosis. On the evening of June 4, 1826, some of his anxious friends went to see him. "Good night, friends," said Weber, "please leave me and let me sleep." The next day he sank into his last sleep. He was buried in England. His remains were taken back to Dresden, Germany, in 1844, when Richard Wagner, who learned so much from Weber that he was called his musical son, spoke at the services.

OVERTURE BECOMES A BILL-OF-FARE

Weber gave opera a big and healthy dose of new life. His instruments and songs express his imaginative plot. He used woodwinds to describe and express feelings with rare skill and beauty. Like Gluck, he tried to treat opera as a bundle of arts, each part having its importance. He advanced the overture by using whole tunes from its opera. Why do you suppose his operas are not given? Probably because most of them are too costly to produce and are too well strewn with spoken words for audiences today. Our audiences seem to say, "When we pay for opera, we don't want words without music, we want grand opera." This is foolish, but so it is.

Weber left a large collection of brilliant piano works, lieder, cantatas, masses and other compositions. Outside of his operas, his *Mass in E Flat* and his "Invitation to the Dance," as well as his "Perpetual Motion," are his best-known works. Had he been less theatrical, his piano works might be more popular today. Yet we should be glad that he had the theatrical in his make-up or he never could have written such picturesque, exciting and fanciful operas.

LUDWIG SPOHR

Few of the followers of Weber were fortunate enough to have their operas live after them. Ludwig Spohr (1784–1859), a violinist and composer, was a man whose mind was not easily led off by whims of the times or of other people. He was a friend of Weber and Rossini and wrote excellent operas, even though he did not accept Weber or Beethoven completely, but he was a great lover of Wagner. His best opera is *Jessonda* (1823). Earlier he wrote an opera called *Faust* (1816).

He contributed to the growth of opera because he was freer in his harmonies than other men had been. In *The Crusaders* (1845), somewhat in the Wagnerian manner, he tried to write a national Romantic opera.

HEINRICH MARSCHNER

Heinrich Marschner (1795–1861) wrote fifteen operas, most of which are in dramatic vein. Among those that have held the German stage is *Hans Heiling* (1833), regarded as an important example of pre-Wagner romanticism.

G. A. LORTZING

With all the drama, nationalism and folklore, the Germans still were writing in the lighter vein. At this time, Gustav Albert Lortzing (1801–51) wrote *Czar und Zimmermann (Czar and Carpenter,* 1837) and *Hans Sachs* (1840), a forerunner of *Die Meistersinger.* These and others show his descent from the beloved German Singspiel. *Czar und Zimmermann* came to the Broadway Theatre in New York, in German, in 1857 and 1882, and to the Metropolitan in 1909.

LILT AND CHARM

Friedrich Freiherr von Flotow (1812–83) was the author of *Alessandro Stradella* (1844, Hamburg) and *Martha.* He fits in beautifully with the opéra-comique feeling of Germany.

Stradella is about the composer Alessandro Stradella, a romantic personality in Naples, who was born around 1642 and was murdered in Genoa in 1682. *Martha* or *The Fair at Richmond* is light and charming and never tiresome.

In five acts, with book by W. Friedrich, it was first performed at the Kärnthnerthor Theater, Vienna, 1847. It was introduced to America, in English, at Niblo's Garden, New York, 1852. A most remarkable vocal quartet sang in *Martha*—Marcella Sembrich for Lady Harriet, Edyth Walker for Nancy, Enrico Caruso for Lionel, Pol Plançon for Plunkett—in the Metropolitan revival of March 9, 1906.

Other descendants of the German Singspiel were Konradin Kreutzer (1780–1849); Carl Otto Nicolai (1810–49) whose opera "The Merry Wives of Windsor" has left us with the delightful and amusing overture and was revived in 1955 most successfully by the New York City Opera Company at City Center; Peter Cornelius (1824–74), friend and admirer of Wagner, who wrote the comic operas *Der Cid* and *Der Barbier von Bagdad (The Barber of Bagdad),* for the presenting of which kindly Franz Liszt lost his hold on Weimer; and Karl Millöcker (1842–99), whose best-known opera is *Der Bettelstudent* (*The Beggar Student*), and a most delightful opera it is.

ROMANTIC POET-COMPOSERS

Robert Schumann (1810–56) and Franz Schubert (1797–1828) wrote operas but did not have success with them, even though they wrote romantic and dramatic art songs. Therefore, while these romanticists have not influenced the development of opera, their effect on song will endure forever.

SCENE VII

Verismo for a Change—
Mascagni, Puccini, and Others

LYRIC FIREBRANDS

WHEN Verdi was writing his operas in Italy, Germany was having difficulty in accepting Richard Wagner with his new theories and the French were producing the romantic and lyric operas spoken of in Scene I. The Italians grew a bit tired of the "naughty" *Thaïs, Manon, Carmen,* and others, so they began to write operas full of fierce excitement, stabbings and intrigue. *Verismo,* a stylish word for "gangster-like," means stark "realism." The men who wrote verismo stretched the bounds of opera and carried shock and excitement far beyond rescue opera or the opera of erring damsels.

MUSIC AND VIOLENCE

One of the first of the verismo operas was *La Gioconda (The Joyous One)* in four acts, by Amilcare Ponchielli (1834–86), which softened the blow of its tragedy by its "Dance of the Hours," probably the most popular ballet music in opera. *La Gioconda* was first given at La Scala, Milan, 1876. Three of the best known songs are: *"Voce di donna"* ("Voice of Woman or of Angel"), an ecstatic love song, *"Cielo! e Mar!"* ("Oh, Sky and Sea"), and Gioconda's aria, one of the most famous in opera, a terrific and dramatic outburst, *"Suicidio! . . . in questi fieri momenti tu sol mi resti"* ("Aye, Suicide, the Sole Resource Now Left to Me!").

In this opera, Ponchielli departs in many ways from conventional Italian methods and often shows Wagner's influence. All this in spite of his employment of the usual ballets, duets, trios, etc.

La Gioconda is set in Venice, at the time of the Inquisition, and the book was taken from Victor Hugo's historical drama *Angelo, the*

Tyrant of Padua by Tobia Gorrio, (anagram on the name of Arrigo Boito) arch-librettist and composer of *Mefistofele*.

Ponchielli influenced the linking of violence with music. *La Gioconda* was first heard in America in 1883, and has been given over and over to the delight of the audiences past and present.

MASCAGNI

An opera, following the shock impulse and of the gangster type, by Pietro Mascagni (1863-1945), is *Cavalleria rusticana* (*Rustic Chivalry*), one of the best examples of verismo or Italian realistic opera. In this it means Blood! It is the story about a faithless lover who abandons his betrothed, and hate and murder are wrapped up in the most beautiful and hum-able melodies!

The intermezzo, between its two scenes; its beautiful *brindisi* (drinking song), "Hail! The Ruby Wine Now Flowing"; and its *"Voi lo sapete"* ("You Know It, Mother") are unforgettably lovely. And the prelude uses the fascinating lure of the song that is sung by the "wicked gal," Lola.

Mascagni's *Iris, L'Amico Fritz, Lodoletta* (*The Little Lark*) and *Isabeau* never approached in popularity *Cavalleria rusticana*. Mascagni died in most distressing circumstances in Rome.

Cavalleria rusticana was first performed at the Costanzi Theatre in Rome (1890), with the book by G. Targioni-Tozzetti and G. Menasci, based on a story by Giovanni Verga. The opera was, according to Pitts Sanborn, a part of "a mad scramble to see who should introduce the lyric firebrand to the United States." It was first given in America at the Grand Opera House, Philadelphia, 1891, and at the Metropolitan a few months later during the same year. This turned out to be the first of thousands of performances, but no cast could better the one which included Emma Eames (soprano) and Emma Calvé (mezzo-soprano), who made her American debut as Santuzza in 1893.

PUCCINI, GREAT STORYTELLER

With Richard Wagner and Giuseppe Verdi, Giacomo Puccini (1858-1924), born in Lucca, Italy, was a master at picking out actable stories for operas. He knew "good theater." Puccini knew how to write exceptionally well for the voice, and his orchestration was original. He, with Wagner, was content to break rules if what he composed made sense to him. This is the way genius advances the scope of art. At first he was criticized. Today, his operas have a tang found in few of those of his contemporaries. His international fame began with *La Bohème.*

He was the first composer in Italy upon whom a bit of the mantle of Verdi might fall. Verdi and Puccini were the gods of Italian opera lovers then and now. When one visits Italy, one realizes this in town and city, hill and valley, among peasants or aristocrats.

Giacomo Puccini did not seem destined to be seated among the immortals, but today, his music has survived in strength and beauty and a front seat will be his lot. He had to fall in love with a story before he used it for a text. He was a great admirer of Wagner and was not afraid to try experiments. Like Massenet, he comes between two eras, after the Romantic Period and before *les enfants terribles* of the twentieth century. He made opera intensely appealing.

AN INDIVIDUAL TANG

His is the music of modern Italy, realistic but softened with a lush melodic line which often rises to passionate climaxes. He made a re- markable advance in getting away from commonplace harmony and rhythms. He employed dissonance and even bitonality beautifully at times; acid major sevenths and other free chords that had not been used except by independent and brave men. His consecutive octaves and fifths made for color as well as coolness, as for example in the snow scene of *La Bohème,* and his tangy use of chromatics won him much unfavorable criticism. His sparkle, piquant harmonies, animated rhythms and his drive made it possible for him to write tragedies like *Tosca* and a fascinating melodic little comic opera like *Gianni Schicchi,* too delicious for even his harsh critic, Busoni, to dis- like.

Puccini uses the leitmotifs in repetition rather than symphonically as Wagner does. Yet, although they are little changed when met again and again, he knows just how much to use them. He can "put over" brutal scenes with entrancing song and orchestration. His spontaneity, rich melody, and his ability to make a gripping scene gripping, has made his *La Bohème, Madame Butterfly* and *Tosca* poignant adorn- ments of opera repertory.

He was particular about his librettos and often spent more time on them than on his scores. He was a man of the theater.

LA BOHÈME

La Bohème (*The Bohemians*) is an exciting, realistic story, with a brilliant mixture of tragedy, pathos and gaiety. It tells of life in Paris, among the artists and so-called Bohemians (freedom-loving and unconventional people), based by Giuseppe Giacosa and Luigi Illica on Henri Murger's *Scènes de le vie de Bohème* ("Bohemian Life"), of gay, but poverty-ridden dwellers in the *Quartier Latin* or Latin Quarter of Paris.

The librettists and the composer of *La Bohème* had to boil down their first fifteen-act libretto to their final four acts! Besides, it was labor to sift the incidents, for the Murger novel was rich and realistic. When Murger produced his play based on the novel, his friends recognized the characters as themselves, with Murger as Rodolfo. As young men, Murger in Paris and Puccini in Milan had had poverty as company and knew Bohemian life. Therefore the story becomes vivid in novel, play and opera. The songs, tinged with the Puccini pathos or joy, go to the heart, and his themes accent the story as it unfolds. The types are the poet, the painter, the musician, the landlord, and a poor little half-starved seamstress, Mimi, who is on the brink of death. The result of the collaboration is an opera realistic yet romantic, well-knit though full of dramatic scenes, and tragic yet with rollicking gaiety at times.

Among the unforgettable songs from the first act are *"Che gelida manina"* ("Your Tiny Hand Is Frozen") and *"Mi chiamano Mimi"* ("They Call Me Mimi"), snatches of which are used like lovely memories in a time of grief as Mimi dies in the last act. The waltz song, *"Quando me 'n vo soletto per la via"* ("As Through the Streets I Wander Onward Merrily"), sung by Musetta, a gay little *grisette* and "girl friend" of the Bohemians, adds color to the lively scene that is prefaced by the patrol of fifes and drums headed by the drum major.

La Bohème was first performed in Turin at the Regio Theatre, in 1896, and it came to America to Los Angeles played by a traveling troupe of Italians in Italian, in 1897; in 1900 it reached the Metropolitan Opera House. It is hardly second to any opera in popularity in America.

INTRIGUE, TORTURE AND SUICIDE

Compared with Floria Tosca, a prima donna, the thrills of the unfortunate maidens, Thaïs and Manon are petty indeed! If ever music made horror palatable, Puccini's music in *Tosca* does so in a blood-curdling, fascinating story.

Luigi Illica and Giuseppe Giacosa first made a libretto of fifteen acts from the much-peopled play of Victorien Sardou. *La Tosca,* his most violent and sensational play, was written for Madame Sarah Bernhardt, French actress, 1887. Few save Puccini rivaled Sardou in knowledge and feeling for good theater and "big scenes." Naturally the boiling down to three acts from fifteen necessitated some omissions. With all Puccini's innate sense of theater, he had been familiar with Victorien Sardou's drama *La Tosca* a long time before he thought of using it for an opera—whose first performance did not occur until 1900.

The action takes place in Rome (1800), when it was badgered by political intrigue. The story hangs on the escape of a political prisoner, Angelotti, who in the opera is Tosca's brother. Tosca's lover assists in the escape and is to be executed. It has a tragic ending, built on a trick played on the lovers by the police commissioner Scarpia, the jealous and crafty adorer of Tosca. It is full of the drama of contrast in story and music.

It opens suddenly with no prelude but with loud and harsh chords, characterizing the vile Scarpia and his vicious deeds, which gives no time for audience chit-chat. One scene can never be forgotten, where Tosca pleads for the life of her lover Mario. She hears him being tortured in the next room. If she promises Scarpia her love, he promises to free her suffering lover Mario. Tosca sings a heartbreaking aria, *"Vissi d'arte, vissi d'amore ..."* ("Love and Music, These Have I Lived For").

Shortly after this aria, as Scarpia writes what Tosca thinks is a pardon for Mario, another bloodcurdling scene takes place. She seizes a carving knife from the table which is spread for the dinner which Scarpia has invited her to share with him. When he tries to embrace her, she stabs him. As he lies dead on the floor, and as she coldly arranges the candles at his head and feet, the most lighthearted melody is heard coming up through the windows from a ball below. A contrast—dramatic indeed! This is as gruesome drama as ever was penned.

In the last act the tenor Mario sings the superb song *"E Lucevan le stelle ed olezza la terror"* ("The Stars Were Brightly Shining"). This is one of the most tragically sweet songs ever written for a tenor. He thinks he is about to die, until Tosca tells him he is to be shot with blank cartridges and that he is to pretend to fall dead when the soldiers fire. Scarpia won! The bullets are real! When she goes to pick up Mario, he is dead! Frantic, she jumps off the parapet to a fascinating, exciting, dissonant and tuneful musical mixture, with the themes of the past happenings blared *fortissimo*. There is everything from love, cannon fire, torture and death in this opera! *Verismo!*

Tosca opened at the Costanzi Theatre, Rome, 1900. Its première in North America was at the Metropolitan Opera House in 1901, and it is now more popular, if possible, than ever. Antonio Scotti (1866–1936) played the part of Scarpia as few singers have done with any role.

MADAME BUTTERFLY

Again Puccini shows verismo tendencies in one of the most heart-breaking operas. For *Madame Butterfly*, not as gangsterish as *Tosca* or *La Gioconda*, has probably caused more tears to flow than many another musical story. It is full of unforgettable and poignant songs. Puccini has used leitmotifs—among them "The Star-Spangled Banner" —to express the mingling of the American and Japanese elements. The story by John Luther Long is a sad one, and the drama made of it by David Belasco is about a little Japanese girl who, in good faith, is married to an American naval lieutenant in a Japanese cere-mony, which the officer did not recognize as binding. Poor little But-terfly did, and is brokenhearted at his faithlessness in marrying an American girl. She retires behind a screen, commits suicide, and falls dead in the sight of the audience. How far our dramma per musica has traveled since the age of Greek drama, when no death was per-mitted to take place on stage!

THE EXOTIC AGAIN!

Puccini has used a few Oriental devices in harmony, and the flavor of his own music carries it in a realistic fashion. Rarely, save with Verdi's *Aïda*, had the exotic and Oriental been so well pictured by a Western composer. Puccini's use of the exotic in both this opera and in *Turandot*, which has a Chinese setting, is remarkable; and the ability to do this is one of the things that gives a peculiar character to all his music, even that which is not Oriental.

Madame Butterfly is always dramatic and always makes its point. The exultant love duet in Act One,*"Dolce notte! Quante stelle"* ("Night of Rapture, Stars Unnumbered"), with all its ecstasy, has in it, too, the foreboding of tragedy. After the lieutenant leaves his little bride, she lives on his promise to return to her. In the meantime she bears his child. She expects him to come back when the "robins nest again," and she sings of his homecoming to her doubting maid, *"Un bel dì vedremo"* ("One Fine Day He'll Come"). This is a song to break the heart, but nothing to the song she sings when she learns that an American warship is in the bay! She waits all night at the little paper window of her typical Japanese home and sings the vigil theme, a Japanese-like melody in the agonizing and withering scene of foreboding.

This music is hardly heard, at times, for it evokes sobs and chokes from the audience. Rarely has a writer of opera been able to make a scene with only two persons in it (the mother and the baby) so devastatingly dramatic and tragic. Indeed, there is no opera whose tragedy seems so *personal*—no epic, no pastorale, no historic story is this!

Madame Butterfly, as an opera, was first staged at La Scala, Milan (1904); in America, in Washington, D. C. (1906), in English, by the Savage Opera Company; and at the Metropolitan in 1907, in Italian.

MANON LESCAUT

With *Manon Lescaut* (which was seen in New York first in 1907), Puccini began to be known outside of Italy (where the opera had its première in Turin, 1893). He was outstripped, however, in this by the *Manon* of Massenet, which is still more popular. In this opera, it was thought that Puccini had not yet struck his stride nor his new musical path. To critics today it shows his brilliance and rare ability to handle plot and music. In his later operas he made his characters more alive. *Manon Lescaut* was his favorite opera and was well received when revived in 1949 at the Metropolitan Opera in New York under Rudolph Bing.

LE VILLI

Puccini's first opera was *Le Villi,* which means "the ghosts of jilted maidens." The book was by Ferdinando Fontana, and it was first produced at Teatro dal Verme in Milan, 1884. It is quite sensational and its wild dance is effective. It was well received in Italy, as was *Edgar* (1889), but both have been little heard elsewhere.

La Fanciulla del West (*The Girl of the Golden West*) was written for the Metropolitan Opera Association (1910). Puccini made a visit to America, saw a popular play by David Belasco and made it into an opera. The "West" here is the American plains. This was not exotic, but meant to mirror the verismo of the Wild West, as blood is even seen dripping from the loft where one poor soul is hiding! It was based on a story by John Luther Long and the libretto is by Guelfo Civinini and Carlo Zangarini. It was one of Puccini's failures—yet, if revived, might be a thriller.

LA RONDINE AND THE THREE

During the war years, in 1917, *La rondine (The Swallow)* was given in Monte Carlo, but it did not approach Puccini's other operas in charm or in success. He did not make another "hit" until 1918, when three one-act operas were given in New York on the same bill: *Gianni Schicchi,* a satiric little comic opera, yet with lovely songs such as the sweet *"O mio babbino caro"* ("Oh, My Beloved Daddy"), which Lauretta sings to her father; *Suora Angelica (Sister Angelica)*; and *Il tabbaro (The Cloak)*. The most winning of these is the first. It is used now in double billing at the Metropolitan, rarely with the other two born at the same time. *Gianni Schicchi* tells a story, in Dante's time, of a scheming crew of relatives who want the money and the estates of a man who is supposed to be dying in the canopied bed. It is full of fun, satire and surprise. The "expecters" form one of the few ensembles in Puccini's operas.

TURANDOT

Puccini's last opera, which he did not live to finish, was *Turandot*. It was based on a Chinese theme and is by many considered his best work. It is romantic. It is exotic. It is built on a larger scale. But somehow, it hasn't his usual singable melodies. It was finished by Franco Alfano (1876–1954), beginning at the duet in the last act between Prince Calaf and Turandot (tyrannical princess) and continuing to the end of the opera when everything turns out fairly well, not counting a poor little victim who kills herself for love.

Ping, Pang and Pong (not a game!) are the three high officials, whose names add a bit of humor. *Turandot* had its Metropolitan première in 1926.

LEONCAVALLO

Another opera writer known for one opera above all his others is Ruggiero Leoncavallo (1858–1919), born in Naples. He was a man of letters, a professional accompanist in café concerts, studied the piano at the Naples Conservatory, was his own librettist, and had the degree of Doctor of Letters. Like Mascagni he reached continuous international success with one opera—*Pagliacci* (*Clowns*). This gory tale rolls up to a climax of intense feeling, backed by beautiful music, which fits the mood and brings the story to a swift and melodramatic finish. It is a play within a play, in two acts, with a book by the composer. Its first performance was in 1892 in the Teatro dal Verme, Milan.

The scene is laid in Calabria, Italy, among the villagers and townsfolk, who are agog to see the traveling clowns give their play. It opens with the famous prologue sung by Tonio, a clown, *"Si puo? Signore e Signori"* ("By Your Leave, Ladies and Gentlemen"), as he steps in front of the curtain. Nedda sings *"Oh! che volo d' augelli"* ("Ah Ye Bright Birds Without Number") leading to the gay *Balletatella*. One of the best-known songs in all opera, *"Vesti la giubba"* ("Now, Don the Motley"), expresses Canio's grief over his betrayal by Nedda, and Canio sings *"Ridi Pagliaccio"* ("Laugh, Clown"), in his grief and sorrow for himself. But apart from these, *"Din, don suona vespero"* ("Ding, Dong, the Vesper Bell"), which a group of villagers sing while waiting for the play to go on, is one of the most enchanting bits in the opera. At the end, Canio, acting with Nedda in a play similar to the play the audience is watching, seizes a carving knife from the table (in the scene) and kills her. The orchestra sarcastically sobs *"Ridi Pagliaccio,"* and as the knife falls from Canio's hand, he says *"La commedia e finita"* ("The comedy is ended"). This is drama! This is tragedy! Leoncavallo, as did Wolf-Ferrari, Mascagni and others, illustrated that the tragedy of the lowly can grip an audience.

Pagliacci's fame spread as rapidly as would a bit of scandal! The opera was given on this continent by some traveling Italian players in California, probably in 1897. A performance was hastily contrived at the Grand Opera House, New York, in June, 1893. Seven months later it opened at the Metropolitan Opera House. It has been presented there ever since!

Pagliacci is usually twinned with Mascagni's *Cavalleria rusticana* to make an evening's entertainment of blood, thunder and melody. Enrico Caruso made a most signal success as Canio.

ZAZÀ

Leoncavallo's four-act opera *Zazà* (1900), with book by the composer, after the play by Berton and Simon, was given in New York. Although Mrs. Leslie Carter, who played it in straight drama, had

sensational success, Geraldine Farrar, in 1920, created a sensation too
in the opera at the Metropolitan, but it was not a success.

ANDREA CHÉNIER

Another man who is known best for one opera is Umberto Giordano
(1867–1948) with *Andrea Chénier,* a story of the French Revolution.
The verismo style was well fitted to this fierce and gory story, written
between the ages of tyranny of monarchs and the new era of people's
rights. It is noisy and dramatic, although tinctured with impressionism. It was thought to be musically revolutionary in its day, but,
as with other art works, time has caught up with it. Among his operas
were two based on plays written by Victorien Sardou for Sarah Bernhardt: the lively and tuneful *Madame Sans-Gêne (Madame Free and
Easy)* and *Fedora,* from which the fedora hat gets its name; also *La
cena della beffe (The Feast of Jests),* with a book by Sem Benelli,
set in the time of Lorenzo the Magnificent of Florence.

ERMANNO WOLF-FERRARI

Wolf-Ferrari (1876–1948) was born in Venice, Italy, of an Italian
mother and a German father. He was more Italian in temperament
than German. With *I gioielli della Madonna (The Jewels of the
Madonna)* he wrote a verismo opera, yet he was a lineal descendant,
in opera buffa, of Mozart! This seems paradoxical, but his music has
the lilt and sparkle, the gaiety and sprightliness of his great prede-
cessor. *The Jewels,* about a terrorist plot and sacrilege, was the third
of his operas. He had been dubbed "Mozartean" previously for his
delightful *Il segreto di Susanna (The Secret of Suzanne),* whose secret
was that she smoked, and *Le donne curiose (The Inquisitive Ladies)*
who spied in their husbands' club only to find them enjoying a good
dinner! This is amusing opera buffa, a twentieth-century encore to
Mozart, Cimarosa, Rossini and Donizetti.

THE JEWELS OF THE MADONNA

For *The Jewels of the Madonna,* an example of delicacy and melody
with powerful drama, Wolf-Ferrari himself wrote the book, with
verses by Carlo Zangarini and Enrico Golisciani. It combines logic,
fiery feeling, murder, theft, realism, religious rites and charm, with
delightful orchestral effects and color. Perhaps this special color quality
was inherited from his father, August Wolf, a painter, who had hoped
his son would be a painter too.

The exciting story of *The Jewels* is set in Italy involving gangster plots. It has a fascinating overture, with pieces from the body of the opera, and even more fascinating intermezzi between the acts, two of the most charmingly devised pieces of music in modern opera. The composer has engaging skill in combining the flute with the harp and other strings. The opera does for Naples something of what Charpentier's *Louise* did for Paris.

The opera was first performed at the Kurfürstenoper, Berlin (1911) in a German version. A performance in Italian took place in Chicago, at the Auditorium in January, 1912, and the Chicago Opera Company brought it to New York a few months later. It was presented by the Metropolitan Opera Company in December, 1925.

RICCARDO ZANDONAI

After Italy had had its share of verismo, Riccardo Zandonai (1883–1944) wrote some operas, the best known among them *Francesca da Rimini* (1914). They are written in a symphonic way, with very few set pieces to interrupt the story, as in the old-style operas. Of course, they did not "take" as well as the aria-filled pre-Wagnerian specimens.

VERISMO IS ABANDONED

Without exaggeration, Italo Montemezzi, born in Vigasio, Italy (1875–1952), proclaimed himself in his *L'amore dei tre re* (*The Love of Three Kings*) one of the greatest modern Italian writers of opera. He abandoned the realistic (verismo) school, and made deep impressions in both Italy and in America with this opera. "He preserves melodic outline, is emotional and dramatic and poignant. Aria, recitative (*musica parlante*) appear as the drama requires. It is not radical, it is always beautiful." (*Music Through the Ages,* by Bauer and Peyser). He never adopts Italian fireworks.

LOVE OF THREE KINGS

This opera is kept moving in spite of its not having catchy tunes, like those of Puccini or Verdi. Montemezzi used new musical ideas in old romantic ways. He took an exciting and intense story, almost veristic in spots, and applied to it a continuous stream of melody, instead of breaking it up into separate songs. *Ecco!* Here is the first Italian who actually did what the Camerata in the seventeenth century tried to do, fit text to music. It took nearly three hundred years to arrive at this pinnacle of Italian *dramma per musica.* Mussorgsky did it in his song-speech for Russia; Wagner did it to a certain extent for Germany; Debussy accomplished it for France to the fullest extent. Its tragedy is so much more elevated than the verismo operas that, with *Aïda* and *Otello, The Love of Three Kings* deserves to live forever. It is "wear-ever" music and affects opera because it gives courage to writers to use the elevated style once more.

MONTEMEZZI SPEAKS

After Sem Benelli told him that he had a story for him, Montemezzi went to Ricordi, his publisher, who had so much faith in both Benelli and Montemezzi that he signed a contract with them for the opera. Montemezzi studied the tragedy with great care and in solitude.... "Owing to the severity I imposed upon myself the work proceeded, though not always easily. Not for a moment could the music advance divorced from the poetry. From beginning to end, *music and poetry must progress side by side.* Only in this fashion could I attain that unity which justified the title 'music drama'. The music had to be the exalta-tion of the drama, augmenting its efficacy; setting poetry in an ideal lyricism and a passion bursting forth with the fury created by the dramatic incidents but all this without having recourse to devices that had nothing to do with effects of a sort that might falsify the title of 'music drama.' This principle I followed through the entire length of the opera." (A letter from Montemezzi to Herbert F. Peyser.)

The Love of Three Kings was performed first at La Scala, Milan, 1913, and had its American première at the Metropolitan Opera House in 1914. It was a perfect medium for Lucrezia Bori's unique gifts.

Of Montemezzi's later operas, *La nave* (*The Ship*), on a Venetian tragedy by Gabriele d'Annunzio, enjoyed some popularity; but *La notte di Zoraima* (*The Night of Zoraima*) won no acclaim. His first opera was *Giovanni Gallurese* in three acts, successfully produced in Turin, 1904, and at the Metropolitan in 1925. These operas added nothing to the development of opera, or to the reputation of Monte-mezzi.

In 1943, his radio opera, *L'incantesimo* (*Enchantment*) was pre-sented by the National Broadcasting System.

SCENE VIII

Light Opera in England and Ireland, and the Strauss Dynasty in Vienna

ENGLAND reached its greatest height in music during the reigns of two queens, Elizabeth I and Victoria. Victoria, like Elizabeth, was very fond of music and dancing. Part German, she doted on the gifted Felix Mendelssohn. Nevertheless, in Queen Victoria's time British light opera or operetta, which has resemblance to Singspiel, opera buffa and opéra bouffe, took a spurt on "its own" after a long stretch of dependence on the operas of Italy, France and Germany.

During the Romantic Period, England followed delightfully the light opera vein of France. Among the first British writers of light opera was Michael William Balfe (1808–70), an Irishman, who wrote *The Bohemian Girl* (1843). This highly colorful, exciting and romantic story is about a child, kidnaped by gypsies, who turns out to be high-born, of course, and all ends happily.

In *The Bohemian Girl,* one of the loveliest light operas, the two songs, "I Dreamt I Dwelt in Marble Halls" and "The Heart Bowed Down" are among its gems.

New York saw it for the first time in 1844, when it enjoyed great success. Even in France it won the Cross of the Legion of Honor. Balfe also wrote a grand opera, *Siege of Rochelle,* much like an Auber opéra comique. Out of his thirty operas, only *The Bohemian Girl* seems enduring. Balfe also enjoyed fame as a singer and composer in Europe.

SPANISH GOLD

Another Irishman, William Vincent Wallace (1814–1865), took his musical gold from Spain, in a masterpiece called *Maritana* (1848), founded on the story of *Don Cesar de Bazan.* Its plot lends itself to

201

beautiful scenery, attractive costumes, excitement, romance and charming songs.

Wallace and Balfe in England carried on the tradition of Jacques Offenbach and the Strausses.

MANY A TRY

Now in England many of her famous composers were inspired to form opera companies. Most of these failed and did not advance opera. Opera singers felt too important to sing any place but in Covent Garden, the Metropolitan (then in its youth) and Monte Carlo. Sir Frederick Hymen Cowen (1852–1935), Sir Alexander Campbell Mackenzie (1847–1935) with his *Cricket on the Hearth,* and Sir Charles Villiers Stanford (1852–1924) with his *Much Ado About Nothing* could not be said to be too successful. But Stanford's *Shamus O'Brien* was successful as a comedy with spoken dialogue.

Around 1909 came Thomas Beecham, now *Sir* Thomas Beecham, who presented *The Wreckers* by Dame Ethel Smythe. This was so successful that nearly all the opera houses in Europe, and our own Metropolitan (1903) produced it. Yet it has not lived. Other works of hers, particularly *The Boatswain's Mate,* have been produced in European theaters.

Grand opera translated into the English language in England and America has not been too successful. Although for other countries it has always been translated into the speech of the nations producing it. *Pelléas et Mélisande* in German seems incongruous! But not more so than *Boris Godounov,* the Russian opera, in an Italian translation as given at the Metropolitan.

THE DAZZLING TEAM

Important among all the other bearers of Offenbach's flag were Sir Arthur Sullivan (1842–1900) and Sir William Schwenck Gilbert (1836–1911). This dazzling team has delighted the world since they wrote their fourteen operettas; among them are: *H.M.S. Pinafore, Patience, Iolanthe, The Mikado* and *The Gondoliers.* Apart from their inimitable music, which we all sing, hum, whistle, and parody, there have been no better lyrics (and rarely as good) as those written by Gilbert for every one of these operettas. They set a high standard for writers of lyrics and so advanced the progress of light opera. Never did a composer have a more accomplished and witty writer. And never did a writer work better with a composer who could, syllable by syllable, and at any speed and rhythm whatever, put music to every word and punctuation mark. Gilbert's lyrics will never be forgotten, Sullivan's melodies, in lovely airs, madrigals, ballads—graceful, sly, satiric, lampooning, haunting, and exquisite—are rich treasures. Among the familiar tunes, to mention only a very few, are "A Wandering Minstrel I" and "Tit-Willow," from *The Mikado;* "When I Was A Lad I Served A Term" (*H.M.S. Pinafore*), "Come Friends Who Plough the Sea" and "Hail, Hail, The Gang's All Here" (*The Pirates of Penzance*).

Arthur Sullivan, later Sir Arthur, was the son of a clarinet player. His ambition was to write serious opera, but his grand opera *Ivanhoe,* based on Sir Walter Scott's story, was a failure. He succeeded far better, however, than he could have imagined with the hymn "Onward, Christian Soldiers" and the song "The Lost Chord."

OTHER BRITISHERS

Sir John in Love by Ralph Vaughan Williams (born 1872) is a story based on *The Merry Wives of Windsor* by Shakespeare, and is probably the largest work for the musical stage that has been written in England. Gustav Holst (1874-1934) wrote operas, but they are given rarely, if ever. *The Immortal Hour* by Rutland Boughton has been popular in his own land.

ARTHURIAN AND NORSE LEGENDS

Not long ago many English composers wrote operas on Norse stories and King Arthur legends, but they did not advance opera materially.

SLIGHT ENCOURAGEMENT

Because of heavy casts and heavier costs, and perhaps for lack of governmental subsidy as other European nations have had, English composers of the nineteenth century have given us few operas of distinction. But in the twentieth century there has been a notable advance in opera writing and audience interest, amounting almost to a renaissance.

THE STRAUSS DYNASTY IN VIENNA

In the making of tuneful, rhythmic, spritely captivating operetta in the nineteenth century, there was a strong trend in Europe, which richly affected the making of light opera long after its birth. Furthermore, owing to its universal appeal it sowed the seeds for the enjoyment of music among the masses as well as among the classes—in other

words, mass enjoyment of music. Without any slur on Jacques Offenbach or on the Gilbert and Sullivan team, the Strauss dynasty influenced the writing of light opera down to our own era. The Strauss
dynasty consisted of "The Father of the Waltz" Johann (1804-49), and
"The Waltz King" Johann Jr. (1825-99) and his talented but far less
talented brothers, Josef (1827-70) and Eduard (1835-1916).

The "Father of the Waltz," Johann the Elder, led his own orchestra,
played the violin as a master, was a gay blade, fascinated Vienna with
his music and personality, but at home was not too popular. He
opposed the musical education of his son although he loved him
tenderly, and had it not been for the son's mother, Johann Jr. as a
musician might never have walked the boards of a stage or written
the beautiful "Blue Danube," the most popular bit of music ever
composed.

The life of the younger Strauss is like a fascinating movie! (It would
be rewarding to read a good biography such as H. E. Jacob's *Johann
Strauss, Father and Son,* Greystone Press, 1940).

His operettas for which he gains admittance to these pages are trivial
in story and so fulfill the light-opera motivation; piquant, sparkling
in melody, stirring in dance rhythm, mainly the waltz; vivid in scenic
design; intensely Viennese in the spirit of the old gay regime; and
swift-moving, in spite of dances and choruses. Three still hold the
stage: *The Bat* (*Die Fledermaus,* 1874); *The Gypsy Baron* (*Der
Zigeunerbaron,* 1885); and *A Night in Venice* (*Eine Nacht in Vene-
dig,* 1883); and eight or nine others are occasionally revived. The waltzes
from *The Bat* and *The Gypsy Baron* are continually enjoyed. Among
the waltzes with names that had nothing whatever to do with their
mood or objective (he wrote many to please potentates) are: "A
Thousand and One Nights," "Wine, Women and Song," "Tales from
the Vienna Woods," "The Artist's Life," five hundred dance pieces
alone (with 498 opus numbers), some with such names as "Telegraph
Waltz," "Roses from the South," "Newspaper Waltz," "Bon Bons,"
and on and on! Apart from these, this Johann wrote hundreds more to
regale the luxury-loving and gay Viennese.

The elder Strauss, who raised dance music to a higher level than
ever before, was blessed with a gift of beautiful orchestration.

The junior Strauss toured Europe, undertook the direction of a
series of important summer concerts for ten years in St. Petersburg
(now Leningrad). He traveled many years giving concerts and rejoic-
ing the hearts of every nation. Triumph was his wherever he played

his waltzes or performed on his violin. As a conductor he had great charm with violin in hand. His reception in America was gargantuan!

In spite of strong opposition, even enmity, from his father, he made his debut as conductor at Dommayer's Garden, in Heitzing at the age of 19 on October 15, 1844. Magnanimously he played his father's popular "Lorelei Walzer." His father, however, had packed the house against him by sending some of his pals to jeer and hiss, but *mirabile dictu!* they who went to damn the boy carried him in triumph on their shoulders while cheers and cries of *encore!* reverberated through the garden.

Johann Jr. was married three times and died after a phenomenally triumphant life in which he was even included as a character in plays!

Following in the Strauss footsteps were Franz Lehar of *The Merry Widow* and *The Count of Luxembourg* fame; Emmerich Kalman who wrote *Countess Maritza;* and Oskar Straus, composer of *A Waltz Dream* and *The Chocolate Soldier.* Many others brought renown to the Viennese school of light opera.

ACT V. Opera Waves National Emblems

PRELUDE

Characteristics of Nationalism in Opera

NATIONALISM

In the nineteenth century, because of unrest after the violence of the French Revolution and many conflicts in France and Germany such as the Franco-Prussian War (1870–71) and the painful birth of Italy as a nation (the *Risorgimento*), France, Germany and Italy began to take stock. They found that each had something different to give to their arts. These differences in music or in any art form may contribute to nationalism.

There are two different kinds of nationalism—one kind is quite unconscious. It doesn't say, "Here now, let's be Russian," or "Come, come, let's be French or German or American." No! Quite naturally, national traits are reflected in old folk songs, in rhythms, tonal combinations, in customs, in the character and even the soul of a people, somewhat in the way traits mark certain families. You could never mistake Walt Whitman's *Drum-Taps* for anything but American, nor the poetry of Robert Burns for anything but Scotch. People who know music can tell a Beethoven concerto from one by Saint-Saëns, a Schubert song from a Debussy, or a Massenet opera from Wagner.

You could tell at once by its buildings that you were on the Champs Élysées in Paris, and not on Broadway in New York. That is because even the streets have their particular styles and national characteristics. You would certainly know the difference between the Paris Opera House and the Empire State Building. One is very definitely European, the other is very definitely American. So, architecture often follows the national need and feeling for design.

CONSCIOUS NATIONALISM

The second kind of nationalism is conscious. This is shown when a composer uses a folk rhythm, song or dance or its counterpart in a composition. The old Singspiel, with its strings of folk songs and folk dances connected by conversation, is an example of conscious nationalism. In *The Bartered Bride* Smetana used the polka of Bohemia to lively effect. Chopin gloried in the forms of Polish mazurkas and polonaises, and Weber used German folk songs. Martin Luther, too (1483–1546), collected German tunes from the people of Germany on which to build his hymns to touch the hearts and awaken the spirit of his people.

During the early years of art music, all the nations used the motet, the madrigal, and later the instrumental suite and the sonata. These were international forms in Germany, France, the Netherlands, Italy, Spain. Nevertheless, each country showed its own colors in flavor or rhythms or tunes. This nationalism grew up through wars and revolutions, victories and defeats. Before Europe was divided into nations and existed only as groups or tribes of the Celts, Saxons, Latins, Goths, Vandals, Huns, Magyars, Norsemen, etc., individual traits had begun to take form and kept on developing.

SERIOUS MUSIC RECEIVES CITIZENSHIP

All through the years the people made pictures of their lives and customs in their national music. In the nineteenth century serious musicians bestowed citizenship on music not only by using their national folk stories and legends, but also by giving characteristics of their folk music to their compositions. Dvorak did this for American Negro music in *The New World Symphony* in which no actual Negro folk songs were used but bits or memories of Negroid musical ideas— for example, the syncopated rhythms of the first theme of the first movement, and the mood of the slow movement which turned the tables on history by being adopted and fitted with words as a spiritual known as "Goin' Home." Folk dances and ancient hymns suggested ideas which led composers to the writing of suites, sonatas, symphonies and operas.

SCENE I

Russian Music and "The Five"

THERE is no history of made-to-order secular or art music in Russia before the end of the eighteenth and the beginning of the nineteenth centuries. The Russians had their old and superb church music, and their vast store of characteristic folk song. This, of course, made them so familiar with their folk music that they were ready to incorporate it into their works, when symphony-and-opera-composing-time came.

The people inherited vivid stories and music from the Slavs and Tartars who had lived in Russia even before the birth of Christ. This music is often wildly rhythmic, as are the Polovtzian dances in *Prince Igor,* and is always vivid, whether tragic, sad, exciting or gay. The Church at first feared that the wild dance and song tunes, and their colorful harmonies, would dull reverence for sacred music.

During the reign of Peter the Great, in the eighteenth century, many foreigners, including music teachers, went to Russia. Catherine the Great (1729–1796) encouraged Italian, Russian and English music and invited foreign composers to settle in Russia. The foreigners brought in their music from Western Europe. While in Russia, Giovanni Paisiello wrote five operas; Domenico Cimarosa, over eighty operas, including one that we still hear, *The Secret Marriage;* Antonio Salieri wrote over forty operas; and François Boieldieu, who supervised French opera, contracted to write three operas a year for the Empress.

Catherine, who was a German, encouraged the use of Russian folk songs and legends. In 1703 was built the first public theater in St. Petersburg in which foreign works were given. It was an Italian, Catterino Cavos, who wrote the first Russian opera, *Ivan Sousanin,* on a Russian fairy tale used later by Glinka in *A Life for the Czar.*

After Russia defeated Napoleon in 1812, and the Russians had saved Moscow by setting it on fire, new political ideas flamed under the Czars. These ideas kept on simmering, with occasional outbreaks, until the Bolshevik explosions after World War I and subsequent Sovietized Russia. All this has affected Russian opera.

RUSSIA IS FIRST

In the early nineteenth century, Russian composers began to write serious music not meant for the Church. Michael Glinka (1804-57) wrote the opera *A Life for the Czar,* the first important piece of Russian made-to-order serious (not church) music. It uses Russian stories and folk tunes. The music of John Field, the Irishman, of Muzio Clementi, the Italian, and other non-Russian composers was beginning to tire the Russians. They wanted their own music. Glinka wanted them to have it. His next opera, *Russlan and Ludmilla,* is another picture of Russia in music and story. Although Glinka was patriotic in the use of Russian music, he wrote two "Spanish Caprices" and was among the first to remind the world of exciting and rich Spanish folk music.

Glinka was expert in his handling of the orchestra. His touch was clear and brilliant. His use of the leitmotif was more general than any composer before Wagner, even if not in Wagner's symphonic style. Glinka was able to produce the splendor and contrast we see and recognize as distinctly Russian.

Intensely Russian are: the fantastic fairy tales, such as *Russlan and Ludmilla,* delighting the soul; ancient bards and astrologers; ancient and archaic melodic schemes, folk song, dance, old church music; Oriental rhythms, tunes, happenings and settings, as in the ballets of *Fire Bird* and *Scheherezade* of Stravinsky and Rimsky-Korsakov; or the brilliant and wildly rhythmic dances of Borodin's *Prince Igor.*

THE RUSSIAN FIVE

Glinka started something. The field of Russian music in due time became a battleground. On one side were "The Three": Piotr Ilyich Tchaikovsky and the two Rubinsteins—Anton and Nikolai. On the other side was a group interested in *Russian* opera, called "The Five": Mily Balakirev, Alexander Borodin, Modest Mussorgsky, Nikolai Rimsky-Korsakov and César Cui—and the greatest of these was Mussorgsky. These "Five" wanted to use new methods—Russian ideas with an emphasis on a new sincerity in Russian music, particularly in opera.

BALAKIREV

Mily Balakirev (1837-1910), founder and the leader of "The Five," was conductor and composer, but unimportant to opera. He knew how to write for both orchestra and piano. He is important only because he insisted on the use in opera of Russian national stories. He also made good use of the Oriental flavor of his country's ancient arts and music.

DR. BORODIN

A writer of magnificent, clashing, sparkling music was a physician, Alexander Borodin (1833–87). His impressionistic qualities place him between Liszt and Debussy. At first, people thought his music to be full of dissonance. Today, we love his songs, his *Second Symphony,* and his flashing opera *Prince Igor.*

Prince Igor was first given in 1890, at the Imperial Opera House, St. Petersburg, and first heard in America at the Metropolitan Opera House in New York, December, 1915.

This work is so Russian and so colorful that when you once hear and see it, you can never forget it. It has dramatic scenes, and occasionally an Italian-styled aria. It is cheerful, romantic, red-blooded, noisy, tuneful and savagely grand. It has intensely rhythmic Oriental war dances, stampings and gesticulations. The Polovtzian dancers are costumed in high Russian boots, and most elaborate costumes, with shields and spears.

With these dance-acts, the Russians began to re-enliven the ballet. No simpering postures in this—but a deepening of the scene and story. Borodin used the Slavic Oriental musical background of his country both in operatic and non-operatic works.

LISZT AND BORODIN

Franz Liszt was the first renowned composer to influence and encourage men in nearly every European country to use their own folk music. He thought that Borodin was the most brilliant of the orchestral writers of the nineteenth century. The recordings of Borodin's music, including the *Second Symphony,* will give you an exciting time.

FROM NAVY TO OPERA

Nikolai Rimsky-Korsakov (1844–1908) wrote the opera *Sadko,* in which you see Sadko descend from his ship into the depths of the waters to ingratiate himself with the King of the Sea, in order to marry the Princess. Sadko was a wandering *gusli* player. A *gusli* is a zitherlike instrument and, with the balalaika, has been much used in Russia.

Sadko is charming, and the Russian love for pageantry, legend, color and beautiful song is evident. In it there is a tremendous whirling dance, to Sadko's *gusli* music, in which the King himself drops dead. Then the coast, or rather the sea, is clear for the brave Sadko to claim the Princess and they live together thereafter in Sadko's palace in Novgorod.

Rimsky-Korsakov was a naval cadet for many years. On one voyage he came to America, and on the return trip he wrote his *First Symphony*.

Rimsky studied music and was no amateur. No one ever called him a dabbler, as they called the others of "The Five." These men, striking out for something new, received all the brickbats that newness in music attracts. Each one had another profession and started out as a musical amateur except Balakirev. "The Five" did not greatly admire Bach, Mozart or Haydn. They *did* admire Beethoven's last quartets, and worshiped Berlioz. In this you see a feeling for a more modern and freer kind of music.

Of Rimsky-Korsakov's *The Czar's Bride* and *Snegourotchka* (*The Snow Maiden*), the latter is the more important. This *Snow Maiden,* a fairy tale, with a few mystic and symbolic touches, was given in St. Petersburg in 1882, in Seattle, Washington (in Russian) in 1922, and in the Metropolitan Opera House (in French) in 1922.

MODES FOR MOODS

Rimsky, contrary to the French, thought with the Italians that the music, not the text, was important. He used motifs not symphonically, but as recurring melodies. He associated certain keys with certain moods, like the Greeks, who too used their modes for moods.

Folk songs and folk tales are favorites of his. His music is rich, vibrant and lyric, and his melodies, poignant and beautiful. His popular symphonic suite, *Scheherezade,* was made into a ballet by Fokine. It tells of the spinner of tales, Queen Scheherezade, from *The Arabian Nights,* a set of highly colored pictures, danced, decorated and postured to rich, rhythmic, fascinating music. It is an integral part of the great Russian revival of ballet which Diaghilev so magnificently brought about later. It did what Glinka did first in his second opera—combined Russian with Oriental elements.

Rimsky was a composer's handyman. He always was called in a crisis to edit or arrange other men's works. He was a friend of Mussorgsky and influenced him tremendously. He directed the "Free

School" organized by Balakirev, and taught the art of orchestration. His methods are important even today, and he is called the "Father of Modern Orchestration." He taught many of the famous men of today, including Stravinsky. This wizard was illustrious in his own time, was appointed professor at the St. Petersburg Conservatory of Music, and was offered a post at the Moscow Conservatory.

While preparing the amusing *Le Coq d'Or* (*The Golden Cockerel*), a sparkling gem for publication, Rimsky had a heart attack. On June 21, 1908, he died—after brilliant accomplishment for Russia, and for the world.

THE GREATEST OF THEM ALL

Modest Mussorgsky (1839-81) was the greatest of the Russian nationalists, and his influence has been international. Because of his modern tendencies, in spite of his belonging in this section as a Russian Nationalist and one of "The Five," we have devoted an entire section to him (Act VII, Scene III).

A SPICY MEDLEY

César Cui (1835-1918), one of "The Five," wrote ten operas. The best known was *William Ratcliffe,* based on a poem of Heinrich Heine. An opera with Russian music, English hero, on a poem by a German, makes a spicy medley. As a maker or developer of operas, Cui was the least important of "The Five."

TCHAIKOVSKY, PERSONAL NATIONALIST

Unlike the many nationalists who could write opera to glorify their country, Piotr Ilyich Tchaikovsky (1840-93) put himself, more often than his country, into whatever he wrote. The moods of his operas, as well as his symphonies, mirrored himself in the grip of depression and melancholy. He was a nationalist in his use of Russian folk music, and in his schemes of music as well, such as the plucked strings so lovely in his *Fourth Symphony,* which is like Russian balalaika music. The scenes of most of his operas were laid in Russia and among Russian people. Yet he, Anton and Nikolai Rubinstein were "The Three" who were antagonistic to "The Five" nationalists.

Piotr was the son of a technician in the Russian government. He was no child genius and when, at the age of fifteen, he applied himself to music, was not particularly brilliant. But, unlike other sires of young composers, who did not approve of their sons' choice of profession, father Tchaikovsky insisted that Piotr enter the St. Petersburg Conservatory of Music, over which Anton Rubinstein presided.

As soon as Tchaikovsky's ability as a composer was recognized, Nikolai Rubinstein called him to the Moscow Conservatory, where at the age of twenty-six Piotr began his eleven years as a teacher. Although his fame as a composer was gradual, his fantasy overture "Romeo and Juliet" brought him acclaim.

THE FAIRY GODMOTHER

The next part of his life was unusual indeed! He decided to give all of his time to composing. Soon he was getting commissions for compositions from a lady. After a spirited correspondence, the "commissioner"—a wealthy widow, Madam Nadejda von Meck—devoted herself to him and his work, and tided him over his financial worries by giving him 6,000 rubles a year for many years. These two never actually met, but glimpsed each other two or three times in public places. Later on, the Czar gave him 3,000 rubles annually.

Tchaikovsky's fame took him all over the world, including America, where he opened Carnegie Hall in New York City in May, 1891. After this he returned to Russia and died two years later (1893) of cholera.

TCHAIKOVSKY'S OPERAS

What interests us mainly are two operas: *Eugen Onegin* and *Pique Dame* (*The Queen of Spades*). He wrote almost a dozen, among them *Vakula the Smith,* rewritten as *The Little Slipper,* now translated by Ruth & Thomas Martin as *The Golden Slippers.*

Eugen Onegin, completed in 1878, was given in America first in concert form by Walter Damrosch in 1908 at Carnegie Hall; in 1920, it was performed at the Metropolitan Opera House in an Italian version Artur Bodanzky conducted, and the singers were Claudia Muzio, (dramatic soprano); Giovanni Martinelli (tenor); Giuseppe de Luca (baritone, in the title role); and Adamo Didur (basso).

Tchaikovsky was not a nationalist by schooling, because of his German training in the Russian conservatories. But he was by nature a firm, convinced Russian, for in *Eugen Onegin* and his other operas, he goes to the adored and most Russian poet, Alexander Pushkin, for his stories.

Eugen Onegin failed at first, and his former well wisher, Anton Rubinstein, was silent about it in hostile fashion. Five years later, in 1884, *Onegin* came back as a conquering hero.

A DEMIGOD

After that, Tchaikovsky, at forty-four, was a Russian demigod. Despite the acceptance of *Onegin* as a master work, it has never been very successful in New York or Philadelphia, where it had one performance in 1940. All that seems to remain of its beauties to the great public are its fascinating waltz, the "Letter Scene" song, and the Polonaise. *Eugen Onegin* is a pathetic and intimate story, with the charm and depth of melancholy that so often impelled Tchaikovsky. It has been produced frequently by smaller opera groups.

THE QUEEN OF SPADES

His other opera, *Pique Dame,* was first given in New York in 1910 at the Metropolitan Opera House, in German, with Emmy Destinn (soprano), Leo Slezak (tenor), and Adamo Didur (basso). In 1922 it was given at the New Amsterdam Theatre in New York, in the original Russian.

It has had less popular success than *Eugen Onegin,* in spite of its being just as ingratiating and more dramatic. Tchaikovsky again goes to the general source of Russian composers, Alexander Pushkin, for his story. He uses an exciting tale of gambling, ghost appearances, suicide, intrigue and love. He even goes so far as to ingratiate his audiences with a ballet and a pastoral interlude in the style of Mozart, and the borrowing of a song from Grétry's *Richard the Lion-Hearted.* One of the characters, the old Countess, sings it in memory of her youth.

Tchaikovsky may not have advanced opera directly, but he enhanced its beauties and drew other Russians toward the writing of it.

SCENE II

French Opera Gets New Life— Saint-Saëns, Massenet, Charpentier, and Others

At the close of the Franco-Prussian War, 1871, France made a mighty oath to become French above all things, so she formed the National Society of Music, to regain the beauties and supremacies she had won in the sixteenth, seventeenth and eighteenth centuries. Once more, her composers became as French as Couperin and Rameau.

Opera now arrives at the important station along its road where the traits of French opera have come to their fullest beauty. These traits have been mentioned before, but a *"da capo al fine"* won't spoil this "piece":

1. Devotion to the text of the opera above everything, with music to intensify it.

2. Interest in, and development of, the ballet with which Lully started French opera.

3. The charm of simplicity, leaving out details, such as Wagner would use in long speeches. Instead, a beautiful, but understandable vagueness and cloudiness of atmosphere.

4. Refinement, polish—nothing exaggerated, either in orchestra or song, stressing understatement rather than overstatement, such as was part of Wagner's and also Berlioz' often too heavy orchestra and vocal vastness in spite of the latter's Frenchness.

CAMILLE SAINT-SAËNS

Camille Saint-Saëns, born in 1835, lived for eighty-six years—an active existence even in his eighties. He brought the Japanese for the first time into Western opera in his *The Yellow Princess,* beating the arrival of Gilbert and Sullivan's *Mikado* by eight years.

He is important because of his *Samson et Dalila* (*Samson and Delilah*). He, too, wrote operas about "naughty" women, Phryne and

Delilah. Delilah it was who betrayed Samson by learning the secret of his strength—his hair. The story, from the Bible, is well told in music. It is like an oratorio with great choruses and a ballet, and it shows Saint-Saëns's orchestration, purity of form and clearness of speech, musical and verbal.

One of the significant songs is *"Mon coeur s'ouvre à ta voix"* ("My Heart at Thy Sweet Voice"). Before the curtain rises, a chorus of Israelites, beseeching the intervention of Jehovah, shows Saint-Saëns's ability to write fugal music. Delilah has an enjoyable song in the first act, *"Printemps qui commence"* ("Spring Voices Are Singing"). And at the end, when she makes an offering to the heathen god, she sings triumphantly, "Dagon, Be Ever Praised." The altar fire flares up and a pagan bacchanale is danced by the maidens, which is finished with an exotic use of the woodwinds. This bacchanale, and the revel of Act II, are vivid uses of the opera ballet in the newer French manner.

The book of the opera is by Ferdinand Lemaire, and its first performance was at the Hoftheater in Weimar, Germany, in 1877. America saw it first at the French Opera House in New Orleans (1893), and it opened at the Metropolitan in New York in 1895.

SYMPHONICALLY EXPERT

Saint-Saëns was a master of symphonic and orchestral music. He influenced opera very little except to impress his followers with the importance of balance—not too much of any one thing (the ancient Greek ideal) and clarity of expression. He came to America as an organist and pianist at the age of eighty-one and played at the World's Fair in San Francisco, New York and other cities. He is said to have worn white cotton gloves when composing!

JULES MASSENET

Of all the collections of maidens in the whole realm of opera, Jules Massenet had the largest. Many of his operas bear the names of these attractive girls who were unhappy or happy heroines, such as *Thaïs,* who had a struggle between her good and her bad nature; *Manon,* who gave in mostly to her bad nature and came to a tragic end; *Sappho; The Queen of Sheba; Mireille; Cendrillon (Cinderella); Grisélidis (Griselda);* etc. He wrote many others, including the captivating *Le Cid (The Lord),* the name given by the Arabs to the Spanish hero Roderigo Diaz de Bivar (died in 1099).

Jules Massenet (1842–1912) was not an opera reformer as were Gluck, Weber and Wagner, nor did he have the genius of Mozart or Debussy. But he did show that a master with a feeling for good plots—who could write tuneful music and clever orchestration—and with a desire to please his audience, could succeed. With nearly thirty operas, all of which were produced before his death, he was unusual because he witnessed his own glory.

He wasn't bothered by theories about music; and no other writer of opera has had such easy success. He told tragic, romantic and often oversentimental stories. He did not write his own librettos, but knew well how to follow the French tradition.

The Massenets were poor when Jules was born. His father died when he was a child, and his mother had to support the family as a piano teacher. She gave Jules lessons which he seemed to like. At eleven he was ready to enter the Conservatory. At twenty-one he began to win prizes. He was clever. In a competition he had handed in a libretto which was turned down, but in 1887 he wrote the opera *The King of Lahore* using the same libretto, changed a bit, with a fantastic Turkish story ending in a fairy tale, and it was accepted.

MANON

Massenet's most successful opera is *Manon,* with book by Henri Meilhac and Philippe Gille. It was given first at the Opéra Comique in 1884, a very tragic opera about a young, refined and charming "moll" of yesterday. She loved luxury and money. She had no conscience, but great beauty and was always able to capture the love of impressionable men. This Mademoiselle Manon Lescaut was a favorite character with the French. The story was written first by Abbé Prevost d'Exiles and was used by several composers, among them Halévy, Balfe, Leoncavallo, and Auber. But the only other successful opera about this engaging sinner was Puccini's *Manon Lescaut.*

Like most of Massenet's operas, *Manon* has elaborate scenery, beautiful orchestration; also—as post-Wagnerian—continuous music, re-use of melodic phrases, lavish decoration; and, unlike Wagner, is lavishly sentimental. Instead of the dry recitative of the past, Massenet likes spoken dialogue over a subdued and pleasant orchestral accompaniment. This is an innovation and appears continually.

The opera is full of melodious songs in which Massenet can paint, paradoxically, impending doom with a lilt! In Act II, the famous dream song, *"Le Rêve,"* is heard. There are many other engaging songs in *Manon* which would take too much space to include here.

The première of *Manon* took place at the Opéra Comique in 1884; *Manon* first bowed to American audiences in 1885, at the New York Academy of Music; and had its première at the Metropolitan ten years later, 1895.

To a colleague who asked him to write his opinions of the new trends in music, Massenet said in a letter: "If you ask me for a melody, I shall do my best to satisfy you, but to write an article is something I cannot do." When his opera *Esclaramonde* (1889) was first produced, a critic called him "Mademoiselle Wagner," to which peculiar criticism Massenet responded, "I shall consider myself fortunate to reach his ankles." He was not a Wagnerian follower, but developed little designs and samples or suggestions of designs placed in the solid color of the cloth. He used the motifs more in the style of Gounod. Although it was continuous music too, it is broken by "take-out-able" songs.

SAGE COUNSEL

Massenet's miracle opera, *Le Jongleur de Notre Dame* (*The Juggler of Notre Dame,* 1902), though given rarely, is one of the most delightful stories ever put to music. One of the lovely and unforgettable songs is in Act II, when the cook, Boniface, sings *"Légende de la sauge"* ("Legend of the Sage Bush"), which tells how the simple sage bush sheltered the Christ Child and how the Savior could love and respect the humble.

The book of the opera is by Maurice Léna, after a story by Anatole France, and the opera was first given in the Théâtre Monte Carlo, 1902. The Paris première was in 1904, and the American opening at Hammerstein's Manhattan Opera House, New York, 1909. Mary Garden played the male role of the youthful Juggler with enchantment, as she did Thaïs, Mélisande, Louise and other parts all differing from each other.

Werther (1903), based on Goethe's *Sorrows of Werther,* is considered by many to be Massenet's best opera. It is a drama dripping with the most intensely Romantic-Period variety of love and intrigue. It ends in poor Werther's suicide brought on by his futile struggle to win Charlotte, the lady of his dreams, who he knew was wed to another. Says H. T. Finck, in his *Massenet and His Operas:*

Thackeray, in his satire on the "Sorrows of Werther" summed up the situation less tragically:

Charlotte, having seen his body
Born before her on a shutter,
Like a well-conducted person,
Went on cutting bread and butter.

Knowing the era in France and the love of Massenet for "soul-tragedy," Georges Hartmann, the poet, suggested to Massenet *The Sorrows of Werther* as a libretto, and said: "...Doesn't this paradox tempt you to give us at least one virtuous woman on your stage...you, who have given us so many courtesans..." (from *Massenet and His Operas*). Massenet acquiesced, and Hartmann within a few days collaborated with Paul Milliet and Edouard Blau, and showed Massenet the sketches. He liked them immensely.

The opera has some exquisite music, and includes the Christmas songs sung by the children. Werther's famous song, "Do Not Wake Me," or "The Song of Ossian," is another high point in the opera. The first performance took place in the Hofoper, Vienna, in 1892. It was introduced to America in 1894 at the Metropolitan Opera House.

THAÏS

Known to most of us is the too-often repeated, but charming intermezzo, "Meditation" from *Thaïs*. Like Mascagni's *Cavalleria rusticana* and even Wolf-Ferrari's *The Jewels of the Madonna, Thaïs* achieved broad-spread fame with the intermezzo. Nevertheless, *Thaïs* is one of the most admired of the Massenet operas. It is the struggle of a gloriously beautiful woman and a pious monk, between their bad and their good natures. The music is in his best vein.

Thaïs, in three acts, is a very good object lesson in the difference between a French drama and an Italian or German opera. Here there is little waste of time with unimportant characters. The drama lies between these two people, and with all its feeling and incident, it never overflows into melodrama or bad taste. This ticklish subject, the love of a monk for a courtesan whom he has reformed, and whose advances he had repelled, is handled with the delicacy of the French. The book is by Louis Gallet, based on Anatole France's famous novel of the same name.

Its first performance was at the Opéra, in Paris (1894). Mary Garden sang *Thaïs* at its American première in 1907 at Hammerstein's Manhattan Opera House. The Metropolitan Opera Company gave *Thaïs* in 1917, with Geraldine Farrar in the name role.

In *Hérodiade,* Massenet deals with not only one "bad" girl, but two —Salome and her wicked mother, Herodias. This is a version of the Biblical story of Salome and John the Baptist, on another version of which Richard Strauss has given a more clashing, sordid, and a more profound musical account. Although Strauss's has a more powerful impact and is a greater dramatic and musical work, Massenet's opera is more tuneful, more polite, and fits the era and pace of the opera-goers of his day.

There is a picturesque, exotic ballet, of course, and the two most important songs are *"Il est doux, il est bon"* ("He Is Kind, He Is Good") sung by Salome in Act I, and *"Vision fugitive"* ("Fleeting Vision") sung in Act II by Herod, who recalls the vision of Salome.

This opera, in four acts, with book by Paul Milliet, Henri Grémont and Georges Hartmann opened at the Théâtre de la Monnaie in Brussels, 1881, and was produced in Paris three years later at the Théâtre des Italien. The American première took place in 1892 in New Orleans, and the opera reached New York in 1909 at Hammerstein's Manhattan Opera House.

This master of poignant pastel shades in music (if such is possible), as Wagner was a master of warm and often hot colors, has given vast pleasure to millions of people all over the world. He was not an innovator, but a server of simple and effectively melodious operatic fare.

Massenet had been honored all his much-enjoyed life. His *Memoirs of a Musician* is fascinating. He composed nearly up to his death in 1912. He lived on, to some extent, in some of his pupils, among whom are Gustave Charpentier, composer of *Louise,* and Henri Constant Gabriel Pierné, composer of the oratorio *The Children's Crusade* and of the well-known "Entrance of the Little Fauns" from the ballet *Cydalise et le Chèvrepied (Cydalise and the Faun).*

CHARPENTIER A FRENCH REALIST

Gustave Charpentier was born in 1860, and lived in France until his death in 1949. The allure of *Louise* is that Paris, the city, is the real character in the opera seen through the media of Louise and her lover, Julien, who are as Parisian as its bricks and mortar. In this play, realism is at its most fascinating point. That is, you get the streets of Paris and their noises and the songs of vendors, the homes and the life in them, and the *ateliers* or shops and the tingling variety of a vibrant city. When you leave the opera *Louise* you almost feel that you have been to Paris.

Gustave Charpentier's music flows without interruption and blesses with lovely songs. It is more modern in tonal combinations or harmony than his master's. His ballets are the street crowds, and when *Louise* is crowned by a group of pleasure-loving Parisians, called Bohemians, the scene is accompanied by a most effective ballet chorale.

In the modern spirit, and a little bit like Wagner, Charpentier brings in, slyly, the questions of morality and the relations of parents and children. Charpentier wrote his musical romance on his own libretto, and it has been one of the most successful in the repertory of French opera. It may have been a forerunner to influence composers in the social possibilities of opera.

He uses leitmotif in the French way, as did Gounod and Massenet, not developed, like Wagner, but accenting the ideas of the plot. The best known song is *"Depuis le Jour"* ("Ever Since the Day"), which Louise sings in the garden of the home that she and Julien have established without the blessing of her parents or the Church. Parts of this song are heard throughout the opera. Other singable melodies are the "Awakening of Paris" and the occasional street cries which paint, in tone, the kaleidoscopic city. It is a love story between Louise and Julien, true childen of Paris. At the end, they refuse to return to her father's home and Julien curses Paris with the song beginning, "Oh, Paris."

Louise is in four acts and was given first at the Opéra Comique in Paris in 1900, on April 12, when Mary Garden in the title role made her first appearance on any stage. She made her debut in America in the same role, at Oscar Hammerstein's Manhattan Opera House, in 1907.

THERE ARE OTHERS!

Among the other late nineteenth century composers who have one or two operas to their credit, are: Edouard Victor Lalo with *Le Roi d'Ys,* and Benjamin Godard, with his *Jocelyn,* whose "Lullaby" is known to everyone.

SCENE III

National Spirit Is Rife—Spain, Bohemia, and Other European Countries; South America and Israel

OF ALL the European nations, Spain seems to have been the last to realize that she had abundant folk song and rhythmic dances. Besides Spain's long use of her dearly beloved rhythms, castanets and guitars gave a characteristic national tang to her music.

ZARZUELAS AND TONADILLAS

As soon as Spain awakened to her "gold mine" of music, she remembered her old *zarzuelas,* a kind of Singspiel or vaudeville, with Spanish songs, dances, and speech. They were often pathetic, however, mostly gay, usually in one act, informal and unimportant. The *Zarzuela Grand* in three acts could be serious. The name *zarzuela* comes from the town of Zarzuela (not far from Madrid), near which these performances were first given in the seventeenth century. They make a colorful basis for a national opera, like the *tonadilla,* invented in 1757 by Luis Misson of Madrid. The first tonadilla was a duet between the landlady and a needy Bohemian. All tell of simple scenes of popular life and are very Spanish.

At first the zarzuelas were given new life by composers such as Francisco Asenyo Barbieri (1823–94), a composer of comic opera. He began to use fifteenth- and sixteenth-century songs and gave Spanish composers their first taste of the enormous Spanish musical "pie." Then he produced over seventy zarzuelas, and influenced not only Spaniards but South American composers as well.

FELIPE PEDRELL

Many composers awoke and joined the nationalistic musical movement. The greatest of them all was Felipe Pedrell (1841–1922). It was not so much what he wrote, although he wrote books and fine music, but what he *did* for Spanish opera, church music, and every other kind of music. He delved years back among the ancient Spanish documents and published the complete works of Tomás Luis de Victoria (1535–1613), who ranks with Palestrina. Yet even in his fatherland, Victoria was practically unknown until Pedrell unearthed him.

Pedrell worked to impress Spaniards that folk music was the basis for a nationalistic music. His operas: *Los Pirineos* (*The Pyrenees*), a trilogy of three dramas; and *La Celestina,* both show consummate skill. He tried to use Wagnerian ideas in Spanish music, but Wagnerians didn't like it.

Pedrell was acknowledged by the world as a great musicologist (student of the history of music). His own people did not appreciate him. Now they know his value. Manuel de Falla (1876–1948) acknowledged him. From then on, his noted pupils, Izaak Albeniz (piano works and orchestral suites) and all the rest, including Granados and de Falla, made superb use of the rich music of Spain, as in the latter's opera *La Vida Breve* (*Life Is Short*), given at the Metropolitan in 1926 in New York.

SPANISH INFLUENCE—GRANADOS

Spanish music is somewhat like American jazz—it travels. You can hear it in the works of other men in other countries, and in the Spain-derived states of the United States; in the operas *Carmen* by Bizet, *Le Cid* by Massenet with its Spanish dances, *L'Heure Espagnole* (*Spanish Time*) by Ravel; *Habañera* by Raoul Laparra; orchestral scores, *Iberia* by Debussy, "The Spanish Symphony" by Lalo, "The Spanish Rhapsody" by Chabrier, "The Spanish Capriccio" of Rimsky-Korsakov, "Spanish Dances" of Moszkowski; and the music of California, New Mexico, and Texas, to say nothing of Latin America. But the first Spanish opera ever given at the Metropolitan Opera House was *Goyescas* by Enrique Granados (1867–1916). It was called *Goyescas* because it was inspired by the characters and canvases of the great painter Goya, as were also some of the tonadillas of Misson. In this opera you can see the national idea in music delightfully. It is a musical painting of Spain, a picture recreated in music.

Granados came to the United States in 1916 for the production of his *Goyescas* at the Metropolitan. As he was returning to Spain, his ship was struck by a shell from a submarine in the English Channel, and he perished. That was one of the grievous extravagances of World War I.

BOHEMIA (CZECH)

The Czechoslovaks (Bohemians) are among the most musical people of the world. Prague welcomed Gluck, Mozart, Weber, and other musicians, and was always an oasis for composers forgotten or snubbed in their own countries before the Russian domination after the Second World War.

SMETANA

Bedřich (Friedrich) Smetana (Smet'-a-na) was born in Bohemia in 1824 and died there in 1884. He was the son of a brewer, and at five could improvise tunes on the violin. Although starting out as a violinist, he became a pianist and composer of small pieces, particularly the polka, the beloved dance of his people. After much opposition he was allowed to study music. He went through hardship for his love.

Smetana took part in the Revolution of 1848, and later was given permission to organize a school of music. Here again, Liszt helped nationalism in music, for earlier he had taught Bedrich, and later gave him the money he needed. Liszt was a "one man national aid society."

THE BARTERED BRIDE

Apart from *My Country,* a series of tone poems for orchestra, in which the wondrous Moldau River music touches the hearts of men, and his string quartet, *"Aus meinem Leben"* ("From My Life," 1855) and other orchestral and vocal works, Smetana started Czech national opera with his amusing and tuneful *The Bartered Bride.* Here he used folk-like music to give the gayest picture of peasant life. It is probably one of the most popular operas outside of its native heath, and its polka and overture are often heard apart from the opera. *The Bartered Bride* is a national musical photograph, filled with characteristic tunes and dance rhythms and the brusque humor of the Czechs. It shows the influence of Mozart in its lilt and gaiety. The difference between the stories of Mozart's comic operas and Smetana's is that Mozart wrote about the middle and upper classes, Smetana about peasants. Some have called him "the peasant Mozart."

Like Beethoven, Smetana became deaf. Unlike Beethoven, his mind became unbalanced before he died. In spreading the power of national traits in opera and helping the young Dvořák, Smetana was a wholesome influence on opera.

The Bartered Bride is neither "hifalutin" nor apart. It is a killingly funny story. In its own country you think that the audience itself is part of the opera! Smetana was adored by his countrymen as the first "really and truly" Czech composer. His music *is* Czechoslovakia, even as Mussorgsky's is Russia. Smetana wrote nine operas.

DVOŘÁK, A BELOVED MASTER

Although Anton Dvořák was a greater man of music than his fellow patriot Smetana, none of his operas is known outside of Bohemia. Yet his *Rusalka* must be mentioned among the Bohemian national operas. Dvořák was a disciple of Smetana, but his choral, chamber, and symphonic works spread out over the world. Whereas Smetana's polkas are to Bohemia what the mazurka is to Poland, or the spiritual and jazz are to America, Dvořák's dances, with characteristic usage of the *dumka* (elegy) and *scherzo,* are international. Smetana kept the freshness of folk art. Dvořák was more sophisticated even though influenced by folk art. He was a master of the orchestra, as "fertile as Schubert." This son of a butcher and innkeeper was one of the world's greatest composers and became rich, famous, and, above all, remained simple in heart and generous in spirit.

Dvořák spent a few years in New York City where he taught and wrote the "American Quartet" and the *New World Symphony.*

SCHWANDA AND JENUFA

But Jaromir Weinberger (1896–) has carried on national opera in his amusing *Schwanda, der Dudelsackpfeiffer (Schwanda, the Bagpiper).* It was given at the Metropolitan in 1931. This, *The Bartered Bride,* and *Jenufa* by Leoš Janáček (1854–1928) are the three Czech operas well-known in many parts of the world. *Jenufa,* given at the Metropolitan in 1924, is of a little corner of Bohemia, very localized and so quite national. It is founded on a play by Gabriela Preissova. It is tuneful, fresh, and engaging in its natural folk music and blithe dances. His *Katia Kabanova* is now (1955) enjoying a revival by Sadler's Wells in England.

QUARTER-TONE MAN

Alois Hába of Bohemia, born in 1893, wrote an opera, *Die Mutter (The Mother,* 1931) on a new series of intervals (quarter tones). No one yet has followed him, so he has contributed little to national opera.

A FEW MODERN ITALIANS

Among the modern Italians who have made their mark in instrumental work are Alfredo Casella (1883-1947), Ildebrando Pizzetti (1880-), and Ottorino Respighi (1879-1936). All three, true to their amazing inheritance, wrote operas which would hardly have made them famous. Casella wrote *La Giara* (*The Jar*), a ballet given at the Metropolitan in 1926; and the opera (1932) *La donna serpente* (literally *The Snake Woman*); Pizzetti wrote, among others, *Fra Gherardo*, given at the Metropolitan Opera House (1929) one year after its première at La Scala, Milan; and Respighi wrote several operas, the best known *La Campana sommersa* (*The Sunken Bell*), based on the Gerhart Hauptmann play, given at the Metropolitan in 1928, *La Fiamma* (*The Flame*), given in 1935 in Chicago.

His opera-oratorio *Maria Egiziaca* had its world première in a staged version by the New York Philharmonic Symphony Society, 1932, the composer conducting.

A MODERN HUNGARIAN

Although Béla Bartók (1881-1945) has written few operas, his influence on twentieth century music has been so important that to leave him out would be unforgiveable. As a nationalist, he and Zoltán Kodály (1882-) made vast researches into the folk music of their native Hungary. A rich store of folk tunes were uncovered which Bartók used with ultramodern harmonies.

His first opera *Bluebeard's Castle* in a text by Béla Balazs had its première in Budapest (1918) and was revived at the New York City Opera at the City Center in 1953, when it made a deep impression on music lovers.

Zoltán Kodály wrote a ballad opera founded upon popular Hungarian tunes which had its premère in Budapest in 1926. The overture is a popular concert number.

NATIONALISM IN OTHER EUROPEAN COUNTRIES

Poland, Scandinavia, Finland, Holland, Switzerland, and other European countries are not mentioned in this book at length only because their operas have had no influence on the development of opera itself, nor have they visited other countries sufficiently to influence the writing of opera elsewhere.

LATIN AMERICA

It would take a book much larger than this one to give an adequate record of the opera of Latin American composers in the twenty countries, even if we considered the works from only Chile, Colombia, and Argentina, where music is going ahead well. Most of these nations for many years followed pretty much the devices of Spain, Portugal, and Brazil. But for the last fifty years their output has been exceptionally high. Most of the composers write better in all other forms than opera, so they have not advanced the art. This is strange when we think of the Latin cousins, the Italians and French, as past masters of dramma per musica.

Nicolas Slonimsky has written an instructive and entertaining book, *Music of Latin America,* to the delight of all those who love its music.

ISRAELI OPERA

Although the new republic in the Middle East is too young to have built a national opera, yet it already recognizes the seeds in its colorful and revered history. Fortunately, this little republic has much local color, today as well as yesterday. That something in the way of opera is developing is demonstrated if only by its latest Festival in Ein Gev (1955) where two operas were given along with instrumental music.

One of these operas was *Vows,* by Karel Salomon, in two acts, finished in 1954. The librettist was the composer; and it was based on the period of Maimonides, who flourished in Islamic Spain and died seven hundred and fifty years ago. He lies buried in Tiberias, Israel, from where this account emanated. The other opera was *The Story of the Exodus,* written as folk opera with scenes of Egypt, Spain, and the Holy Land, with music by Menahem Avidon and the book by Leah Goldberg. Both these operas are rich in color of the Orient and the history of Israel, and the music is pleasantly modern.

Apart from their own operas they have welcomed old and new stage works of others, among them the première of Darius Milhaud's *David.* What more appropriate setting!

It is safe to augur well for Israeli opera and other types of music if only based upon the artistic contributions of those of Hebrew ancestry in America and other countries.

ACT VI. Opera—A Bundle of the Arts

SCENE I

The Librettist's Lot Is Not a Happy One

THE ways of composers with librettists are as changeable as the ways of a maid with a man. Some are overexacting; some are tyrannical; some choose the story and let the librettist write it; some accept an idea for a plot, as Massenet with *Werther* and Richard Strauss for *Der Rosenkavalier;* some outline a story for the librettist; and some write their own. There are as many ways to make a libretto as there are ways to skin a cat. And sometimes the skinner is the librettist; sometimes the cat is the opera; and sometimes the audience gets the skinning.

American laymen are often set against the opera librettist. They are prone to cast horrible aspersions on all opera librettos because they have often bought badly translated "books of the opera" in theater lobbies and therefore discredit the librettists. It is forgotten that at first the libretto was the chief consideration, and that their authors were important from Rinuccini through Molière, Metastasio who did too many, and Scribe (who followed with overproduction), to Boito, superb librettist for Verdi's *Falstaff* and *Otello;* and von Hoffmansthal, librettist for Strauss's *Elektra* and *Der Rosenkavalier.* Then, of course, there was Wagner, whose librettos are heavy reading, telegraphic in brevity. Nevertheless, they are worth more than being cast aside, for they are the bone of their operas. Therefore, it behooves opera-goers to read the libretto before condemning it. Better and better librettos should be forthcoming, if new operas are to live, and there are, unexpectedly, a few very good ones.

Sardou's play, *La Tosca* and Anatole France's *Thaïs* have been preserved through the operas based on them, because the librettist trusted the composer and relied on him for stressing and tying up points which the original plays neglected.

Yes, the librettist's life is not a happy one, and as for reputation, he gets little. Try to find the names of Carré, Meilhac, Ludovic Halévy, and others in music encyclopedias or even in many of the librettos offered for sale. Even when tied to their composers, most of their first names are missing.

MOZART AND LIBRETTISTS

Even Mozart, who complained no little of the treatment he received from people, rarely honored his librettists. Yet he did mention Caterino Mazzolà in connection with *The Clemency of Tito* (*La clemenza di Tito*), saying on the score that he had made a real opera out of it. Indeed, he had made it from a vapid Metastasio libretto, which, as usual, was all sunshine and starlight. But Mazzolà rescued it. Mozart acknowledged it. Alfred Einstein, in his noble volume *Mozart, His Character and His Work,* says: "This was an honor he did not even pay to Lorenzo da Ponte for his excellent *Marriage of Figaro, Don Giovanni,* or *Così Fan Tutte.* Only for *The Magic Flute* did he remember to mention the librettist's name, Schikeneder!"

It is not surprising, then, that da Ponte used the word "my" when speaking of the operas he wrote with Mozart. This is shown in his story of a friend who always went to sleep at operas but "who not only stayed awake all through my *Giovanni,* but all through the ensuing night." But there is no doubt with all respect to librettists that Mozart's constant warning, "Make it shorter," contributed to the life and glitter in his music and librettos.

Few librettos can stand without being hitched to an operatic score. Even those of Wagner, who wrote his own, are rarely read for pleasure, including the excellent one for *Die Meistersinger.* Naming the utterly independent libretto is not easy. Probably *Pelléas et Mélisande* would be listed along with some delightful English translations by Ruth and Thomas Martin, George Meade and Marion Farquhar. The fault, dear reader, is not in the poet or in the composer, but in the difficulties encountered when two or three try to write as one, each one in his own medium.

GOOD THEATER AND MOUNT NEVER-REST

There are some composers who know "good theater." Among them are Mozart, Wagner, Massenet, Puccini, Verdi, and Menotti and the best judge of these is Verdi. There are other composers who do not know what good theater is, and their operas fail because even librettists with dramatic instincts, poor souls, have been forced to contrive a story that will not act. But whatever he writes, or whoever writes it, the composer is or should always be the boss, the librettist always the. *under* writer. Yes, the librettist's lot is not a happy one. The only one with an unhappier lot is the composer himself. Should you want proof, without taking into consideration the "blood, sweat and tears" over composition itself, read H. W. Heinsheimer's *Menagerie in F Sharp* (Doubleday), in which he tells of the physical labor in writing the orchestral score alone, of its hundreds of pages, in which each instrument gets its own line. In addition to this there is the score for the chorus, the score for singers, and the later schedules and confabs on stage business, vast lighting plot, costumes, and scenery; all of which mounts into thousands of pages, a Mount Never-rest of work!

WHO IS WEISKERN, WHO IS HE?

Truly the librettist is the stepchild of opera. In one book on the history of opera, for example, the author speaks of the Singspiel written by Mozart at the age of twelve, *Bastien et Bastienne*. He tells us that it was based on a French vaudeville comedy by Favart. It required, of course, a tedious search to find the poor man's given name—Charles Simon (1710-92). His comedy was *The Love Affairs of Bastien and Bastienne*. It parodied Jean Jacques Rousseau's opera *Le Devin du village* (*The Village Soothsayer*). But who translated it into German? The writers, after much sleuthing, dug up two translators and librettists: (1) Andreas Schachtner, a valued assistant of Mozart from childhood on, and (2) Frederick Wilhelm Weiskern. This information is not vital, but it illustrates how neglected are the librettists and translators, unless, before contact with the composer, they have gathered some glory for themselves.

"NO THANKS"

In some cases the librettist is a well-known poet or writer. When asked by Aaron Copland to write a libretto, a writer snapped, "No thanks, no playwright wants his fine prose messed up by music." This may be an excellent reason, but there are others. Some can't work in harness, some dodge the drudgery of working with a composer to get scant acknowledgment and scanter royalties. The composer should always be the commander. The librettist has to be subservient, unless he be an extraordinary writer, or dramatist, or poet with experience, as for instance, Boito or von Hofmannsthal or Oscar Hammerstein II. But such librettists are hard to find.

AN IRRITATING TASK

The writing of an opera, with its libretto, is an irritating task, and a big one. Competitions for librettos have proved this. Hundreds have been submitted but rejected by composers. This may or may not have been owing to the librettist's lack of skill. It may well be because few composers know a good libretto when they get one. Those who choose librettos that will never "act" kill their operas. If all this were not true, there would be fewer new operas today that die on limping feet after the first, second or third production. Yet the composer wonders why!

A MIRACULOUS TRIO

A great librettist and a great composer can be seen at work by comparing a version of Shakespeare's *Othello* with Arrigo Boito's libretto for Verdi's *Otello*. The first thing to be noticed is that the libretto does not begin with Act I of the play. Far from it. Indeed, one act from it. Boito plunges into the second act of Shakespeare's drama. Why? Because, considering that it is to be used with music, it will *act* better. An arrival of a prince from the tempests of the sea is more dramatic in opera than a street scene where a few gentlemen chat. Yes, this has more drama, more punch, more interest, more glamour—when used with music. Many an opera writer forgets that glamour for opera, as for women, is the allure. A reading of the last two acts of *Othello* and the last pages of the libretto of *Otello* will illustrate the sense of drama, imagination, and ingenuity of Boito, librettist.

In the opera (fourth act and last) Boito concentrates events leading up to the murder, and the murder itself in the one act. Shakespeare does it in two acts (the fourth and fifth) because the interest is in the verse. Before the jealous, maddened husband arrives on the scene, Desdemona tells her handmaiden to lay her wedding sheets upon her bed. She tells Emelia of her youth in the most tender reminiscence. Then she sings the simple "Willow Song" in childlike Italian folk-music vein. Set to music, this scene shatters the audience. The naïve little song begins with the words, "The poor little soul sat pining." After this, she sings her tragedy-laden prayer, Verdi's unforgettable *"Ave Maria,"* ending in her plea for her adored Otello's salvation. This scene is one of the most soul-stirring in words, music and tenseness in the whole library of opera. Not only this, but it serves as a superb dramatic device to excite the audience, create suspense, and intensify the hatefulness and the inevitability of the murder which is intimated to the audience. The contrast of the simplicity of Desdemona with the horror to come is realized in every increasing wave of the music.

In the play there is no long Prayer Scene. This scene in the opera is one of the most poignantly written in all music drama. In the Shakespeare version, when Othello reaches Desdemona's bedside to strangle her, after a long and horrible dialogue about her impending doom, she merely asks for a respite before her death—"while I say one prayer." "It's too late," says Othello, and forthwith strangles her.

The comparison of the libretto of Boito with the play of Shakespeare is a rewarding adventure. It is a glimpse of what may make a drama act on the spoken stage, and what is needed for drama that acts on the lyric stage. Yet with all the high qualities this demands on the part of the librettist, how many realize that this libretto came from the pen of Arrigo Boito, composer of *Mefistofele?*

PELLÉAS ET MÉLISANDE

Maeterlinck's *Pelléas et Mélisande* is far less changed for Debussy's opera than was Shakespeare's play for Verdi's *Otello.* This may be because the play and the music of Maeterlinck and Debussy are both of the impressionistic era or the era when impressionism and mysticism instead of "hot" drama dominate "art." Boito, of course, could not pull Verdi and Shakespeare into the same art period. Being of the same era may account, too, for the miracle that the Pelléas of the libretto and the Pelléas of the opera seem to have been born for one another. Both words and music are of gossamer tissue, mystical, and serenely punctuated with understated climaxes. In this case the reputation of the dramatist, Maeterlinck, had been made before Debussy set the play to music.

THE MUSIC IS THE THING

Skills are indispensable to mate the syllables and accents of all languages to the dramatic situations and to the needs of the same music when adapting a libretto from one language to another. For the major battle between gifted librettists and gifted composers is the mating of the action, the syllable and the word to the individual note. Furthermore, the difficulty of getting a librettist sufficiently equipped (or one who can give his time to this most meticulous task) is tremendous. For besides all his skills he must enter into the emotional states of the composer and his music, only to be forgotten as have been so many librettists, including Ghislanzoni, librettist of *Aida,*

Nahum Tate, librettist of Purcell's *Dido and Aeneas* and Salvatore Cammerano, librettist for *Il Trovatore*.

If it be difficult to fit word to note, it is equally difficult to fit words to action. For example, the librettist has to give the acting singer the correct amount of time for "stage business." Barbier and Carré, those excellent librettists, gave Marguerite (*Faust*) in the Jewel Casket Scene just enough time to get her earrings out of the box and into her ears before she has to sing "The Jewel Song."

How then is a collaboration made? This is as difficult to outline as to tell you how married couples make marriage a success. There are many combinations of methods, but no set method. Some composers get the idea of a story, of a poem, of a book, of a play, of an incident, and mull it over in their minds and think, "This might make an opera." If there is a writer or a poet or a dramatist who thinks he is equipped to write a libretto and is convinced that he has a good idea, and knows the right composer, he may give him the idea, as Georges Hartmann did for Massenet's *Werther*. After long or short and tedious or delightful discussion, librettist or composer or both may make outlines of the poem or prose play to be set to music. It may, however, be done just the opposite way. The composer may have the idea, and have his opera sketched, and ask the librettist to write the poem or the book. He may have only a rhythm scheme. Then they get together and make the marriage as perfect as possible between word and music, and librettist and composer, even to doing what Lully did to the poet, Quinault—make him write scenes over as many as twenty times!

AN UNHAPPY LOT

Here is an instance of a little problem. The name of this scene is "The Librettist's Lot Is Not a Happy One." It parodies the line from Gilbert and Sullivan's *Pirates of Penzance* ("A Policeman's Lot Is Not a Happy One"). At first the title of this scene was "The Librettist's Lot Was an Unhappy One." Compare the one chosen. Notice how it swings. The "an" and the "un" coming together in the first version of the title is as unhappy as the lot of the librettist.

From Act III of *The Pirates of Penzance,* sing these two titles with the proper word put in: "A Policeman's Lot Is Not a Happy One." Note how this distinguished line might have been made awkward, and then forgotten. This seems to be a small problem, but it isn't, of course, and is only one of the complexities that come up to cause friction and trouble between the librettist and the composer. Collaboration takes maturity combined with mutual understanding, mutual respect and patience.

Another host of agonies occurs when an opera's libretto is changed from one language to another.

A LIBRETTO'S A LIBRETTO FOR A' THAT

The libretto is designated in many ways:

1. Libretto "after" the French of du Locle by Ghislanzoni, as was *Aïda.*

2. Libretto "after" the drama *Faust,* which means that the librettist made changes in Goethe's *Faust* for Gounod's opera.

3. The libretto may be called a book, and it may be by the composer or by a librettist, or with verses only supplied by librettists, as in the case of Wolf-Ferrari's *The Jewels of the Madonna,* with book by the composer and verses by Carlo Zangarini and Enrico Golisciani.

4. The libretto may be built on more than one play or book, as was Verdi's *Falstaff,* based chiefly on Shakespeare's *The Merry Wives of Windsor* with bits from *Henry IV* and put together brilliantly by Arrigo Boito.

5. When "words by" is used, it can mean the story or book.

6. When the libretto is "based on," it usually means that the idea has been taken from a narrative or poem.

7. "Book" usually means the book or the story which the librettist writes for the opera or the book given to a librettist to change into a libretto.

VERDI AND LIBRETTIST AT WORK

When Verdi was considering the opera *Il Trovatore,* he wrote to his librettist, Salvatore Cammerano: "The subject I should like and which I suggest is *Il Trovador,* a Spanish drama by Gutierez. It seems to me very fine, rich in ideas and in strong situation. [Note Verdi's emphasis on strong situation, or "good theater."] I should like to have two feminine roles. First the Gypsy, a woman of unusual character, after whom I want to name the opera; the other part for a secondary singer. So be up and doing, young man, and on with the work. It can't be hard to find the Spanish drama . . ."

This is the way the collaboration for *Il Trovatore* began. It will be noticed that Verdi did not in the end call the opera *Azucena* (pronounced As-you-*chai*-nah), after the Gypsy, but *Il Trovatore.* How much argument went on between Cammerano and Verdi is not recorded.

Here is Verdi writing again to his librettist, Salvatore Cammerano, about an opera, *The Battle of Legnano* (*La Battaglia di Legnano*), given in Rome in 1849, a few months before his better-known *Luisa Miller,* and two years before *Rigoletto,* his greatest success up to that time. Notice how courteous the young Verdi was, when he asked a difficult task of his librettist:

May I ask a favor of you in connection with the last act? At the beginning, in front of the temple of Saint Ambrose, I would like to bring together two or three different melodies; for example, I would like both the priests inside and the people outside to have a text in the same poetic metre, and Lida a song with a different metre. Leave the task of putting them together to me. You might even (if you think right) give the priests some little Latin verses. Do whatever you think best, but be sure that this situation makes a dramatic effect.

Here is another letter. Note Verdi's definite command to be dramatic, which, too, is no easy task:

I am still waiting for an answer to my letter acknowledging receipt of the Third Act. I particularly asked you in that letter to add a scene for the prima donna. I hope you will be so friendly as to do me this favor. In case you didn't receive the letter, I repeat my wishes here. Since the lady's role doesn't seem to me to have the importance of the other two, I would like you to add, after the *Death Chorus,* a great agitated recitative, in which she expresses her love, her despair at Arrigo's being doomed to die, her fear of being discovered and so on. After a beautiful recitative, have the husband arrive and do a moving little duet. Have the father bless his son, or something of that sort and so on.

One more last tiny favor I want: At the end of the Second Act, I should like four verses....

I want these verses powerful and vigorous. I should like them to express the following idea: "A time will come when your descendants will shrink in horror from bearing your name."

Here Verdi became anxious and exceedingly definite. He even thinks he is being exacting, for he says, "One more last *tiny* favor." This, to any layman, does not seem a tiny favor, nor is it a tiny favor, to have to meet the inward urge of a great composer. Then again he says in this same letter to Cammerano:

And tell me, too: don't be frightened! I need another voice in the ensemble of the introduction, a tenor. Could we put in one of Arrigo's shield-

bearers? I should think we could use him in the finale too. He could
support Arrigo when he is wounded. Answer me this too.

Here again, Verdi, implying that he does not want to overwork the
librettist, does so in spite of himself for the good of his drama.

In the same letter, he says:

I know you are rehearsing *Macbeth* and since it is an opera which interests
me more than all my others, you will permit me to say a few words
about it.

Here the librettist is seen at the opera house assisting in the production of an opera, the play by Shakespeare and the opera Verdi's.

(Excerpts from the letters above are taken from *Verdi, The Man in
His Letters,* edited by Franz Werfel and Paul Stefan.)

AUDIENCE INTEREST

Nowhere does it seem more evident than in the building of *Manon*
by Jules Massenet that audience interest with all other technical
problems must be considered. There is no doubt that Puccini built an
excellent opera in *Manon Lescaut* and that Auber too made a good
opera out of the same Abbé Prevost's *Tragic History of Manon Lescaut
and of the Count des Grieux*—so attractive that Dickens doted on it.
But Massenet's librettists, with uncanny skill, made the "naughty gal"
less wicked than attractive, and lured rather than alienated audiences.
Auber, Balfe, Halévy, Piccinni, Puccini, Massenet and others wrote
operas based on Manon's tragic tale, but the most popular of these is
Massenet's. He was lucky to have Henri Meilhac and Philippe Gille
for librettists, but who knows it? Even Balfe's opera on the same
tragedy hasn't lived and "The Laughing Song" in Auber's *Manon
Lescaut* didn't act as a preservative! Puccini's favorite opera, *Manon
Lescaut,* is revived often and gets righteous acclaim.

STRAUSS AND VON HOFMANNSTHAL

Richard Strauss had his disagreements with von Hofmannsthal but
they were always resolved. Strauss thought that the first draft of the
libretto for *Der Rosenkavalier* was gay, but he didn't think it would
"pull" a real laugh from the audience. Yet he made it known to his
librettist that he didn't want to make the opera an imitation of *Figaro*
or *Die Meistersinger.* Then again Strauss didn't want a too literary
second act which couldn't rise dramatically. All these things and many,

many more made for argument and discussion. Rightly, Strauss won out. Von Hofmannsthal was big enough to realize that the composer must be the final arbiter. So this librettist both for Strauss's *Elektra* (after Sophocles) and *Der Rosenkavalier* made a mature collaboration ending in two of the greatest operas of the early twentieth century.

THE BIRTH OF LIBRETTISTS

The first opera librettist may be said to have been Ottavio Rinuccini, who was born in Florence in 1562 and died there in 1621. He was a poet who wrote the poems for Peri's *Dafne* and *Euridice*. He was a member of the Camerata (see Act II, Scene I). He wrote the libretto for Monteverdi's *Arianna* and did himself proud in the ballet *Ballo dell' ingrata*. The librettist at the time of the Camerata had the new task of fitting poetry to a new method of music and a new kind of musical speech (recitative).

LIBRETTO INDUSTRIES

It wasn't long before libretto "factories" began to standardize stories for opera to the point of fatiguing audiences. Dante, Petrarch, Boccaccio and Ariosto had not long been left behind when Apostolo Zeno (1668–1750) began writing librettos for Venetian operas. He was a poet of highest standing and a laureate to the King, besides taking part in important historical research. Yet with all his attainments there is but a half a line in the *Encyclopaedia Britannica* and nothing in Grove's *Dictionary of Music and Musicians*. Thompson's *Cyclopedia of Music and Musicians* gives eight lines, but doesn't mention any composer with whom he collaborated.

METASTASIO

Then followed Pietro Metastasio, a laureate, beloved of Voltaire, and writer of graceful and charming but not too dramatic verse. He tried to cure the rash of humor that spread all over Venetian opera. He succeeded far too well, and helped to stiffen opera. Yet this did not keep the European world of music from using his librettos. With few changes, his stories and verses were used over and over again. In whatever opera, site, legend, nationality or characters, the plots were practically the same! There were, however, a few differences in color and style of costumes! The same kind of voices sang the same kind of song, and everybody married the right mate in the end. Exciting! In such librettos there was no suspense. The audience knew what was coming, so you can readily understand how opera became static and almost unpalatable. It was at this point, suggests the erudite Dr. Edward Dent, that the Victorian opera in England "took off" with its staid and circumspect plots and moral conclusions.

Pietro Metastasio was known all over Europe. He was born in Rome in 1698. (This was close to the time of the Salem witchcraft delusion in Massachusetts and he lived until six years after the American Declaration of Independence was signed.) He wrote for the known and unknown composers of his time, Hasse, Mozart, Dr. Arne in England, and the famous Nicola Piccinni who lost his contest with Gluck. His masterpieces in verse finally put the hand of death on their operas. Few or none of them, mated with his super-conventional poems, tread the stage today. Metastasio's plots were too exasperatingly goody-good! Nearly all the complexes were founded, not on too much villainy, but on too much chivalry. Indeed, *Après vous, Gaston!* ("After you, Gaston!") was a Metastasio and Zeno basis for librettos, but not for the conduct between the singers. "*Me* first!" was their motto.

Opera in the days of the poets Zeno and Metastasio had slipped from the dramatic antique to the opera of luxury and splendor. Zeno's librettos stressed the softer side of the picture while Metastasio gloried in killing off his heroes!

EUGÈNE SCRIBE, THE SCRIBE

If ever there was a good name for a librettist who was an inveterate writer (scribe) Monsieur Scribe (1791–1861) had the best. He did a bigger business in libretto manufacture than anyone before or since. Before 1830, when he was thirty-nine years old, he had furnished to one theater in Paris over 150 plays or librettos! He had a well organized industry. He employed a number of aides; some wrote the stories, others the dialogue, and yet others the jokes. He is said to have sent many sums of money for copyrighting ideas to men who didn't even realize that he had annexed their material. At least Scribe was honest! He wrote independent dramas of every kind. After Scribe's death his work was gathered into seventy-six volumes, including three complete operas of his own. Among the men for whom he wrote librettos were: Boieldieu, Auber, Verdi, Meyerbeer, Halévy and countless others. He was famous enough to have a street in Paris named for him! (Every American knows rue Scribe.) This "industrialist" was lucky to have been born in Europe when new operas were as frequent, and of as little permanent value, as new movies are today in America.

Scribe died in Paris in 1861, a few months before the fall of Fort Sumpter in the American Civil War.

CONCLUSION

What would have happened to the advancement of opera by Gluck had he not met Raniero di Calzabigi?

What would have happened if Mozart had not met Lorenzo da Ponte (1749–1838) whose libretto for *The Marriage of Figaro* is as sparkling now as it was in his own day? He composed this long before Cesare Sterbini wrote the libretto for Rossini's *Barber of Seville,* both of which were founded on comedies by P. A. Caron Beaumarchais—*Le Mariage de Figaro* and *Le Barbier de Seville.* Da Ponte was banished from Europe, went to New York and became a professor of Italian at Columbia University.

What would have happened if Giuseppe Verdi had not had the good luck to have Arrigo Boito write the libretto of his two greatest operas, during what might have been Verdi's declining, but were instead his transcendent, years?

What would have happened if Sir Arthur Sullivan had not met William Schwenk Gilbert? For, as lovesome as is the music of these gems, the librettos are even more tangy. Furthermore, these librettos are among the few that can "stand without hitching" to operas. Few librettos like these Gilbert lyrics are treasured for themselves alone.

Would Amilcare Ponchielli's *La Gioconda,* the best of his operatic brood, have lived had not Arrigo Boito, under the anagrammatic (rearranged letters) name of Tobia Gorrio, written the libretto?

The subject of librettos and librettists is vast. This is hoped to be but a peephole into the complex relationships of librettist, composer and audience. This much, however, is certain:

There are some librettos that are good and cannot act. There are poor librettos that can act. These are the facts that the new opera writers must learn. Mozart, for instance, could turn a poor libretto into a beautiful opera. Aaron Copland and Howard Hanson and others as erudite have not as yet demonstrated that power, although the fine quality of their music cannot be denied.

SCENE II

The Song of Opera

THE GROWTH OF SONG

FROM the time the Camerata attempted to set a story to music in the early seventeenth century, until the early eighteenth, song was music's chief element. This is partly because the song could better carry a story and partly because instruments were still in their infancy and were not yet as expressive in an ensemble as the voice. As the skills of composers advanced and instruments became more expressive, a tussle arose between voices and instruments. The voices won, because they had strong advocates among the sopranos and tenors who domineered over librettist and composer up through Handel's time—and even later. The struggle is still on!

THE "RIVER OF SONG"

Consider the following when listening to singing. W. J. Henderson, onetime music critic of the New York *Evening Sun,* said, "... to sing beautifully demands first and foremost a perfectly pure tone delivered in the sustained and smooth stream [of sound]. This is the true river of song. Upon its surface the shimmer of sunlit wavelets, or ornament or passage work, shall float calmly and securely, diversifying its beauty, but not fundamentally altering it."

A famous singer of long ago (200 years) said, "... the voice must come forth neat and clear, without passing through the nose or being choked in the throat." He might have added too, that it is most important to sing in tune!

IN THE EARLY DAYS

Singing is older than speech, if we consider as a form of singing: shouting, grunting, war whoops and squeals. So, it is safe to say that

245

THE GENERAL CLASSIFICATION OF VOICES

*Tenor an octave lower than here written.

These ranges are flexible in either direction. (Contralto is low vocal range for women's voices.) Adapted from *Early History of Singing* by W. J. Henderson, Longmans, Green and Company.

what we call singing today, the essential of opera, began very early in the march of the human race and on the conscious road of opera.

FOLK AND COMPOSED SONGS

From the earliest times there was the song of the folk in simple expressions in music of work, play, sorrow, sickness, love, crime, punishment, worship and every ritual known to mankind. Popular songs, rising spontaneously from the people, took hold, even as today. As time went on and people became more educated, if not more civilized, the song that accompanied dances, games, the hunt and other pursuits, began to stand alone as art songs, or as *composed* songs for shows, spectacles, and finally opera. So we have two kinds of song; the song composed by *Mr. Nobody Knows Who* and by the Composer. Today songs of Irving Berlin and Stephen Foster are also among the composed group, yet they are for the most part in the folk-song class.

THE CHURCH STARTED IT

Singing as an art had its start in the religious music of the Church. Its business was to mirror the feeling for God, the saints and morality, and to accompany rituals. It did not use intimate music to reflect human care, tragedy and fun, as our music does today. Therefore, the noble and stately Gregorian chant (originally sung in unison without accompaniment) was unexcelled for the purity of religious ecstasy, but later, when music was used in opera for stories, like Monteverdi's *Arianne* or Gluck's *Orfeo et Euridice* and human feelings, the chant didn't do at all.

Because of the unison singing maintained by Gregorian or plain chant, the solo song had no easy road to travel. Plain song or chant led singing away from the rhythm of strophic or verse-structured song and action. Notwithstanding its influence, however, secular songs, such as those of the folk and the minstrel, were sung with accompaniment of instruments, and in solo form. And, according to Dante and Boccaccio, solos were sung by the "higher ups" to the accompaniment of lute or pipe (flute) as early as the fourteenth century. These solos were songs with verses (strophes) and refrains—the popular frottola dressed up. With all these solo song beginnings, the art of song and instrumental accompaniment went through many stages. It traveled from Organum and Discant up through Polphony to Harmony with tune and accompaniment and to Twentieth-Century Song, which must fend for itself against wayward instrumental accompaniment or difficult vocalization. (See *Music Through the Ages,* by Bauer and Peyser.)

Gregorian music, too, had become elaborate and gathered to itself trills, runs and passage work.

DESCANT

Ornamentation in the singing of church music began to dislodge its simple strength. The troubadours, many of whom were trained in the Church abbeys, sang their secular ballads and songs with the same florid ornament that the Church had adopted. Church music remained slow-moving and quite logically religious in feeling.

As time went on, a change came about. One singer carried or held a melody, while one or more sang other parts around it. Among other names, this was called *descant.* The melody or music that was sung by the tenor was called the *cantus firmus,* or the fixed tune. This kind of singing, after song had gone through the stages of from three to eight voiced madrigals and the *frottola,* the song with a refrain, spread to music outside of the Church and helped, in the long run, to create the harmonic style.

These *descanters* were the ancestors of the *virtuosi* (top opera singers) of Handel's day. One of the early criticisms of the florid singing and the theatrical gesturing was made by a Scottish clergyman who complained bitterly of the gestures, the rolling eyes and the "singers' whinnies, like horses!"

In 1323, about the time the Hundred Years War began in Europe, Pope John XXII, realizing the harm that over-ornamentation was to pure Gregorian chant, forbade it.

THE FIRST SINGING SCHOOL

A hundred and fourteen years after the destruction of Rome (476) Pope Gregory (590–604) organized a singing school called the *Schola Cantorum.* Here boys were taught singing and Latin and other branches of learning for nine long years. They had to memorize the words and the music of more than six hundred chants to become specialists in the art of Church song, because there wasn't any adequate method of writing music at the time. These boys sang with the trained men and clergy in the choir. There was no variety except in the way that different registers of the sopranos, tenors, altos and bassos sounded. Usually they were given the pitch by the leader, who twanged an instrument of one string, a monochord. The organ was in its infancy and few existed. So they sang, unaccompanied, in the chapel. To this day singing, without an instrument, is called *a cappella* (or chapel) singing. Never get mixed up and say *a cappello* because that would mean in the style of a hat, and *not* in the style of a chapel, nor *capello*— that would mean hair!

At the start of the Crusades, the Church called secular song "lascivious and nimble."

COMPOSER-SINGERS

When song began to grip writers of music, the composers themselves were singers because there were no adequate instruments. Among the singers and makers of secular songs of great beauty were the yet unexcelled composers, the great contrapuntalist Josquin Després of Burgundy, then of the Netherlands (1450–1521), Adrian Willaert of Flanders and Venice (1480–1562) and many others of the countries of the Lowlands and France. These men, although not opera writers, were good exemplars to men of the seventeenth century in the making of songs, after the decline of the madrigal in opera. Claudio Monteverdi, one of the first of the great Italian opera composers, was a violinist as well as a singer. He was influenced by the men of the Lowlands.

SINGING STYLES BEFORE OPERA

In the fifteenth century, before there was any opera, singers were trained for Church services and they took part in the pageants also. Particularly well sung was the pastoral drama *Orfeo* of Poliziano, given in Mantua about 1474, a century before the first operas (Peri's *Dafne* and *Euridice,* 1594) were written. In *Orfeo* they had vocal solos, as well as ensembles. At this time, however, popular music and folk song in verse form (strophic) such as the people's frottola, and other secular songs, produced fine singers. The solo song very rapidly became popular, because the one-tune song with accompaniment (homophony) rose in favor after the madrigal (woven song strands) began to wane. Then, recitative ushered in by the Camerata made the sung story, solo or ensemble, more interesting because it could move along. So compared to the madrigal drama, the first operas could more or less express feeling. Song soon slid out of the Church style. Recitative or *stilo parlando* was gradually adopted. This required control of the breath so that the singer could produce *legato* (smooth) tones, instead of choppy singing. Italian singers had learned the smooth tone-making in Church music, and in this style attained great skill, which they have always retained.

The Italian language, with its lovely vowel sounds, produced what is called *bel canto* (beautiful song). And this has always been the Italians' first consideration in opera. After they had acquired a beautiful *legato,* it was possible for the voice to become agile. During the singing lesson there was no accompaniment. The words had to be intelligible and smooth. In the treatises on early singing, no one mentions volume or power. This was thought, no doubt, to come naturally, if the voice was properly produced.

Up to the sixteenth century, outside of the Church, both folk song and minstrelsy with their tunes and accompaniments were unconsciously developing a one-melody music. In the seventeenth century, instruments were reaching a new perfection. The voice began to be accompanied by instruments playing voice parts—offstage. This was new and convenient, for in the past a singer of serious music had often been accompanied by two or more voices. It seems strange that it took many years to bring about this development, when popular songs and troubadour songs were accompanied by instruments. They were accompanied by the fiddle, a close relative to the violin, popular with the strolling musician. The violin, indeed, had a hard time to win respectability because its family had had a long life with the gay and often shiftless wandering minstrels. It was only accepted when its beauty, achieved by the makers in Cremona and elsewhere, made it a nobler, more brilliant and more useful instrument as the larger theaters began to replace the smaller chambers of the nobles and kings for concerts. Yes, opera is now on its way with the instruments "keeping company" with the voice and with music written especially for them.

OPERA SINGERS

Any church singer of the sixteenth and early seventeenth centuries was able to sing the stage works of his time, for when anything like opera came, all that was new were the stories and recitative. The new texts were attempts to satisfy the yearning for the expression of human, rather than ritualistic feeling. But opera was still using plain chant melodies and madrigals. The church singer, too, had been schooled in decoration, trill and passage work, and was proficient in the beloved vocal gymnastics.

A VOICE PROBLEM

At the end of the sixteenth century, there was the craze for the Madrigal Drama, such as Orazio Vecchi's amusing *L'Amfiparnaso* (*At the Foot of Mount Parnassus,* 1594). This was given as an opera in 1954 at the Berkshire Festival at Tanglewood. It required a high soprano voice for the principal part and hereby hangs a long story. Women were not allowed to sing in the Church. How to get soprano voices for operas that needed a more mature tang than boys' natural soprano! Boys could hardly take the place of women, although they had been trained for years and were proficient in singing. The young men called *castrati* retained their beautiful and ethereal high voices, which were not so warm as women's, but were sweet and powerful, and like our boy sopranos in color (white). They kept their voices sometimes for forty years. The French opera did not use *castrati,* yet even in France women sopranos had not the social recognition of the male soprano elsewhere.

SINGING

At the end of the seventeenth century, famous singers were as thick as stars in the Milky Way. Earlier, Peri and Caccini of the Camerata were singers. Peri with the first operas, and Caccini, who wrote the epoch-making book of madrigals for one voice and thorough-bass accompaniment, *Le Nuove musiche* (*The New Art of Music*), helped develop the art of song. He was father to Francesca, a composer and famous singer of dramma per musica.

Unfortunately, however, exhibition singing set in. Beautiful expression went out about 1640. It wasn't all smooth sailing. At first there was opposition to *castrati* (or *evirati*) singing women's parts, but gradually it grew fashionable. Coloratura opera singers were hailed as baseball stars and movie actors are today. The wealthy nobles and the princes of the Church vied with each other in entertaining and housing the singers with high voices and athletic vocal chords. The more florid and scintillating the triller, the more popular was he. This singer worship lessened the possibility of writing librettos that would make opera a world of real make-believe. But like it or not, owing to the demand for dazzling singing, the noble art of song, so recently brought to beauty by the Florentines, took a deep nose dive! It was not alone, for with it, in these days, architecture, which had become beautiful in proportion and composition, became heavy with ornament, baroque in style. To realize the difference compare the Parthenon or any Greek temple with the Santa Maria de la Saluta Church in Venice.

Even the Florentines, inventors of opera, whose ideal had been expressive singing, and who shared with the ancient Greeks the desire to interpret the texts faithfully, used men for men's parts and for women's parts as well. To sing poetry with expressiveness would not permit florid singing with vocal fireworks, yet these masters encouraged it.

LANDI

Steffano Landi, one of the foremost Venetian opera writers, in his opera *The Death of Orpheus,* in 1619, was the first to dare to use men for male characters, and women for female characters! This must have made a more realistic piece. But soon he too lost his nerve, for in his opera *St. Alexis* (1634) the saint was sung by a male soprano, and all the other parts, for men and women, were taken by male soprani. From this time on, from Scarlatti and Handel and occasionally into the middle of the nineteenth century, *castrati* were more or less used for any female character.

Although Handel used many of the great women singers of his

day, he also used cool and clear-voiced *castrati* for his gods, half-gods and even for warriors and other important characters. In those days the composer had to truckle to the singers, who were far more popular and better-known than the composers. Yet today, one reason why Handel is not sung more often is owing to the fact that the parts were written for the powerful male *castrati,* not for women.

THE FIRST OPERA HOUSE (1637)

In the opera *Andromeda* by Francesco Manelli, given at the opening of the first opera house in the world, the San Cassiano in Venice, Manelli himself took the part of Neptune. Madalena, his wife, took the part of Andromeda. But for the sake of their audience, reveling in the scintillating high tones of the male sopranos, the parts of the other actors, gods and goddesses were sung by men.

In the seventeenth century Monteverdi, master of recitative, of instrumental effectiveness, and portrayer of human feeling, used a male soprano in his *Orfeo.*

But logically enough, during Monteverdi's day, devils and lords of the underworld, such as Pluto of Greek mythology, were always sung by bassos practically unused in serious opera, and almost forgotten until opera buffa gave them a place in the sun. Gounod, much later, followed Monteverdi's example and used a bass baritone or bass for Mephistopheles in his *Faust.*

SINGERS OF HANDEL'S DAY

The castrati were no more popular, however, than for example the great sopranos of Handel's day such as Mesdames Faustino and Cuzzoni. Signore Farinelli and Detto Caffarelli were the most popular castrati in their world. A certain lady exclaimed when she saw Farinelli, there is "one God and one Farinelli." Niccolo Porpora, composer and teacher, and a rival of Handel's, taught Caffarelli and other great singers of his day. It is said that Porpora gave Caffarelli a single sheet of paper on which all the stunts that could be performed by the voice were recorded, and kept him at it for six solid years! When he came the last time to see him, he sent him off with these words: "Go, my son, you are the greatest singer in the world." (Adapted from Grove's *Dictionary of Music and Musicians.)*

SCARLATTI AND COMIC RELIEF

The opera had grown staid and stale with its noble but somewhat monotonous recitative. It was not as interesting as it had been at the height of the Florentine period.

Alessandro Scarlatti (1659–1725), the most famous of the Naples group of opera writers, yielding to the public demand, added comic relief to serious operas. Between the acts, or even during the opera, comic types would be added, such as a funny old man singing deep bass or using a false or falsetto voice in squeals that made everybody laugh. Sometimes an old woman, a male tenor, would accompany the old man.

In spite of the popularity of the castrati and high vocal calisthenics, the da capo aria was probably as much of a goad to vocal fireworks as the high-voiced men, because of the lure of ornament and high tones and overuse of the aria form. The art of song was declining.

OPERA BUFFA A BOON TO SONG

It is reasonable to expect that serious opera would have been more sensible than opera based on buffoonery. But it took opera buffa to iron out some of the ridiculous kinks and hurdles that had grown up to throttle serious opera. Delightful paradox!

Opera buffa became more direct because the plot was so fast-moving that it didn't have time for trills and passage work to slow down action. Also it used the bass voice. Yet, in an opera like *The Marriage of Figaro,* which Mozart called opera buffa, he used a girl singer for the character of Cherubino, the boy page. This was somewhat logical, because he needed a character who would be timid, effeminate and innocent. All the other comic operas of Mozart used men for men's roles and women for women's roles. The comic operas or opera buffa of Pergolesi were sensible, because everybody was familiar with the characters taken from everyday life, who had not come from Mount Parnassus, Hades, the Elysian Fields or from the holy places mentioned in the Bible.

It is well that opera buffa was popular, or we might today be having Indian chiefs and racketeers speaking with women's voices or male sopranos as they pull out their tomahawks or their tommy-guns. But don't be fooled. High voices with ornament and trills are not much less favored in our own days but they are women's voices, not *castrati*.

Vocal calisthenics are among the reasons why people still adore nine-teenth-century Italian opera.

THE YOUNG MOZART

Mozart was fourteen years old when he wrote *Mithradates, King of Pontus*. Mithradates was sung by a castrato. When he was sixteen, in the opera *Lucio Silla,* his Roman hero, Silla, and his Senator Cecilio were male sopranos, but Mozart, a young boy, naturally wanted his operas to be liked and so followed the fashion. But as soon as he grew up, he became too much the character painter to have men sing women's parts, or permit high voices to characterize men save in the case of Cherubino, the Timid.

STYLE CHANGES

Style in singing has changed almost as much as costumes. Can you imagine a singer of a madrigal opera singing a Wagnerian part, such as Brünnhilde or Isolde, or even Elsa? No. Wagner, in the great variety of his singing styles, demanded his own kind of singing, which Caruso said *he* would sing only at the very end of his career when he wouldn't care if he did strain his voice. There were few choruses in olden days because of the rulings of the soloists against them. Handel, however, began to use choruses masterfully as well as ballets in his operas in London.

THE ARIA

The *aria,* or air, or song, had come up through many forms, some of which were: the madrigal or polyphonic song, the strophic song which repeated the verses, and the two-part song which occasionally repeated the first section. This latter finally developed under Scarlatti into the da capo aria. At the time of Handel, arias had assumed many traits which distinguished them from one another:

1. The tender *aria cantabile* had simple and telling music and gave the singer opportunity to "emote" or use feeling in control.

2. The *aria di portamento* strongly marked in rhythm was beautifully flowing and gave little chance to singers to embellish its graceful lines. It was very expressive.

3. The *aria di mezzo carattere,* less pathetic than the *aria cantabile,* and less stately than the *aria di portamento,* expressed greater depths of feeling or passion than the others and usually took its second part a little faster than the first part.

4. The declaiming type of aria was the *aria parlante,* with richer accompaniment and ability to express agitation, fury and intense emotion, from which it took some special names.

5. Now comes the beloved of singers, the *aria di bravura* or *d'agilità* with its show-off rapid passages and *fioritura* (ornamentation). Handel had to write these for his high-tempered singers.

These are the principal arias into which the eighteenth-century song can be divided. There were also the aria of imitation, which mimicked sounds of animals, battle, etc.; the *aria in unisono,* an aria accompanied by one instrument playing the same melody as the voice (see "They Walked in Darkness" by Handel in *Messiah,* original version). There were, too, an aria without accompaniment and an elaborately accompanied *aria parlante,* called *aria di concertato.*

SONG SPECIALISTS

Late in the nineteenth century when so much became known scientifically about the structure of the throat, methods of breathing, and head tones, supporting tones, and so on, the voice became more specialized and less instrumental than it had previously been. It has become characteristic that the singer today, who can sing Brahms well, doesn't always interpret Mozart well, and the singers who are great in opera are often inept as interpreters of German songs (*Lieder*). Rarely, in fact, is the lieder singer, save in a few instances like Lotte Lehmann, an excellent opera singer. Furthermore, in olden times, a singer was able to sing any kind of music. Today there are so many kinds of vocal music that it is not difficult to understand why the vocal instrument is less able to sing in some media than others. So it is easily seen how this specialization has made of the vocal art a very different thing from that of the eighteenth century. Whether it is good or bad—it is the situation now.

TEACHING

In our own day, violent controversy still rages about voice teaching. The golden era (*bel canto*) of singing of the nineteenth century is mourned for as lost. Its singers, "they" say are gone from us, as are the great coloraturas of Mozart's and Bellini's day. It is hard to cast modern singers in the old dramas which demand the kind of technique that was used in the era in which they were composed. Yet much royal singing is done today in such difficult roles as in *Don Giovanni* and

Norma, and others. The singers who, like Rosa Ponselle, could sing the role of Norma, difficult because of its slow coloratura, are today few and far between.

SINGERS

Without the singer, opera could not have progressed, for opera is a sung story with orchestra. Great singers with great teachers of song have been part of the bone and sinew of opera. It is often said that our singers are not as great as they used to be. Only a few of the older ones can say this, and distance often lends enchantment. Hereafter the recordings of voices will tell the story, and memories will no longer be the link between today and the past. Were we to pay adequate tribute to the singers who have contributed to the growth of opera, it would take a book thrice this size.

A FEW TERMS USED IN MUSIC

Here are some of the terms heard often in connection with music, song in particular.

Coloratura   Decorated song with trills and runs, usually for display. The same word is used with instrumental music. The singer who specializes in this decorated song is called a *coloratura.*

Fioritura   The literal translation is "flowery." It is music with embellishments, improvised by the singer, or written by the composer, to decorate a basic melody.

Rubato   This in origin means "robbed," for it is a momentary disregard for strict tempo. The time is robbed from one part of a measure by another.

Legato   The holding of tones in smooth motion so that there is no realizable pause between them. It is the opposite of *staccato,* in which the notes are released almost immediately.

Cantabile   In a singing, almost caressing manner.

Bravura   This is mostly used in instrumental music, such as a Liszt piano concerto. It is music, wherever found, of broad, ornamental, elaborate passages needing great skill, and a sort of bravado ("bravery") in execution, as the word *bravura* connotes; usually very loud.

Trill   The rapid alternation of a tone with its upper neighbor, played or sung in the same time value as the original note. A *shake* is similar to the trill.

SCENE III

A Whirl Through Ballet

THE ballet which was a basis of French opera is not a trivial or frivolous factor of opera. It emerges in twentieth-century opera as one of the most alluring ways of telling a story, when used as part of the plot or action.

IMPORTANCE OF THE DANCE

John Martin, dance critic of the *New York Times,* said about Paul Draper, who invented the ballet tap and elevated tap dancing to concert pitch, "He uses the floor like the keyboard of a piano." This shows what the art of the dancer can be, in and out of opera.

Dancing has its roots in primitive life. Savages danced before they could speak, using it as a way of prayer and play. The Greek chorus danced to express the play's meanings. The Bible records that David danced before the Ark in the Temple, to atone for his sins.

In old Spain, a religious dance, performed with all solemnity and seriousness, was used in connection with the Mass. It was but little removed in intention from the dance of early Greece.

During the early days of dramatic spectacles, which unwittingly led to opera itself, the people danced to their rough and melodious songs. The Church clamped down hard on dancing because of the vulgarities that had crept into it.

By degrees the dance of the people caught on among the nobles of the opera-making countries of Europe. Italy unconsciously began to experiment with opera in the fourteenth and fifteenth centuries. Her festivals, secular and religious, were made up of song and round dances. France by now had begun her invaluable and often permanent contributions to the ballet leading to opera. In the fifteenth and six-teenth centuries, to compensate for her empty treasury, and to divert their minds, the peers and the kings of joy-loving France took part in theatricals and in garish ballets.

LE BALLET COMIQUE DE LA REINE

The first French ballet was given in 1409 with pantomime, declaimed speech, acting and dancing. In 1581, however, all histories record that *Le Ballet comique de la Reine* (*The Comedy Ballet of the Queen*) was given at the Court of Catherine de Medici, wife of Henry II of France. It has been considered the first ballet, with dance, verse and music molded into one production. On it was modeled later the *ballet de cour* or court ballet with its seeds of opera. It was the work of Balthaza de Beaujoyeulx, for the betrothal of the Queen's sister Marguerite of Lorraine to the Duke de Joyeuse. (Aren't these names of joyousness like music itself?) The ballet, based on the legend of Circe, cost three million six hundred thousand francs. Ten thousand guests witnessed it from 10 P.M. to 3 A.M.

The *ballet comique* in France was so called only because it was not tragic. It was an early stage spectacle with dance, song, speech, plot, costuming and elaborate scenery. As extravagant as it was, we as heirs should rejoice that ballet was given so colorful a start, because it became the ground work of France's aristocratic and artistic life. More important, however, Lully later studied it from the manuscript published in 1582 and used it as the steppingstone to French opera.

As yet there was no opera in France, but stage works like the *ballet comique* were given by Baïf and his co-workers.

CROSS-FERTILIZATION

In this early seventeenth century, Italy was having her first "tries" at opera (dramma per musica). She had made only a little attempt at ballet, sometimes with speech and sometimes with music only. When the Italians were invited by Cardinal Mazarin in 1645 to give Peri's *Euridice* in Paris, they caught the germ of elaborate ballet from the French. On the other hand the French were inoculated with the germs of Italian opera, which they soon threw out for their own "make."

From these Italo-French happenings, the opera and the ballet world received the impetus with which to dance ahead up to our own time.

ENGLISH MASQUES AND FESTIVALS

Don't think that England didn't have her dancers and masques and festivals from as early dates as Italy and France. She had most elaborate and royal presentations as well as her simple folk dancing. These too, gave ideas to makers of ballets in Europe, but not of course as directly as did the French and Italian brands.

THE FIRST DEFINITE ADVANCE

Lully, the kitchen boy, "made good." Besides creating opera, he was the first to make an art of the ballet on which he built French opera. He was also the first to admit women as dancers (1681). The first ballerina is believed to have been Madame La Fontaine. Heretofore men dressed as women had danced.

Nothing in King Louis XIV's reign could be too elaborate. When he grew heavy and did not take part in ballets, interest in ballet waned at court. The scene was shifted to the universities and colleges, with ballets written by Lully and the poets Quinault, Racine, Molière, and others. Lully also composed *entrées* (introductions) to Molière's plays, and wrote the ballet *Le mariage forcé* (*The Forced Marriage*), and danced in it with Pierre Beauchamp (1639-1705).

UNIFICATION

We hear much about unification today in all lines of work. Lully in his day unified the ballet. Under his leadership ballet became not a suite or string of dances by a half-dozen poets and composers, but was a mimed play in a succession of dramatic scenes, tied together by a unifying plot taken from myth, fable, fantasy. He favored the lively and active rhythms of their familiar dances such as the *gigue, passepied* and *bourrée*. The Royal Academy of Music, in which Lully established a department of the dance, survived in France, and influenced Europe through the ages with its high standards. Later it was somewhat paralleled by the Russian Imperial Ballet.

BALLET REACHES UPWARD

Lully's ballet, made up mainly of declaimed speeches, marching and some quick dances, always dignified and formal, nevertheless, helped to establish many new techniques. It was a feast for the eye, rather than of motion or emotions, and was like a gigantic pageant or equestrian tournament or a masque with or without speech.

The dances had been typical in spirit of the stately and dignified *basse dance,* the father of the minuet.

Lully permitted the dancers to express themselves with their arms and bodies. Thus the "dance of elevation" came to expand the ballet. These high jumps and leaps, or good *ballon*—the act of staying in the air for some time—gave the ballet a sense of soaring, flying, and the dimension of height (or verticality). The dance of elevation has taken years to develop, and is still developing.

Pierre Beauchamp, one of the most accomplished choreographers of this period, and dean of dancers, was made Lully's assistant, and the Dancing Master to Louis XIV.

Beauchamp said that the way "pigeons in his dovecote" ran to feed in different groups, gave him ideas for composing his ballet groups. He did his best to get more freedom of movement, but not until Noverre grappled with the cumbersome costume was there much improvement. In Lully's and Beauchamp's time the heavy court costumes with wigs and masks worn by the dancers curbed motion.

FAMOUS BALLERINAS

The techniques developed in the Lully *Danse d'École* (Classic Dance) came down to us through such dancers as: Marie Camargo (1710–70), the sturdy dancer who wore shorter skirts for freedom, soft slippers and an undergarment the ancestor of tights; Marie Sallé (1707–56), who used a light muslin garment, wore her hair down, unornamented, and believed in natural expression; Marie Taglioni (1804–84), the most famous dancer of the Romantic Period, who made her debut in Vienna in 1822 with Fanny Elssler, one of the most "glorious names" in ballet.

In addition to these ballerinas there was the Vestris family of which Gaetan Vestris of the Paris Opera (1729–1808) was one of the world's greatest dancers.

FANNY ELSSLER

Born in 1810, Fanny Elssler was a daughter of Joseph Haydn's valet and music copyist. To help support the six children, her mother had to take in washing. But Haydn did send Theresa and Fanny to ballet school. Elssler brought into vogue the character dance, such as the passionate Hungarian, Spanish, Russian and Polish dances. She came to America in 1840 and set the cities agog. In two tours she visited almost every important American city, including Havana. She died in 1884 and left not a trace of her art in the United States where ballet remained merely a stunt until much later.

Anna Pavlova (1881–1931) of the Mariinsky Theatre in St. Petersburg, the daughter of a peasant and a laundress, was one of the geniuses among dancers in ballet of modern days.

CHOREOGRAPHICS

To go back, Louis Pécourt (1655–1729) succeeded Beauchamp, and he was actually credited with Raoul Feuillet's book *Choréographie*. In this was begun the invention of a notation by means of which steps could be set down so that a ballet once produced could be repeated. The first English edition of this book, *Choreography, or the Art of Writing Dancing,* came out in 1728.

At present (1955) a dance notation has been realized. It looks queer to a novice but the dancer will use it as the musician uses a music score.

During the reigns of Henri II, Louis XIII and Louis XIV, ballets were the ancient substitutes for our political junkets. Statesmen, and even cardinals, used the ballet to flatter their monarchs or visiting grandees of Church or State. Lully made almost satanic use of choreographic "soft soap."

Some of the most elaborate ballets were given outdoors. Before and at the time of Lully, the costumes and scenery were most elaborate in which great painters and architects were engaged.

RAMEAU'S CONTRIBUTION—OPERA BALLET AND BALLET OPERA

When Jean-Philippe Rameau, composer and author of a book on harmony, the new system of musical theory, entered the scene, Lully had established French opera. Now the ballet became more amusing and was used not only as a separate entertainment, but was put into opera with more diverting than sensible intent. It usually spoiled the pace of its opera, and for years remained to do little more.

Lully emphasized the music of the ballet and developed it into French opera. Rameau introduced the opera ballet, the form of ballet in which this book is most interested, with *Les Indes galantes* (*Gallant India,* 1735). Rameau, both practical man and musical theorist, gave this opera ballet its most decisive form. He used sharply marked rhythms, melody, and well-mated music and dance.

Rameau tried as well as he could to make the ballet more expressive. He wrote, with Voltaire, the comedy ballet *La Princesse de Navarre* (*The Princess of Navarre,* 1745), and with Jean-Jacques Rousseau, *Les Fêtes de Ramire* (*The Festivals of Ramire*). Rameau, with Gluck and Wagner (in opera) and Stravinsky (outside opera), in varying degrees, stressed the dramatic in the ballet.

With all Rameau's attempts at dramatic unity, the ballet became interruptive and as stiff as the lamp-shade-shaped skirts made of several layers of tarlatan, silk, or both—the *tutu*. It slowed up and broke the continuity of the plot. Indeed, the *Maître de Ballet* seemed to forget the opera! Even the scene designer forgot the matrix for the jewel. It wasn't long before the actors became halfhearted, and the ballets diluted and dispirited. After Rameau, the opera ballet had again become fixed, formalized in music and content. If it was a Parisian in Mexico or a Mexican in Paris, the changes were only in scenery or clothes and not in the character or elements of the dance.

JEAN GEORGES NOVERRE

Again art is rescued. This time by Noverre (1727–1810), a dancer and ballet master, born in Paris. Noverre, after struggling in provincial capitals, went to Paris to use pantomime and gesture in the ballet. He was valued by Gluck, whom he helped with his delightful *Don Juan Ballet,* given in Vienna in 1761. This proved Noverre to be a master of the heroic ballet style. It is so beautiful that it was revived in 1936. Noverre, in this, as in everything, tried to give to the dance a human significance, and to the body a dignity apart from jumps, leaps, and geometric figurations.

In 1747, he produced his first ballet for the Opéra Comique. He had worked in Berlin and London, and had revolutionized the art of the ballet. It was fortunate that Gluck and he could team up, in separate ballets as well as in the opera ballet, *Iphigenia in Aulis* (1774), for Gluck maintained, with Noverre, that not only opera but ballet too was becoming too stiff.

BALLET WITH MEANING

After Rameau, Gluck, as well as Noverre, started the building of opera ballet as quite distinct from the ballet outside of opera. They meant it to express something definite. For example, the "Ballet of the Happy Shades" and the "Ballet of the Furies" in *Orpheus and Eurydice* are not athletic spectacles. They show in excellent choreography the happiness of the Happy Shades and the suffering of the Sinners. This contributes to the action of the opera. This is what ballet in opera was expected to do and what it does today.

It is told that Gluck was very peremptory with Vestris, who was then a czar of French opera. He had criticized Gluck's opera *Armide*. Said Gluck, "There is to be no fancy dancing in my opera," and with vehemence added: "An artist whose entire learning is in his heels has no right to criticize an opera like *Armide*." (*Some Musicians of Former Days,* by Romain Rolland. Henry Holt.) Gluck did not recognize that the learning of a good dancer is not only in the heels!

Through David Garrick in London, Noverre, having left ungrateful Paris, was given instruction in the art of acting, which led him to create his famous *Ballet d'Action* (*Ballet of Action*), in which there were no spoken dialogues or interludes, only dumb show, which had been popular with the Romans and still obtains in our ballets in and out of opera. Up to this time, speaking was common in the ballet (and shows signs of returning to modern ballet). Later, Noverre went to Stuttgart, and made that city the center of the world of dancing.

Noverre wrote delightfully and

1. Revived the ballet as Gluck revived opera, and Gluck took advice from his famous *Lettres sur la Danse et sur les Ballets* (*Letters on the Dance and on the Ballets*).

2. Demanded more dramatic librettos.

3. Freed the dance from the starched stiffness of the tutu and farthingale (a long hooped-skirt contrivance).

4. Introduced unlimited expression into the dance, making it more heroic when necessary, or more lyric.

5. Did away with the leader of the ballet, and substituted a scheme in which music, painting and costume, under suitable masters, became the auxiliary of dancing.

6. Was the last of the classic ballet masters, because of the Revolution, which ended large expenditure of monies.

7. Opposed the wearing of masks (an ancient custom), which was discontinued in 1773—when the famous dancer, Maximilian Gardel, discarded his at the Paris Opéra.

8. Made the ballet a part of the opera, and thereby reinforced the opera. The ballet became an adjunct to the chorus as well as to the soloist.

Noverre influenced the writing of ballet up to the twentieth century. Even as late as Michel Fokine's time has he been a factor. During the eighteenth and nineteenth centuries the classical ballet was established and has endured, often to hurt the opera as well as enliven it.

The rest of the story of ballet is of the Russian School, for the French ballet declined and was reconditioned in Moscow and in St. Petersburg.

REFORM WANTING

European opera ballet in the early nineteenth century needed reform. It is apparent by what one critic said: "French opera is a spectacle where the whole happiness and misery of people consists in seeing dancing about them." Before this, Jean Jacques Rousseau said, "The manner of conducting the ballets is quite simple. If a prince is happy, all share his joy and dance. If he is unhappy, those around try to cheer him up, and they dance. There are also many other occasions for dancing, and the most serious actions of life are accompanied by it. Priests dance, soldiers dance, gods dance, there is even dancing at burials—"

VARIETY LACKING

There was a long period when the dances or the ballet were all about the same. They were monotonous and boring and it was quite obvious why Wagner denounced the ballet as throttling opera.

BALLET—"A SOMETIME THING"

During the nineteenth century, the ballet, like Porgy's woman, was "a sometime thing"—sometimes used for *divertissement* and occasionally to help the story of the opera. There are many operas whose ballets contribute to the plot. For example, in *Masaniello* or *The Dumb Girl of Portici* (Auber) the Dumb Girl, Fenella, is the prima ballerina in the ballet. This role was danced in America in 1915 by Anna Pavlova.

The "Orgies of Brocken" in Gounod's *Faust* would probably be weaker were it not for the "Witches' Ballet," and the ballets in *Aïda* contribute much to the feeling and color of its story, to say nothing of the fascinating and illustrative under-sea ballet in *Sadko* by Rimsky-Korsakov.

But an ironic twist (considering Wagner's dislike of ballet) is that Massine made a ballet from Wagner's *Tristan und Isolde*, *The Mad Tristan* in 1944; and previously (1939) *Bacchanale* from *Tannhäuser*. David Lichine made the ballet *Cain and Abel* from Wagner's "Siegfried's Rhine Journey" and "Funeral March" from *Die Götterdämmerung*.

DANCES FOR THE SAKE OF PLOT

Meyerbeer attempted to make the ballet stem from the opera plot. From this time on, opera ballet seems to understand its function. This condition lapsed, and the ballet in opera became once more a hindrance rather than a help to action. For example, masquerades, in *Mignon;* peasant dances, as in *The Bartered Bride;* and fiestas.

Saint-Saëns used the ballet as a heathen orgy in the temple, to fire Samson to feel his kinship to Israel and so to destroy the heathen edifice. This ballet gives poignancy to the internal conflict.

Again in the "Bacchanale" from *Tannhäuser,* the action portrays the feelings of the senses. The dance and revels in the "Venusberg Music" are in contrast to the feeling of the Pilgrims, whose attitudes are so solemnly "marched" during the "Pilgrim's Chorus." It will be remembered that Wagner was forced according to Parisian custom to put in a ballet.

RUSSIAN BALLET—NINETEENTH CENTURY

Ballet in Russia in the early nineteenth century was fundamentally French and Italian, but it borrowed from every nationality which gave it life. It especially admired the brilliance, not the technique, of the Italian ballet and its dancers. The Italians sacrificed grace to skill.

The Russian Imperial Ballet School is marked for its stringent methods of training. No means were spared, no hardship softened, to train the dancer who finally proclaimed to the world the splendidness and thoroughness and grace of the Russian Imperial School.

Charles Ludwig Didelot (1767–1837) of Stockholm, son of the first dancer and choreographer of the Swedish Royal Theatre, brought the French ballet to Russia. "Charles" made his name and debut in Paris. After him came Marius Petipa (1822–1910), choreographer and dancer in the Russian Imperial Ballet, a Frenchman, called "father of the dance-ballet in Russia." He was a contemporary of Tchaikovsky and knew well the kind of music required. Certainly, Tchaikovsky wrote three of the most well-fashioned (outside of opera) ballets of his day: *Swan Lake* (1876), *The Sleeping Beauty* (1889) and *The Nutcracker Suite (Casse-noisette)* (1891–92). Petipa made a big contribution in the ballet in and out of opera, by realizing the limitations of music on gesture and gesture on music.

Russia invited Antoine Titus to design a ballet for the new opera by Michael Glinka, *A Life for the Czar.* Titus introduced Polish national dances, such as the *mazurka* and *krakoviak,* and costumed and motivated the ballet in the classical Italian style. It was not used. Nicholas Goltz, however, staged an immortal masterwork for it.

RUSSIA—DIAGHILEV

But the man who gave Russia and the world a new ballet was Serge Diaghilev, who was born in Russia in 1872 and died in Venice in 1929. He became legendary in his own time. His friendship with Nijinsky did well for the ballet. Nijinsky's dismissal at his marriage made it necessary for Diaghilev to get somebody in his place. Leonide Massine was elected. Although not a Nijinsky, he was a gifted choreographer and a superb dancer. He has been seen in the film *The Red Shoes* (a story of the ballet, 1949), based on a fairy tale by Hans Christian Andersen.

Diaghilev, before he became interested in the ballet, had been editor of an art magazine. Among the painters that Diaghilev used for his ballets were Bakst, Benois, Derain, Picasso, Sert, Rouault. His composers were Ravel, Tcherepnine, Glazunov, Prokofiev, Debussy, Auric, Satie, Milhaud, Nabokoff, Dukelsky (Vernon Duke), and Stravinsky. Diaghilev set Stravinsky on the highway to success with his first ballet, *The Fire Bird,* after he had arranged for him *Les Sylphides* on Chopin's music.

Diaghilev was not at first interested in the ballet, even though he saw it prosper in the imperial theaters in Russia, over which he presided as a "functionary for special missions." But one night he saw Virginia Zucci dance at the Imperial Ballet and "forever after" gave his attention exclusively to the ballet.

Among the choreographers to whom Diaghilev gave opportunities were: Michel Fokine; Vaslav Nijinsky; Leonide Massine; Adolph Bolm; Bronislava Nijinska; and George Ballanchine, who is now important in American ballet.

THE UNION OF MUSIC AND DANCE

To be sure, Diaghilev's ballets were mostly independent of opera, such as *La Sacre du Printemps* (Igor Stravinsky); *Les Sylphides* (Chopin); *Till Eulenspiegel* (Richard Strauss); *Scheherezade* (Nicolai Rimsky-Korsakov); *L'Oiseau de Feu* (*The Fire Bird*) (Stravinsky); *L'Après-midi d'un faune* (Claude Debussy); *Giselle* (Adolphe Adam); *Petrouchka* (Stravinsky); *Le Spectre de la Rose* (Carl Maria von Weber); *Swan Lake* (Tchaikovsky); and many, many others. Yet the ballets for the operas, such as the "Polovtzian Dances" in *Prince Igor* (Borodin); the ballets of *Ruslan and Ludmilla* (Glinka), and that of Stravinsky's *Le Chant du rossignol* (*The Song of the Nightingale*), give him a place in this book because he welcomed a union of dancing, music and scenery.

Among the performers Diaghilev featured in his many tours in Europe and his productions in America were Karsavina, Anna Pavlova, Adolph Bolm, and the two most unique of them all—Vaslav Nijinsky, probably the world's greatest dancer, and Michel Fokine, dancer and probably one of the world's greatest choreographers. But in or out of opera, those who saw Anna Pavlova in *The Dying Swan* or Nijinsky in *L'Après-midi d'un faune* (*The Afternoon of a Faun*) or in *Till Eulenspiegel,* and in the many other things he did, will realize, for example, the difference between "The Dance of the Hours" in *La Gioconda* and the ballets mounted by Diaghilev.

THE NEW ERA IN BALLET

Anatole Chujoy says in his excellent Dance Encyclopedia that "Diaghilev was the greatest impresario ballet has ever known . . . he gave Western Europe and the United States Russian ballet" . . . and "he made the Russian ballet a Cosmopolitan art form . . . which Western Europe and America had thought dead for more than half a century" save for some ballets in opera, *La Gioconda* and *Carmen.*

There has been in the Soviet Union little of value in the ballet. Some ballets on Pushkin themes, Aleko and Prokofiev's *Cinderella,* and some standard ballets, have been produced. Men like Michel Fokine succeeded in reviving ballet only outside of Russia.

Soviet ballet and dancing today (1955) have retrogressed from delicacy, which they now abhor, to muscularity, which they celebrate in every step, from grace to power, and from art terms to physical terms. Skillful beyond words are their dancers but devoid of the grace and elegance cultivated by the Imperial Russian Ballet.

All ballet today in Russia tends toward the political aims of the State, often to silliness in story. The emphasis now in the Soviet ballet is weightiness, numbers, energy, muscularity, melodrama and lack of subtlety. Politics instead of elegance seems to be the aim of the once unsurpassed ballet.

OTHER MODERNS

Among other dance proponents in Europe during the twentieth century are the greatest of German dance theorists and the author of a new dance notation, *Schrift Tanse* (1928)—Rudolph von Laban, and his pupils, Mary Wigman (1886–) and Kurt Jooss (1901–).

THE DANCE IN SPAIN

The Spanish Dance has been a highly organized art, but it needs little place in this book, for it has not been used as much in opera as ballet. We are familiar with the *jota* of Valencia and Aragon, the *sevillañas* of Andalusia, the *fandangos, boleros* and *cachuchas;* the *flamenco* dances of Indian or Gypsy origin, such as the *tango,* the *zambra.* In Spain, too, were the school dances in which the *bolero,* the *seguidillas,* the *malagueñas* and other dances were used in court ballets, with all the intricacies of the French ballet. In later times, twentieth century, a new type of dance grew up under the influence of Otero, which included the concert dance so magnificently performed by La Argentina, who set the old school dances of Spain to compositions of Albeniz, Falla, Turina and others. Soon, this revival inspired such men as Falla, who gave us the dance dramas *El Amor brujo* (*Love, the Magician*) and *The Three-cornered Hat.* The Spanish dance owes it power to the emotional expression of a proud, sensuous people, with a highly developed sense of rhythm. The carriage of the head, the torso and the arms is of vital importance.

As far as Western opera is concerned we have among a few other instances the seguidilla danced in Verdi's *La Forza del Destino;* the seguidilla and *habañera* (born in Cuba), danced and sung in Bizet's *Carmen;* the ballet in Massenet's *Le Cid;* and in Granados' *Goyescas.* There are also Spanish ballets which never had operas, such as Ravel's *Bolero* and Chabrier's *España.*

The popular dances today with such phonetically catchy names as the *mambo, samba,* etc., are not yet of operatic dimensions but may arrive to give color to the twentieth-century ballet.

FOKINE, THE "FATHER OF MODERN BALLET"

Michel Fokine (1880–1942), brought to fame through Diaghilev, was a reformer of the ballet. He was educated, as were most of the great Russian dancers of his day, at the Imperial Russian School of Ballet. He held some posts in Russia, but as he did not have there the opportunity to break away from traditional ballet, he went "on his own" with Diaghilev. *Scheherezade, Fire Bird, Petrouchka, Les Sylphides, Cleopatra, Carnival,* and many others, showed the greatness of Fokine, who made a strong alliance between dancing and the other arts. With him the ballet (in opera) seizes its independence by refusing to be a slave to the other arts. Yet he never adds a character out of keeping with the plot of an opera.

His first ballet was the *Pavilion of Armide*. It had three scenes and was written by Nicholas Tcherepnine, and costumed by the painter Alexander Benois. Fokine danced in it with Anna Pavlova and Vaslav Nijinsky. What a trio!

REFORMS

Fokine demanded inspired music, in the fusion of dance, music and painting. He used the whole body, including the brain, as well as the hands, feet and head, to express the music and the story. The group and groups became important, as well as the soloist. He had no use for any ballet that was just "stuck in." It had to tell a story in mime and dance, with all the resources of the body. Among the opera ballets for which he did the choreography are the "Polovtzian Dances" of *Prince Igor,* the dances in *Ruslan and Ludmilla* of Glinka, and the ballet opera *Le Coq d'Or* by Rimsky-Korsakov.

KINSHIP OF OPERA AND BALLET

Fokine's *Le Coq d'Or* proves that opera and ballet are again growing together. This opera requires singers who can dance and dancers who can sing. In many cases, this is not possible or has not been needed. When it was given at the Metropolitan Opera House, the singers were arranged in sloping tiers of seats erected on both sides of the stage, and the dancers acted the parts in the center of the stage.

Richard Strauss's *Ariadne auf Naxos* (opera with ballet), *Legend of Joseph* and his *Schlagobers* (*Whipped Cream*) are all indicative of the twentieth-century trend to ballet and ballet opera and the Fokine spur or inspiration.

Ballet became a dramatic, exciting, storytelling medium, which today is essential in operas, plays and most popular "on its own." Fokine, father of modern ballet, died in New York in 1942 after returning from Mexico City, where he had revived his *Petrouchka* (Stravinsky).

Doris Humphrey, Charles Weidman, Jerome Robbins, Eugene Loring, Agnes de Mille, Martha Graham, Harold Kreutzberg, Katherine Dunham, Hanya Holm and others were somewhat affected by Fokine. They profited too in the spirit if not technique of the modern dance from Mary Wigman, Rudolph von Laban, but especially from Ruth St. Denis and Isadora Duncan. Even Fokine's deviations from the "classical ballet" are thought to have been inspired by the work in Russia of Isadora Duncan.

ISADORA AND THE INNER URGE

Isadora Duncan (1878–1927) is not strictly speaking a master of ballet in or out of opera, but because she dramatized the necessity of the *inward urge* to express what was in the mind and senses of the dancer and composer, she has assisted in giving the dance a new meaning and carrying power. She helped kill the Romantic tutu and the farthingale, and used flowing Greek robes and the garb of Greek boys. She was at war with the old balletomanes, and was criticised by those of the old school and the new. Her dance was essentially pantomime. Yet her audiences came away filled with emotion and the beauty and meaning underlying her performances. There were no set movements, no formulated systems. The inner urge alone was commander. She died a tragic death in France, by as weird an accident as ever befell a human being. She was strangled by her own scarf which somehow had become twisted in the wheel of her motorcar!

OTHER AMERICAN DANCERS

Isadora Duncan and Ruth St. Denis broke from tradition, and St. Denis, with Ted Shawn (Dennishawn Dancers) developed such dancers as: Charles Weidman, Martha Graham, Doris Humphrey and other moderns, who invented their own "dance"—severally—all of which might be called individualistic expressionism, a possible boon to modern opera.

THE BALLETOMANE OF BALLETOMANES

Lincoln Edward Kirstein (1907–) is the "god from the machine" of the American ballet world. It would be tedious to give the list of the publications he has written or a recital of his efforts for the cultivation of the ballet and the dance in this country. Of all Americans of our time, no one man has done more. Besides his many books on the subject, he has organized and supported new groups, societies, movements and publications. Kirstein without a doubt, has made American ballet not only possible, but beloved and popular.

REALISM VS. DIVERTISSEMENTS

Opera has the tendency of becoming painfully realistic, as in Alban Berg's *Wozzeck*, in Darius Milhaud's *Christophe Colombe*, and others of the present day. Therefore, it is doubtful whether the old-fashioned opera ballet, except as a museum piece of *divertissement* in a program, will ever come back. Yet Antony Tudor, supreme choreographer and dancer, attempted (and not too successfully) to rebuild a "Walpurgis Night" ballet (long omitted) in *Faust* at the Metropolitan Opera in the season of 1950–51.

CAROUSEL AND AGNES DE MILLE

Although not in an opera, but a musical comedy, *Carousel,* a twentieth-century ballet (by choreographer Agnes de Mille) portrays with such poignancy the sorrow and confusion of a little girl (in the plot) badgered by other children because of her father's bad reputation, that it not only helped the story of the play, but made every sophisticated spectator suffer for the child, even weeping. This choreography of brain and body is of the most important kind, and augurs well for its use in opera. Ballet has departed as just a divertissement and has become a plot carrier to engage the mind and the heart, rather than just the eye. This is a step ahead, and is most American.

Agnes de Mille's list of musical plays for which she has created the ballets is too long to include here.

COMPOSERS AND CHOREGRAPHERS OF TODAY

The American composers of today have been making such excellent story ballets outside of opera that it is to be hoped that the next operas to be written, should they use ballet, will engage composers who have written so well, such as Aaron Copland (*Appalachian Spring* and *Billy the Kid*); Leonard Bernstein (*Fancy Free*); Virgil Thomson (*Filling Station*); William Schuman (*Undertow* and *Judith*); Paul Bowles (*Yankee Clipper*); Jerome Moross (*Frankie and Johnnie*); and Norman Dello Joio (*On Stage!* and *Wilderness Stair*). And to step a little further outside of opera, and further back in the twentieth century, John Alden Carpenter, in his ballet *Skyscraper,* told a story of American life with impressionistic music and realistic action worthy of the Soviets for their ballets of today (1955). Opera, too, can make use of the practiced choreographers, such as: (1) Balanchine, "one of the most brilliant choreographers of our generation, and the only one who has a genius for pure ballet," says Chujoy. This is proven by his *The Nightingale, Apollon Musagete, The Prodigal Son, Orpheus, Symphonie Concertante,* etc.; (2) Martha Graham, the list of whose well-known dance ballets outside of opera is too long to be included here; (3) Agnes de Mille (*Rodeo, Tally-ho, Black Ritual, Billy the*

Kid and *Fall River Legend*); (4) Eugene Loring, soloist and chore-ographer who danced in *Billy the Kid, Yankee Clipper* and *Filling Station* (choreographer, Lew Christensen, and music by Virgil Thomson); (5) Antony Tudor, English choreographer and dancer (*The Great American Goof, Undertow, Time Table of American Ballet, Pillar of Fire, Romeo and Juliet*); (6) Michael Kidd, choreographer and dancer who staged the dances for *Finian's Rainbow,* danced principal roles in *Aurora's Wedding, Billy the Kid, Interplay,* choreographed *On Stage!*; (7) expert Todd Bolender; (8) Jerome Robbins, choreographer and dancer in *Interplay, Fancy Free* (Bernstein music), *Mack Sennet Ballet, High-Button Shoes, Till Eulenspiegel* and many others which he either danced or choreographed or both. Space doesn't permit the long list of ballet charmers in this country today, where ballet is as fresh and thrilling as if it were a new art!

SOME AMERICAN DANCERS

Besides the choreographer-dancers mentioned above are the following who may also be choreographers but are known best for their dancing: Jacques d'Amboise, Tanaquil LeClerq, André Eglevsky. Jean Rosenthal is no dancer but as a lighting expert she makes the stage to dance, to rest, or to twinkle. (These are members of The City Center in New York.)

THE BALLET GOES ON!

You can see how many centuries of ballet have gone by since French shepherds and masked ladies and gentlemen took part in the ballet, or even how many have passed in the history of ballet since Tchaikovsky's old-fashioned fairy tale *Swan Lake* with its airy-fairy, toe-dancing maidens in their stiff tarlatan skirts, and the formal ballets of the romantic operas. Now America is using her own ballet subjects; whether greasy with oil, or perilous with guns, they are her own—fit to energize opera as well as stand on their own feet.

The choreographer today must, with the stage director and the composer of the opera, conspire in every detail to make the opera a unit. If there is to be a ballet, it must be as important a part of the opera as the song and the orchestra. The dancers have to remember that they cannot be only athletic, unless the ballet were in an opera about the Olympic games or is telling a "sports" story.

America has forged ahead in ballet and is still developing choreographers and dancers to make opera even more rewarding.

SCENE IV

The Opener or the Overture

THE OVERTURE, whether well-known or unknown, is often the ignored of opera. The poor thing is rarely heard, because of the hubbub in the opera house made by the latecomers. If it is familiar, like the overture to *Tannhäuser,* why should anyone listen? If it is unfamiliar, why bother? Those of the audience who care are therefore almost deprived of knowing whether there is an overture or not.

Used as it first was with opera and with oratorio as well, the overture takes its name from the French word to open: *ouvrir.* The French themselves call it the *ouverture* and *prélude* too; the Italians—*overtura;* the Germans—*Vorspiel* or *Einleitung* or *Prelude.* But an opener by any other name opens equally well. Primarily it should set forth the idea or spirit of the opera, whether it uses its melodies or not.

The first operas in the late sixteenth and early seventeenth centuries had no overtures. The so-called operas in Italy, or ballets, opened with a brief *sinfonia* which simply meant a pleasant sounding together of instruments. Sometimes they opened with a *toccata,* which means a "touchpiece" to distinguish it from the long prevalent and familiar *cantata* or "voice-piece," or the earliest *sonata,* a "sound-piece." The *sinfonia* was played on an instrument, most often a harpsichord or gravicembalo. It was used in opera, oratorio, ballet and the suite.

ITALIAN AND FRENCH OVERTURES

Monteverdi, in his *Orfeo* (1607), used a nine-bar prelude which he called a toccata, and repeated it three times. It was, possibly, only a time absorber for the instruments before the performance began. The nobles, who were probably already seated, had to be amused. But Alessandro Scarlatti, about 1690, used a three-part form as overture or sinfonia with the first part lively (usually in fugal or imitative style), the second part quieter, and the third part lively (fast-slow-fast).

In France, the early operas and ballets and masques had very short pieces by way of a prelude. Lully used the first real *ouverture* in his *Alcide* and laid the foundation of this important form in which the first part, slow and majestic, was followed by a faster piece in the manner of a fugue; and finished, usually with a short, slow coda-like section. Sometimes, the Lully overture included one or even two sections in dance form, a minuet or other dance.

The Germans liked Lully's overture and so did Purcell and Handel. It had an effect on music throughout Europe. In Scarlatti's land it seemed natural to perform the first part of a piece in a lively manner to wake up interest, the scond part in a quieter manner for the sake of contrast, and the third again with liveliness to proclaim that all is well.

The Italian sinfonia or overture, popular in the second half of the eighteenth century, has led to the development of the new sonata form. This in turn became the accepted form of the overture replacing both the earlier Italian and the French types.

THE EARLY OVERTURE

At first, the overture had little relation to its running mate, the opera. For often an opera would mate up with an overture written for an entirely different work. It was merely a musical lever to open the lid of a piece.

The main difference between the French and the Italian overtures was that the French began with a slow movement and the Italian with a fast movement. Not only was the overture, as it developed, used for opera, but it helped in the development of the mighty symphony and its interpreter the orchestra.

Overtures come in four varieties.

1. Those that still live happily with their operas, like the overture to Mozart's *Magic Flute,* or the Vorspiel (prelude) to Wagner's *Lohengrin.*

2. Those that have almost lost their operas, as far as modern audiences are concerned; Weber's overture to *Oberon;* and Auber's overture to *Fra Diavolo,* Otto Nicolai's *Merry Wives of Windsor,* and Gluck's superb *Iphigenia in Aulis.*

3. Overtures such as Beethoven's *Coriolanus* and *Egmont* overtures intended originally for incidental music to plays.

4. Overtures that are quite guiltless of ever having been promised in marriage to any opera, such as "Fingal's Cave" by Felix Mendelssohn and "Manfred," Robert Schumann's overture to Byron's poem of the same name.

GLUCK AND MOZART

In the overture to *The Magic Flute* Mozart pictures the overall spirit and feeling, not the melodies which are used in the opera. Gluck and Mozart, however, made the overture a relative (even when not a bill-of-fare) to its opera. Indeed Gluck often connected the overture to his opera as in *Iphigenia in Tauris,* where the overture slides into the first act. Wagner's prelude to *Tristan und Isolde* does the same thing. In Mozart's *Idomeneo,* the overture also glides into Act I. He began to use samples of his opera in his overtures, as for example in *Don Giovanni;* a bit of the scary theme of the statue which came to life is heard in overture. Both Gluck and Mozart used three sections but did not let the plot or drama interfere with the beauty or form of the overture. Hence its ability to stand alone.

OVERTURE A PARENT TO SONATA FORM

Not only did the overture start the opera "politely" but it helped develop classic sonata form in ternary form, or in three sections. In the first section of the first movement, the sonata announces two themes which are contrasted in feeling; the second section enlarges upon these two themes and develops them according to the skill of the composer; the third section brings them back somewhat as they appeared in the first section. The sections are known as: Exposition, Development and Recapitulation.

Sonata form appears in the classic sonata, symphony, concerto, quartet, etc. Developing a small sample into a great web is its basis. In Haydn's time, his first symphonies were often called overtures, no doubt because the overture gradually took on the elements of sonata form. This type entirely replaced the Italian type in opera and oratorio.

BEETHOVEN'S FOUR

In Beethoven's "Leonore III" is found one of the loveliest examples in all overtures of symphonic sampling as well as one of the greatest pieces of instrumental music. Beethoven wrote four overtures to the opera now called *Fidelio*. Their order and identification is very puzzling, even to experts. There are three "Leonore" overtures and one "Fidelio."

The opera was produced in 1805 as *Leonore*. The overture used at this first performance is known as "Leonore II." After the first production of *Leonore*, the opera was shortened, staged again and Beethoven wrote another overture for it. This one is called "Leonore III"! It was played in 1806 when the opera appeared with a new and more original name, *Fidelio*. To be more confusing, the overture known as "Leonore I" was written for a performance scheduled for Prague which never took place. This overture was published as Opus 138 five years after Beethoven's death. When the opera was given in 1814, in the version we know now as *Fidelio*, in two acts, a fourth overture was used, the one known as "Fidelio." This one is used now to begin the opera, and the beautiful "Leonore III" is given between the acts.

"LEONORE III"

There is no argument about which of the overtures is the most perfect. "Leonore III" is the very pinnacle in beauty of the sampler symphonic overture, in which are given not only samples of the opera tunes but many versions of them, developed with Beethoven's consummate symphonic skill.

After Beethoven's time, composers seized upon the idea of giving samples in the overtures of operas to which they were mated. Indeed, they now became definite menus of the opera, with their best dishes shown. There is, however, very little symphonic development.

WEBER

Weber was definitely the first to write the sampler overture in *Der Freischütz*, which is perfect in unity and form. Weber invented the dramatic fantasia in the overtures to *Der Freischütz, Oberon* and *Euryanthe.*

Some of the most beautiful openers of opera occur in the works of Wagner. He puts the listener into the mood of the opera with miraculously woven bits of two or more samples. He uses many names for the openers. The Vorspiel to *Lohengrin* ranks second in the minds of the writers to Beethoven's "Leonore III." It uses one theme which dominates the opera in angelic shimmering and ethereal use of violins divided into many voices. You are transported to the domain of the Holy Grail.

The overture to *Tannhäuser,* although one of Wagner's early works, is a marvelous example of the use of antagonistic motifs which foretell the struggle in the story of the opera. The story is symphonically and glitteringly developed, and its importance in the overture stresses the high spots in the coming drama.

In *Tristan und Isolde,* the introduction (called the Prelude) uses seven samples, all of the leitmotifs or "calling-cards" of the principal themes, such as: The Confession of Love, Desire, The Glance, The Love Potion which causes all the mischief, The Death Potion which could have stopped the opera before it began, The Magic Casket out of which the potions had been taken and mixed by Brangäne, Isolde's companion, and finally The Deliverance from Death motif so gorgeously declaimed throughout. This prelude, like the rest of the opera, woven into a symphonic musical web, is amazingly moving. The opera enters as a continuation of the prelude.

Quite the opposite kind of overture are the ones of *Das Rheingold* and *Die Walküre.* In the first is heard a great, rolling musical figure based on one tone, which gives the picture of the mighty undulating River Rhine, in which is hidden the gold, the "root of all evil in The Ring." In *Die Walküre* is heard primarily the flight through the air and the neighs of the horses on which the Valkyr maidens (*Walküren*) carry their heroes to Valhalla (*Walhalla*), the home of the gods. This introduces the exciting atmosphere of the opera and gives the first taste of the "Ride of the Valkyrs." Then appear "The Incantation of Thunder" and "The Tempest." Here, too, there is no break between the Vorspiel and its opera.

Some acts are introduced by an opener to set the scene. For example, the third act of *Die Walküre* is opened by the "Ride of the Valkyrs." But among all act-openers, or preludes, there is none in all music drama that sets a scene better than that which introduces Act III of *Tristan und Isolde.* The scene to come is pictured in cold, stark music, which steeps the audience in the mood of foreboding. The bleakness of the visual scene to follow is drawn in the music.

In recent years there has been no set style in overtures. Many composers are making and have made overtures without operas, such as Walton's overture "Portsmouth Point," and Tchaikovsky's "Fantasy Overture, Romeo and Juliet." Such overtures are more like tone poems than opera openers.

SCENE V

The Orchestra and Teamwork

AFTER many years of slavery to the voice, finally instruments were freed and organized as a team, and became the orchestra, with its rich and varied responsibilities—a huge instrument of both individualistic and communal activities. The importance of instruments is due to the development and greater needs of composers and the resulting better instrumental construction. Which was cause and which was effect? Did the composer write better because of the improved instruments or were the instruments improved because of the demands of the composer? Furthermore, were it not for the influence of the dance, instruments might still be only "playing second fiddle" to the voice.

The orchestra owes much of its development to opera. The needs of this grasping "bundle of the arts," had to be met by a responsible group of instruments, as a bulwark to the voice, mood, and every vocal expression. It had to develop as a painter of sadness, gladness, fear, joy and every other feeling of the human breast. Besides, it had to fill in when the voice or action lagged purposely or by chance. For this the orchestra had to grow in gracefulness, nimbleness, power and glory, which it certainly has done. Today there are few aggregations of men who work together as a unit as do the musicians and the leader of the orchestra. Consider the coming of the more brilliant violin substituting for the older and more reticent viol; the clarinet, which was still a new instrument in Haydn's day; the development of the old hunting horn into the modern valve horn; the saxophone, which has not quite achieved high respectability in the modern symphony orchestra; the muffled bell of horns and trumpets of Berlioz' invention without which our jazz bands could not have functioned; the celesta as used by Tchaikovsky; and so on. Opera and concert have needed brilliant instruments, so the orchestra as an organization has logically assumed the responsibility.

INSTRUMENTS IN BANDS

Instruments of different kinds, like people, flock together in orchestras and bands—military, symphonic, jazz and swing. For a long time all groups of instruments were called "bands." It meant a group of players "banded" together. The bands played "on the march," in market places, at country fairs, at celebrations, and on military expeditions. The players were not seated; therefore the instruments had to be small and light.

The main difference between the band and orchestra today lies in the kind and number of instruments used, and even this distinction is waning—for the band is absorbing orchestral elements and the orchestra, band elements. The orchestra, when a band, had a few players only. Today it often has one hundred and ten and more. Hector Berlioz boasted that he had written a work for four hundred! And Gustav Mahler wrote a work for orchestra and chorus that is called the *Symphony of a Thousand*.

THE ORCHESTRAL TEAM

An orchestra is like a team with its squads and star players. The enjoyment of an orchestral work of any kind is increased by the knowledge of the duties, abilities and general character, kind of sounds and scope of each of the instruments, even as a baseball game is appreciated more when you know the positions and abilities of each player.

One way to know and enjoy the orchestral team is to hear and see it often in action. If this cannot be done, listen to the records such as Benjamin Britten's "The Young Person's Guide to the Orchestra," and others, on which examples of the sounds of all the instruments can be heard.

COMPOSERS AND PLAYERS

The composer makes the rules. The conductor must know the score. The team follows what the conductor orders from the musical score. The composer must know the sounds and timbre of sound, and the range and habits of each instrument; how each behaves when played loud, soft, fast, slow, for long stretches and for short stretches, and how they can blend with other instruments. The audience, to enjoy the orchestra fully, must learn to appreciate the different functions of these instruments, even as the baseball fan knows what to expect from the catcher, or the football fan the responsibilities of the halfback.

THE LEADER OR CAPTAIN OF THE TEAM

Before Felix Mendelssohn's day, in Germany and Italy, the orchestra conductor, or leader, sat at the harpsichord and played it occasionally. With hands, when free, he directed the orchestra. Sometimes the leader played the violin. Mendelssohn popularized the style of conducting without playing an instrument. Today, in nearly every case, the leader with a baton stands in front of his players in the manner, strange to say, begun by Lully in France. He has before him the score for the team and each player has his own part. Look at the left side of the score beginning with the names of each instrument. It gives directions to the leader or conductor. This is what he has to read as he leads the team. If he doesn't use a score, he must have a picture of it in his mind and ear.

He reads from the top to the bottom of each page, to know what instruments are to play, and his eyes must follow the music as it moves across the page from bar to bar. He knows the spot of entrance of each instrument to a split second. The score is marked so that the conductor can, with his baton, give entrance orders, or cues, to every instrument at the proper time.

A "ONE-WORLD" TEAM

Every individual and group of instruments adds its character to the whole in a sportsmanlike or most democratic union of effort. The piccolo player may have to sit through a long work and play only eight or ten tones, yet he does not complain. His piccolo with its own peculiar quality is as important to the good of the team as the violins, which may play almost continuously. The tuba player, in spite of George Kleinsinger's delightful "Tubby the Tuba," may have but three notes to play, yet he, too, is not jealous of the busy violins.

Opera too, owes much to the leader of the orchestra. He holds the unifying command of the actor-singers and is often moderator in questions of musical expression, rhythm, pace and accent. He can tell too in a dress rehearsal what sounds well as it is sent forth from the stage.

PRIMITIVE MAN'S INSTRUMENTS

Primitive man had all of the types of musical instruments that are in use today—the drum, the pipe and the lyre. He invented the different species with the exception of the keyboard. He clapped his hands,

Page from full orchestra score, Act II of *Der Rosenkavalier* by Richard Strauss.

stamped his feet, and slapped his body, thus using his natural percussion instruments. Soon he hollowed out tree trunks and covered them with skins of animals. Small pieces of bone such as animals' teeth and horns, nutshells, gourds, or hard seeds, when enclosed or strung together, were wonderful noise-makers. In another stage of development, man blew on reeds and bamboo and whittled pipes from twigs. Precursors of trumpets were hollowed pieces of wood, horns of animals or large conch shells that made frightening noises. Finally in the course of his evolution, the twanging of his hunting bow may have suggested the invention of stringed instruments. Between prehistoric time and the twentieth century there have been thousands of varieties of the rattle and drum type (percussion), the pipe type (wood winds and brasses), and the lyre, or string, type (strings and harp).

INSTRUMENTS AIDED EARLY OPERA

There was a time when no instrumental art existed. For so many centuries music was dominated by the Church, and under its influence vocal polyphony was brought to a high degree of perfection. When a secular instrumental art was developed and monody (one-line music) was introduced, the earliest operas, oratorios, and ballets needed the aid of instruments in order to function properly.

The early accompanying orchestra consisted of any instruments available at the time and place, but as the violin replaced the viol, the strings became the backbone of the orchestra even as they are today. The string orchestra put the lute and other species of the lute like the theorbo and the chitarrone, as well as the viol family, out of existence. These instruments, along with the harpsichord, spinet, or organ, served to accompany the opera efforts of the Camerata in Florence around 1600. They supplied the instrumentation of the thorough-bass (*basso continuo*) period. Recitative and vocal solos were accompanied by light chordal parts indicated by a figured bass.

At the time Peri and Caccini were making their first experiments with opera, Giovanni Gabrieli, organist of St. Mark's in Venice, was writing *sacrae simphoniae* (sacred symphonies) for ecclesiastical performance. His orchestra consisted of from two to six trombones, two or three *cornetti,* one or two violas, and sometimes a bassoon. The *cornetto* was not our cornet, but was descended from an instrument made of the curved horn of an animal, later replaced by wood or ivory. A similar instrument is still used by shepherds, Dr. Kurt Sachs says, in Finland, Esthonia, Sweden, Norway and Yugoslavia.

MONTEVERDI'S ORCHESTRA

A list of the instruments Claudio Monteverdi used in the score of his first opera *Orfeo* will be found on page 34. It might be worth while to reread the passage in order to realize what an orchestra was like in the early years of the Baroque Period. It will be recalled that Monteverdi created a new effect in the *stile concitato,* known to us as the *tremolo* or *vibrato.* He was also credited with *pizzicato* playing, or plucking of the strings of the violin, viola, violoncello and double bass.

When the players were confronted with the tremolo they would not take it seriously, and could not see why they should have to repeat the same note sixteen times by moving their bows up and down in the same spot, instead of sustaining one tone. Monteverdi had to use persuasion to make the men play the passage as he had written it.

The opera writers who followed Monteverdi stressed the string orchestra. Viols were still used but always as independent instruments, never as part of the violin family. The strings were rarely used as solo instruments, but the string section became better balanced under the followers of Monteverdi.

LULLY FOLLOWS THE RULES

In the second half of the seventeenth century, Lully and his French colleagues established the existing rules. They did not invent or discover new effects and ideas. Lully's orchestra was famous for *Les vingtquatre violons du Roi* (The twenty-four violins of the King). By 1700, flutes, oboes and horns became a well-defined group. And Lully clearly foreshadowed the combining of the wood winds and bassoons into a family group, although he still had them duplicating and did not play independently as they do in modern orchestration. Lully stood as a model for those who came after him in France.

BACH AND HANDEL CLOSE BAROQUE PERIOD

Bach and Handel, who closed the Baroque Period, also ended the use of a style of orchestration known as the contrapuntal. Bach's orchestration consisted largely of a duplication of string and wind parts, equally distributed. Neither Handel nor Bach knew what a standardized orchestra meant. Bach had to write according to the orchestral resources at hand. In Leipzig he had an orchestra of eighteen or twenty, and his strings were in four parts, which means that the violoncello and double bass were always doubled. In early eighteenth-century scores one finds the stereotyped use of two oboes doubling the first and second violins, and the bassoon doubling the bass.

RAMEAU MAKES INSTRUMENTS INDEPENDENT

Rameau, a contemporary of Bach and Handel, increased the independence of flutes, oboes, and bassoons, and he used clarinets, thus leading to the coloristic effects of the modern orchestra. The composers of the late eighteenth century followed Gluck's advice that "instruments are to be introduced in proportion to the degree of interest and passion in the words," and that "instruments are to be employed not according to the dexterity of the players, but according to the dramatic propriety of their tone." This made the use of instruments dependent on the dramatic situation on the stage. Adam Carse says that Italian opera in particular "had strayed so far from dramatic truth that almost every witty author of the time found its conventionalities a ready target for ridicule. . . ."

BIRTH OF THE "CLASSIC" ORCHESTRA

The style of instrumentation in the first part of the eighteenth century changed gradually with the changing style in composition that was on its way to classicism. The seeds of the new classicism were sprouting while Bach and Handel were still at their height. In Mannheim, Germany, the birthplace of the modern symphony orchestra, the old thorough bass accompaniment gave way to the new written-out orchestral parts, and Johann Stamitz (1717-57), conductor of the orchestra, was responsible for a new style of orchestral music and performance. As forerunner of the Classical Period, the Mannheim School is of greater value than are the works turned out by its members.

The modern orchestra, as evolved in Vienna by Haydn and Mozart, dates from the last twenty years of the eighteenth century, and profited by the experiments and achievements in Mannheim. The opera orchestras of Naples and Paris are numbered with the famous orchestras at Mannheim, Dresden and Berlin. The Mannheim Orchestra was known for its *ensemble* and for its tonal effects of *crescendo* (growing louder) and *diminuendo* (growing softer). This effect greatly increased the expressive powers of performance which happily were reflected in opera. Mozart wrote symphonies for the orchestras at Salzburg and Prague, and Haydn for his patron Prince Esterhazy at Eisenstadt, and later for the Salomon concerts at London.

By the end of the century the thorough-bass system had passed out of existence and with it the harpsichord. In opera the pianoforte was used for *recitativo secco* but in the opera pit, keyboard instruments were almost nonexistent.

In Paris, the Italian opera was conducted from the piano about 1778 but the French opera was conducted with a stick. In Lully's day, time was marked by pounding the floor with a heavy stick, which accounts for his death. In 1810, it was reported that Louis Spohr beat time with a roll of paper, "without the least noise, and without the slightest contortion of countenance."

Clarinets made their appearance in the middle of the eighteenth century with Rameau (1756), but were not generally included until its end. Trombones were used in operas and in church services before they were members of the orchestras. In Haydn and Mozart's time, the string section numbered fewer players than later, but there were more wood winds: three to six oboes and bassoons, three or four flutes and four horns. The wood winds must have overbalanced the strings.

As the orchestra became standardized more strings were added and the number of winds were reduced. Late symphonic works of Haydn, Mozart (with exceptions) and many Beethoven scores call for two each of flutes, oboes, clarinets, bassoons, horns, trumpets, timpani, and the usual strings. The piccolo, the English horn, the basset horn (tenor clarinet) and the double bassoon put in occasional appearances. Bass drums, cymbals and triangle are found once in a while in opera scores. Mozart used a mandolin in *Don Giovanni* and bells in *The Magic Flute*. Also, clarinets, which he loved, appear in most of his operas, but in only five symphonies.

The later operas by Mozart, Haydn's oratorios, and sacred choral works of both composers "represent the more highly colored orchestration associated with the stage, or the broader treatment required in combining the orchestra with choral voices," writes Adam Carse. In the operas of Mozart richer orchestral effects and more dramatic coloring are to be found than in his symphonies.

ROSSINI "LETS FRESH AIR AND LIGHT" INTO THE ORCHESTRA

Gioacchino Rossini is unusually important in opera orchestration. He wrote clearly and brilliantly, and displayed the solo instruments to advantage, making them stand out against harmonic accompanying backgrounds. He knew his horns because he had been a horn player himself. He was also famous for having been one of the first to write extended crescendos, for which effects he was regarded as a model.

Carse says that Rossini "let fresh air and light penetrate into the heart of the orchestra. . . ."

With the growth of the Romantic style, the orchestra grew in warmth of color and sensuous beauty.

THE ORCHESTRA'S DEBT TO BERLIOZ

The French Romanticist Hector Berlioz (1803–69), was the first composer to devote himself almost exclusively to orchestral and vocal compositions. Little wonder he was called the father of the modern orchestra! He had a genius for orchestration that had never before been equaled and has rarely been surpassed. From his day, composers of orchestral music built on what Berlioz knew and presented. In 1844, he published his *Treatise on Modern Instrumentation and Orchestration,* a book that is still basic as well as entertaining. He explored the tone color and characteristic qualities of every instrument, he studied blend, contrast and balance, and he treated the various choirs—wood winds, brass, percussion and strings—as independent entities. He invented new ways of using instruments. He elevated the viola to its estate as a solo instrument. He opened the way for Liszt, Gustav Mahler, Richard Strauss, and even for Richard Wagner.

WAGNER'S CONTRIBUTIONS

Richard Wagner (1813–83) had a greater influence on orchestration in the nineteenth century than his contemporary Berlioz. Berlioz' star has risen in the twentieth century surprisingly, and it is almost safe to say that the Berlioz influence is today more popular than the Wagner in the use of orchestration and instrumentation.

Wagner developed and enlarged the Beethoven orchestra. The Harvard Dictionary of Music says that the Wagner tubas made specially for use in "The Ring" "combine the agility of the cornet with the mellow timbre of the true tubas." They are not in general use today outside of Wagner scores, but may be heard in the symphonies of Bruckner and in Strauss's *Elektra.*

When Wagner wanted more noise, he added more instruments— eight horns, four wood winds, four trumpets, more drums and extra harps, etc. His method might be described as group orchestration. Wagner operas are notably hard to sing, against such an array of instruments. They require voices of heroic proportions, wide ranges, tremendous power, and powerful physiques.

In *Tristan und Isolde* all the maturity of Wagner's art is reflected in his tempered use of the orchestra. He seems to have developed it into a medium of rich timbres (tone colors) and used the interweaving of instruments to produce expressive effects instead of exaggerating the blatancy of brass and wood winds. He handed down to those who followed him, Richard Strauss in particular, a mellowed orchestra of great richness of sonority, a tapestry of multi-colors, characteristic of the high Romantic Period in which he lived and which he helped to make. Wagner left a legacy of a vastly original and expanded orchestral language.

Gustav Mahler and Richard Strauss followed Wagner in demanding an enormous orchestra. Although one of the greatest opera conductors, Mahler never wrote an opera. Strauss, than whom no composer for orchestra has been greater as a craftsman, loved to work with a gigantic orchestra. In the International Cyclopedia of Music and Musicians, Philip James wrote: "He established a new standard of orchestral performance by taxing the players to the utmost in making frequent use of intense upper registers sometimes beyond the legitimate ranges of the instruments, and made an extension of technique in every voice; in his aim for realism we have a new delineation in the extra effects of all instruments." He added greatly to the orchestrator's "bag of tricks."

RIMSKY-KORSAKOV LEADS INTO THE TWENTIETH CENTURY

In the meantime, a new school, or method, of orchestration had been growing up with Rimsky-Korsakov (1844–1908) of the Russian "Five." Like Berlioz, Rimsky wrote a book, *Principles of Orchestration,* which definitely turned the tide from a mammoth orchestra to a smaller palette characterized by brilliancy, clarity, directness, and a new evaluation put upon the solo instruments for timbre and effect. Rimsky's influence has extended far beyond the Russian border into France, where it reached Debussy, Ravel, and practically all the composers of Impressionism.

Rimsky wrote in 1891: "Our epoch, the post-Wagnerian age, is the age of brilliance and imaginative quality in orchestral tone coloring." He names Berlioz, Glinka, Liszt, Wagner, Delibes, Bizet, Borodin, Balakirev, Glazunov, and Tchaikovsky as having brought "this side of musical art to its zenith; they have eclipsed, as colorists, their predecessors, Weber, Meyerbeer and Mendelssohn, to whose genius, nevertheless, they are indebted for their own progress." Tonal resonance and orchestral combination are also subjects of his investigation.

STRAVINSKY BRINGS US UP TO DATE

One of Rimsky's pupils was Igor Stravinsky, who studied orchestration with him from 1906 to 1908, laying a traditional foundation from which he branched off. He was an innovator in his employment of instruments, no longer using them as a medium for coloristic effects, but choosing each instrument because of its individual timbre. These timbres are not blended but are treated as separate strands of sound, a polyphony of tone colors. To Stravinsky, orchestration is not a thing apart but is itself the music. He no longer views the orchestra as a means of expressive effect, but to him, a composition is itself the "musical object."

It is said that in his home in Switzerland, Stravinsky had a collection of all the instruments of the orchestra, and he learned to play a scale on each of them. He studied their possibilities in range, timbre, and eccentricities, all of which he made use of. How do you suppose the neighbors liked these experiments? "His knowledge of all the technical possibilities of each instrument," Alexandre Tansman writes in his book *Ivor Stravinsky: The Man and His Music,* "the sonorous value of each register, the relationships between instruments, whether united or contrasted, the emotional value of their mode of emission, joined to an admirable gift of intuition and divination, are made use of by the composer with rare and infallible success."

Stravinsky has been the leader of today's generation of composers. He has been called a neo-Classicist because he, with many others, has returned to eighteenth-century ideals in form and methods of composition—the term "neo-Baroque" explains the root of his research into the past. In his successful attempt to rediscover and to restore instruments to their original character, he has been a neo-Classicist in the art of orchestration also.

"No contemporary musician has contributed more wealth, more variety in the instrumental combinations," says Tansman, "and more novelties in the choice of timbres than Igor Stravinsky."

SCENE VI

Scenery Interprets

As THIS story of opera has progressed, scenery has been mentioned, but this will be the shortest section in the book in spite of the intensely important role scenery has in opera and all theater. Without appropriate scenery an opera can be very much weakened, not only in atmosphere but in action. A column, a door, a wall, or a chair, or a false color or combination of colors in the wrong place can block the continuity of the plot and thwart the imagination of the onlooker.

In passing, we might mention that costumes, too, are important. It is obvious that to dress an actor in the toga of a Roman general to play the part of an American senator would be absurd! The costume as well as the scenery must be appropriate in detail.

The subject of lighting has been a problem all through the ages, from the time of outdoor and indoor pageants and plays when torches and thousands of candles lit inadequately the stage or area of operations. Today, with the vast electrical equipment, the book of the "light plot" is often hundreds of pages thick and yet lighting experts maintain that they are only just beginning to light adequately. The problem of making scenery, music and costumes into a unit is a problem indeed.

EARLIEST SCENERY

Some scenery and some props have been necessary, from the use of the little altar in worship of Dionysus to the cinema *The Robe,* and the elaborately simple scenery of Expressionists, who exercise the actors on flights of steps leading back to architectural devices which can signify anything from a house to pillars of doom. These sets often, too, are used without a curtain. Scenery is important. It is another key to the interpretation of opera.

THE ANCIENT THEATER

The early Greeks built their theater, fed by the imagination of its audience and its knowledge of the story, with very little scenery, although it had to use some, such as the *deus ex machina;* boards painted white for lightning flashes; a little platform on wheels drawn from backstage for showing interiors (see page 6). Then came the medieval custom of play-giving "on location" with its natural scenery.

During and after this era the theater was, like the Shakespearean theater, "in the round." Scenic construction ran into problems when the proscenium arch was first used in theaters and space was restricted, both up-and-down and horizontally.

Since this time there have been various experiments not only to make scenery add pictorially to a performance, but to achieve this without killing the imagination of the spectators. In this new theater, with the realization that all the audience can never see all the stage, the problems of lighting and scenery are profound.

The theater to the Greeks was their most "vital creative expression" (Kenneth MacGowan). For "pure theater" they have never been surpassed. The mysteries of life and the tragedies went beyond their humdrum life and their comedy is so exaggerated as to seem vulgar to us today. The modern theater does not so much feed our imaginations or emotions, for we live in an age where we get stimuli outside of the theater. Therefore, it is important that the eye be somewhat satisfied in the theater to communicate the proper feeling and atmosphere of the play or opera. For this reason, various devices and schools of scene-making have sprung up during the last fifty years. Among the names of these schools are the Constructionist, Expressionist, the Realistic, the Theatric, and many more, according to the amount and type of scenery used; some having practically no scenery but curtains, different stage levels, flights of steps, and a few well-placed columns—and to the designer of lighting in all its color and variety comes the problem of creating the illusion of softness, hardness, bulk, mystery, reality, fantasy, and down-to-earthness.

The drama has gone through all the stages of scenic experiment from the symbolic type, *They Brought the News to Mary,* to the new, realistic setting for *Andrea Chenier* at the Metropolitan Opera House in 1955.

Scenery in the last analysis must feed the eye, help the story and yet not block the imagination. What the imagination is can be well explained by the vast enjoyment derived from a good play, well presented on the radio. The listener unconsciously fills in the appropriate costume, lighting, and environment (scenic props), with the aid only of his imagination. Without the use of this sixth sense, visual drama would be impossible to present even by the most accomplished scenic artist. He needs the help of the imagination of the audience.

ACT VII. Opera Is Led by Great Commanders

SCENE I

Wagner the Magician

EVERY now and then there comes a man, admired and hated, who is saint and sinner; a magician in his work; a demon in his everyday relationships; a man who, through a persistent dream-driven urge, in debt and out of debt, in misery and frustration, with little or no help where most needed, succeeds grandly to the glory of the world. This was Richard Wagner, who before he died had his own theater built to his own order, in which were held festivals of his operas that attracted music lovers and composers from all over the world!

Unlike other men, his life was derived from his work instead of his work from his life.

Few have been penetrating enough to understand his amazing brain and its reactions. No one has been able to follow him in opera, yet many have used his ideas, such as leitmotifs, continuous melody and some schemes of harmony. He was four men in one: one of the first to write his own librettos, his own music, direct his operas, and plan to the exact inch his own scenery—to the despair of the designers! Richard Wagner, "poet and thinker," as he called himself, created and peopled worlds of his own. He takes us with him into a universe of heroes and heroines, artists and muddlers, the lovelorn, the lover, gods and goddesses, saints and sinners, magic swords, magic fire, magic rings, magic potions, but above all, magic music. He told his stories, which usually had a moral, with music lavishly rich, brilliant, tender, loving, striking, mild, wild, always colorful.

MUSIC OF THE FUTURE

Wagner believed in himself beyond everyone and everything and he also believed in what he called the "music of the future" which must unite all the arts (*Gesammtmusik*) in the service of music-drama (not opera). He was finished with what had been called opera. In Wagner's lifetime, Germany was using French and Italian operas, as in Mozart's time. Up to 1900, French opéra comique was popular in Germany, but German operas had had a hard time. So Wagner's final victory in his homeland was all the greater.

Ernest Newman in *Wagner as Man and Artist* says that Wagner, in his essay "A Pilgrimage to Beethoven," saw that music could in the future renew its vitality only by being "fertilized by poetry and that real music drama will be continuous tissue." Wagner, in a bit of journalism, cleverly makes Beethoven say of the making of opera: "Were I to make opera after my own heart, people would run away from it, for it would have no arias, duets, trios, or any other of the stuff with which operas are patched today; and what I would put in their places no audience would listen to. . . . Anyone who should write a real music drama would be taken for a fool."

Between 1830 and 1900 there were 600, more or less, popular German operas! Few, however, were played except those of the poverty-ridden, luxurious spender of other people's money, proud, unpleasant, much-criticized, and finally lionized, Wagner.

WAGNER THE YOUTH

Richard Wagner, the ninth child in his family, was born in Leipzig, Germany, in 1813. He came into the world after our Revolutionary War. And most important, he lived during the Napoleonic years after the French Revolution, when men were freer to express their opinions. He lived when the operas of Gluck and Weber were no longer given, but he so loved Weber and studied him so diligently that Weber has been called his "musical grandfather." The boy Wagner knew every word and every note by heart of *Der Freischütz.*

It was well that he was born after instruments had reached a high stage of development. He must also have been familiar with Berlioz' orchestra and treatise on orchestration. But it was Beethoven's *Choral Symphony* (the Ninth), that convinced Wagner how vocal and instrumental music should be symphonically treated. In other words, he learned how to use and develop a few notes into magnificent and refreshing patterns, and weave them into a mighty polyphony, as colored strands in a variegated rug. In short, this weaving or developing of a small design into a larger one and into one great whole is the central idea of the elements in Wagner music-drama. In this symphonic scheme Wagner considered himself the direct descendant of Beethoven.

Unlike Mozart, Richard was not a child prodigy. His father died when he was less than a year old, and his stepfather, Ludwig Geyer the actor-painter, died when he was eight. Fed upon Geyer's stories and trips to the playhouse with him, Richard developed an overwhelming love for the theater. He fell in love with its make-believe. This love increased with his understanding and sustained him in his work, for a proper presentation of make-believe, or "good theater," is the essence of opera.

His school report was never more than fair, yet by the time he was thirteen he had become a good Greek scholar. He was scholarly only in the subjects which pleased him. He was no lover of formal education and very difficult to teach. He was so interested in Homer's *Iliad,* with its Greek myths, that later in life they fed his love for legend and impelled him to study and interest himself in the Norse and German sagas which he was to use magniloquently.

His people evidently had no idea of his capabilities or sensibilities, nor could they excuse the peculiarities of this boy not yet fifteen with definite learning but with no evidence of genius. Before he was eighteen, he had had very little formal education, and none at all in music. He implored his family, then living in Dresden, to let him go back to school at Leipzig. He was so persistent that they permitted it. His family regarded this explosive, anxious, sensitive child as a rapscallion and a devil.

When he went back to Leipzig, he was put in a lower grade than he had been in, in Dresden. This soured him. His life in the future was consistent with this. He was constantly being hurt by people who did not mean to hurt him.

Up to now he had been writing lurid dramas, and at fourteen he begged his family to let him study music. But they didn't think he was suited to it, nor did they welcome the idea, so insecure did they consider this profession. In time few music instructors would teach him, for he was too hostile. So this one-man educational institution, Richard Wagner, for the most part, was self-taught.

As a young fellow, he spent most of his time in libraries, where he studied orchestral scores of Mozart, Bach, Haydn, Weber, and Beethoven. He copied all nine of Beethoven's symphonies. He learned from these scores the use of instruments; from his beloved Weber, the use of legends near home; and from Beethoven, the development of short themes into a mighty work. Beethoven's *Ninth Symphony* with its choral and instrumental parts, helped to give the Wagner epoch to the world.

Richard entered the university in Leipzig in 1831. He had read so many plays and legends, and reveled so wholeheartedly in romance and tragedy that he could not help, in the dramas he was writing, but outdo in the spectacular all the writers he read. At sixteen Wagner wrote a play, *Leubald,* so gory that he had to bring back most of the forty-two characters from the dead, as ghosts, in order to finish it!

While attending the university, Richard, the firebrand, became interested in the political upheavals. Germany was in the throes of becoming a unified nation. His writings began to be tinged with the idea of freedom in art and music, and he wasn't bashful in expressing what he thought. Before the police caught up with him, the hot-headed boy decided to go to Vienna (1832), but soon returned because he couldn't stand hearing the Strauss waltzes and Hérold's popular opera *Zampa.* By this time he had written his *Symphony in C Major* and a poor opera, *Die Hochzeit (The Wedding,* 1832), which he tore up the next year.

By twenty, Wagner had had a few works performed. When his "Overture in B Flat Minor" was played (1830), it had so many timpani beats that the audience became hysterical. This embarrassed him greatly, but it can be seen that Wagner's music began to have what is vulgarly called "guts."

But the poor lad was suffering the tortures of poverty. Beautiful surroundings, whether in his home, in clothing, or in the landscape, induced in him a dreamlike state which seemed to develop his tremendous drive. In spite of his poverty, his favorite drink was champagne, as it was Schumann's. They both drank too much of it for the health of their pocketbooks!

CHORUSMASTER

Wagner took a job as chorusmaster at five dollars a week when he was writing *Die Feen (The Fairies).* He often began operas which he didn't finish until some years afterwards because something would remind him of another story, and the *daemon,* or spirit in him, would urge him on to the new, although he never forgot the old. *Die Feen,* inspired by Weber's *Die Freischütz,* was given when Richard was twenty-one. In this fantastic story of fairies and comical folk, he tried to show how the romantic, comic, and tragic sides of life are indivisible and could move the soul of the spectators. In this he preached and moralized, as he continued to do throughout his life.

A MOMENTOUS OCCASION

One of the events in Wagner's life that exerted a tremendous influence on him was his meeting in 1834 with the singer Madame Wilhelmine Schroeder-Devrient, and hearing her in the role of Leonore in Beethoven's *Fidelio*. He maintained to the end of his life that she gave him the inspiration to form music and poetry into an unbreakable union.

In order to eat, Wagner had to make money, and this he did by conducting. It was beneficent, for he learned the needs of the orchestra, the alliance between the orchestra and the voice, an experience given to few young composers.

While conducting at Magdeburg, he wrote *Das Liebesverbot* (*A Ban on Love,* 1836), based on Shakespeare's better story, *Measure for Measure*. He suggested, childishly, doing away with all usual behavior dictated by our codes of decency and politeness. In this free-for-all exiling of the conventions, young Wagner had a field day. He let loose his early ideas for man's freedom. Its music echoed Bellini and Auber, but who can blame a young man of twenty-one for not being original!

RICHARD AND MINNA

Soon Wagner was off to conduct in Königsberg, in East Prussia (1837). The year before he had married pretty Wilhelmina Planer, a young actress. They led a miserable existence, for she (as any other woman probably would have) found it hard to be happy with an eccentric and a genius, a man driven to work, and just as ready to borrow money as to eat, who could curse those who wouldn't understand him, and bought luxuries when he needed shoes. Probably his love of luxury spurred him to write luxuriant and rich music. We recognize him as a genius. But it must have been difficult to see one who didn't pay his debts with purple velvet curtains in his study. We forgive the genius, who was thought in his day to be a cad.

In Königsberg with Minna, he went through the usual financial crisis. He was anxious to raise the musical standards at Riga, but he was soon dismissed because of his debts. This was disappointing, for he had hoped to make money and achieve fame. So, with Minna and Robber, his beloved dog, a Great Dane, he went to Paris via the perilous seas.

RIENZI

While in Paris, he started the opera *Rienzi* with his own libretto based on Lord Bulwer-Lytton's novel, *Rienzi, The Last of the Tribunes,* a semi-historical study of ancient Rome, full of unrest and glamour. Nothing of it is given now but its overture. If this overture has lost its opera, it is only following the composer's example, who repudiated it! In this bill-of-fare overture you hear the splendid trumpet flare, which rouses the populace; the beautiful "Prayer of Rienzi" ("Almighty Father"), the Rienzi motif, and the turbulent and romantic musical interweavings which paint confusion and beauty. *Rienzi* has a strength all its own, even if a bit like the Meyerbeer pageantry and old-fashioned opera mill—dances, mass effects, and exciting finales.

In his anxiety to get *Rienzi* produced, Wagner, with not enough to eat to keep himself alive, did everything in his power from writing and arranging music to singing very badly in a chorus. Over and over again he went to see Meyerbeer, who was then manager of the French Opéra, and from whom, as from every other man in authority, he received only empty pledges of help. In these agonizing months of disappointment and hardship, he felt his powers increasing. He spoke frankly of this in *Mein Leben* (*My Life*), a fascinating diary of a man who knows his own value.

During his agonies of starvation and humiliation, he saw Jacques Offenbach, the grotesque figure of the Paris boulevards in "all his glory" successfully presenting his operas. This didn't make things easier. In his misery, he wrote a "Faust Overture," which is still played and is prophetic of *Tristan and Isolde.*

During his first unhappy visit in Paris, he did have an overture, "Columbus," produced (1841). But it failed.

Wagner decided (1842) to go from Paris to Dresden. There he knew he would be able to get his "goddess and songbird," Madame Schroeder-Devrient, to sing in *Rienzi,* which was given with great success in 1842. At the third performance, the conductor handed the baton to the young composer, who had his first taste of glory, but little money. The poet Heine heard it and said that "with this opera Wagner had placed himself in line with the worthiest masters . . . Some loathsome Italianized fools were of the opinion that the work 'surpassed even the divine Donizetti.'"

New York was introduced to *Rienzi* at the Academy of Music in

1878, and three years after Wagner died, it was given at the Metropolitan Opera House (1886).

THE FLYING DUTCHMAN

Yet, in spite of all his suffering, urged on by his *daemon,* he started work on *The Flying Dutchman,* stimulated by his memories of the perilous and stormy trip in the tiny ship *Thetis,* during which the sailors told him stories and legends of the Northlands. From these tales, his own experiences, and perhaps from a story of the poet Heine, and one of his own, he was ready to write *Der Fliegende Holländer* (*The Flying Dutchman*), which tells the story, in three acts, of a captain of a sailing ship with red sails, who blasphemed against God and was destined to roam the seas until redeemed by the love of a woman who would sacrifice her life for him. In this, Wagner glories in his self-appointed mission of preaching sacrificing love as a savior of mankind. Here, too, he uses a few themes or little melodies as calling cards, or leading motifs (leitmotifs) to represent each character, occurrence, thing or idea, such as the storm, spinning, the Dutchmen as they enter or are suggested. Not yet does he use them as he will later, changing their forms, colors, moods, into a mighty web, but keeping their individuality, as his tapestry grows in magnificence. In *The Flying Dutchman,* too, we hear Wagner's first really great dramatic monologue, differing from the decorated arias because of its directness and freedom from repeats of sections and other fatiguing repetitions then prevalent in Italian and French opera.

The overture breathes excitement. You feel the gale and hear the waves as the music gives you the bill-of-fare leitmotifs of the opera to follow. Among the motifs are those of the Flying Dutchman, Senta's "Ballade," the germ of the whole opera, and the Spinning theme. "It is," said Ernest Newman in *Wagner's Operas,* "the first real sea picture in music and today the best of its kind." After he had written *Tristan und Isolde,* he went back to his overture and gave it a better ending.

A BIG STEP

In *The Flying Dutchman* Wagner took a long step from Meyerbeer and started to write opera with continuous music, less interrupted by arias and Italian flights into coloratura and "whatnots." This tuneful and magnificently lurid opera still has some of the dramatic devices of Weber, particularly the reliance on magic, as well as some of

Bellini, Auber, Halévy, and other writers of opéra comique, with which Wagner was drenched. For example, his Senta sacrifices her life for love by jumping off a cliff into the sea to redeem her bewitched Dutchman. This is not unlike Bellini's Norma, burned on the funeral pyre with her lover, or Auber's heroine, Fenella (from *The Dumb Girl of Portici*), who jumps from a royal balcony into the hot lava flowing from Mt. Vesuvius. Romantic!

This opera was meant to be in one act. Therefore, when the critics say it is overstuffed, it might appear so, because Wagner, in order to satisfy producers, may have filled it in. Whatever and however it is now, it is vastly interesting and has germs of the imperishable Wagner to come.

The Flying Dutchman landed first at the Hoftheater, Dresden (1843). It was first given in English at the Academy of Music, London (1877). The Metropolitan Opera gave it in German (1889) and rarely again until 1950 under Rudolf Bing, impresario.

TANNHÄUSER, THE MINSTREL KNIGHT

Wagner's love for the ancient tales of Germany led him to write *Tannhäuser and the Song Contest at the Wartburg* (*Tannhäuser und der Sängerkrieg auf dem Wartburg*), which he called not opera or drama, but *Handlung* (action). This shows that he intended to write a new dramatico-musical form. Yet, from its general make-up, this work is still too closely related to the past to be an example of the music drama of "the future." He wrote this after a long "build-up" through travel and sightseeing, which always affected him. It is said that when he passed the Wartburg, in which Luther had been imprisoned and where in medieval times the great Festivals of Song had been held, he was enamored of the massive structure and later remembered it so vividly that he gave an exact picture of it to the scene painter, who reproduced it, detail for detail, in the production of *Tannhäuser*!

Wagner's sixth opera is of a minstrel knight who lived in the thirteenth century, and with other minstrels had taken part in a song tournament at the Wartburg Castle in Carinthia. The story tells in colorful, melodious, and rousing music the tale of Tannhäuser, lured from his exemplary mortal bride-to-be, Elizabeth, by Venus, the goddess of love, and how he was redeemed. Here again Wagner is the moralist, pitting the good against the evil, and weaving a love tale such as he had never experienced. In a most ingenious combination of legend, magic, love, religion, ballet, and melody, with the richest orchestration up to this time, the opera has remained a recompense for eye and ear.

THE OVERTURE OF TANNHÄUSER

This overture, of the bill-of-fare type, is a condensed table of contents of the important ideas of the drama and the development of two main themes in magnificent combat: "The Pilgrims' Chorus," sung by the holy men, and the motif of the Venusberg, the abode of luxury and unholy joys. Then the "Hymn to Venus" bursts out, and after some changes of coloring or of key, reverts to "The Pilgrims' Chorus," accompanied by strident passages on the violins, and ends in a brilliant finale. Of course, the good pilgrims have won. Wagner must spin a moral—but in what "glorious sheen"!

Among the well-known and well-loved songs of *Tannhäuser* are: "The Pilgrims' Chorus"; Elizabeth's song, *"Dich, teure Halle"* ("Thou, Dear Hall of Song"); Elizabeth's Prayer; and Wolfram's song to the evening star. The Venusberg music is highly flavored. This opera, a mixture of the seductive and the sacred, is a well-put-together dramatic "show."

INFLUENCE OF WEBER

Again Weber's use of magic influenced Wagner in *Tannhäuser*. In the first act the pagan revels end in the Venusberg with a terrible crash. Tannhäuser, repentant, finds himself in a beautiful valley with the Wartburg in sight. There is magic in the last act, too, wherein the cross or rod that he carries from Rome blossoms with leaves as a sign that he is forgiven.

WAGNER'S CHORUS

In the second act is seen and heard Wagner's superb use of the chorus. When the people come in to the Hall of Song different sections do different things and express the emotion of human beings, not of puppets.

CONTINUOUS MUSIC

Wagner now attempts to follow his own dictates and not repeat words and phrases. He departs in many ways from the old-fashioned melody, and begins an elementary use of little calling-cards or motifs, developed more fully in later works. The Venusberg, "The Pilgrims'

Chorus," Elizabeth, Wolfram, and others, and The Damnation of
Tannhäuser each has its own motif, repeated and modified in various
forms throughout the opera, giving one comfortable familiarity with
the action.

TANNHÄUSER'S FATE

The reception of this opera when it was first given in Dresden was
stormy. When it was produced later in Paris (March 13, 1861), a
writer said, "Wagner came in for one of the chief tempests of his
career."

After persistent and not too well stapled-down wire-pulling, the
composer obtained an imperial order (from Napoleon III) for the
production of *Tannhäuser* at the Grand Opéra. Wagner was so thrilled
to know that his drama was to be produced that he composed a special
ballet for the first act (1861). This bacchanale was to be danced in the
mountain grotto of Venus, during a love scene between Tannhäuser
and the goddess. A bacchanale in ancient Greece was a wild dance
performed in the worship of Bacchus.

When the manager realized that the ballet was placed in the first
act, he was enraged. He ordered Wagner to put it in the second and
dress it up with the usual operatic claptrap. Wagner refused, even
though it threatened the success of the coveted Paris performance. Paris
at that time was the heaven of all operatic composers. The manager
said that the Jockey Club, a group of fashionable Parisian young men,
always came too late to see a ballet in the first act, and they would
spoil the performance by interruptions. The young blades heard about
this "outrage" of placing the ballet in the first act, before they had time
to finish their coffee, and when they entered the Paris Opera House,
they made such a rumpus that Wagner thought it was to celebrate the
Emperor's arrival. Instead, it was a riot set up against his "impudence."
As a result the opera was mangled. The conductor wasn't any too
good, and it was not until a full generation later that the now popular
opera was appreciated. This was one of the most notorious first-night
fiascos along the road of opera.

Wagner wrote, after the failure and the spiritual loneliness of that
night, "A feeling of complete isolation took possession of me. It was not
my vanity; I had deceived myself with my eyes open, and now I was
quite stunned by it. I had only one thought: to bring the public to
understand and to share in my views, and to accomplish its artistic
education." Again he is the mentor!

Tannhäuser was first given at the Metropolitan Opera House in 1884 and inaugurated the German era there. Leopold Damrosch, father of Walter, directed. Not until 1889 was the Paris version heard in New York. It was conducted by Anton Seidl with Lilli Lehmann as Venus. In the Paris version the overture slides into Act I without pause.

REVOLUTION

Into the revolution of 1848 in Germany Wagner jumped with "both feet." Whatever he did, he did furiously. His station (reminding us of Shostakovich's in the Battle of Leningrad, as an observer of the Battle of the Streets) was in the tower of the *Kreuzkirche* in Dresden, three hundred feet above the ground. His duty was to observe what was happening and to conduct fighters over the barricades, deliver messages and food to them, and collect hand grenades. Like the musician he was, said he to a buddy, "The view is splendid. The combination of bells and cannon is intoxicating." When warned to be careful, he replied, "The bullet that could lay me low has not yet been cast." (*Mein Leben,* by Richard Wagner). Even in duels or whatever danger he incurred, Wagner seemed destined to be spared.

VON BÜLOW

After Wagner had completed *Tannhäuser* and it had been produced, *Die Meistersinger* began to stir in his brain, and at the same time he made sketches for *Lohengrin*. Wagner often worked on several things at a time. The same year that he began the composition of *Lohengrin* (*The Knight of the Swan*), he conducted Beethoven's *Ninth Symphony* in Dresden (1846) and met Hans von Bülow for the first time. Von Bülow and Wagner were destined to know each other under very difficult circumstances, yet von Bülow never lost his faith in the composer and artist, if he did in the man.

LOHENGRIN (KNIGHT OF THE SWAN)

It would sound queer to call Wagner a backward composer, but he did write *Lohengrin* backwards, doing the last act first, and in the four operas known as "The Ring of the Nibelungen," he wrote the prologue, "*Das Rheingold,*" last. While taking a cure in Marienbad, he had started writing the *Lohengrin* poem and by August, 1847, had finished the score. This opera is a Wagnerian mixture of history, mythology, and legend about Lohengrin and the Holy Grail, the cup out of which the Savior drank at the Last Supper. It has magic music and a moralistic ending, with its settings among knights, ladies, charms, and dreams. One of the sources on which Wagner based the libretto was the life of Wolfram von Eschenbach, a minstrel knight of the thirteenth century, who also "helped" Wagner in *Tannhäuser*. This drama took the place of one he wished to write on Jesus of Nazareth.

Lohengrin is one of the loveliest fairy tales in music. The celestial overture, or prelude, whose leitmotif stands throughout the opera for the Holy Grail, glows like a vision of iridescent light. It is the most shimmering musical example of the whir of angel wings, and a picture of a halo.

This prelude is meant to describe the descent of the Holy Grail to the mountain of the pious knights, and its return to Heaven in the midst of a band of angels. As Gustave Kobbé well said, you get a "glimpse of supernatural radiance." It starts softly in the high regions of the violins, divided into twelve choirs or parts. These violins, divided as they are, give the ethereal shimmer. Then the melody goes to the other strings, to the wood winds and brasses, and after a tremendous crescendo, denoting the ascent into Heaven, dies into a radiant softness in the muted violins. Its celestial quality cannot be described. It must be heard. It opened a new vista in spiritual representation in music. It is like a bridge carrying the mind, heart, and soul toward heaven. As Bach opened a new vista of spiritual feeling in his music in his *B Minor Mass,* Wagner in one short instrumental prelude opens another vista as his soaring orchestra acts without vocal help. Furthermore, he already had enough dramatic instinct to drop the "Swan Song" into the last act, to make the drama end with a direct climax.

Among the familiar and well-loved bits is the "Wedding March" of the third act. It is difficult to think of any wedding having taken place before Wagner wrote this march, so inevitable is it now, linked up with Mendelssohn's "Wedding March" from *The Midsummer Night's Dream*.

Then there is "Elsa's Dream" in the first act, where she tells the King and a tremendous crowd of people of the hero who is going to come "in shining armor" to save her from punishment for the murder of her brother which she had not committed. The King's song in this act, sung by a basso, is so fervidly melodious that its melody has been used as a hymn in some Protestant churches. Another beautiful song is Lohengrin's farewell to his bride, who has, by her curiosity in trying to learn his identity, lost him. Here follows the leitmotif, the mystery of the name which had figured so beautifully in Lohengrin's opening address when he stepped out of the Swan Boat to save Elsa. As Lohengrin said good-by to Elsa, so Wagner said good-by to the old time making of operas.

The first performance of *Lohengrin* was in 1850, at the Hoftheater in Weimar, and in America it was first given in German at the Stadt Theater (as was *Tannhäuser*) in New York in 1871. In 1874 it was heard in Italian at the New York Academy of Music, and it entered the German repertory of the Metropolitan Opera House in its first season, 1883.

At the time *Lohengrin* was to be produced in Weimar, Wagner, wanted by the police because of his radical ideas, was forced to leave Germany. He fled to Zurich, Switzerland, missed the performance of his *Lohengrin,* conducted by Liszt, and did not hear it until years later.

ZURICH

Back in Zurich with Minna, Wagner was again very unhappy. As always, when most unhappy and most uncomfortable, he worked the hardest. He began to write his many pamphlets and articles as well as books, to rationalize his exile and explain his theories of art and politics. Among the things he says are that Art is not for pleasure but a record. He also defends his beliefs in the music drama as a union of all the arts. And logically enough, during the following twelve years we see him fashioning his own librettos and designing his own scenery for the next and greatest period of his career.

THE ARTS BUNDLE

In his exile Wagner had time to think things through. After *Lohengrin* he was about ready to pursue his new theories. His over-all idea was *Gesammtkunstwerk*. His aim was to make opera a bundle of the many arts. One of his devices was the leitmotif, which in a few notes developed and enlarged in variation, foretells, introduces, or reintroduces an idea such as redemption or love; a person such as Brünnhilde or Wotan; things such as the Sword or the Tamhelm which makes the wearer invisible; and very often the music in its pace and rhythm denotes quality, such as the quality of heaviness, as in the giants, Fafner and Fasolt. The calling-cards, too, often give insight into gestures and deportment. In the whole "Ring" there are dozens of these leitmotifs, which, if you know them and hear the operas, is like having a musical libretto because you can easily follow the story in whatever language the opera is given. Here you see concretely music as an almost universal language. For example, when Siegfried appears, you hear his motif, and as the drama progresses, or where he is thought of or mentioned, it is changed to meet the occasion. Valhalla, the home of the gods, in the beginning is represented in its motif as glorious and mighty, but when in *"Die Götterdämmerung"* Valhalla collapses with the downfall of the gods, it becomes tragic.

When his music dramas were rehearsed, he nearly drove his fellow workers mad. The mixture in him of dreamer and realist made him want things to be real and yet to have a fairy-tale atmosphere. His demand for a realistic dragon breathing fire and smoke and lashing out at Siegfried was a mammoth problem.

A FEW OF WAGNER'S GIFTS TO OPERA

Here are *some* of the things that Wagner did or wanted to do in his music dramas:

1. He wrote his own librettos to make his dramas unified.

2. He showed the possibility of *continuous* symphonic song and orchestra.

3. He proved that action need not be interrupted with songs to show off the stars' skill, as did Rossini, Donizetti, and even Verdi in earlier operas. Indeed, to sing Wagner's music takes skill enough!

4. Whereas Beethoven forgot his drama for the moral, Wagner was able to forget neither his drama nor the moral. He became a preacher in spite of critics.

5. Wagner introduced the practice of no waits between scenes, to the distraction of his scenic assistants.

6. Against the will of the audiences, he insisted upon the theater being darkened before the first curtain went up. Even as late as 1890, in England, the people fretted when Covent Garden was darkened. But Wagner's ideas prevailed because the darkness bathes the audience in the mood of the drama.

7. In particular, he enlarged the orchestra and made it one of the characters of his drama, an actifier instead of a filler-in. He went on from where Beethoven left off to make the orchestra as important as the singer. Wagner appreciated the values and greater possibilities of brass instruments (see page 286). He said himself that he had "out-

Meyerbeered Meyerbeer" in colorful orchestration. As he progressed in the writing of magniloquent drama-with-music, he developed the brass choir in the orchestra by giving it messages of force, beauty, nobility, gloom, sometimes humor; expanding always the powers of expression of *all* the instruments, including the bass clarinet. His use of wood winds, too, is sometimes little less than magic (for example, the mournful English horn for the Shepherd in the last act of *Tristan* relieved by the happier tones of the oboe when Isolde's ship is sighted), but one can say this of all the instruments under Wagner's miraculous direction. All orchestration has profited from his example.

8. The motifs, interwoven into beautiful textures in orchestra and voice, give unity. People have attempted in vain to copy Wagner. Humperdinck, his friend and editor, comes nearer than many to the Wagnerian style but is still far off.

9. The orchestra acts as much as the voice. Each instrument or group has its say. Each strand carries its own character. If the motif be of sadness, it grieves; if of gladness, it rejoices. Both the accent, the loudness or softness (dynamics), and key changes are used to create and establish character, mood, color, and action.

10. His division of the orchestra into choirs (the violins in the Prelude to *Lohengrin*) and letting them answer each other with glint, fire, and feeling is something that few composers have done as well. No one, not even Bach, has surpassed him in magnificent polyphonic melody (song and orchestra). In *Die Meistersinger* is this found to be most superbly true.

11. Wagner's colorful innovations in harmony are usually in the use of chromatics—twelve half steps within the octave. Thus a chord, interval, or progression may be altered. Wagner used chromatic intervals skillfully to enhance color, for emphasis, strangeness, and even to tinge a character. This is beautifully illustrated in *Tristan* and "The Ring."

12. Wagner changed the corroding custom of catering to singers. His singers had to be interested in what they were singing, not in themselves. No Wagnerian singer interrupts her song with pyrotechnics to display her skill. The voice is the servant of the story and the music, not the master, as in either Handel's or Rossini's time. Neither does the chorus strut; it helps tell the story. Not one part of the opera —scenery, orchestra, singer, or chorus—is the buttons on the cloak, but part of the cloth itself.

13. The singer's solo is not really a solo because the orchestra takes

over much, sometimes too much, of the telling of the tale. The recitative, too, is glorified and powered by the orchestra. His singers declaim in ecstatic music, the finest examples of which are the "Love Duet" and the "Love-Death" in the second and last acts of *Tristan und Isolde.* The da capo aria has been abandoned. The lovers speak of love from their hearts, not by formula.

14. He actually used the chorus as a character—making it not a military drill and/or a parade, but giving it gesture and music to "express emotion and human conduct."

15. Wagner decried making the singer repeat the same lines over and over again. Writing the librettos himself assured him of his kind of song and text. His librettos are not always good poetry, but his aim was to help the singer in short, compact lines. Here are a few "telegraphic" examples from *Tristan und Isolde:*

> *Denkt dich das!*
> *Ich weiss es anders*
> *Doch kann ich's dir nicht sagen.*

> Thinkst thou thus!
> I know 'tis not so,
> But this I cannot tell thee.

16. He cut out dazzling trills. He demanded that singers sing not only smoothly but robustly, when necessary, in very difficult stage situations and in a very difficult new kind of music which flowed continuously without stops. Singers found Wagner's music very tiring. Once, after fifty rehearsals of *Tristan und Isolde,* the performance was given up. He was implored to change some of the parts, but he wouldn't change a note. Even his goddess, Madame Schroeder-Devrient, said, "You write such queer stuff, it is impossible to sing it." But she did, and singers today sing it and "ask for more." He stuck to his guns while the battle raged about and around him, yet for years he was "box-office."

"THE RING OF THE NIBELUNGS"

Wagner was enticed by the story of Siegfried in the Norse and Germanic sagas, or myths. He started writing a drama about Siegfried's death and became so engrossed in the wonder and magic in it that he decided he would lead up to it by telling the story of Siegfried's youth. The same thing happened again. He felt the need for further explanations of Siegfried's parentage and his connection with the gods of Valhalla. These he intended to form into a trilogy, or three music dramas. But eventually he added a prologue, which made it into a tetralogy (*tetra* means "four" in Greek), or cycle, known as "The Ring of the Nibelungs" (*"Der Ring des Nibelungen"*).

Between 1853 and 1874 Wagner was working on these four music dramas for which the librettos had been written in reverse order: *Das Rheingold* (*The Rhinegold*, 1853–54); *Die Walküre* (*The Valkyrs*, 1854–56); *Siegfried* (1856–71); and *Die Götterdämmerung* (*The Twilight of the Gods*, 1869–74).

This is a four-ring musical circus *serial* You meet a dragon breathing fire; horses flying through the skies with women warriors upon their backs, carrying fallen heroes to Valhalla; a dwarf turned into a serpent and into a frog; a bird that can disclose vital information; a magic fire; a rainbow bridge; beautiful maidens, daughters of the Rhine, swimming and singing in its depths.

DAS RHEINGOLD

The Rhinegold, prologue to "The Ring," opens with its own prelude, one of the most impressive spots in the four dramas. This is composed exclusively on the holding of a colossal chord (E flat), over which the music flows and ebbs, expressing the ceaseless roll of the waters of the Rhine. It symbolizes the element of water, from which life's struggles and passions emerge. First is heard the single mysterious note, very grave and drawn out. This Wagner meant to picture Nature asleep. To the first tone is then added its fifth, and after a long interval, its octave. New instruments are added and gradually the orchestra itself is one with the Rhine in surge and flow. This chord, often called the Primeval Element, personifies the Rhine in the four dramas. On this chord of "personification" many leitmotifs are built. This is no accident. Wagner is writing a mystical drama, proclaiming the disintegration caused by greed. Everything in these four dramas has a reason. He fulfills the malediction of the grasping Alberich, the Nibelung dwarf, that whosoever possesses the gold stolen from the Nibelungs will be torn by anguish. The Gold Hoard, which motivates the action of "The Ring," ends in the idea that Love, not Gold, conquers the world. So Wagner ends the drama with the downfall, or twilight (*Die Götterdämmerung*) of the greedy gods.

Briefly, *Das Rheingold* serves to introduce many of the characters—gods, giants, and the Nibelungs (gnomes); to establish the mythical atmosphere; to show the pride and chicanery of the gods, and the theft of the gold.

Das Rheingold (four scenes) was first performed in 1869 at the Hof-und-National Theater, Munich. It burst upon America, in the original German, at the Metropolitan Opera House, in 1889, with Anton Seidl conducting.

DIE WALKÜRE

Die Walküre introduces Siegfried's parents and begins the weaving of the complicated web of the life of the coming hero, Siegfried. It also discloses the relation of the warrior-maiden, Brünnhilde, favorite daughter of Wotan, the god of gods, to Siegfried throughout the whole tetralogy.

Die Walküre was first performed in the Hof-und-National Theater, Munich, 1870, and its American première took place at the New York Academy of Music, 1877. The Metropolitan Opera Company first gave this music drama in 1885.

SIEGFRIED

In *Siegfried* is revealed to the young hero, in a series of magical happenings, his foreordained tasks which culminate in this opera with his release of Brünnhilde, who has been put to sleep in punishment by her father, Wotan, on the rock of the Valkyrs, protected by a ring of fire, penetrable only by a hero without fear—Siegfried.

Siegfried's first performance was held in the Festspielhaus, Bayreuth, 1876, its première in America was at the Metropolitan Opera House, 1887.

DIE GÖTTERDAMMERUNG

Die Götterdämmerung shows the trickery that separated Siegfried from his lawful mate, the events leading up to the murder of Siegfried, the annihilation of the treacherous plotters, the return of the gold to the Rhine maidens, and the fall of the gods—thus fulfilling Wagner's theory that greed is a destructive force in the life of man and overcome only by love.

The first performance, in 1876, was at the Festspielhaus, Bayreuth, one day after the opening of *Siegfried;* its première in America was at the Metropolitan in 1888.

TRISTAN UND ISOLDE

As far back as 1854, while he was writing *Die Walküre,* the idea of *Tristan* had possessed Wagner, along with the fiery articles on "Art of the Future." In 1857, *Parsifal* came to his mind, and about this time he was also considering *Die Meistersinger.* Such was the mind of this man. He was very much upset about politics, his bad luck, and his penury, but his beloved Madame Mathilde Wesendonck, on whose estate he and Minna had been living, is said to have inspired him to write some lovely songs, as well as *Tristan,* a story of the fulfillment of love in death. Minna naturally was jealous of Madame Wesendonck, and conflict became so unbearable that Wagner fled to Venice. He was sick with longing for Mathilde, and the music conquered him before he had written it. And so he turned from other ideas and wrote the greatest music-love drama.

This is a legend of Tristan and Isolde found in the Celtic stories of King Arthur's Court and other legends. Wagner's sources for his stories were international. *Tristan und Isolde* became a story of love, unfulfilled on earth, fulfilled in Heaven. It was an expression of his own starved heart which longed for an idyllic love.

Most frequently you hear the "Prelude," which begins the opera, joined to the "Love-Death," which ends it. There is the sumptuously quiet scene in the second act, backed by the sounds of the tufty hunting horns in the distance. The lovers are discovered by Isolde's husband, King Mark, singing a more luscious love melody than had ever been conceived. The effulgence of this web of sound is impossible to describe. It is continuous in vocal conversations, rather than in songs. Its richness, compared to other operas, is like a plum pudding compared to a sponge cake. The opera is a story of love potions, impatience, tragedy, courage, cowardice, loyalty, gallantry, elation and transcendant love. In the Wagnerian way, the two lovers who have suffered disappointment and heartbreak through separation are united in death.

Tristan und Isolde (called by Wagner a *Handlung*—action—in three acts) had its first performance at the Hof-und-National Theater in Munich in 1865. Its première in America took place in 1886 at the Metropolitan Opera House.

THE MASTERSINGERS—FUN AND SATIRE

If *Tristan und Isolde* is the greatest love drama ever set to music, *Die Meistersinger von Nürnberg* (*The Mastersingers of Nuremburg*) is a colossally great comic opera. Wagner had thought of it for a long time, but had been so occupied with getting *Tristan und Isolde* produced, he had had to lay it aside. But when he was in Venice his friend, Madame Wesendonck, suggested that he go back to it; he did, and fell in love with it.

Then he went to Paris with money loaned to him by a publisher, but soon he was in dire want. For the next two years his work went very slowly. Life in garrets did not feed Wagner's soul, but in 1862 he did finish the book for *The Mastersingers,* a sarcastic, brilliant, and witty poem, the best libretto he ever wrote, which few, if any, have approached. In it Wagner attacks the critics who seemed to resent any attempts to change art, particularly music.

Two years later (1864), when he was beginning to be popular, with the help of King Ludwig II of Bavaria, Wagner retired to the village of Triebschen, near Lucerne. Now he lived in comfort, with the financial assistance of the King, under the happiest conditions of his poverty-torn life. Here he finished the score of *Die Meistersinger* (1868).

King Ludwig, in Wagnerian and fairy-tale fashion, visited him constantly, disguised as a commoner, for his subjects resented the expenditure of so much money on the composer. Yet for this, Ludwig has gone down in history as a world benefactor! Economy can be very wasteful.

The story of the opera is set among the ancient Mastersingers in the trade guilds, such as goldsmiths and cobblers. Wagner pits these, led by the stuttering, concrete-brained Beckmesser (opposed to all change), against the mellow shoemaker, Hans Sachs (see page 62) and his friends.

So the brilliant-scened story unrolls as Walther von Stolzing, Knight of Song, aided by Hans Sachs, wins the contest with his "Prize Song" and is awarded the lovely Eva as his bride. The contest is amazing, as it presents Beckmesser with his ridiculous, meticulous rule-keeping and vocal dribbling; and Walther's song, which did not observe the ancient rules of the Guild, but did the laws of sincerity and beauty. Here again enters the Wagnerian love of morals: You will win with sincerity and beauty, not with claptrap because it is old or because it is new!

The music throughout, from the first note of the prelude to the last note of the finale, is probably the finest Wagner wrote. Never did he weave a more magnificent fabric in counterpoint. The motifs represent most amazing series of developments, and "tell-tale" activities.

The prelude starts pompously to show how stiffnecked the Master-singers are. In it are entwined their special motifs, in brassy flares: the motif that denotes Awakening of Love between Eva and Walther, and then Confessed Love with the Impatient Order of Love. All these motifs are the foundation later of the glowing "Prize Song." So, by the time you hear the complete "Prize Song," you are already intimate with it, for Wagner has tossed it, turned it, and woven it throughout in transforming splendor and variety.

There is one very amusing motif: The Beating. The composer heard a street fight and transformed it into music. It represents the punish-ment Beckmesser is given when he attempts to sing a serenade in a chirpy voice outside the window of lovely and unattainable Eva. The funny part is that it is made out of music of Beckmesser's "Serenade" —so seriously sung to Eva before his beating! This is one of Wagner's clever and humorous musical tricks! The music is cast in the form of a huge fugue.

The opera was first performed at the Hof-und-National Theater, Munich, in 1868. It was a success, for Hans von Bülow was a great conductor, and *Die Meistersinger,* a great opera. In spite of the fact that von Bülow was about to lose his wife to Wagner, whose secretary she was, von Bülow loved music better than coddling his own heart-ache. In 1886 *Die Meistersinger* had its première in America, in the original German, at the Metropolitan Opera House.

A THEATER OF HIS OWN

Wagner conceived the idea of building his own theater because of the unprecedented and elaborate scenery his dramas required. The people of Bavaria were making an outcry against Ludwig's "extrava-gance," so Wagner societies to collect funds were started all over the world. He was determined to have the theater. Subscriptions came in even from America and the Festival Theatre (Festspielhaus) was finally built in Bayreuth. Its cornerstone was laid on Wagner's fifty-ninth birthday, May 22, 1872.

STAGING

Staging Wagner's dramas even today is no small task. Imagine what it was in the days without electricity! Not only did the lack of the yet unknown electrical devices make things difficult, but the presence of tyrannical Wagner made everything nervewracking. His peculiar mixture of realism and fantasy drove his scenery builders almost mad. It is hard to understand how they managed to have flying horses, magic fire, swan boats changing into princes, double-story scenes, and everything removable to keep Wagner's pet theories in practice—plus the continuous flow of music with no interruptions for scene changing.

The first performance of the cycle, or the four dramas of "The Ring of the Nibelungs," was given at the Festival Theatre in 1876. Before each act, trumpets blared a fanfare. Previously, "The Ring" had never been given as a whole. But now Wagner's music dramas were presented as if they were sacred rites, and he the high priest.

PARSIFAL, A FESTIVAL PLAY

Wagner's last work was *Parsifal*. It is presented as if it were a sacred drama. The audience is asked not to applaud. It is Wagner's last gift to the world and the crowning point of his life. Debussy said: *"Parsifal* is one of the loveliest monuments of sound ever raised to the serene glory of music." This he said after condemning the story. It was given its first public performance in 1882, a year before the composer's death.

The legend which possessed Wagner for thirty-one years is rooted in the history of the Holy Grail. It is a mixture of Christian morality; *Percival le Gaulois,* or *Contes de Grail (Percival the Gaul* or *Stories of the Grail* by Chrétien de Troyes in the late twelfth century); *Mabinogion* (Celtic stories of the thirteenth century included in the King Arthur legends); and Wagner's own inventions. Added to the ingredients of his other dramas: magic, myth, love, glamour, adventure, he now adds the element of moralizing *religiousness.* The moral of the great story he unfolds in uninterrupted flow of sound and elaborate scenery is that *only the pure in heart win the rewards.* Parsifal is the "guileless fool," the hero, who because of his innocence is the only one who can save Amfortas, the Knight of the Holy Grail, wounded by a wicked magician, Klingser, who caused the Knights to break their holy vows of chastity.

The drama tells the story of Parsifal's adventures on his way to the home of the Knights in Montsalvat. It takes place mostly on Good

Friday, and the "Good Friday Spell" is one of the most beautiful pages in the music of Wagner. The magnificent leitmotifs of the Eucharist, Faith, the Spear which had wounded Amfortas, and the Grail are superbly woven into the prelude to the opera, which is introduced by a magnificent blare of trumpets.

Among the beautiful numbers are the song of the Flower Maidens, Parsifal's song about his mother, Herzeleide, and the music for his march (on a moving platform) to Montsalvat—with the great bells of the temple sounding, interweaving, and transforming many of the leitmotifs of the whole drama. The scene of Parsifal's glorification at the end of the opera is served by a two-story scenic setting from which rises the singing of Knights and the choir. This was one of Wagner's ideas and had not been used since the sixteenth century. It is interesting to realize that the Faith motif was modeled on the bell motif of a church in Dresden, the town which Wagner knew so well, and is used often for the final *Amen* today in many churches.

Parsifal (in three acts) had its first performance in the Festspielhaus, Bayreuth, in 1882. Wagner wished to limit its presentation to Bayreuth, where it could be given with the proper reverence. After his death, it was not released for production until Cosima Wagner approved. Concert performances, however, were given in London and America, and it had a formal debut on Christmas Eve, 1903, at the Metropolitan Opera House, under the management of Heinrich Conried, ten years before it was supposed to be released.

WAGNER'S DOUBLE ASPECT

One of Wagner's relatives gives a good picture of the man. ". . . The double aspect of this powerful personality was shown in his face: the upper part beautiful with a vast ideality and lighted with eyes which were deep and severe, gentle or malicious, according to circumstances; the lower part wry and sarcastic. A mouth cold and calculating and pursed up was cut slantingly into a face beneath an imperious nose and above a chin which projected like the menace of a conquering will." He was a man who could not separate himself from his art, and created most often in his most perturbed states of mind. Thwarted in love, too often hungry and ill-clad, he pictured in his dramas the life he craved.

INTERMEZZO

Some German Writers After Wagner

WAGNER seemed to end Germany's greatness in opera. She had gloried in her *Singspiel,* her Mozart, her Gluck, and her Weber. Now, among others, opera slid into the hands of merely delightful composers such as Otto Nicolai (1810–49), with such works as *The Merry Wives of Windsor,* the overture to which is the part most frequently heard; and Peter Cornelius (1824–74), a friend of Wagner's, with his delightful *Barber of Bagdad,* in which he kept his own individuality. Wagner exerted some influence over all opera makers, however, whether or not they tried to copy him.

Two years after his death, composers began again to use myths as had Wagner, from Greek, Hindu, or Germanic mythology. They used the leitmotif in their own ways. They used more continuous music, but they lacked the originality to move opera much further along. They did, however, keep opera "going" in Germany until the time of Richard Strauss. There were a few exceptions among the post-Wagnerian opera writers. Among these were Engelbert Humperdinck, with his fairy opera *Hänsel und Gretel* and Wilhelm Kienzl, with his once very popular *Der Evangelimann* (1857).

HÄNSEL UND GRETEL

Never was an opera so strangely born. Out of a few songs for a children's party Engelbert Humperdinck fashioned the fairy opera *Hänsel und Gretel!* Their adventures in the woods, with the wicked witch and the gingerbread house, are loved by both children and grown-ups. It has become a festival play in America, usually given around Christmas time when holidays permit children to enjoy the theater.

Humperdinck was born in Siegburg near Bonn in 1854, and died in Neustrelitz, Germany, in 1921. He wrote several compositions, edited Wagner's *Parsifal* and absorbed some of the Wagnerian ideas, such as the use of the leitmotif. Yet, like others, he did not use them with Wagner's richness.

His music is a happy mixture of German folk music, leitmotifs, and counterpoint (polyphony). It mixes together the delightful ingredients of the folk dance, sentimental and simple chorales, songs, fantastic scenery and magic.

"The Evening Blessing" ends the sweet opera with this rhyme in German: "When need is greatest, God stretches forth His hands." Here, too, you see the Wagnerian delight in moral endings.

Humperdinck wrote four operas, none as successful as *Hänsel und Gretel*. He was knighted and held many honors. No honor was as great, however, as delighting the children and grown-ups all over the world with his fairy opera. He came to New York when his *Königskinder* (*Children of the King*) was played at the Metropolitan Opera House in 1910, with Geraldine Farrar as the Goose-Girl.

Hänsel und Gretel had its first performance at the Hoftheater in Weimar, 1893, and in an English version was first given in America, in New York, at Daly's Theatre, 1895. Its première at the Metropolitan was in 1905, with Louise Homer as the wicked Witch.

FERRUCCIO BUSONI

Ferruccio Busoni, born in Empoli, Italy, 1866, was a pianist, composer and arranger who spent most of his life in Vienna and Berlin and died there in 1924. It should be said here that his opera *Doctor Faustus* (1925) is rewarding for those who appreciate scholarly music. Enlightened critics say that it is a spiritual and mystic composition. So if it be dull to some, it may become, in spite of its lack of dramatic power, something of value in the future. It has had of late (1954–55) some happy revivals.

Earlier, *Arlecchino* (*Harlequin*) was given in 1917 in Frankfurt. It might have been more popular, says Professor Edward S. Dent, save that it takes "unusual alertness of mind" for full enjoyment. Yet it was of great importance to Busoni for he regarded it as his most "individual and personal work." (Kobbé's *Complete Opera Book,* New York: Putnam.)

FRANZ SCHREKER

Among many other German composers is Franz Schreker (1878–1934), best known for his *Der Ferne Klang* (*Distant Sound*), somewhat impressionistic in feeling. He is also somewhat like Richard

Strauss because of the rich texture of his orchestra. He is quite twentieth century, for his plots make research in abnormal mental reactions. Another of his operas is *Der Schatzgräber* (*The Treasure Digger*). Like a few other composers, he wrote his own librettos.

HANS PFITZNER

A contemporary of Schreker and a composer of about his caliber is Hans Pfitzner (1869–) best known for his opera *Palestrina,* a musical legend to his own libretto. Its première was in Munich (1917) and it has been popular in German opera houses. (See Act VIII for other German opera writers.)

SCENE II

Verdi the Showman

VERDI came to the opera world at the end of a long line of Italian practitioners of varying abilities. Italy had been supreme in the art of song from the time of Monteverdi.

Verdi and Wagner were the pinnacles of romantic opera in Europe. Wagner, high priest of the symphonic opera, despised Italian opera with its arias and giddy trimmings. And Verdi was continuously annoyed at Wagner for despising it—for, after all, Wagner had thrown a throttling wrench into the wheels of Italian opera, yet Verdi had been accused of copying him. But Verdi outlived Wagner by almost a generation—so now to Verdi!

Giuseppe Verdi (1813–1901) is the man who straddled public life and his ivory tower to plead for freedom and emancipation for Italy. It is said that his mother took him in her arms soon after his birth and fled the Austrian terror. Later Verdi did all he could to help Italy against Austria, and to cement his country into one nation, instead of many city-states. His superbly rhythmic and melodic music became the most beautiful rabble-rousing medium ever known to politics.

Giuseppe Verdi was born in La Roncole, near Busseto, Italy. Like Beethoven and Mozart, Verdi became an organist when only a lad, taking his teacher's place. He believed he could be a success in music and worked hard. His father, a keeper of an inn, pleased that his son loved music, gave him a spinet. Giuseppe loved it, but one day, it is said, his father found him trying to hack it to pieces because he couldn't find a chord he had once struck. Fortunately, father Verdi saved the instrument, which Giuseppe loved all his life.

At the time he was playing the organ at the church, he lived in Busseto with his father's friend, the grocer, Antonio Barezzi, who was interested in the local Philharmonic Orchestra. Verdi became part of this orchestra. With his work in Barezzi's store, his playing in the

Philharmonic, and his Sundays at the cathedral in La Roncole, to which he walked, he was a busy boy. When he was fifteen, Verdi began to compose for celebrations and religious festivals. The love of writing for special occasions never left him.

He had a gift for making friends and keeping them. This best of friends, Barezzi, later his father-in-law, thought that Giuseppe ought to go to Milan to study, so he and some others raised a fund. But Verdi, who was to write twenty-seven operas, was refused admission to the Conservatory of Music in 1832. It is generally stated that the examiners thought he had little talent for music and that his piano playing did not come up to their standard. But a new biography by Carlo Gatti, (published in New York by G. P. Putnam's, 1955) states that Verdi was rejected because he was over age (he was eighteen instead of four-teen) and he was "a foreigner," that is, he was neither from Lombardy nor from Venice. This was one of the first obstacles that the composer met during his long life of tragedy and happiness.

He studied privately with Vincenzo Lavigna, who became a close friend. Lavigna, a prompter at La Scala Theatre in Milan, introduced Verdi to great polyphonic music, as well as to performances of opera at La Scala. (A prompter in the opera sits in a little box, unseen, and only seldom heard, with the score and the words of the opera, to prompt the singers should they forget their lines.)

OBERTO, HIS FIRST OPERA

One day Lavigna took Verdi to a rehearsal of an amateur choral society giving Haydn's oratorio *The Creation*. The conductor failed to arrive. The chorus was assembled and everybody was anxious. Giuseppe, before he knew it, was playing the accompaniment on the piano, and conducting the chorus, to the joy and applause of all. This wasn't mere flattering applause, for he was asked to conduct the public concert at the Teatro Filodrammatico, where the manager asked him to write an opera on the story, *Oberto, Conte di San Bonifacio,* by Antonio Piazza. He did not like the book, which made it difficult, and furthermore, he was itching to accept a proffered post as choirmaster in Busseto. As an honorable young man, however, he finished the opera.

The production of *Oberto* in 1839 was no triumph, but it did establish him as a promising writer of opera. Indeed, traces of three or four of his future operas can be seen in this first attempt. He seems here to be developing his unique gift of revealing the workings of the minds of his characters. In addition, he was blessed with the Italian gift of melody.

Oberto was also a friend to Verdi, for Bartolomeo Merelli, manager of La Scala, because of it, ordered three operas for La Scala and Vienna.

The first libretto he was asked to set to music was a comedy by Felice Romani, *Il finto Stanislao, ossia un Giorno di Regno* (*Stanislaus,* or *The Pretender's Day of Power*). With his beautiful wife, Margherita, and his little son, Verdi went to Milan to write the opera. They were suffering from the recent death of their first child, a daughter. Verdi fell ill. He, who was to live to be eighty-seven, had a slight heart attack! Then the boy sickened and died, while Margherita, as in a Greek tragedy, died of brain fever. When Verdi recovered he was a heartbroken, discouraged man. Little wonder that the opera buffa was a failure. It was indeed *un giorno di regno,* for it had only one performance.

NABUCCO

Although Verdi decided he would never write again, Merelli decided otherwise. Persuasion did no good. One day while in Milan he casually showed Verdi Solera's *Nabucodonos,* and asked him to read it. It was based on a Biblical story of the Jews under Nebuchadnezzar. Verdi saw it as his first chance to spread his gospel of freedom. Besides, he liked it because it was from the Bible—which he loved.

Now he decided to dedicate himself to the freedom of Italy and its rebirth as a nation. He called the opera *Nabucco.* It was given in 1842 at La Scala, Milan. The rallying cry of the "Jews' Chorus" roused the people of Italy. Here we see the signs of the coming Verdi, both in the music and in his use of singers, stressing the mezzo-soprano and baritone roles. In this case, Giuseppina Strepponi sang Abdigaille's (Abigail's) part, but later she played the greatest part in her life as the mate of Giuseppe Verdi, for whom she gave up her career.

ERNANI

Up to this time Verdi's librettos had not been too good. But for *Ernani* he was more fortunate. Francesco Piave's libretto was based on Victor Hugo's play *Hernani.* According to the censors, this opera and *I Lombardi alla Prima Crociata* (*The Lombards at the First Crusade*), like *Nabucco,* are drenched with political feeling. In a letter from Venice, where *I Lombardi* was given in 1844, Verdi wrote that

"I Lombardi is a grand fiasco, one of the really classic fiascos." But its success was greater than he expected.

Ernani (Verdi's opera) was first given at the Teatro la Fenice in Venice in 1844. In 1830 a jolly good fight had taken place between the conservatives and romanticists when Hugo's play was given in Paris. In Italy the choruses from *Ernani* and *I Lombardi* were used in anti-Austrian demonstrations. Verdi became a national figure.

In the original Italian, *Ernani* came to America at the Park Theatre in New York in 1847, and eight days later it was performed in Boston. The first Metropolitan performance was in 1902. It was revived in 1921.

HIS FIRST SHAKESPEARE

In 1847 Verdi wrote the favorite opera of his youth, *Macbetto* (*Macbeth*), based on Shakespeare's tragedy. It was first given in Florence. Had the libretto by Piave been better, the opera might have been more popular, although it has been successfully revived in recent years. Verdi revised it for Paris in 1865. This gory tale was the turning point in the practices of this great musical showman. Here he displays ability to join story and music as he never had done before.

Macbeth was given in New York, in the original Italian at Niblo's Garden, April 1850, and wasn't performed in New York again until during the nineteen-forties!

While *Macbeth* was in rehearsal, Salvatore Cammarano received a letter from the Master in Paris saying he regretted that the management had selected Tadolini to sing Lady Macbeth: "Tadolini has too great qualities for this role! Perhaps you think that a contradiction!! Tadolini's appearance is good and beautiful. I would like Lady Macbeth twisted and ugly. Tadolini sings to perfection, and I don't wish Lady Macbeth really to sing at all . . . for Lady Macbeth I should like a raw, choked, hollow voice. Tadolini's voice has something angelic, Lady Macbeth's voice should have something devilish." (*Verdi, The Man in His Letters,* edited by Franz Werfel and Paul Stefan.) Note the double exclamation points after "contradiction." This man is dramatic even in letters.

LUISA MILLER

A new stage in Verdi's growth was *Luisa Miller,* in three acts (1849). It was an adaptation of Schiller's play *Kabale und Liebe* (*Intrigue and Love*). The score is beautiful and gives intimations of *Falstaff,* which comes forty years later. In *Luisa* Verdi is able to express more intimate and poignant feeling than ever before.

Luisa "stepped out" first in Naples, at the San Carlo Theatre, in 1849, and came to New York in an Italian version in 1854, at the Castle Garden Theatre. *Luisa Miller* appeared at the Metropolitan in 1929 with Rosa Ponselle, Tullio Serafin conducting.

A BRILLIANT SUCCESS

In 1851, his most brilliant success up to this time occurred in Venice —the production of *Rigoletto*. It took Verdi only forty days to write it. Again the story was from Victor Hugo. This time it was *Le Roi s'amuse* (*The King Amuses Himself*). This was, however, a time in Italy when kings were sensitive, and the censors more sensitive. The police were afraid of the uprisings which were forming without encouragement from Verdi's operas. So Verdi was forced to demote the king to a duke. He was prevented from calling the opera by the original title; the king had to exit! So he called it *Rigoletto,* after the name of the King's Jester.

In *Rigoletto* he reveals intense, human feelings of passion, of love, of frustration and calamity. This is magnificently brought to a head in the last act, in the best-known quartet in any opera *"Bella figlia dell' amor"* ("Beautiful Woman of Love, at Your Feet..."), sung by Gilda, Maddalena, the Duke and Rigoletto.

Although *Rigoletto* is the most popular among Verdi's popular operas, when it was first given it was considered repulsive. It had, nevertheless, one hundred performances the first year.

It made its first bow in America at the New York Academy of Music in 1855. It was given in German at the New York Stadt Theater in 1870, in English at the Academy of Music in 1874, and a Russian version was given in 1922 at the Second Avenue Theatre in New York. Since 1883, the Metropolitan's first season, on November 17, *Rigoletto* has been in the repertory.

As Verdi advanced, his most important gift to opera was that he improved the people's taste by taking "the wooden and the tinkly" out of grand opera and by fitting the action to the feeling of the characters and to the music. He also made opera grow because of his uncanny use of rhythms and meters and of individual instruments. For example, in the song *"La donna è mobile"* ("Fickle Is Woman Fair"), although it has been overplayed since the street-organ days, he paints in its rhythm and meter the picture of a fickle or change-able human being.

Nothing can destroy or mar the value of the mood-expressing-songs: *"Questa o quella"* ("This One or That One to Me Is the Same") in which the Duke tells of his nonchalant existence; Gilda's *"Caro nome"* ("Dearest Name"), a soprano song of ecstasy on her lover's name; and the fiery *"Si, vendetta,"* a song the distracted father, Rigoletto, sings swearing vengeance on his daughter's seducer.

A GREATER SUCCESS

Then came probably the great popular success of his life, *Il Trova-tore* (*The Troubadour*), given at the Apollo Theatre in Rome in 1853. There are no political ideas in this. It is a fanciful and romantic drama, if ever there was one! A tale of gypsy love, adventure and intrigue, so complicated that it is difficult to unwind. Were it not for the magic of the music, one wonders how it might have fared. Verdi shows uncanny ability to hold the listener's attention, in spite of the fact that he condenses scenes and music for brevity, the spice of drama to him—as it was to Mozart. Furthermore, he still uses one scene to sing an aria—on an empty stage—while the drama stops.

In this opera, of complicated story, there is no dead wood in the music, in melody, counterpoint or instrumentation. In the last scene of the fourth act, Verdi's genius flames to one of its highest peaks of splendor and excitement. Song to express emotion is rarely better used than in this white-hot story.

Il Trovatore is in four acts, with a book by Salvatore Cammarano, based on the Spanish drama of chivalry by Antonio Gutierrez. The Rome performance had an instantaneous success, in spite of the rain-soaked people who lined up in the mud and water of the Tiber, which had overflowed. Later it was given in London (in English), as *The Gypsy's Vengeance,* in 1856, and in Paris in 1857. It came to New York at the Academy of Music, in Italian, in 1855; at Burton's Theatre, 1858; the New York Stadt Theatre in 1870, in German; in French at the Lyric Theatre in New York in 1912; and at the Metropolitan in 1883, during its first year, where it is still in the repertory.

Toscanini conducted a famous revival in 1915 at the Metropolitan. It has been the tool of burlesque from Walt Disney's pompous Hen to Alec Templeton's clever parodies, but nothing can dim its lustrous melodies, with its "Anvil Chorus," its "Troubadour Serenade," the effectively chanted *"Miserere,"* and one of the most lovely duets: *"Ai nostri monti"* ("Home to Our Mountains") for mezzo-soprano and tenor instead of the usual soprano and tenor.

Now we come to *La Traviata* (*The Misled One*). It opened for its première in Venice (Teatro Fenice), 1853, with little success. The book is by Francesco Piave, in three acts, after Alexandre Dumas' *La Dame aux camélias* (*The Lady of the Camellias*). It is about Violetta, a glittering and erring maiden, but an unfortunate victim of love and tuberculosis! Yet she shows her nobility by giving up her lover because his father wishes it for his family's good.

In this are heard some of Verdi's finest music and songs, and the opera's overture and prelude to the third act are what the jazz publicists would call "super-duper." The song Violetta sings when dying is some of Verdi's most effective realism embroidered in romance. Indeed, this is one of the beautiful inconsistencies of opera. Opera is naturally unnatural, overvivid, and sensational and therefore has to be made with supreme skill.

Although *La Traviata* was not at first highly successful, it has made up for its losses ever since. It now can be seen as a play, as a movie, in television, and as an opera—again and again.

La Traviata had a hard time because it was denounced as immoral by pulpit and press. It was forbidden in London because of its "foul and hideous horrors." But it has persisted in spite of censorship.

One of the most expressive songs is Violetta's aria, *"Ah fors' è lui che l'anima"* ("For Him, Perchance, My Longing Soul"); another is Germont's moving plea for his son, *"Pura siccome un angelo"* ("Pure as an Angel").

The first performance of *La Traviata* in America was at the New York Academy of Music in 1856; at the Metropolitan in 1883. At Oscar Hammerstein's Manhattan Opera House, in the winter of 1907, Melba took the part of Violetta and Maurice Renaud played Alfredo.

With all Verdi's genius and political fervor, he loved farming, and during the first part of the Italian Revolution he stayed close to his estate at St. Agatha, near Busseto, where, with Madame Strepponi (later his second wife) he lived happily, composed, farmed and took care of his land. All this time he was in touch with his former father-in-law, Barezzi, whom he loved as a father, and who loved him as a son. Sometimes they had serious disagreements but never lost touch with one another.

SIMON BOCCANEGRA

Verdi, at this time, had become not only a national, but an international character. He was a power in politics because of his fervor and he was becoming a center of musical interest. Indeed, his reputation was so great that the musical Mecca, Paris, was actually calling to him. He was asked to write an opera for the opening of the Paris Exposition in 1857. Instead, he remained on his beloved Italian estate and wrote one of his noblest works—*Simon Boccanegra* with a prologue and two acts. It is set in Genoa in the fourteenth century—its most picturesque days—with glamorous effects on an epic scale. It will never be as popular as the operas with lighter melodies, but to opera lovers it is a joy. The story is a bit obscure, but it means to tell of a band of men who wish to make a *doge,* or ruler, of Boccanegra, a Corsair in government service. He becomes doge, finds his long-lost daughter and the drama unfolds in which plotters for his daughter's hand finally poison Boccanegra.

Best-known is the bass aria *"Il lacerato spirito"* ("A Wounded Heart" [or Soul]), another instance of Verdi's writing for someone other than tenors and sopranos.

Boccanegra was first presented at La Scala, Milan, 1859. Unfortunately, the tenor and baritone fell ill and couldn't appear. Verdi considered it a fiasco and withdrew it. In 1881, with libretto revised by Arrigo Boito, it was given at the same theater. Verdi rescored most of the music. The cast was magnificent in the annals of great singing: Victor Maurel, French baritone, as Simon; Francesco Tamagno, a baker who became a famous tenor, sang in many Verdi operas and later created the role of Otello; Edouard de Reszke, most illustrious bass; and Signora d'Angeri. New York saw it first in 1932 at the Metropolitan, with Lawrence Tibbett (Simon) baritone; Giovanni Martinelli, tenor; Ezio Pinza, bass; Maria Müller, soprano. This opera demands great breadth of song and gesture.

A NEW HIGH, EVEN FOR VERDI

The greatest height to which Verdi had risen by 1859 is marked by *Un Ballo in maschera* (*A Masked Ball*), with its première in Rome in 1859. Its book is by Antonio Somma. Here Verdi becomes political again.

A Masked Ball was supposed to have had its debut in Naples during the Carnival of 1858. The attempt on the life of Napoleon III by Orsini made the censors watchful, and since the original story called for a conspiracy resulting in the murder of the king, the management made all sorts of excuses and wouldn't house it. Verdi held out against the management, but finally changed the scene to Boston, Massachusetts! (The setting has gone back to Italy, with a few English names remaining.)

VERDI—POLITICAL STANDARD BEARER

At this point the people of Naples began shouting in the street Viva Verdi. He became a symbol of the unity of his country—the longing to make a united Italy. On the walls of the city were written *Viva Verdi.* It was an acrostic—

V
I
V iva
A
V ittoria
E mmanuele
R e
D '
I talia

(which means "LONG LIVE VICTOR EMMANUEL, KING OF ITALY," who united the nation in 1870.)

A MASKED BALL

In *Un Ballo in maschera,* Verdi shows again his great understanding of orchestral writing. The drama seems to rest more on the orchestra than did his other operas. This is a valuable development in Italian opera. Yet the songs continue to give the various shades of feeling, if not so obviously as heretofore. Its overture has great charm, and its use of the solo flute is effective. Indeed, Verdi seems now to appreciate instruments "on their own." For the first time, too, he shows that he can be amusing, although Rossini said he couldn't. The Conspirator's "Laughing Chorus" proves his skill at humor. Later, of course, with the even greater *Falstaff,* he proves himself to be the writer of one of the most distinguished comic operas in history.

The best-known song is the baritone solo, *"Eri tu"* ("It Was You").

A Masked Ball had its première in Rome in 1859. It was presented in Italian in New York at the Academy of Music in 1861, and in English in 1871. The Metropolitan Opera House gave it in German and later in Italian. In December 1954, Marian Anderson, first Negro diva to sing on the Metropolitan stage, appeared as Ulrica, the prophetess.

MUSIC, POLITICS AND WAR

For Verdi 1859 was an exciting year. In it occurred Italy's war of independence against Austria, and his marriage to Giuseppina Strepponi. The next year he became deputy to the National Parliament. In 1865 he resigned and five years later became a revered Senator at sixty-two—after he had written *La Forza del destino* and *Don Carlo*. Politics was no bar to Verdi's accomplishments.

THE FORCE OF DESTINY—OPERA 22

La Forza del destino has some lovely songs and a sample of wit vested in the person of a grumpy friar, that Verdi developed to greater girth in *Falstaff*. Then there is the popular but tragic song for soprano *"Pace, pace, mio Dio"* ("Peace, Peace, Dear God"). In this too we see a favorite departure in his duets for tenor and baritone. Among these the best-known is *"Solenne in quest' ora"* ("In This Solemn Hour"). Then there is a most effective overture or sinfonia which begins with flashing trumpets signalizing Fate. It uses themes from its songs among which is *"Madre Pietosa Virginie"* ("Oh Holy Virgin"), sung by the soprano Donna Leonora kneeling in the moonlight near a convent from which is heard the chant of the priests. How well Verdi does such scenes!

In this and in *A Masked Ball* Verdi has reached the second station in his own march of dramatic power.

The libretto by Piave in four acts is on a Spanish play. It was first heard at the Imperial Theatre, St. Petersburg, 1862. In New York, it had its première at the Academy of Music, 1865. In 1869, it was given at La Scala, revised by Antonio Chizlanzoni to make all gory events occur "offstage"—as in ancient Greek tragedy. This version was presented at the New York Academy of Music in 1881, and at the Metropolitan in 1918.

DON CARLO

Verdi's next opera, *Don Carlo* (1867), a tragedy in five acts originally, was written for the Paris Opéra which Verdi called in derision the *Grande Boutique* (Large Shop). It is important not because of novelties or new styles but because it was something like an experimental laboratory, for he wrote it three times, never being entirely satisfied. The work on *Don Carlo* prepared him for *Aïda, Otello* and *Falstaff*—his three greatest! Indeed in *Don Carlo,* in the "Inquisition March" in the Church Square, you get a premonition or sample of the vast triumphal scene in *Aïda.*

Don Carlo with its theme of Liberty took hold of Verdi's imagination; he wrapped it in a love story—and it became the ingredient of a dramatic, if gloomy, romance.

It is based on Schiller's *Don Carlos* (the Italian form *Don Carlo* is used in the opera) and the book was written by Joseph Méry and Camille du Locle. It was no shining success, without doubt because it was enveloped for the most part in a basic gloominess. The consensus is that *Don Carlo* is a "good show" when as admirably given as it was by impresario Rudolf Bing when he revived it in 1950 as his first production for the Metropolitan Opera in New York. The scene of the play is the Inquisition in Spain, during which Philip II and his son Don Carlo became enamored of the same princess, and Philip hands his unhappy son over to the Inquisitors to be killed. Colorful, but far more colorful is the Schiller drama.

It is vast in scale, sometimes in the manner of Meyerbeer but not in the style of Wagner, even if Verdi can establish a mood with a phrase used and reused as in the third act (second version) in the King's desolating singing of *"Ella giammai m'amo"* ("She Never Loved Me"). Also the scene with the Grand Inquisitor is a triumph of opera-making at its highest point. There are few operas surpassing it for sheer power, pathos, and skills in both orchestral and vocal music.

Later in the same act the contralto sings the most popular piece in the opera, *"O don fatale"* ("Oh Fatal Gift") inveighing against her gift of beauty to which she ascribes her sin—betrayal of her queen. This song is certainly of full-blown Italian style—but original and in the best tradition. The devotion of Carlo and Roderigo is heard in a few songs, particularly the one in Carlo's cell. A beautiful prelude is given to Act III, and in Act I (second revision) the contralto sings a Morisco (Moorish) song in fascinating rhythm with a tangy "blue" leading note.

As this opera takes place during the times of the superlative painters El Greco and Velasquez, the scene painters and builders have opportunities to create magnificent sixteenth-seventeenth-century architecture and costumes. In the 1950 version (the second) the El Greco and not the Velasquez coloring was generally used . . . duller than Velasquez' but fitting the plot.

New York heard it first, in Italian, at the Academy of Music in 1877, and again at the Metropolitan in 1920. Rosa Ponselle in her golden voice sang Elizabetta, Margaret Matzenauer in her brown-gold voice sang Princess Eboli, Carlo was sung by Martinelli, Roderigo by de Luca. In 1922, Feodor Chaliapin interpreted Philip as no one had before, or since, and Leon Rothier as the Grand Inquisitor gave it added distinction. In spite of its superiority, Enrico Caruso and Antonio Scotti made "Oh Lord By Whose Desire the Soul Knew Love and Hope, . . ." almost popular!

AÏDA (1871)

Verdi learned much from the writing of *Don Carlo,* in which a more continuous music was evident, and he used this knowledge in his pre-eminent *Aïda.* The Khedive (ruler) of Egypt asked Verdi again and again to write an opera to celebrate the opening of the Suez Canal, but he didn't seem to like the idea. Finally, at the persuasion of a friend and collaborator, Camille du Locle brought him a story of his own based on a sketch by the Egyptologist, Mariette Bey. Du Locle won him over and he (Verdi) accepted the commission. He, his wife, and Antonio Ghislanzoni composed the libretto. Mariette Bey brought to the production of *Aïda* his knowledge of old Egypt: ". . . revived Egyptian life of the time of the Pharaohs; he rebuilt ancient Thebes, Memphis, the Temple of Phtah; he designed the costumes and arranged the scenery. And under these exceptional circumstances, Verdi's new opera was produced." (*The Complete Opera Book* by Kobbé.)

Aïda was a year late in production, for the French scenery and costumes, owing to the outbreak of the Franco-Prussian War, could not be shipped from Paris to Cairo. The manager conquered the unconquerable in difficulties.

Aïda, in four acts, is operatic magnificence to the nth power, with sumptuous scenes, rich, flashing music and fascinating story, all of which hang together as they should in a well-behaved opera. It has the feeling of great defeats and great victories, great love and great deception, great song and great orchestra—altogether great!

The scene, made more exciting particularly in Act II by the blaring brasses, and hundreds of richly dressed men, women, with horses and even elephants (!) is unforgettable. The ancient Egyptian architecture, the Orientally garbed cast, and the religious music with its Oriental feeling and the ballets add to the thrills. If Verdi has not used actual Egyptian music, his Oriental intervals give the illusion. Few Italian operas, except Verdi's own, approach it in beauty, in glamour, in entertainment, or in music. So in *Aïda* this magical composer built something greater than even he thought could be done.

Verdi tried to use a more continuous narrative, less broken by separate arias, than in his other operas. Whether admitting it or not, he was somewhat influenced by Wagner's uninterrupted musical speech.

The world would be poorer indeed, musically, (1) had Verdi never written *"Celeste Aïda"* (tenor solo) which he had the courage to put early in the first act; (2) had Verdi never written *"Ritorna vincitor"* ("Return Conqueror"), sung by *Aïda* (soprano); (3) had he never written the Orientally styled "Sacred Chant" in the first act, and the Temple of Isis music in the last act. The last wondrous song sung by the hero, Radames, before he and Aïda are confined to a living death in the vault is unforgettable. This opera is what the movies claim to be stupendous, gigantic, terrific!

Aïda was produced in Cairo in 1871. It opened first in New York, at the Academy of Music in 1873, and at the Metropolitan, where it has received more performances, it is said, than any other opera, because of the singers, or because of its rich and melodious music and "super" scenic effects.

After he had written his record-breaking *Aïda* at fifty-eight, Verdi, with the same luck that Gluck had in meeting Calzabigi, was fortunate to collaborate with Arrigo Boito, the composer of *Mefistofele,* who persuaded him to write an opera based on Shakespeare's *Othello.*

Verdi had not been idle since he wrote *Aïda.* For at sixty-one he had composed the *Requiem Mass* (1874) in honor of his friend the poet Manzoni. In this, the third and last stage of his development began. In spite of his use of operatic methods, it is one of the best examples of modern sacred music.

OTELLO (1886)

So with the collaboration of Boito and his wife, Giuseppina Strepponi, he wrote the opera *Otello.* He made, not a graft of music on a great play, but recreated musically an *Othello* that stands and falls by its own poetic and dramatic qualities. (For the libretto that makes *Otello* superb as a music drama, see Act VI, Scene I.)

Whereas *Aïda* is a sumptuous and glamorous opera, *Otello* turned out to be a music drama (with apologies to Wagner!). In it he more nearly arrives at the continuous drama he attempted in *Aïda*.

For power, brevity, mystery, positiveness, for profoundly deep and beautiful melody and continuous action and music, he surpassed himself. The song in *Otello* is not the popular, surface, catchy tune that characterized the operas before *Aïda*. Here he becomes eloquent and passionate, and achieves a deeper poignancy of feeling than he had ever reached before. In this his orchestration transcends the marvels that even he had accomplished, for he gives more power to the musical web. In short, *Otello* ranks with the five or six greatest music dramas ever written. Records of Desdemona's "Willow Song," and her "Prayer," in the last act, or Otello's passionate plaint in the second act are most satisfying and touching. Among the other great songs in this is the one that Desdemona sings when she is swearing her constancy: "Upon My Knees before Thee."

When Otello enters, before the strangling scene, he is accompanied by a powerful passage on the double basses. This is only one of the many instrumental colorings that are spread soul-deep and graphic throughout this opera.

At seventy-three, Verdi wrote this masterpiece of masterpieces, and was yet to write *Falstaff*.

Otello was produced at La Scala, Milan, in 1887, with Francesco Tamagno, tenor, in the title role and Victor Maurel as Iago; and in New York, at the Academy of Music, in 1888, with two great singers: Eva Tetrazzini, sister of the more famous Luisa, and Sophia Scalchi, an Italian contralto, who had made her debut in *The Masked Ball*. At the time it was given in New York Italo Campanini, tenor, was manager of the Academy of Music. *Otello* did not reach the Metropolitan until 1891, and after that some of the most eminent singers, including Nellie Melba, sang in it.

MERRIMENT FOLLOWS TRAGEDY

Merriment followed tragedy in the list of operas by this versatile man—farmer, senator, composer and fighter for liberty. His last opera, at the age of eighty, was written with Boito as librettist, on two plays of Shakespeare: *The Merry Wives of Windsor* and *King Henry IV*, and was named *Falstaff*. This rotund winebibber, friend of Prince Hal, later Henry V, had made musical copy for Mozart's enemy, Salieri, in Vienna; for the Irishman Balfe in London; for a number of others, including Otto Nicolai in his amusing *The Merry Wives of Windsor,* but never more brilliantly, more amusingly or gayer in spirit or as well composed as in Verdi's opera.

In *Falstaff* (1893) Verdi uses continuous musical narrative. All scenes are connected as advocated by Wagner, but not with the Wagnerian type of symphonic music. This has the dash and spirit and an amazing youthfulness that Wagner never could have accomplished with his heavier orchestration. "I wrote it for fun," Verdi said in a letter. "The opera is wholly comic."

Falstaff may not have the tuneful set pieces, like the "Anvil Chorus," "Miserere" in *Il Trovatore,* or the Table Scene in *La Traviata,* but it has a sprightliness in musical dialogue, added to its engaging orchestration, which at times has the blitheness of a Rossini opera.

Falstaff, like *Otello,* is a music drama, where song does not win out over orchestra, or orchestra over song. In the music drama, song and orchestra are partners, and each is of importance. In music drama, the orchestra acts and sings as in *Otello* in a continuous stream of interpretation.

Instead of cutting *Falstaff* into various songs, Verdi uses characteristic episodes or scenes in which the singers, with their songs, paint occurrence and sentiment, also in a continuous stream. For example, in the episode of the letter (for Falstaff writes a love letter in a misguided moment) there is an unaccompanied quartet for women, which begins "Tho' shaped like a barrel he fain would come courting." In short, *Falstaff,* to be colloquial, "is a scream."

After *Falstaff,* Verdi, at eighty-five, wrote *Pezzi Sacri (A Few Sacred Pieces)* which show a deep reverence for God and Palestrina.

Verdi resented the accusation that he was copying Richard Wagner because of his continued uninterrupted musical narrative, now brought to a climax in *Falstaff.* He could no more be accused of copying Wagner than he could of copying Meyerbeer or Gounod, from whom he certainly did get some ideas. He was Verdi, and Verdi *only.* He did not write symphonic opera. He did write Verdian opera and music drama.

ITALIAN SONG VS. GERMAN ORCHESTRA

He inherited the responsibility of bringing Italian song to a victory over German instrumental music, such as the symphony or symphonic opera. This was a hot war and not always accompanied by the sweetest melodies, for the Germans and Italians clashed on theories of opera. Verdi in his developing might from *Nabucco* to *Otello* and *Falstaff* brought operatic song to its pinnacle in action and beauty. Now anger, passion, roughness of humanity, subterranean rumbles are heard as well as sweetness both in song and in orchestra. At the end Verdi makes melodious song and orchestra partners. He left behind the "tingling agility of Rossini, and early Verdi, the divinely gentle melancholy of Bellini, the sensually ecstatic drama of Donizetti. His charm is almost purely Italian." (Pitts Sanborn, *The Metropolitan Book of the Opera*.)

SOME VERDIAN CONTRIBUTIONS

Respect for separate instruments and small groups of instruments is a contribution that Verdi made to the Italian opera orchestra. In *Ernani*, at one point, Verdi lets a cello sing alone during the third act, and as mentioned, has a flute solo in the overture to *The Masked Ball*. In *Otello*, and especially in *Falstaff*, he gave large groups of instruments beautiful combinations and melodies which another would have given to a solo instrument. Verdi could make small and large groups sing gloriously together without any seams showing. Yet, as he grew old, his music became simpler, deeper and more lovely, with less surface glitter. He used fewer notes and fewer words—should you ever wish to count them!

That Verdi had a gift of melody is as true as that Titian, the painter, had a gift of color. Some people who understand the amazing qualities of *The Masked Ball*, *Otello* and *Falstaff*, make light of *Ernani*, *Rigoletto*, *La Traviata*, *Il Trovatore* and others, because they are easy to listen to. Operas, however, that are easy to listen to, which have good stories, and delighting melodies in spite of out-dated rhythmic formulae, should not be underrated but treasured.

Verdi was the boss with his librettists, managers and singers. From the very beginning he was ready to throw back a libretto or a score to the management and give up production if they wanted to change even a punctuation mark. He never agreed to add or subtract a thing, nor did he ever write additional songs at the singers' requests. He was not writing to enhance the popularity of singers, but to write concisely and dramatically. He was a man of the theater with an iron will. He knew what would act, and what would not act. Probably no one approached the magnitude of this gift as nearly as Puccini—certainly not Wagner!

A REMARKABLE TIME-TABLE

Read this time-table and be it never admitted that anyone is obliged by age to stop working:

Oberto, Conte di Bonifacio, November 17, 1839, Milan.
Un Giorno di Regno (or *Il Finto Stanislao*), September 5, 1840, Milan.
Nabucodonos (*Nabucco*) March 9, 1842, Milan.
I Lombardi alla Prima Crociata (*Crusader*) February 11, 1843, Milan (revised as *Jerusalem*, November 26, 1847, Paris).
Ernani, March 9, 1844, Venice.
I Due Foscari, November 3, 1844, Rome.
Giovanna D'Arco, February 15, 1845, Milan.
Alzira, August 12, 1845, Naples.
Attila, March 17, 1846, Venice.
Macbeth, March 14, 1847, Florence (revision April 21, 1865, Paris).
I Masnadieri, July 22, 1847, London.
Il Corsaro, October 25, 1848, Trieste.
La Battaglia di Legnano, January 27, 1849, Rome.
Luisa Miller, December 8, 1849, Naples.
Stiffelio, November 16, 1850, Trieste.
Rigoletto, March 11, 1851, Venice.
Il Trovatore, January 19, 1853, Rome.
La Traviata, March 6, 1853, Venice.
I Vespri Siciliani, June 13, 1855, Paris.
Simon Boccanegra, March 12, 1857, Venice, (Revision March 24, 1881, Milan).
Aroldo, August 16, 1857, Rimini.
Un Ballo in maschera, February 17, 1859, Rome.
La forza del destino, November 10, 1862, St. Petersburg.
Don Carlo, March 11, 1867, Paris.
Aida, December 24, 1871, Cairo.
Otello, February 5, 1886, Milan—at seventy-three!
Falstaff, February 9, 1893, Milan—at eighty years of age!

SCENE III

Mussorgsky the Realist

MODEST Mussorgsky (1839–81), foremost genius among Russian opera writers, was the grandson of a serf, and son of a landowner and officer in the Royal Guards. Baby-sitting might not have been a trade nor an art in Modest Petrovitch Mussorgsky's day, but his nurse not only sat with this baby, but fed him Russian folklore, and folk song! The nursery songs he wrote subsequently are enchanting. Through these he came to understand the power of tenderness and humor in music. Long before school age his mother taught him music, and his father suggested teachers. As his mother thought he should go to school first he went to St. Petersburg, and by eleven he showed genuine musical talent. In one instance at an affair for charity, his teacher rewarded him for his magnificent performance with a copy of a Beethoven sonata.

Next, this modest Modest Mussorgsky was sent to a school for cadets, but he was unfit for the harsh and impersonal training. He wanted to study, but his companions thought study ill suited an officer. One of them said to him—looking upon him with disgust as he was reading—"My dear Modest, what sort of an officer will *you* make!" Nevertheless he learned Old Church music in the cadet school, which enriched his late compositions.

Modest became more and more possessed with music, and was lucky enough to meet Alexander Borodin, then a doctor in the military hospital. This same Dr. Borodin composed the opera *Prince Igor*. It wasn't long after that Modest met Alexander Sergievitch Dargomijsky, who suggested that a new Russian music, with a new flavor and *song-speech* should be built. This had a profound influence on Mussorgsky's work and was a factor in the development of "The Five" so influential in making the new nationalistic Russian music.

Dargomijsky and his group wanted to do something new but something Russian. Their aim was "truth in music."

338

Dargomijsky wrote *Russalka,* on the same theme as Glinka's *Ruslan and Ludmilla,* but it was not as good. He is noteworthy, not so much for operas as for the inspiration he gave to young Russian composers. He wanted to use Russian themes for both comic and serious opera. This fired Mussorgsky, who could write satirically and humorously, as for example "The Song of the Flea" (Goethe's poem), as well as incomparable, tenderly sweet nursery songs sung so delightfully by Maria Kusenko.

Dargomijsky's *Stone Guest,* on Pushkin's *Don Juan,* was supposed to carry out his ideas of song-speech so often sought by writers through the ages. This was not accomplished by Dargomijsky, but by a pianist-composer in France—Claude Achille Debussy—and to a wonderful extent by Mussorgsky (in *Khovantchina*).

STRIDES AHEAD

Mussorgsky had tried his hand at an opera based on *Salammbô* by Flaubert. As this was romantic and far from realistic, he decided thereafter to use his own texts or alter others to suit him. His friends thought him an idiot. And here he did something that Pergolesi had done—he wrote music picturing "regular" people, not only the privileged. He also tried hard to get a realistic song-speech. Mussorgsky lived among peasants with his sister on the little that was left of her estate.

Then Mussorgsky attempted a farce, *The Marriage.* He set this in drab, realistic, uncomfortable surroundings. He painted character amazingly, and went far from the romantic fairy tale and folk operas of the recent past.

TRUTH IN MUSIC

Liberated from old styles, he felt confident and free enough to satisfy his passion to tell the truth in music, to try to recreate Russian life, and rouse the public spirit not only with ancient legends but with current actualities. He and his family were impoverished by the freeing of serfs in 1861, two years before Lincoln freed America from slavery. In spite of his personal suffering Mussorgsky believed in the emancipation.

Now he was ready to tackle *Boris Godounov,* for which he wrote his own libretto, based on a drama by the poet Alexander Pushkin. (Pushkin has been loved in Russia as Shakespeare, Goethe and the Bible are loved in the West.) It gave him the scope he was seeking in fitting music to a politico-social theme. He also adapted the story to his own liking and started Russian music on the social and realistic road, as Pushkin had poetry. Boris, so the story went in the days of old Russia, had seized a throne which didn't belong to him. This brought on intrigue, sorrow and calamity to the people and to the nobles. It has typical Russian scenery, typical Russian crowds and noises, and ends in as great a tragedy as the mind of man can represent. As Charpentier's opera *Louise* made Paris a part of the plot, so Mussorgsky's *Boris* (*Khovantchina* too) made Russia the main character. He pictured the "common" people, beggars and insane victims as human—so not to be neglected.

BORIS GODOUNOV EXCELS

The opera is powerful and uses the moving, moblike choruses almost as if they were part of an ancient Greek drama. The surging crowds of Russian people feel and prophesy tragedy in a manner somewhat similar to that of the ancient Greek chorus. Mussorgsky sometimes uses melody, sometimes recitative, and the listener is carried away by the profound beauties of the songs. Characteristically, the "Nurse's Song" to the children is one of rare loveliness, intensified by the background of the alarming tolling of the Kremlin bells, so rich in color.

Mussorgsky uses the old Russian modes, along with the scales we use, folk and folklike tunes as well as religious. He wastes no musical phrases and puts recitative where he sees fit, copying no one—and no one seems to have been able to copy him. His orchestra can engulf you with great waves of ravishing sound such as you have never heard, or it can purr like a kitten. *Boris Godounov* is a pulsing pageant, yet full of human pathos and drama.

Strange as it may seem, the manuscript of this opera was so original that it was considered to be harmonically and instrumentally rough and uncouth, and was given to self-sacrificing Rimsky-Korsakov to edit after Mussorgsky's death. For some time *Boris* was produced in the Rimsky-Korsakov edition, in which he changed some of the scenery schemes and made it conform a little more to usual operatic customs. Shostakovitch was also given a turn at editing this great opera. But now, owing to more understanding, the manuscript is presented very nearly as Mussorgsky wrote it. The Metropolitan used the Rimsky-Korsakov version until 1953, when Karol Rathaus made a revision more faithful to the original.

It is produced in all its magnificent, so-called "uncouthness" and neglect of the singers' wishes. He made a basso the hero—an unheard of thing.

Indeed, there is no finer modern opera of any nationality than *Boris Godounov,* unless it be his own *Khovantchina.* Nor is there a bass role so darkly lustrous as in *Boris.* Feodor Chaliapin made the part so remarkable, so unforgettable that when one thinks of *Boris* today, one thinks of this incomparable Russian basso.

For fifty years, *Boris,* this work of beauty, "slept on shelves" (Olin Downes). It was indeed a sleeping beauty! It was not revived as the composer wrote it until after the Russian Revolution of 1917. At first it was refused for production because it contained too many choruses and too many ensembles and not enough principal roles to satisfy a cast. Doesn't this sound somewhat like the complaints of the singers in Handel's time?

Boris Godounov was given first at the Mariinsky Theatre in St. Petersburg in 1874, and later in New York at the Metropolitan Opera House in 1913, in an Italian translation directed by Arturo Toscanini. The cast had Adam Didur, basso, as Boris, Louise Homer, contralto, and Paul Althouse, tenor. In 1921, at the Metropolitan, Feodor Chaliapin sang Boris in Russian and the rest of the cast sang in Italian. Strange things happen in opera.

Mussorgsky wasn't a great technician. He was a composer who wrote just as he wished, making unconventional jumps and skips to carry out his own ideas as a painter uses his colors. He wished to mirror both human nature and nature. His influence on Debussy is very evident.

KHOVANTCHINA

Plots of Russian operas in the nineteenth century were never easy to follow, but Mussorgsky's own libretto for *Khovantchina* is the most bewildering. It is easy to understand, however, when one considers Russian novels with their long complicated plots like those of Tolstoi and Dostoievsky. Both librettists and novelists look at their stories from many sides, and purposely do not confine themselves to easily followed plots. In many of the Russian operas the story is a familiar one, as are many of our stories, such as that of John Alden, the assassination of Lincoln, Franklin and the kite, and so on. If it is understood that the plot unfolds in scenes instead of in continuity, it isn't difficult to follow. Tchaikovsky, indeed, gave to his opera *Eugen Onegin* the subtitle *Lyrical Scenes.*

The story in this magnificent work, *Khovantchina,* is of Mussorgsky's beloved people ground between the traditional and Peter the Great's new and radical ideas and ruthless acts.

The scenario is dated 1682 as the beginning of the action. This makes Peter the Great only ten years old, too young for introducing reforms or for making the term *Khovantchina* apply to the princes Khovansky who were spearheads of revolt. Therefore, the plot is the more complicated by distorting history. Yet Mussorgsky has made a significant opera—again the triumph of musical genius over a distorted libretto.

The choruses so important in Russian opera are written superbly for men, women, and mixed voices, bringing color and meaning to the episodes they celebrate, in rich, ringing song.

Marfa in this plot is a peculiar creation. She is part soothsayer, part frustrated woman who bewails her "many sins and wickednesses" and goes to her death in spite of her witchcraft with the man whom she loves and who betrays her. She dominates the opera as her story weaves in and out, enriching the scenes. One of the finest with beautiful music is where Marfa prophesies Prince Galitzin's baleful future in an incantation over a bowl of water.

Nothing is omitted in *Khovantchina* that makes for drama, contrast and color in scenes and music. If the plot is complicated, Mussorgsky achieved a continuous music, and a melodic musical speech. Whereas Debussy, influenced by Mussorgsky, succeeded eminently with his vague unitalicized half chant, half speech, Mussorgsky used a song-speech which was more song than speech and more rhythmic and definite than Debussy's.

In Act III of *Khovantchina,* Scene II, Mussorgsky's use of continuous music in dialogue is beautifully illustrated. In the series of verses or sentences, beginning "I, a thoughtless maiden, went through the field," Marfa sings to a folk tune, which is not developed like Wagner's, as she speaks and is interrupted by others, but each time her verses are heard the background or matrix of the verse gives it freshness and new poignancy. This, of course, takes a versatile composer. In his hand this kind of song-speech works. It tells the story of her betrayal by Prince André Khovansky, the son of the leader of the incoherent masses of people.

In the fourth act, the Persian Dances are sumptuous. Why they are not as well known as the dances in *Prince Igor* is hard to say.

Mussorgsky uses folk tunes from traditional sources as well as his own folklike music sown in his Russian consciousness. His music is at times so much like folk song that it is hard to tell which is which.

How beautifully and tunefully the opera starts with a familiar prelude which suggests daybreak along the Moskva River! Then follows a lovely theme used in five variations and quoted later (at the end of Act II). The music keeps on playing while the stage remains in semi-darkness wherein naught but the half-asleep sentinel is apparent at first.

The first performance of *Khovantchina* was in 1885 (1886?) in St. Petersburg. Emil Cooper conducted the first performance of *Khovantchina* at the Metropolitan Opera House in New York in the winter of 1949–50.

AN UNFINISHED COMIC OPERA

After Mussorgsky had finished *Boris Godounov* (1869), he started (in 1874) on *Khovantchina* and sometime later on his comic opera, *The Fair at Sorochinsk*. He said he needed relief from the two operas in which he had told tragic stories of his beloved Russian people. Unfortunately, he worked too hard on poor rations and bad health and died before they were finished. At his death (1881) he had nearly finished the rough draft in a vocal score of *Khovantchina* and several scenes of *Sorochinsk*. Other composers have had a hand in completing *The Fair,* which had its first performance in Moscow in 1913.

Modest Mussorgsky believed and followed the new ideas and was the greatest of "The Five," as proven by his operas, *Boris Godounov, Khovantchina,* and other works. They show originality, a new approach, grandeur of ideas and colorful handling. As Debussy did later, Mussorgsky said what he wanted to say in the way he wanted to say it, in spite of being told he was hollow, idiotic and so on!

A TRAGIC END

Mussorgsky was too frail a man to stand the wear and tear of composing and government office work, so he gave up his job. Once a military man and a dandy, Mussorgsky died of drugs, drink, illness and long subjection to poverty, at the age of forty-six. It is tragic that one so greatly gifted, who left his imprint on composers, should have had so unhappy an end. What a pity that the government in his day didn't take care of its composers as it has done in the Soviet regime! But at least Mussorgsky was a free man and could write as he wished, without governmental supervision.

SCENE IV

Debussy, Glinting Impressionist

THE WORD AND MUSIC ARE EQUAL

How hard the Camerata struggled with their limited musical tools to fit words with music as in the ancient Greek drama! How sincerely the early Italian poets and critics tried to fit the word to the action! How long and for how many years did Gluck, Weber and, most noisily of all, Richard Wagner, declare that opera must be continuous, not blocked in action by arias, duets and ballets, with voice not canceled by the orchestra; orchestra ever present and not made insignificant by the voice, and so on, and so on! None of them accomplished all of these things. Gluck and Weber did much toward making opera more lovely, and Wagner made many more changes which no one could or wanted to follow completely. He did use a few choruses and duets—and the song sometimes dominated the orchestra, and the orchestra sometimes drowned the song. But the men who put into practice in differing degrees their loudly sung theories were Mussorgsky, realist, in Eastern Europe; and Claude Achille Debussy, glinting Impressionist, in the West. These made words, music and scenery tell their stories with equal power.

Debussy was born in the right era, when painting and poetry freed themselves from the lonely cow in the meadow, the girl strewing flowers, and other old forms of sentimentality. So why shouldn't music change with a changing world?

PINNACLE OF FRENCH OPERA

Debussy was born in St. Germain-en-Laye in 1862, died in Paris in 1918, and was buried during a German air-raid. He reached the pinnacle of French opera with his tragic, mysterious story, *Pelléas et Mélisande*. This is an "impressionist tone picture" in five acts, "unique and isolated in the history of opera" (Pitts Sanborn). It lives in a tone world of its own—a shadowy world, half-ghostly in half-real and secret places. Debussy tried to make his continuous music fit the poetic essence of the Maeterlinck drama. So well did he succeed that you can take a copy of the Maeterlinck play to the opera, instead of a libretto, for with few exceptions it is like the play. The story of Maeterlinck's and the opera are one story, one opera—and a miracle!

The story is akin to *Tristan und Isolde* and *Paola and Francesca,* in which are told the tragic results of two men with ties of blood or friendship desiring the same woman. Because at first critics heard no clashing of cymbals and blaring of trumpets, they called *Pelléas* "jelly-fish," "sound wraiths," and "stammering phantoms." Compared to most operas, it seems pale and vague. It tells a story of the soul rather than the struggle of physical characters, and is the composer's impression of the tragic and mystic meshing of events. There is no orchestral clash, nor human outcries, even in the most intense moments. It is played in gloom, occasionally shot through with exquisite musical impressions of light. There are no arias or choruses in the old way, or ballets. The tale is told in translucent, limpid, gracile French. Nearly any opera libretto might be translated into English, or other languages, but it is difficult to conceive of *Pelléas et Mélisande* sung in anything but French. Each syllable and phrase has its own "musification" or musicality. The French language, with its slight stress or accent, flows continuously in half-speech as gently as an undulating stream of silver light. At times it is like a whisper, and at times it is stressed and accented into more forceful statements. It is what the Camerata tried to do with Italian in the early days, and what Wagner thought ought to be done. The opera rarely reaches fortissimo, even at its climactic moments, such as when Mélisande's wedding ring falls into the fountain, or the tragic crisis in the bed-chamber in the last act, where Mélisande lies dying and her half-crazed doubting husband probes her for what he calls "the truth" about her love for Pelléas. Occasionally, musical interludes interrupt the narrative, to foretell the mood or to revert to a mood. These interludes, which carry on the feeling and give time for scene changes, are a part of the story itself.

THE MUSIC—AN ADVENTURER

Edward Lockspeiser, a biographer of Debussy, says that he "wandered into new worlds of tonality and musical coloring." The opera is based on primitive matter, sensation, and overtones, both in the soul and in the music.

There is much written about the scale that Debussy used, its vagueness and its beauty. It's enough for us to know that he used, for the most part, a scale that moves in whole steps or tones, six within an octave. Furthermore, he used interval sequences that are like the medieval *modes* akin to the melody of Gregorian Chant. In other works he used also Gregorian Chant with its old-time beauty. Like Mussorgsky, who influenced him, he used what he thought was expressive. He wanted to get away from the old tonalities and keys. He was an adventurer.

To use the Pelléas story was not simple, even for Debussy. In his letters to Chausson (1894), he complains how difficult it is to picture Mélisande, who is so finely "spun." He complains too of the old man Arkel, who troubles him even more, and says, "he has the otherworldly, far-seeing tenderness of those who will soon disappear, and this must be expressed by means of *do, re, mi, fa, sol, la, si, do.*" (*Revue Musicale,* Special Number, May 1, 1926.)

In another letter to Chausson, Debussy says "The color of my soul is iron-grey. Sinister bats wheel about the belfry of my dreams. My only hope is in *Pelléas et Mélisande,* and God alone knows if this hope will not end in smoke." It did not end in smoke, but in diaphanous, translucent mists of exquisite music and drama.

The orchestra never dims the voice (in continuous song), nor the voice the orchestra. The story is one of mystery with vague glints coming from no one knows where. No one knows where Mélisande comes from; no one knows how she reached the gloomy forest, the gloomier palace; and how she came to wed the middle-aged Golaud, old enough to have been her father. Excitement is intense with silences, with understatement; soft music, ancient and pastel harmonies. The excitement is in the enmeshment of the souls of the characters, rather than in the self-effacing orchestra, the carrier for the tragic web of the story. The over-all feeling, when you see this opera, is that you have actually been to the "Never-Never Land," down with Pelléas into the mysterious caves and gloomy forest with only an occasional glinting shaft of music lighting the soul and mind. The vagueness of the music is matched only by the vagueness about Mélisande, who does not seem to understand of what she is accused, so innocent is she.

Although *Pelléas et Mélisande* was accepted for production in 1898, Debussy took back his score many times for remodeling. This delayed the presentation for four years. It was produced first at the Opéra Comique in Paris in 1902. Mary Garden played it with enchanting simplicity. New York saw this powerfully "pale" drama when Oscar Hammerstein produced it at the Manhattan Opera House in 1908. One critic said of it that Debussy's tone combinations "sting and blister and pain and outrage the ear." How anything as flowing and gentle could do these violent things is hard to understand, but it shows again how new things may torture some ears, and heal others. Since 1925, when it was first presented at the Metropolitan, *Pelléas* has been an occasional feature of the Metropolitan repertory. Edward Johnson was Pelléas and Lucrezia Bori was Mélisande, in this first performance.

IN OTHER FIELDS

Debussy is important as a writer who advanced the scope of opera. Needless to say, he is an eminent and original composer in other musical fields. His symphonic poem *L'Après-midi d'un faune,* used also for a ballet for Vaslav Nijinsky, is in delicate yet vivid colors. After you have heard this you will never forget its haunting mysterious flutes and wood winds. For Debussy had the power of using instruments to make us hear the glimmering sunshine, vague gloom, mysterious darkness and impending perils and joys. He was almost able to make you, in music, smell the warm lush grass where the indolent faun lay stretched in the sunlight. And you could feel the velvet of his delight as he warmed himself in the sun and heard the sound of distant revels.

Debussy's piano *Préludes* are gems of impressionism—short tone poems in which are reflected the ethereal quality and iridescent colors that make *Pelléas et Mélisande* a penetrating experience in opera.

After Debussy finished his "Sonata for Violin and Piano," he appeared as a pianist in public for the last time in May, 1917. As a youth he had taught piano in the household of Madame von Meck, the friend of Tchaikovsky, where he met Borodin, one of the Russian "Five." He must have heard Mussorgsky's music and probably had a taste of other Slavic music and the beauties of the sacred and secular song of Russia.

DEBUSSY'S IMPRESSIONISM

Debussy, like Wagner, has been imitated in opera by few, but many composers have followed in his tonal path. He and his followers, if they can be so called, were writing music at the time that the impressionists were painting pictures and the symbolist poets were writing impressionist poetry. This word *impressionist* means that these men expressed in their work their own feeling about something, rather than exact descriptive details of the subject, whether in music, painting or poetry. "Debussy . . . tried to suggest in tone a mental image—a thought, an emotion, a definite object, a poem, a picture—used not to reproduce tangible or concrete things, but the *emotion* aroused by the image." (*Music Through the Ages,* by Bauer and Peyser.)

Among the few that can be called followers, because they wrote impressionistic music, is Paul Dukas, best known for *The Sorcerer's Apprentice.* His opera *Ariane et Barbe-Bleue (Ariadne and Bluebeard)* was also based on a play of Maeterlinck's. One critic called it "an allegory of the Women's Rights Movement." It's about Bluebeard and his wives whom Ariane delivers from bondage and, after she gets what she wants, leaves to fend for themselves.

It was given first at the Opéra Comique in Paris in 1907, later at the Metropolitan Opera House in New York, 1911, with Geraldine Farrar as Ariane and Arturo Toscanini as conductor.

RAVEL HELPS FRENCH OPERA'S FRENCHNESS

The most illustrious composer in France, after Debussy, is Maurice Ravel (1875–1937). France was a long time pulling out from under alien musical influence, particularly that of German romanticists, and it wasn't until after the Franco-Prussian War that she did. Ravel, with others, rebelling against Wagner's influence, helped to restore France to her former grace, formality and beauty.

Ravel is much liked for his popular "Bolero," and his enticing, colorful and charming ballets. Among these are the shimmery, glittering *Daphnis and Chloë,* and *Ma Mère l'Oye (Mother Goose).* Among many other works are exquisite songs and the choreographic poem, *La Valse.*

He wrote two operas. One, *L'Enfant et les sortilèges (The Child and the Sorceries),* tells of a bewitched and naughty child who "sees the light."

His opera *L'Heure espagnole (Spanish Time),* text by Franc-Nohain, is laid in Spain in a tick-tock shop of active clocks. It tells the story of a too flippant wife who flirts with other men when her husband is away, and hides them in the big grandfather clock. It is gay, and the music is as witty and as sarcastic as the text itself. It is one of the little masterpieces of modern times, and its one act is full of delights.

It was given first at the Opéra Comique in Paris in 1911, later in

America in Chicago, as well as in New York by Hammerstein in 1920 at the Lexington Theatre. In 1925 the Metropolitan gave it with Lucrezia Bori and Lawrence Tibbett.

In *Spanish Time* (which Ravel called a musical comedy) he again is the master of orchestration, as in all his other works. He can make an ordinary piece of music so colorful and so beautiful that it seems like another thing from what it started out to be. His orchestration of Mussorgsky's "Pictures from an Exhibition" is almost as original as is the piano work. People have compared Ravel's works to formal, symmetrical French gardens, beautifully arranged and designed.

Maurice Ravel was somewhat influenced by Claude Debussy, yet he went his own way. He used more definite rhythms and kept to more definite forms and shapes than Debussy.

SCENE V

Richard Strauss, Romantic Realist

RICHARD STRAUSS is the most eminent German opera writer in the twentieth century. He went farther along the paths of new tone combinations than had any other opera writer, and took advantage of what had been before him. He horrified people with his operas *Salome* and *Elektra*.

Yet, with dissonance, with contrasting sweet measures, with every resourceful device of the composer, with Strauss's skill at making a tune in the smallest tonal compass, or spreading it over a wide range, he reveals a new, free phase, a new station on the road of opera. This man's work, which repelled many thirty years ago, is now embraced, and at his death in Germany, 1949, he was mourned as a genius.

Richard Strauss, born in Munich in 1864, was the son of a horn player who had been in the orchestra when Richard Wagner conducted his operas. When the child showed signs of musical genius, Franz Strauss insisted on his having a classical training, because he did not approve of the methods of Wagner, and wished to protect young Richard from the influence of "musical degeneracy"! But fate worked differently.

Richard became assistant conductor to Hans von Bülow of the Ducal Court Orchestra at Meiningen in 1885. There he met Alexander Ritter, a poet, musician and distant relative of Richard Wagner. Ritter was enthusiastic about the "new" music of the early eighties and turned his young friend, classical training notwithstanding, toward Wagner, Liszt, and Berlioz. The result was that before the end of the century, Richard Strauss had written tone poems and songs that marked him as a musician of profound gifts. The bulk of his opera writings belongs to the twentieth century, although his early sallies in that field were of the 1890's.

It took a long time for the world to revere Strauss, for his music was considered often to be in bad taste. If ever any one seemed to make a business of "startling the natives" (or as the French say it, *"épater le bourgeois"*) it was Strauss! He combined modern experiments in dissonance with harmonic commonplaceness; he horrified with his shocking subjects, especially in his operas later; he seemed to take pleasure in sensational effects and realistic devices in his orchestral works, including an imitation of an alarm clock, spanking the baby and signifying its crying in the *Symphonia domestica* (*Domestic Symphony*). What was regarded as artistic heresy yesterday, today is recognized as a remarkable portrayal of "realism in music," with Richard Strauss as its high priest.

There was such a din in the Battle Scene in *Ein Heldenleben* (*A Hero's Life*), in which he told his own story, that the critics rose up against him. They were disturbed also by his use of a wind machine and of his imitation of bleating sheep in *Don Quixote*. And yet few composers have been as successful in musical protraiture and character sketching as Strauss.

Audiences today are accustomed to far greater flights from the traditional and they take them without dismay. Now Strauss stands out as one of the original composers of his day.

EARLY OPERAS

The resourceful Richard Strauss, along with other of his contemporaries, followed Wagner's ideas of going back into German legend and myth for opera plots. His first, eleven years after Wagner's death, was *Guntrun* (1894, Munich), for which he wrote the libretto, following Wagner's lead, even to having a moralistic theme of redemption of humanity through "something." In this case the "something" was song, not love. This opera was a failure. He was so depressed that he didn't write another for seven years, but composed one symphonic poem after another, which brought him fame.

Then he wrote a one-act opera, *Feuersnot* (*Fire Famine,* 1901, Dresden), with libretto by Ernst von Wolzogen. This was ironic, and in somewhat dangerously Rabelaisian or in what might be called a "naughty" vein, which the librettist counteracted by placing the story in the thirteenth century in Munich. It is a fantastic tale of magic and candlelight in which is a scene where the lady love traps the magician lover in a basket hanging from her window. It might be interesting to hear this opera today in order to measure the younger Strauss's progress as we can that of Verdi and the young Mozart.

SALOME

In his third opera, *Salome* (pronounced Sa'-lo-may), Strauss reached the height of the psychopathic and crass horror. The magnificence and richness of the music makes even more emphatic the morbidity of the story of the beheading of St. John the Baptist to satisfy the sensual passion of Salome, daughter of the salacious Herodias, and step-daughter of Herod the degenerate monarch.

The libretto for *Salome* was on the play by Oscar Wilde, translated by Hedwig Lachmann. While based on the Bible story it wanders far afield in its (un)"poetic license." The Wilde version supplied Strauss with material for erotic, direct and perverse "drama with music." This too beautiful princess has been of interest to painters and writers, such as Albrecht Dürer, Leonardo da Vinci, Flaubert, Heine and Ernest Renan. And it is claimed that Wilde was inspired by a painting of Salome by Titian in the Prado (gallery) in Spain.

Salome is at the pinnacle of realism, known in Italian opera as *verismo*. It is a typical revolt from the spiritual vagueness of French impressionistic opera, such as *Pelléas et Mélisande* by Debussy and *Ariane et Barbe-Bleue* by Dukas, to the naked expression of the physical and unwholesome.

What is not done on the stage to shock the audience is voiced by the orchestra which brilliantly fills out the picture of horror. "The Dance of the Seven Veils" is a thriller! Its unforgettable theme and bits of it are used again and again in the opera. In a panther-like dance, Salome removes veil after veil in a sort of morbid, classical(?) "strip tease," that offended the Church and even national governments. Neither Boston nor London would allow its appearance. Furthermore the scene in which the head of John the Baptist is delivered to Salome on a silver salver banned the opera from the Metropolitan stage for years. First the newspapers claimed that it had outraged morals and should be dropped. Then the directors, led by Anne Morgan, thought it immoral and sacrilegious, and threatened to break the lease of Heinrich Conried (manager) unless he withdrew *Salome*. It was withdrawn.

Olive Fremstad, the Swedish-American soprano, had created a sensation in the role. "A sleek tigress, with seduction speaking in every pose, gesture, look and utterance," wrote H. E. Krehbiel of the New York *Tribune,* although he denounced the opera after its première, January 22, 1907.

In 1909, the unique singing actress Mary Garden appeared as Salome under the management of Oscar Hammerstein in his "amazing fine" company at the Manhattan Opera House in New York City. On January 13, 1934, the opera was given again at the Metropolitan with Artur Bodansky conducting and Göta Ljüngberg as Salome. Another revival took place in 1949 under Edward Johnson's management with Fritz Reiner (conductor) and Ljuba Welitch (soprano)—an exciting team.

THE ORCHESTRA OF STRAUSS

After Wagner's chromaticisms, the age of dissonance was dawning, and unusual harmonies began to enrich music. Strauss uses a heavy orchestra and leitmotifs somewhat like Wagner. He also uses the old styles, such as having a dance in the middle of an act, as is seen in the "Dance of the Seven Veils" in *Salome*. He was not afraid to go back, nor to go forward. Of dissonance there is much; of jumps and skips there are many. We are now accustomed to it, but we were not prepared when *Salome* and *Elektra* came among us!

ELEKTRA AND VENGEANCE

Elektra (Dresden, 1909) is a story of vengeance as practiced by the Greeks. The libretto was the first one by Hugo von Hofmannsthal with whom Strauss was to collaborate in several operas. Von Hofmannsthal went to Sophocles for his basic material.

Outraged by the murder of her father, Agamemnon, at the hands of her mother, Klytemnestra, and Aegisthus, her mother's paramour, Elektra realizes that she is too frail to kill the guilty pair. Orestes, Elektra's brother, returns from a long absence, and, incited by his sister's dramatic pleading for vengeance, strikes down Klytemnestra and Aegisthus offstage, with the accompanying frenzied crowd onstage and shrieking commentary from the orchestra. Elektra's pleading with Orestes is one of the most eloquent pages in Strauss's music. The opera closes with Elektra's hysterical dance of triumph on her father's grave upon which she falls senseless. Morbid, yes—but how dramatic!

One of the authors saw the first performance of *Elektra* in New York at the Manhattan Opera House, 1910, where, after the final curtain, a girl just behind her said to her friend: "My Gawd, Goit, but that was one big noise!" And so it seemed—in 1910, with its new, clashing, cataclysmic, acid bursts of Strauss's exciting instrumental eruptions.

In a way Richard Strauss could be compared with Henrik Ibsen, for these men composed psychotic drama revealing the morbid compulsions of human beings. Wagner himself told heroic stories with a deep sense of romance, myth and sin; but Wagner's characters were never human as were those of Strauss—so full of terror and even of depravity.

Had we, however, been on hand when the Greek dramatists Sophocles and Aristophanes had their plays performed, we might have called them in bad taste, because beauty, comedy and tragedy were often wrapped in horror—yes, and the Greek comedies of Aristophanes would often seem pornographic or "off color" to a modern audience.

Elektra in French had its American première at the Manhattan Opera House, February 1, 1910. It did not reach the Metropolitan until December 3, 1932, since when it has been revived occasionally. It has won a growing audience although it never "caught on" as did *Salome,* which made Strauss as famous as an opera writer could become until *Der Rosenkavalier* entered.

TONE-POEM OPERAS

The basis of both *Salome* and *Elektra* is the symphonic or tone poem. Each might be described as an orchestral tone poem, with vocal obbligato for "programmatic explanation" (Paul Bekker). Both operas are short, hardly more than two hours, and each has only one act and one stage set. The orchestra describes, explains, and carries the emotional impact of the story. The dance, according to the Strauss habit, is used advantageously. The voices become a part of the orchestra, and the word helps to underline the action, but is not of primary importance as in earlier operas.

"The *Elektra* music should *not* be compared with that of *Salome,*" Herbert F. Peyser wrote in *Opera Lovers' Companion,* "which is rather subtle and aims at something like the effect of changeable silk. There are few subtleties in the score of *Elektra,* which is bigger and vastly more terrible in its impact, more somber in its dark ecstasies, more grandiose and immense, so that even its essentially lyrical quality is shaped on a larger and bolder scale."

FROM HORROR TO WINNING ROMANCE

If ever a composer made an about-face it was this versatile Richard Strauss, when he wrote the Johann Straussian, Mozart-like *Der Rosenkavalier* (*The Knight of the Rose*). In this he is winning and charming. Much of the music is based on waltz rhythms. These fascinate because of salty use of instruments and harmonies. With all its delectable writing for harps, celesta, flutes and violins, it always has a sharp-edged harmony which tempers the sentimental and touching parts of the story, without marring the feeling, and makes naughtier the "naughty parts." In all, *Der Rosenkavalier* is a crowning glory of opera writing in the early twentieth century. This tragicomedy is a most captivating mixture of humanity and artificiality on one of the greatest librettos ever penned.

How brilliant it was of Strauss to get von Hofmannsthal to write both *Elektra* and *Der Rosenkavalier!* Here was a genius who could join a morbid story with Viennese grace and glamour.

Der Rosenkavalier was first performed in America in 1913 at the Metropolitan Opera House, where it is given over and over again, to the refreshment of every listener.

In the creation of this comic opera, Strauss may have had Wagner's *Die Meistersinger* in mind, although the two works bear no resemblance. Strauss felt closer to Mozart and blended some Mozart essence with his own twentieth-century methods.

In his criticism of *Der Rosenkavalier* in the *New York Times,* Richard Aldrich wrote: "It was natural that the composer of *Till Eulenspiegel* and *Don Quixote* should before long arrive at comic opera, with all of the means at his disposition to express in music, humor, fantasy, lively movement and brisk activities."

He handled the human voice with more regard to its possibilities than he had either in *Salome* or more particularly in *Elektra.* Von Hofmannsthal placed his story in "Baroque Vienna" in the early eighteenth century, with its unique manners and customs and even its Viennese dialect. He also created several unforgettable personalities in the Marschallin, a great lady approaching middle age; Baron von Ochs, a sensual, impoverished member of the old nobility; and in Octavian, the young man with whom the Marschallin is enjoying a clandestine affair.

Strauss went back to the convention of the eighteenth-century theater and wrote the Octavian role for a woman, *à la* Cherubino in Mozart's *The Marriage of Figaro* and Gluck in *Orfeo ed Euridice.* Where Octavian finally falls in love with a young girl, Strauss wrote some of his most delectable music. Here it is singable, simple, a cross between folk song and Mozart.

One does not easily forget the glamour and magic of the entrance of the bearer of the silver rose (Octavian) and the shimmer of the music. The motif of the Silver Rose with its modern harmony has been imitated by many twentieth-century composers.

BURLESQUE

During a festival in his honor, Strauss's serio-burlesque opera, *Ariadne auf Naxos,* on a libretto by von Hofmannsthal, was given at the newly opened Hof Theater in Stuttgart in 1912, directed by Max Reinhardt. It was originally written as a concluding entertainment piece, or divertissement, to *Le Bourgeois Gentilhomme* (*The Would-be Gentleman*), Strauss's opera on the Molière comedy, and as such it was given. It was revised in 1916 with a new first act or musical prologue, instead of a spoken one, and in this new version, it began to live "on its own" without the Molière story. The incidental music he had written for *Le Bourgeois Gentilhomme* is preserved in an instrumental suite under the Molière title.

Here Strauss turned to burlesquing. He parodies the heroic opera of the seventeenth century as written by Lully and his contemporaries, and combines it with commedia dell' arte. Again he proves himself, for in the opening piece, where Ariadne sings her lament, he writes lovely music. Furthermore, his burlesque of mad scenes is brilliant. One of the opera's most famous bits is the tricky coloratura aria sung by the soubrette Zerbinetta. This conscious mixture of opera seria and opera buffa stands alone for the originality of its music and treatment.

Strauss was probably unaware that a generation later, *Ariadne auf Naxos* would be pointed out as one of the first operas in a neoclassic style. Neoclassicism marks a return to eighteenth-century conventions using twentieth-century musical methods.

It has an amusing scene in the music room of a Viennese who suddenly has amassed wealth—a *nouveau riche*. The composer and stage director and singers and ballet dancers bustle about to prepare the stage props for a performance of a serious grand opera. In the midst of the preparation, the crew is shocked to learn that a troop of comedians has arrived and a comic divertissement is scheduled to follow the grand opera. Then, to the dismay of all, it is decided to run the two operas together! A grand-style overture opens the opera, which then proceeds to enliven the audience.

Antony Tudor used Strauss's *Burleska* in his ballet *Dim Lustre* in 1943, and in 1944, *Le Bourgeois Gentilhomme* (*The Would-be Gen-*

tleman) was used by George Balanchine. *Ariadne auf Naxos* was introduced to America by the Philadelphia Civic Opera Company in 1928, directed by Alexander Smallens. It was given in English in New York first at the Juilliard School in 1934, and later at the City Center of Music and Drama, New York City. In 1955, the National Broadcasting Company Opera Theatre produced *Ariadne on Naxos* in a television version in which the direction used the first half of the original based on scenes from Molière's play with the incidental music composed in 1912 for the spoken comedy and combined it with the second part of Strauss's revision of 1916.

Strauss had the ordeal of living through Hitlerdom, from which he seemed to escape into a world of his imagination, with no attempt to interpret his country's dilemma.

BALLET FOR DIAGHILEV

In 1914, Strauss conducted a ballet, *Die Josefslegende* (*The Joseph Legend*), for Diaghilev's Baroque Ballet Russe in Paris, danced by Nijinsky, but it was not a success.

OTHER OPERAS

The rest of Strauss's operas were of a lesser breed, except, perhaps, *Die Frau ohne Schatten* (*The Woman Without a Shadow,* Vienna, 1919). The libretto by Hugo von Hofmannsthal is an Oriental legendary tale, a "sophisticated *Magic Flute*," in which an elaborate stage apparatus is used.

Intermezzo is a realistic picture of home life, a sort of operatic *Sinfonia Domestica* with the libretto by a man who knew good theater —the composer. He completed it in Buenos Aires in 1923. It is a combination of light opera and tragedy.

Die Aegyptische Helena (*The Egyptian Helen,* 1928) with libretto by von Hofmannsthal, was not destined for popularity. It had its world première at the Dresden Opera in June, and was given at the Metropolitan in November. Many critics found the composer, the last of the famous Germans, musically bankrupt.

ARABELLA

Before Hugo von Hofmannsthal died in 1929, he wrote one last libretto for Strauss, *Arabella*. New Yorkers have recently had the opportunity to judge of its merits for themselves, as it was given an elaborate and handsome production by the Metropolitan Opera Association in an English translation by John Gutman in February, 1955. It is a musical comedy about life in old Vienna, even as *Der Rosenkavalier,* but without its sparkle and dash. It has not the originality in musical treatment and invention of *Salome, Elektra* and *Der Rosenkavalier,* yet much of the music has charm and expert craftsmanship especially in the handling of the orchestration. The difficult role of Arabella gives opportunity to a soprano who, like Eleanor Steber, has the power, range and musicianship to execute it successfully. Strauss again wrote for a woman disguised as a male in Arabella's sister. The main male role in the opera is for a baritone.

TENORS LOSE CASTE

Strauss was one of the first composers to demote the tenor from a lover's role to that of a character part, "hysterical, pathological, almost possessed," Paul Bekker wrote. He cites Mozart's Don Basilio as "perhaps the stem from which the entire line of such figures sprang. . . . The sound of the tenor voice," according to the same writer, "arouses thoughts no longer of tenderness but of the singular and the grotesque." "Be that as it may," audiences are still stirred by a tenor's high C's in *Carmen, Faust, La Gioconda,* et al!

The first performance of *Arabella* was at the Dresden Opera, July 1, 1933, and in America at the Metropolitan, February 10, 1955.

Four other operas swell the list: *Die Schweigsame Frau (The Silent Woman,* 1935), with libretto by Stefan Zweig based on *The Silent Woman* by Ben Jonson of "Drink to Me Only with Thine Eyes" fame; *Der Friedenstag (The Day of Peace,* 1938), in which appears a hymnal chorus celebrating peace, with libretto by Joseph Gregor; and interestingly enough, he wrote an opera about the nymph *Daphne* (1938) (beloved of the Camerata) for which Joseph Gregor also furnished the libretto; and *Capriccio* (1941).

CAPRICCIO

Strauss's last stage work was *Capriccio,* Opus 85, subtitled *A Conversation Piece for Music,* in one act. It was first produced in Munich in 1942 by Clemens Krauss, the conductor, who was also its librettist. Its workmanship is perfect and it has pages of exquisite beauty. It went far to explode the idea that Strauss was a tired old man who could only repeat himself. The subject matter would hardly seem suitable for an opera, as it is a discussion between a poet and a composer as to which is more important, the words or music of an opera. No solution! The text was based on an Italian opera by G. B. Casti of the eighteenth century, called *Prima la musica e poi le parole* (*First the Music and Then the Words*). The scene is Paris about 1775. A young countess has two suitors, a poet and a composer, but the opera ends without her making up her mind as to which she will have.

Capriccio was produced for the first time in America in English by the Juilliard Opera Theatre in April, 1954.

Of Strauss's thirteen operas, only seven have been heard in the United States: *Salome, Elektra, Der Rosenkavalier, Ariadne auf Naxos, The Egyptian Helen, Capriccio* and *Arabella*.

STRAUSS'S GIFTS TO OPERA

Strauss set opera ahead by contributing to it the unusual in story and in music. His texts present a vast array of contrasts in plots and scenes. He inaugurated the startlingly neurotic in opera. He gave courage to composers to be daring and gave warning to critics of what might be "in the offing." Starting as an offspring of Wagner, as early as 1912 he had shed the "Wagnerian music armor." He thanked Hugo von Hofmannsthal for having "opened up an entirely new landscape ... the territory of the un-Wagnerian opera of play, soul and humanity" (Letter quoted by Max Graf in his book *Modern Music—Music and Composers of our Time*).

He showed the world how to use the morbid; also, that some parts of an opera may be all "sound and fury," yet there can be spots of sheer loveliness. He produced music to make one gasp and music to draw tears because of its beauty.

He used music to do his bidding and express feelings and ideas, such as irony and frenzy, as could few composers. Wagner was grandiose and epic in fury, Strauss was physical and human. Following the French impressionism, Strauss's energy and color were valuable and wholesome contributions. Indeed, looking back, Strauss is seen to be the overture to twentieth-century noises, irony, melody, rhythm, dissonance and drama. He is a descendant of Berlioz (program symphony), Wagner (music drama), Liszt (symphonic poems), and Ibsen (drama). His one great fault, which he deplored, was to use so rich an orchestra that it veiled the voice parts.

IF

In his early years Strauss excelled in tone poems, song and opera. In his later years he was condemned for his lack of inspiration, to which he confessed, although his technical skill remained supreme. But might it not be that had Pergolesi, Mozart, Schubert and Bellini lived into their eighties, they, too, would have lost some of their inspiration?

ACT VIII. Opera "Goes Modern": Twentieth Century

PRELUDE

A Plea for the New in Music—From Consonance
to Dissonance

Now we have arrived at our own century—the twentieth, when music has stretched itself mightily, when it has gone from consonance to dissonance. Composers had been dominated by the old music. They needed new ways of expressing themselves. Many thought that the three B's—Bach, Beethoven and Brahms—had said all there was to say in the diatonic modes (major and minor scales). Diatonic music had been in use for so long that it no longer seemed suitable to express feelings, ideas, manners, and customs that had undergone vast changes, that had created a new way of life. The consonance of the old music was seeking a more pungent, a more dissonant language.

Since the Middle Ages art had attempted to reflect life and nature. For the first time in 400 years all humanity seemed to rebel against existing things and was seeking change. Small bonfires had started from time to time, but they had not developed into a conflagration that threatened the world. Music that had pictured a stately dance at court did not fit a jitter-bugging, bebopping age. Music produced in the age of the sedan could not keep up with airplanes and atom bombs. In civilization it was a fight against social, political and even religious conditions, a protest against a world that had threatened to destroy itself with wars and revolutions. In art it became a fight against conventionalities and traditions, a resistance to worn-out forms and an absence of spontaneous expression.

After the first World War (1914–18), European musicians were scattered far and wide, and suffered cruel experiences owing to the devastation of heart and home. Much refreshment and aeration of our music came through the misfortunes that forced eminent composers to come to the United States after World War I and during the Nazi domination. Schoenberg, Stravinsky, Hindemith, Krenek, Bartok,

Korngold, Kurt Weill, and innumerable others became valuable citizens. Whereas they have influenced us, they too have absorbed some Americanisms, and all have been enriched.

The artificial search for the new and the strange is only one side of the panel, however. On the other side are those whose slogan is "back to nature," who believe that salvation for art lies in the commonplace, in the folk expression, in the "grass roots": that art is communication and must be in a language that all can understand, in a form intelligible to the "masses." These two points of view have found followers in the makers of opera as well as every other field of art. If only composer and listener could see eye to eye, we might arrive at important results!

After the world had gone through two wars, the Hitler regime, the Russian Revolution, and a depression, the Metropolitan Opera House had found a new audience, made up mostly of a younger generation. For these young people and operatic "raw recruits," *La Traviata, Carmen, Faust, Rigoletto, Lohengrin,* etc., had the same thrills as they had had for their parents and grandparents. A new singer who wins acclaim attracts the public regardless of the opera in which he or she appears. But a new opera rarely does. Opera-goers do not trust "new wine in old bottles," and tasters in the guise of newspaper critics are lukewarm, indifferent, or negative in their reactions. So what can the poor public do but fall back on the old "wear-evers"! Unless novelties have the encouragement of "good box-office returns," they cannot make headway. Most operatic and orchestral organizations run into deficits, so managements have to cater to audiences, and must give them music that they think they want.

What the audience wants to hear and what the composers wish to write are sometimes poles apart. What compromise can art make in order to bring them together? Unfortunately we have neither government nor private subsidy which might make the management independent of the box-office.

Only a small proportion of the public is interested in experiments even though many composers of necessity must be. But the large public pays the bills and therefore dictates policies.

EARLY TWENTIETH-CENTURY OPERAS

Do not forget that in these pages we have already discussed a good many twentieth-century operas. Puccini's *Tosca* and Charpentier's *Louise* closed the nineteenth century in 1900. Richard Strauss opened the twentieth with *Feuersnot,* to be followed in 1905 with *Salome,* in 1909 with *Elektra,* and 1911 with *Der Rosenkavalier.* Debussy, after ten years of hard work, finished *Pelléas et Mélisande,* which was produced in 1902. Strauss and Debussy did much to open new paths in music. In 1902 Massenet's *Le Jongleur de Nôtre Dame* saw the light. *Madame Butterfly* increased Puccini's fame in 1904. Another impressionist opera, Paul Dukas' *Ariane et Barbe-Bleue,* was presented in Paris in 1907. During the next year, 1908, came the unusual success of the Russian Rimsky-Korsakov's *Le Coq d'or;* also Wolf-Ferrari's *The Secret of Suzanne.* In 1912 appeared *Der Ferne Klang (The Distant Sound),* by an Austrian composer, Franz Schreker, whose works have never reached the American stage, in spite of an immediate success in Vienna and the critics having hailed him as a successor to Wagner. Montemezzi's *The Love of Three Kings* dates from 1913. And in the war year 1914 came Igor Stravinsky with his opera *Le Rossignol (The Nightingale).* *Mona Lisa* by Max von Schillings (1915) was heard in America four times in 1923 and once in 1924. It was not a success. Hans Pfitzner's *Palestrina* (1917) never was given in this country. By the end of the war a new era in opera was established.

Yes, a new era was established, but in the few major opera companies such as the Metropolitan and those in Chicago, San Francisco, Philadelphia, Boston, Cincinnati, etc., the repertory, for the most part, still consists of operas written before 1900, and nothing after 1910 lasts for more than a season or two.

From Hans Heinsheimer's amusing and clever book, *Menagerie in F Sharp,* we quote: "The United States, the most up-to-date country in the world, where a car, a refrigerator, a suit, a railroad, a bridge, a fountain pen, a job, and a wife are old and heading for the junk pile after they have been in use for a year or two, is feeding on the most conservative and old-fashioned operatic diet."

The theaters are much more successful in producing novelties than are the opera houses. And curiously enough, the ballet, with new, up-to-date music by twentieth-century composers, even by men born in the twentieth century, has found a large and enthusiastic audience. Why not opera? Some of its detractors claim that opera, after three hundred years of existence, is finished!

The twentieth-century listener with nineteenth-century ears is convinced that no previous era had to wrestle with the problem of dissonance and "ugliness" with which he is faced. He forgets that all through the ages men have composed new kinds of music that seemed "too modern" to those to whom it was unfamiliar. Mozart's editor corrected some of his finest quartets. Franz Schubert's songs were called unmelodious by his publishers! Of Beethoven it was said, "Poor man, he is so deaf, he cannot hear the discords he is writing"! Wagner's music was criticized for having no melody. Someone said that Debussy's music sounded as though it were "Butterick perforated patterns played on a player-piano." Now Debussy is thrice welcome. But opera after opera has been hissed before it has been accepted. *The Barber of Seville* and *Tannhäuser* were hissed. The ballet *Le Sacre du printemps* (*The Rite of Spring*) by Stravinsky created an unprecedented scandal in Paris at its première in 1913. A pent-up storm against "modernism" broke with such antagonism that the performers could not hear the playing of the orchestra, and Nijinsky standing on a kitchen chair in the wings had to direct the movements of the dancers on stage. Lawrence Gilman in a New York Philharmonic Symphony program in 1930 wrote that the work "teaches us again the inexhaustible responsiveness of music to new ways of apprehending life, new adventures of the imagination, new conceptions of sensibility and truth and beauty."

If water in a cistern is not renewed or aerated, it grows stagnant. The same is true of the arts—they must renew themselves to be kept wholesome and representative of life.

AN EDITORIAL BY PAUL HENRY LANG

As though in answer to a special request, Paul Henry Lang writes an editorial entitled "The Public—Old and New" in the New York *Herald Tribune,* April 17, 1955, in which he looks "at some of the past attitudes of the 'public' that is declared to be a sworn enemy of progress, and of everything new in art." Starting with the eighteenth century, "which offers the prelude to the political and intellectual emancipation of the bourgeoisie," Dr. Lang dwells on the fact that opera had moved out of the courts into public theaters and had proved to be more at home in its new surroundings than in its old.

"Naturally, this enlarged public encouraged a new orientation on the part of the composer, for this middle class and lower middle class audience was not interested in 'dynastic' opera and mythology; it wanted worldly themes and a dramatic atmosphere that was palpable and was suffused with allusions to contemporary life." This was not within the territory of "old music," as many writers on music regard this period, but "both taste and style changed rapidly and within one generation." " 'Good' was practically synonymous with 'new.' This bourgeoisie [middle class] of the eighteenth century was progressive— even revolutionary—and it responded to music that expressed this spirit of adventure. The composers, even though still in the pay of princes and archbishops, were by inclination in tune with the public whose social status they shared, but they were never artistically sub- servient to that public."

Comic opera, especially in Italy, caught this spirit. The audiences were amused by the play and the lilting music but also by "the constant allusions to political and other topics of the day." These works "are not so innocent as the uninitiated believe them to be. . . . It is unfor- tunate that this modern attitude, delighting in everything that is contemporary and alive, came to be unfashionable." Opera in the nine- teenth century had to be " 'noble' and detached from the vulgarities of life; its subjects must deal with mythology and history of the dim past." Dr. Lang points out that when *Carmen* was first performed the Parisians found it too vulgar for an opera!

"Our composers who still try to set to music classical, Biblical, or medieval stories in order to satisfy the public's artistic code might well emulate Gian-Carlo Menotti, his *Consul* and his *Saint of Bleecker Street.* . . ." Dr. Lang makes this suggestion, not because of their in- trinsic value, but "[because] that's the stuff our life is made of. . . . It is not always the composer who refuses to give the public a chance to understand contemporary life in opera, but the public misled by silly theories, silly books and silly musical instruction, refuses to lend an ear to such works."

In conclusion, he says: "Let us not be afraid of our own reflection and let us look into the mirror that is contemporary life in art. After a while overalls, bicycles and cocktails will seem as natural and familiar on the operatic stage as are armor, swan-drawn barges, and love potions."

SCENE I

Modern French Opera—Satie, Honegger, Milhaud

THE PEAR IN MUSIC

ONCE upon a time, not so long ago, there was an interesting and witty composer, Erik Satie (1866–1925). He did not compose operas, but he did produce several ballets, and he was so influential in the life of French composers that he insists upon an entrance in this act.

Satie tried to make composers stop trying to be impressive. He introduced humor even into late nineteenth- and early twentieth-century serious, so-called classic music. He also renewed and re-animated the musical spirit, and introduced American jazz into polite European society. He taught by laughter and by a proper use of the past. He encouraged musical freedom of thought, and advanced the idea of polytonality or writing in two or more keys at a time. Like Schoenberg, the father of atonality, Satie sought to abandon the home tone as "gospel," as used for centuries in diatonic music. He anticipated, or perhaps paralleled, Debussy's methods. He wrote works with such names as *"Pièces en forme de poire"* ("Pieces in the Form of a Pear"). A pear is used in French slang as Americans use "lemon." In his musical cartoons it is hard to know whether he laughs *at* or *with* the poor old world.

Although he worked with many forms, his importance is not in what he wrote, but in what he did to encourage the younger composers to stretch French music, leave impressionism behind, and strike out into polytonality or anything that freed music. "The Six"—Arthur Honegger (1892–), Darius Milhaud (1892–), Francis Poulenc (1899–), Georges Auric (1899–), Germaine Tailleferre (1892–), and Louis Durey (1888–)—were under Satie's influence. As were also our American Virgil Thomson, and a group called after the place where Satie lived, *L'Ecole d'Arceuil,* which included Henri Sauguet (1901–), Henri

Cliquet-Pleyel (1894–), Maxime Jacob (1906–), and Roger Désormière (1898–).

THE GROUP OF SIX

The composers forming "The Six" had no common musical aims or ideals except their desire to get away from impressionism. They loved Debussy but not his imitators. They were not a school as were the Russian Five. Young, enthusiastic, gifted, and radical, they easily fell under the spell of Satie and his friend Jean Cocteau, a French critic and writer, who urged them to a musical declaration of independence. They did not function as a group although they have remained friends and every ten years they have a reunion in a radio program. Jean Cocteau wrote a ballet scenario *Les Mariés de la Tour Eiffel* (*The Couples at the Eiffel Tower*) for which each of the six composed a part. It was a clever bit of publicity rather than an artistic achievement. The names of Honegger and Milhaud are frequently associated, as are those of Poulenc and Auric. Tailleferre and Durey have dropped out.

Honegger and Milhaud are the most important figures for this story of opera as painters of large musical canvases. Francis Poulenc is a disciple of Satie in having achieved elegance and polish in short forms—songs and piano pieces—which he handles with a light touch and a delightful sense of humor. Georges Auric has gone his well remunerated way as a writer of music for films, many of which have enjoyed famous careers, as for example, *Cesar and Cleopatra, The Baker's Wife,* and *À nous la liberté.*

ARTHUR HONEGGER

This man of France, Arthur Honegger, born at Le Havre in 1892 of Swiss parents, was one of *Les nouveaux jeunes* (The New Youths), as Erik Satie called "The Six." Honegger, however, did not approve of the rules laid down for them by Jean Cocteau in 1919. He was a classicist at heart and Bach was his model. He did not desire, as did Satie and his satellites, to return to simple harmonies in their fight against impressionism. He was interested fundamentally in the musical line and rhythm, and did not want to sacrifice form to literary or pictorial ideas.

Honegger proved this point of view in his compositions, especially his stage works, in which he handles orchestra, chorus and solo expertly. One of his best-known compositions is the symphonic psalm

"Le Roi David" ("King David," 1921-23), written originally as incidental music for a poem by René Morax, and staged in Switzerland. Later he cast it into oratorial form. It is one of the finest works of its kind for power, movement and individuality. It met with instantaneous success in Paris and became a "box-office attraction."

That he was trying definitely to get music away from impressionism may be heard in his orchestral "Pacific 231" (1923), which is realistic in describing a huge American locomotive in music that almost breathes steam!

His opera *Judith* was based on a Biblical poem by René Morax to which Honegger had written incidental music. In it he showed his profound talent for choral writing. He claimed that when some of the young musicians returned to the style of the old Italian opera buffa, he was led to the early Italian background of opera seria. He writes neoclassic opera.

Judith was first performed in Monte Carlo in 1926 and in Chicago by the Chicago Opera Company in 1927.

ANTIGONE

In a continuous and symphonic opera with recitative, and without interruptions by arias or ballets, Honegger's *Antigone* (1927), "freely adapted from *Sophocles*" by Jean Cocteau, is important. It was one of the first operas to be given in Paris after the liberation. The theme is stark and tragic, and the music, appropriately dissonant is backed by percussion instruments. The declamation is accented with rare originality which makes for unusual and arresting effects. The rapid recitative is somewhat like the early Italian *quasi parlando* (almost spoken) style. With all the earnestness of the first French opera writers, Honegger attaches great importance to the mating of words and music. He also used the electric instrument *Onde-Martenot,* with its individual, if a bit ghoulish, timbre and smoothness in *Antigone,* as well as in *Jeanne d'Arc au bûcher* (*Joan of Arc at the Stake*).

JEANNE D'ARC AU BÛCHER

When Charles Munch, the French conductor, visited New York, before he became Serge Koussevitzky's successor as director of the Boston Symphony Orchestra, he won acclaim for an extraordinary presentation of an extraordinary work, Honegger's *Jeanne d'Arc au bûcher* (1948). The form approaches that of oratorio, but it is a moving spectacle performed with stage setting with both singing and speaking roles, a mixed adult chorus, a children's chorus and orchestra. The text is by Paul Claudel, poet and diplomat, and the work is dedicated to Ida Rubinstein who recited the lines of Jeanne in the early performances in Paris (1938). In hearing this "mystery" play one feels as if admitted to a region of beauty, courage and holiness.

This may not be typical grand opera but it unites the dramatic stage with operatic and orchestral resources in a monumental effect that sounds a new note in operatic history.

DARIUS MILHAUD—CHAMELEON

How fitting for a composer to have been born in the beautiful country of the troubadours! This twentieth-century troubadour, Darius Milhaud, was born in Aix-en-Provence, France, in 1892. Among his chameleon-like qualities is a strong lyrical gift and a romantic strain, which he may have inherited from Provençal folk songs, seeming to carry him into neoromanticism.

Milhaud, however, refuses to be pigeonholed: neoclassicist, neoromanticist, postimpressionist, polytonalist, a Hellenophile, a jazzist, an innovator. He is all these and more, for everything he does is stamped with his own personality and his singular genius. He is a mixture, swinging from the lofty to the commonplace, from the gay to the gloomy, from dissonance to very understandable melody, from the polite to jazz. As he has often said, he writes as the idea or the story or the poem dictates, turning from Greek mythology to history in the Old and the New World, to the Bible, to the past, to the present. Sometimes the head rules, sometimes the heart. Yet here again he is hard to pin down, for some of his music is so rhythmic and full of feeling that the brain seems to give way to the nerves.

MILHAUD'S EARLY STAGE WORKS

Before he was twenty, Milhaud was at work on his first opera, *La Brebis egarée* (*The Lost Sheep,* completed 1913), on a text by Francis Jammes. It was impressionistic and not far removed from Debussy in style. But by the time it was produced in 1923, Milhaud had completely changed his method of writing. In the meanwhile he had met Erik Satie and was identified as one of *Les Six* (The Six); had come under the influence of Jean Cocteau, the literary spokesman of the group; and had met Paul Claudel, poet-diplomat-dramatist.

During World War I, Milhaud was a member of the French Diplomatic Corps in Brazil where he worked under Claudel. He came in contact with the dance rhythms of South America, and before he returned to France was obsessed by American jazz, which he said was like a beneficent thunderclap clearing the art sky. He listened to jazz in Harlem, bought all the records possible, decided that here was a new rhythmic means of expression and determined to make experiments, not in popular, but in art music. This culminated in his Negro ballet, *La Creation du monde* (*The Creation of the World*), written in 1923, a year before Gershwin's "Rhapsody in Blue" shot its bolt.

It sounds incredible but another influence in *La Creation du monde,* in addition to that of jazz is Bach! In Paris a "Back to Bach" movement was going on among the composers who were calling themselves neoclassicists. One of those who turned back to baroque ideals and was imitating Bach was Stravinsky, as may be seen in his early "Sonata for Piano" and his first piano concerto. Works carrying neoclassic labels were supposed to have returned to eighteenth-century classic models. But this unnatural combination of Bach and jazz in both Milhaud and Stravinsky seems almost laughable!

Among Milhaud's early stage works are the ballets, *Le Boeuf sur le toit* (*The Nothing-Doing Bar,* the name of a famous Paris restaurant), and *L'Homme et son desir* (*Man and His Desire*). The former was a "cinema-symphony on South American airs" on a book by Claudel. The latter, written in Brazil with Claudel, was danced by Nijinsky in Rio de Janeiro with the Ballet Russe. Before the Brazilian sojourn, Milhaud had written incidental music for Claudel's satirical drama, *Protée* (*Proteus, 1913–19*). This "Aristophanesque buffoonery" appealed to the young composer and brought out humorous, colorful, fearless, almost violent, expression.

At the same time Milhaud was working on music for Claudel's translations of Aeschylus' *Oresteia: Agamemnon* (1913); *Les Choëphores,* (*The Liberation Powers*), "drama, chorus, percussion and orchestra"; and *Les Eumenides* (*The Furies, 1917–25*), an opera in three acts for very large orchestra (with sixteen percussion instruments —page Hector Berlioz!) and large chorus. With characteristic versatility, Milhaud "turned from the hilarity of *Protée* to the savage power and frenetic passion of Aeschylus as translated by Claudel. He caught the violence, the spirit of vengeance, the frenzied horror, which he translated into some of his most powerful music. The choral declamation, more speech than song, of *Les Choëphores* and of *Les Eumenides,* produces an effect that is not to be forgotten." ("Darius Milhaud," by Marion Bauer, *Musical Quarterly,* April, 1942.)

POLYTONALITY

Although Darius Milhaud did not invent polytonality, his name is closely linked with its development, and he established its usage. The basis of his polytonality is melody, usually diatonic. In combining two or more melodies in different keys, the clash of dissonance occurs; Satie was an advocate of polytonality, and Ravel and even Debussy planted some of its seeds. In an article Milhaud wrote in the Paris *Revue musicale* in February 1923, he pointed out Bela Bartok's use of two different signatures—four sharps for a violin part and four flats for the cello. Prokofiev wrote *"Sarcasmes,"* short piano pieces, with different keys in the two staves. This is bitonality (two keys). Stravinsky, Poulenc, and many other twentieth-century composers write polytonally.

In Milhaud's piano pieces, *"Saudades do Brasil"* ("Souvenirs of Brazil," 1920–21) he combined Brazilian-like melodies and rhythms with bitonality. Milhaud claims that polytonality frees music, but like fantasy, resists being fastened down by rules.

Two more ballets, *Le Train bleu* and *Salade,* with voices, won the Paris public. The program of the latter stated that this union of dance, painting, music, and poetry, tended "to reveal the new soul and the latest aspect of France." The chameleon quality of the man was displayed in the way he could turn from his earlier dramatic works to the light music of his ballets.

Milhaud found an interesting problem in short experimental operas such as *Les Malheurs d'Orphée* (*The Sorrows of Orpheus,* 1924), an up-to-date version of the Greek myth, which had its première at the Théâtre de la Monnaie in Brussels (1926); a comic opera, *Esther de Carpentras,* on the Biblical character (1925; presented at the Opéra Comique, 1938) both of which are on texts by Armand Lunel; and the three *opéras minutes* (small operas) *L'Enlèvement d'Europe* (*The Abduction of Europa*), *L'Abandon d'Ariane* (*The Desertion of Ariadne*) and *La Délivrance de Thesée* (*The Rescue of Theseus*) on texts by Henri Hoppenot, composed in 1927 and performed in Baden-Baden and Wiesbaden. These small operas parodied Greek myths in the style of the early eighteenth-century theaters.

Le Pauvre matelot (*The Poor Sailor,* 1926) is a collaboration of Milhaud and Cocteau in a highly condensed drama lasting less than an hour. It was given at the Opéra Comique in 1927, and has had many performances in this country. It has only four characters and the accompaniment is for chamber orchestra.

Milhaud wrote the short operas in protest against Wagnerian music drama, and he felt that composers turned naturally to earlier forms such as the *opera da camera* which were well suited to the neoclassic spirit of the twentieth century.

CHRISTOPHE COLOMB

In the spring of 1930, Milhaud's greatest opera to date, *Christophe Colomb,* had it première, curiously enough, in Germany, when Erich Kleiber presented it at the Berlin State Opera, the only institution interested enough in experiments to be willing to produce it. In this, Milhaud stretched dramatic expression by using for the first time the moving-picture screen in an opera score in addition to complicated stage machinery with twenty-seven scenes, a huge chorus, fifty characters and orchestra. The chorus strides backwards to Greece and forward to the twentieth century, for it speaks, sings and chants, explains the story, asks questions and argues, acting as both commentator and audience. Paul Claudel, Milhaud's collaborator, broke away from the traditional opera libretto and wrote what might be called a Catholic Mystery. Claudel explains the chorus as one "which stands on consecrated ground to mediate between priest and congregation" of the Roman Catholic Church. It even declaims quotations from the Bible.

The life of Columbus and his discovery of America are pictured and the effect of these events on his own time and on the future is depicted. On his deathbed, Columbus reviews his past, and in a vision the effect of his accomplishment is revealed to him. Claudel's treatment of the play upon his name, Colomb, and the Biblical dove (*colombe*) is mystical and poetic.

A narrator reads from a book the events presented by means of the moving-picture screen while the chorus explains the drama on the stage. Columbus is shown on the screen as a youth, as middle-aged, and as an old man.

After *Christophe Colomb,* Milhaud had a première in Paris in 1932 of his opera *Maximilien,* based on a novel by Franz Werfel and made into a libretto by his wife, Madeleine Milhaud. The hero is the ill-fated Archduke of Austria who became Emperor of Mexico.

Another of Milhaud's works and one of the best-known in America is *L'Annonce fait à Marie* (*Tidings Brought to Mary,* 1934), incidental music to the drama by Claudel, presented first in Brussels, and later in a beautifully stylized setting by the Theatre Guild of New York. It looked like a canvas of blues, reds and gold of the old Sienna school (Italy) of painting.

A new act in Milhaud's life began on July 4, 1940, when he, his wife and young son arrived in the United States where they were to make their home. The curtain had been rung down a month before on the première of his opera *Médée* (*Medea*) in Paris, although two more scheduled performances took place after the German occupation. Ironically enough *Médée*, a one-act opera on a libretto by Madeleine Milhaud, had been commissioned by the French government, the first time in its history that it had decided to encourage composers by attempting to bring about a renaissance of opera.

For a number of years Milhaud has held a chair of composition at Mills College, California. He still occupies that post but he has been dividing his time between a year in Paris and in California.

In an article in the *Juilliard Review,* Abraham Skulsky, an authority on contemporary opera, said that in *Bolivar* (1943), libretto by Madeleine Milhaud from a book by Supervielle, Milhaud had written "a great work, in which the composer came closer to real opera than ever before, by means of true operatic forms and real dramatic situations."

The most recent of Milhaud's operas is *David* (1952) on a text by Armand Lunel. Its first public performance was in concert form at the Festival of the International Society for Contemporary Music in Jerusalem in the spring of 1954. In five acts with twelve scenes, it shows King David's life from his anointing by Samuel to the crowning of Solomon. The cast consists of eighteen singers, and there are two choruses, one of which called "Israelites of the year 1954," is in modern dress and "comments on the historic spectacle from the point of view of our own times and of recent developments in the Holy Land, where the action takes place," Mr. Skulsky writes. "By using this chorus Milhaud lends a contemporary significance to this historic pageant. It is used not only in certain interludes which separate the scenes, but very often during the course of the opera, when parallelisms arise between historic and contemporary happenings." This would seem as though *Christophe Colomb* and *David* must have similar and entirely original treatment.

SCENE II

Stravinsky Blasts New Roads

"OCCASIONALLY there appears a creator of such force, originality and genius that whether his works prove to be lasting or not, he becomes a part of the future through his influence. Such is Stravinsky, innovator, musical iconoclast, scientist, realist, rhythmist, non-sentimentalist. . . . No composer of the Twentieth Century has been more condemned, more imitated than Stravinsky, whose works have been performed in all the music centers of the world." (*Music Through the Ages* by Bauer and Peyser.)

Stravinsky has written important ballets and has contributed as well to the development of modern opera. The ballet—a kind of storytelling dance—has given new ideas to the lyric stage. Stravinsky is important because by expression and invention of bold ideas he stretched the means and power of music, and was a model for others.

Experiment is the keynote of his good offices to opera—for example his *L'Histoire du soldat* (*The Story of the Soldier,* 1918), a secular story, is told by a narrator and staged as a play with an orchestra of only seven instruments—a cantata of the twentieth century.

STRAVINSKY'S HERITAGE

Igor Stravinsky's immediate musical ancestors were Russian folk music, Rimsky-Korsakov and Mussorgsky. Stravinsky is rougher and freer than Mussorgsky; and he learned much about the orchestra from Rimsky-Korsakov, the stimulant and abettor of other composers. Stravinsky led the music world from complication to simplification, and sometimes, in the opinion of many, to "uglification." Whatever he has done, he did with plan and design.

IMPERSONAL

"He (Stravinsky) strikes an elemental chord throbbing with vital, passionate, exuberant life. . . . his pictures are impersonal, without sympathy or expression of opinion, for what he depicts is without attempt to preach." (*Music Through the Ages.*) He uses folk song, folklore, folk dance. He presents peasant life in Russia, at times vulgar, sensual, cruel, amusing, hysterically gay, often violent, morbid, but never sentimental.

INSTRUMENTAL BATTLES

The orchestras of Hector Berlioz, Richard Wagner and Richard Strauss make great masses of sound by accumulative volume, but Stravinsky builds his climaxes by opposing instruments one against another. His superb clash and dissonance in his use of instruments soloistically have cleared the air for young composers in which to stretch their musical muscles. He links instruments together which have always belonged to warring families, and he creates novel effects, never for novelty's sake, but to carry out an idea.

Stravinsky almost jerked people out of their seats at the first performances in France of his ballet music *Le Sacre du printemps* (*The Rite of Spring,* Paris, 1913). They walked out, shocked and hurt by what they called "demoralizing noises"!

Igor Stravinsky was born in 1882 at Oranienbaum, in Russia, near what is now Leningrad. He became a French citizen in 1932, and is now an American citizen and lives in California.

His father was a bass singer in the opera, so he must have heard opera in his home during his early childhood. Although not musically trained, he had deep delight in playing and reading scores of operatic and symphonic music. Like Robert Schumann, however, he was forced to study law. Later, he was lucky to meet in college Nicolai Rimsky-Korsakov's son, whose famous father advised the boy to study composition, and later became Igor's teacher of orchestration.

After he had left the university, Igor went to Paris where he met musical people, the most significant of whom, for the history of music, was Serge Diaghilev (1872-1929), director of the Ballet Russe. Diaghilev put Stravinsky on the "music map," but Stravinsky supplied him with something new and amazing. When Diaghilev heard Stravinsky's "Fantastic Scherzo," he immediately recognized that Stravinsky was the man for whom he was looking. The two changed the "rules of the music game" of the twentieth century. So marvelous were the fruitful twenty years (1909-29) that Stravinsky was able to match, in new and striking harmonies, the paintings of Bakst, Picasso, Derain, Matisse and others who worked with him and Diaghilev on the modern ballet. The first ballet he did was for *Les Sylphides* when Diaghilev gave him two pieces by Chopin to orchestrate.

Among his ballets were: the colorful, glamorous and sometimes even tender *L'Oiseau de feu* (*The Fire Bird,* Paris, 1910); *Petrouchka* (Paris, 1911); the epoch opening of *Le Sacre du printemps* with the elemental clash of music and dance picturing ancient and pagan Russian rites of spring; *Pulcinella* (Paris, 1920), a ballet with singing in which this innovator goes back to Pergolesi for his themes; *Les Noces* (*Russian Wedding Rites* of ancient days, Paris, 1923), in which four pianos and many unusual percussion instruments make strange effects; *Apollon musagète,* done first in an ancient-modern Greek setting as a commission from Mrs. Elizabeth Coolidge, in Washington, D. C., 1928; *Le Baiser de la fée* (*The Fairy's Kiss,* Paris, 1928) in which the composer takes Tchaikovsky themes and brings them into the twentieth century with grace, tang and charm; *Jeu de cartes* (*Card Game,* New York, 1937), a game of poker related in musical variations; *Circus Polka* (New York, 1942), originally for band, commissioned by Ringling Brothers and Barnum and Bailey Circus, and presented in Madison Square Garden; *Scènes de ballet* (*Ballet Scenes,* New York, 1944) commissioned by Billy Rose and used in part in his show *The Seven Lively Arts;* and *Orpheus* (New York, 1948), written for the Ballet Society.

STRAVINSKY STRETCHES MUSIC

It took *Petrouchka,* the poor little puppet typifying the "little people" of the world who are pushed around, it took this little fellow to stretch music itself. In this ballet Stravinsky uses what is called the "Petrouchka chord"—two chords at once from two different keys, or polytonality, or more precisely, polyharmony. The music in *Petrouchka,* reflecting a Russian fair with all its hurly-burly, fun, tragedy and romance, is alternately melodic and dissonant, amusing, but flashy and pathetic. He paints here with tremendous fidelity a conglomerate, colorful, palpitant scene.

With polytonality, music now reaches the point where composers need not designate a key. Unfortunately, lesser men trying to copy Stravinsky have in some cases prejudiced the public against so-called "modern music." Whereas Stravinsky might be said to have composed sensational yet sincere music, many have written unimaginative copies. Some have only imitated his brutality and ugliness and at times made twentieth-century music obnoxious. This is often what occurs in the arts when a giant is imitated by pygmies.

STAGE WORKS

Beside the ballets, which made him famous, Stravinsky wrote orchestral compositions and a few works staged as opera or oratorio.

Foremost among what might be called "chamber music opera," to be given with few instruments in small halls, is *L'Histoire du soldat.* In this interesting and exciting tale, a narrator relates the return from the wars of a soldier, and of his meeting a stranger (the Devil) who offers him a book of knowledge in exchange for his fiddle. The Soldier, the Devil and the Princess act in pantomime, or dance, to the accompaniment of a chamber orchestra of seven instruments. This is one of the scores in which Stravinsky combined imitations of Bach or Handel with jazz, the result of his coming in touch with the music in vogue in Paris at the time. In *L'Histoire* one finds marches, ragtime, tango, waltzes, etc. The influence of Paris' musical life turned him away from the grandiose, complex scores that reflected the folklore and music of his Russian heritage. C. F. Ramuz wrote the text of this work that shows the effect Stravinsky could achieve with slender means.

Les Noces was the last of the great ballets dealing with pagan Russia. It differs from the earlier Diaghilev ballets in its use of voices on a text written by Stravinsky.

Le Renard (*The Fox,* 1917) was based on Russian folklore and was commissioned by the Princess de Polignac as a stage work. It might be called a "sung ballet." It was played by silent buffoons, dancers, and acrobats, with the voices of four men as part of the chamber orchestra. It was performed in 1922 at the Paris Opéra along with *Mavra.*

One hears little about the short opera *Le Rossignol* (*The Nightingale,* 1914) based on a story by Hans Christian Andersen, in which Stravinsky used Russian elements in an exotic way. The story is Chinese. The music is a mixture of Stravinsky, Debussy and Rimsky-Korsakov. It was presented at the Metropolitan in 1926 and 1927. In 1920, the music was produced in Paris as a ballet under the title of *Le Chant du Rossignol,* and the score is occasionally heard in concert.

OPERA BUFFA

With a book based on Pushkin, Stravinsky wrote a short, satirical opera buffa, *Mavra* (1921), in an attempt to imitate the style of early nineteenth-century opera. He dedicated it to Tchaikovsky, Glinka and Pushkin. It was hard for the public at that time to realize that the composer had simplified his style and that the Stravinsky of *Le Sacre* and *Les Noces* was gone forever. He had become a neoclassicist. *Mavra* was first performed in Paris under the Polish conductor, Gregor Fitelberg, in 1922.

OEDIPUS REX—NEOCLASSIC OPERA-ORATORIO

It was said that Stravinsky discovered the eighteenth century too late. With all his "newness," he went back to the old classic forms and is therefore called a neoclassicist with Schoenberg, Hindemith, Milhaud, Prokofiev, our own Aaron Copland, and many others.

Again Stravinsky showed courage in using new ideas, imagination and skill in dramma per musica. With Cocteau and the painter Picasso of the early twentieth century, he actually put into practice a mechanical, unemotional drama in the opera-oratorio *Oedipus Rex* (1927). The play, originally by Sophocles, the libretto by Jean Cocteau, was translated from the French version into the Latin by J. Danielou. There is a dramatic text for a narrator, and soloists and a chorus of male voices, but in masked, marble rigidity. The League of Composers and the Philadelphia Orchestra under Leopold Stokowski gave the first stage performance in America in 1931 with giant puppets. In 1948, it was given by the Juilliard School of Music with live actors. There is in this Greek legend of Oedipus, who unknowingly kills his father and marries his mother, tragedy and terror and mystery that demands the stark music that often is Stravinsky's.

Many of the works after *Mavra* were experiments in the development of a new style. "The master was willing to become the apprentice again, in a self-imposed discipline, in order to reach another stage of mastery. *Oedipus Rex* would indicate such a psychology. . . . No longer in transition, Stravinsky had perfected a new language as gripping and individual as was *Le Sacre,* but more profound and less dissonant . . ." (*Twentieth Century Music,* by Bauer).

A WORK OF FAITH

Stravinsky, arch-innovator, branched out in works like *The Symphony of Psalms* (1930), for chorus and orchestra. In it, he becomes a staunch neoclassicist. It was "composed for the glory of God and dedicated to the Boston Symphony on the occasion of the Fiftieth Anniversary of its existence." In this new form of classicism he again becomes an innovator, for he uses no violas or violins. In Alexandre Tansman's book *Igor Stravinsky: The Man and His Music,* we read: ". . . the *Symphony of Psalms* is the sum of his maturity in which a constant tension is allied to the unforgettable serenity of the last movement. . . ."

PERSEPHONE

Tansman says: "It is surprising that no music critic ever tried to slip a 'Greek' period into the evolution of Stravinsky's art." And so it is! For here added to *Oedipus Rex, Apollon musagète* and a later *Orpheus,* is a melodrama and "an epic of redemption," music written at the request of Ida Rubinstein for André Gide's play *Persephone.* A "feminine counterpart of *Oedipus,*" Robert Craft calls it in the book edited by Minna Lederman, *Stravinsky in the Theatre.* He also states that "Its real subject is not Persephone's fall to the underworld, but her sojourn there and her ascent, in the second and third parts, which resemble the same sections of Dante's poem." Craft also calls attention to the fact that "Persephone's own words are always accompanied by the sound of flute, harp and solo string quartet . . ."

THE RAKE'S PROGRESS

To the fourteenth International Festival of Contemporary Music at Venice, Italy, fell the honor of presenting the première of Stravinsky's full-length opera, *The Rake's Progress,* on September 11, 1951 (the catalogues of Boosey and Hawkes, music publishers, give September 8 as the date).

A few years ago, Stravinsky was attracted by a set of engravings by William Hogarth entitled *The Rake's Progress.* He saw them as possible scenes of an opera. The poet W. H. Auden collaborated with Chester Kallman on a libretto with which the composer was well pleased and he worked for three years at writing the score.

The principal characters include Tom Rakewell, the "Rake," whom Guido M. Gatti, a leading Italian critic, in a *Musical Quarterly* review (January, 1951) describes as a blend of Faust, Don Giovanni and Peer Gynt; Ann Trulove, Tom's fiancée, who like Wagner's heroines, brings his turbulent life to a peaceful death through her steadfast love; Nick Shadow, a prototype of the Devil; and Baba the Turk, the bearded lady of the circus whom Tom marries out of bravado.

Stravinsky wished to write an opera in eighteenth-century tradition with all the discarded baggage of arias, duets, trios, ensembles, choruses and recitatives, with an orchestra of chamber size including a harpsichord to accompany the recitatives. This very statement of his aims has led to great controversy. His audience constituted "a house divided against itself." Probably the "no's" have it, for the general public (especially in New York where it was given at the Metropolitan) refused to accept the work. Many musicians and scholars, however, found it refreshing and an extraordinary feat that a man of his experience and reputation could refute his own past, and borrow "raw material," as it seemed, from Gluck, Mozart, Bellini, Rossini, etc.

The score is not as simple as it seems on the surface, and frequent hearings reveal qualities that do not appear at first. Only a highly gifted composer could carry off his plan to carry the twentieth century back to the eighteenth with an individuality that remains Stravinskian. "But the whole opera," says Signore Gatti, "is full of pages that are not only valuable for artistic and technical mastery, but rich in emotional life."

And so Stravinsky has added another enigma to a long list of works that have always posed problems.

Stravinsky's way with music has irritated many people, but he has made music march ahead and has given it new power and force, wherein he and other composers in opera, ballet and other forms are free to express the speed, drive, clash and uncertainties of the present day.

Igor Stravinsky has been one of the greatest musical forces as well as influences in music in the first half of the twentieth century.

SCENE III

Schoenberg, Berg, Hindemith and Krenek—
Atonalists

ARNOLD SCHOENBERG: INNOVATOR

LIKE the men of the Camerata, Arnold Schoenberg (1874-1951), started something. He was once considered a Bad Boy of Music. He opened up new fields in harmony and became the teacher of some important opera composers in Europe, among them Alban Berg (1885-1935), who wrote *Wozzeck;* Egon Wellesz (1885-) who wrote *Bacchante;* Anton von Webern (1883-1945); Kurt Weill (born in Dessau, Germany, 1900, who wrote many operas and was living in the United States until he died in 1950); and Paul Pisk (1893-), now living in California.

EXPRESSIONISM

Schoenberg is an Expressionist. Expressionism is the *ism* which exiles realism! You don't have to show a house on fire because it is in the plot, you show what you feel about it. You only have to show the idea or symbol.

Schoenberg was a painter and through his painting he came in touch with Wassily Kandinsky of Munich, Germany. As Debussy had been influenced by the impressionist painters and symbolist poets, so Schoenberg was affected by a group whose aim was "the expression of the *soul* of nature and humanity." And Schoenberg worked out a philosophy of *expressionism* in music in his search for freedom, a freedom that resulted in a new approach to the technique of composition. Expressionism is the outward reaction to an *inner* impulse. It differs from Impressionism, in that impressionism is a reaction to an *outer* stimulus.

383

His theater pieces are some of the seeds by means of which Schoenberg impregnated music and opera.

Diaghilev and Stravinsky introduced the short ballet; Schoenberg introduced a condensed and shortened opera. He may have realized that with this new style it would be hard to hold the attention of the listeners for long, so he may have "tempered the wind to the shorn lamb," the listener, by making these works mercifully short.

Schoenberg's music is more difficult for the unaccustomed ear than for the open mind. Although it may still be looked upon by many as impossible to understand, he gave music a shot in the arm. We must try to understand it through our minds, if we do not get it through our ears and emotions.

Schoenberg once wrote in the older ways, and always retained deep respect for traditional music, and great teacher that he was, he demanded that students conquer the methods of the past in order to have the foundation on which to expand music. The labels—atonality, polytonality, dissonance and consonance—disturbed him, and he hoped the time would come when they would disappear. And yet those labels help to explain the newer ways.

Arnold Schoenberg, born in Vienna, filled an important place in Europe until World War II. At first he was very poor, but did what he could to earn a living. He had little formal training. He had been playing the violin and the cello in amateur chamber groups. He wrote music that was received with opposition from the beginning of his career, even though today his early songs which were "booed" and ridiculed are considered beautiful and in line with Wagner, Brahms, Mahler and Strauss. Audiences do not want to be shaken out of a comfortable acceptance of idioms and moods with which they are familiar. They try to stifle anything that is bold or unusual.

TRANSFIGURED NIGHT

In 1899, Schoenberg began to compose *"Verklaerte Nacht"* ("Transfigured Night"), the sextet for strings on a poem by Richard Dehmel, which sounds like *Tristan und Isolde* in many spots; and the *Gurre-Lieder*. But he had to stop work on these to write potboilers in order to eat. Before long, he held high posts as professor, composer and conductor in distinguished institutions in central Europe.

Schoenberg did not dive directly into the new kind of composing, for he first wrote romantic melody such as you find in his *Gurre-Lieder (Songs of Gurre Castle)*. This vast, romantic cantata (1910) was on a poem by Jens Peter Jacobsen. When heard in 1932 in this country, it sounded old-fashioned, yet for a man of twenty-six it was a magnificent work. Wagner is not forgotten here either! It uses a tremendous orchestra, soloists, narrator and chorus. The writers recall that the score for this work requires sixty-six staves!

Schoenberg had a restless spirit, a brilliant intellect, great sincerity, tremendous physical vitality, an inquiring mind, and a fanatical love of art.

Max Graf in *Modern Music* writes that he "moves out of romanticism straight ahead into territory never before touched by man— considered a desert by his contemporaries—where he seems to know every spot of soil."

TREATISE ON HARMONY

Schoenberg wrote a book *"Harmonielehre"* or *Treatise on Harmony,* which he said he had learned from his pupils. He tried to enlarge the scope of composition without destroying its solid foundations. At the end of the volume he discussed "Fourth Chords" without going deeply into this early method he used to stretch music. Building chords in the traditional thirds quickly used up the diatonic scale: c-e-g-b-d-f-a-c. He discovered that in building them in fourths, they covered a much wider range: c-f-bb-eb-ab-db-gb-(cb)-b-e-a-d-g-c of three octaves and included all twelve tones of the chromatic scale. He built chords in fourths in three, four, five voices (c-f-bb, c-f-bb-eb, c-f-bb-eb-ab), etc. This led to new and unfamiliar sounds that many composers liked and used—Satie, Milhaud, Hindemith and many others. Schoenberg used the chords-in-fourths in his second "String Quartet" in which he brings in a voice, an excellent example of his early atonal style.

THE ATONAL STYLE

Schoenberg evolved what is known as an *atonal* style, although he himself objected to the term *atonality,* which means literally and erroneously an absence of tonality. Tonality is the relationship of all the tones of a scale or mode to a central keynote. Schoenberg claimed to have substituted twelve keynotes or centers for one; that is, the only relationship that exists is that which each of the twelve tones has to each other. *Pan*-tonality (or all tonalities) might be a better term than atonality.

The basis of his technique was counterpoint, the counterpoint of Bach carried far from the tonal principles that governed composers

before the twentieth century. Many dissonant effects in modern music
are the result of individual vocal lines coming together in chords
that do not sound like the familiar teachings of harmony textbooks.
Thus the possibilities of music were stretched by Schoenberg, Berg,
Hindemith and many other composers of the twentieth century. The
use of twelve tones is not new. Bach wrote a "Chromatic Fantasy and
Fugue" based on the twelve-tone, or chromatic, scale. But Schoenberg
invented new ways to arrange the twelve tones in rows, out of which
to make melodic patterns and to construct whole compositions.

PIERROT LUNAIRE

But before he had worked out his twelve-tone technique, Schoenberg perfected atonality as may be seen in his three "Piano Pieces,
Opus 11", and "Six Little Piano Pieces, Opus 19." *Pierrot Lunaire* is
written in an atonal, or *pantonal,* style. This melodrama for recitation
(1912), is on a text called *Thrice Seven Poems* translated into German by Otto Erich Hartleben from the French by Albert Giraud. In
this Schoenberg uses the *Sprechstimme,* or the voice part half-spoken,
half-intoned (sung), blending with the tones of the instruments:
piano, violin, viola, clarinet, flute (and piccolo), bass clarinet and
cello. It was an experimental, untraditional, new tone medium. Those
who were hostile said that the voice not only acted as an instrument,
but as an instrument of torture!

Strange to say, in 1937, a Japanese periodical brought out a special
Schoenberg number!

(For details of Schoenberg's atonal methods and twelve-tone technique see *Twentieth Century Music* by Marion Bauer.)

ATONAL OPERA

In 1934, Arnold Schoenberg, a recent refugee from Nazi-ruled
Berlin and Vienna, in which cities he had worked and taught, spent
the summer at Chautauqua, New York. There he sampled American
musical life and saw a cross section of its culture. (Incidently he heard
his first Gilbert and Sullivan opera as presented by the Chautauqua
Opera Association, and was delighted with it!) He expressed himself
on many subjects to one of the authors of this book, and on one occasion he said, "Of course I am a romanticist, how could I be other
than a romanticist and write operas?" And he discussed two early
experiments in operatic form, *Erwartung* (*Waiting,* 1909) and *Die
Glückliche Hand* (*The Hand of Fate,* 1913). In both of these com-

plex scores he developed his twelve-tone theories, which found full expression in later works.

Schoenberg's romanticism is patent in *Verklaerte Nacht, Gurre-Lieder* and the tone poem *Pelleas und Melisande* (inspired by Maeterlinck's drama). There was no phase of romanticism that he did not know.

Erwartung, on a text by Marie Pappenheim, is called a monodrama, because he experimented in making one (mono) soprano carry the whole drama. The plot tells of a woman going to meet her lover in the forest at night only to come upon his dead body! A half-hour of gruesome terrifying drama with music!

The Hand of Fate is quite as horrifying and even more fantastic. A high baritone carries the principal role in a nightmare setting in which the man is being overcome by a mythical beast, a chimera, glowing with a green light. The chorus in the orchestra pit chants in a *Sprech-chor* (speech chorus similar to the solo voice in *Pierrot Lunaire*). Another man, a stranger, and a woman, the embodiment of earthly happiness, do not sing but act in pantomime. The opera is symbolic of man's fight between spirituality and materiality.

This opera for which Schoenberg wrote the text was presented by Zemlinsky, Schoenberg's brother-in-law and only teacher, at Prague in 1924 at a Festival of the International Society for Contemporary Music (I.S.C.M.); a few months later Dr. Fritz Stiedry conducted it in Vienna; it was given in Breslau in 1928 with great success; and in 1929 at Duisberg at a music festival where it won such acclaim that it was repeated two days later; and in 1930 it was presented in New York under the auspices of the League of Composers by Leopold Stokowski and the Philadelphia Orchestra on a program with the first stage performance in America of Stravinsky's *Le Sacre du printemps.*

TWELVE-TONE OPERA

While Schoenberg was still in Germany (1929–30), his *Von Heute auf Morgen* (*From One Day to Another*) was given. It was a happy little opera in one act, of fifty minutes' duration. But it was a source of much dispute, because an opera written in the twelve-tone scale proved to be agreeable! There are four characters; each one has his own melodic line and his own rhythmic pattern. Schoenberg had a good time experimenting with arias, recitatives, contrapuntal passages and an orchestra expanded by piano, saxophones, mandolins, guitars and flexitons (a metal plate that shiveringly whines under the pressure of the player's thumb, usually found in jazz bands).

SCHOENBERG'S IDEALS

Schoenberg wrote in every form. He used every device to tell the story in symbol, vision and suggestion. Someone said with twelve-tone technique he seemed to inhale air from the planets.

In America, Schoenberg wrote in different styles. In some pieces, he even abandoned his twelve-tone technique and used the diatonic (our accustomed) scale, in a masterly contrapuntal way. Yet again, he used twentieth-century harmonies and was probably trying to discover still another way of expressing himself. He deplored the pinning down of musical composition to systems, techniques, or any other "stylish" word. Music is music, and expression is expression to Arnold Schoenberg.

Schoenberg's "inquiring mind" gave him no peace until he had evolved new means and forms and had uncovered the laws and rules governing the forms he had conceived "as in a dream." Those who think that Schoenberg's music is all brain and no heart are mistaken, for it was the outcome of his sincerity and of his feeling. He believed that a real composer writes because it pleases *him,* and because he is "driven to say something whether or not there exists one person who likes it. . . ."

A DISCIPLE'S OPINION

Ernst Krenek, a disciple of Schoenberg, says of Schoenberg's twelve-tone music that it isn't any more difficult than the old polyphonic music writing of 1500 from the pre-opera era. Krenek also says that this sort of woven writing is taught to our music students, who do not find it difficult, and he thinks it is the best way of creating atonal music or music which is not written in any set key.

Wagner himself stretched the scale and was most deft with the chromatic scale which can be heard in the *"Liebestod"* ("Love-Death") in the last act of *Tristan und Isolde.* So did Chopin use chromatic harmonies. But they never lost the feeling of key relationships as did Schoenberg's.

In spite of the people's sharp opposition to his "hard to listen to" music. Schoenberg enjoyed the friendship of Richard Strauss, Gustav Mahler and other pre-eminent contemporaries. As a painter he exhibited his pictures in Vienna in 1910. This man became professor of a master class at the Prussian Academy of Arts in Berlin, where he taught with honor until the city became too small for himself and Adolf Hitler. His works were put on the list of *degenerate art* by the Nazis!

Schoenberg was forced to emigrate to America in 1933. When he arrived here he was received with reverence and enthusiasm. Concerts by the League of Composers in New York City and the Library of Congress, in Washington, D. C., were given in his honor. In 1940, he became an American citizen. He taught in California the last years of his life.

A POSTHUMOUS OPERA

Arnold Schoenberg left a posthumous opera on a Biblical subject, *Moses and Aaron*. The first two acts had been written in 1930–32, and although the third act was never finished, the monumental score forms an entity "important enough to make the work one of the most distinctive compositions of the first half of our century." So writes Karl H. Wörner, a German author, in the July, 1954, *Musical Quarterly* (Current Chronicle).

Its première in a concert version took place in Hamburg, March 12, 1954, conducted by Hans Rosbaud. The story from Exodus is a document of the struggle between spiritual and material power, the former represented by Moses, the latter by Aaron. "Life is identified with truth and spirit." He has probably never written a more important work, never a more definite declaration of faith.

Until we have heard a performance in this country, we must accept someone else's opinion that the music has greatness, power of artistic concentration, universality in its exploitation of all the possibilities of expression, unlimited melodic, harmonic and rhythmic richness.

Moses and Aaron is in twelve-tone style, based on one row. It makes difficult listening because of the complicated contrapuntal writing. "On the other hand," Wörner states, "the innumerable melodic details on the stage and especially in the orchestra are organized to serve a dramatic purpose. In this respect the work is an opera in the full sense of the word."

The part of Moses is for a singer-narrator, not unlike the Sprechstimme of *Pierrot Lunaire*. The role has solemnity and dignity.

"The opera consists of scenes of three different kinds. There are scenes for soloists, especially the scenes of Moses and Aaron, the large scenes of the people (choruses), and one scene for orchestra (the

'Dance of the Golden Calf')." The entire work is a synthesis of opera and oratorio. Wörner compares the choruses to "Bach's polyphony and Handel's grandeur and dramatic power." The solo scenes are treated in "the dramatic and psychological language of Richard Wagner. The orchestra, especially in the Golden Calf scene, is possessed of a rhythmic energy recalling Stravinsky and Bartok, yet always contrapuntal." Wörner calls the performance "an event of historical importance. The large audience was deeply impressed..."

Arnold Schoenberg no doubt will go down in history as one of the prophets in music—one of the few composers of any age who had the courage and the conviction to burn his bridges (old methods and formulae) and to build anew. Out of his experiments and ideas have come new paths that will be trod by future music makers. Even today the stone he dropped in the pond is making ever-widening circles.

BERG—SIGNIFICANT PIONEER

Alban Berg, one of the twentieth century's most gifted composers, was born in 1885 in Vienna, where he died suddenly in 1935.

Berg was a pupil of Schoenberg. Although written by one of the kindest and most sincere men, his songs, so difficult to understand, caused a riot when given in Vienna in 1913. He struck out on different paths from Schoenberg, although he used Schoenberg's atonality and twelve-tone technique. He made expressionism stronger because he was influenced greatly by Wagner and Bruckner, and more so by Gustav Mahler.

WOZZECK, THE TRAGIC

Wozzeck, in three acts and fifteen scenes, with text by Berg, based on a dramatic fragment by Georg Buechner (1813–37), was probably the most important experimental opera since *Pelléas et Mélisande* of Debussy.

Berg has set a new music on the old classic forms. Note the old forms in the following, as analyzed by Dr. Willi Reich:

Act I. Five characteristic sketches: Suite, Rhapsody, Military March and Cradle Song, Passacaglia, Andante Affettuoso (quasi Rondo).

Act II. Symphony in five movements: Sonata form, Fantasie and Fugue, Largo, Scherzo and Rondo Martiale.

Act III. Five Inventions: on a Theme, on a Tone, on a Rhythm, on a Key (D Minor), on a Persistent Rhythm (perpetual motion).

With all this, Berg's chief trait is in the power of his drama rather than his newer (Schoenbergian) music. In some places, he enlarged the possibilities of the theme by using the *cancrizans* (or crab) method of playing the theme backwards. This was a game or stunt of musicians before Bach's time.

"From the moment the curtain parts until it closes for the last time," Berg stated, "there is no one in the audience who pays any attention to the various fugues, inventions, suites, sonata movements, variations and passacaglias—no one who heeds anything but the social problems of this opera, which by far transcend the personal destiny of Wozzeck." All the listener is aware of is the remarkable characterizations and the coherence of the score.

There is no smooth singing or bel canto, or sweet moonlight scenes. Indeed, the most memorable scenes are those of horror, where Wozzeck kills his Marie while their child, unaware of what is happening, continues at play.

SOMETHING OF THE STORY

Berg uses for this opera a gory, sensational plot about a poor wretch of a soldier, stupid and clodlike—Wozzeck. Deceived and betrayed by his "girl friend," whom he murders, he drowns himself in the lake. He is an example of frustration and of a sick mind, a symbol of an underprivileged human being. The rest of the cast is symbolic as well as realistic: the Captain, a fear-tormented, commonplace moralizer; the Physician, a demon of materialism, indifferent to the struggle between man and his spirit; the Drum Major, the beast in man; and Marie, a victim of forces stronger than herself.

Wozzeck is modern in declamation and melody, an unusual feat in its experimental way, almost as great but not as inviting and elusive as *Pelléas et Mélisande*. The work is a mammoth conception and a new trend in opera. For the first time, atonality was used in an extended operatic work. After Berg, atonality was used everywhere. He said ". . . I never . . . expected that *Wozzeck* would become the basis of a school. I wanted to compose good music; to develop musically the contents of Buechner's immortal drama [*Wozzeck*] . . . to give to the theatre what belongs to the theatre."

POWER WITH FREEDOM

Berg put more feeling and passion into opera than Schoenberg. His use of folk music, of the grotesque, and his freedom to wander harmonically added to his power. *Wozzeck* is exciting with touching and impressive scenes, such as Marie's reading of the Bible, and the music when she is killed, suffused by one tone—terrific in its insistence. The final *hop-hop* of the child playing with the other children in the face of the tragedy is unforgettable!

The first performance in 1925 in Berlin under Erich Kleiber brought Berg fame. In 1931, Leopold Stokowski with the Philadelphia Orchestra presented it in New York and Philadelphia with sensational effect.

By 1936, it had been given in 29 cities—about 166 times. The United States Library of Congress owns the original score.

In the magazine *Modern Music* for November-December, 1927, Adolf Weissman wrote, "Despite the protests of reactionary spirits, a work which denies the old tradition of bel canto and relentlessly pursues its own direction in a search for truth, has miraculously achieved not only a first night success, but an enduring place in the opera repertoire...it is, in the finest meaning of the word, an independent and original work."

ANOTHER OPERA

Wozzeck no doubt mirrors a world, the Germanic world, that was torn with wars, was agitated and stark and faced with ruin and dissolution. The German dramatists, according to Max Graf, were dissatisfied with society, disappointed in the world that was driving toward chaos and self-destruction—"horror of the apocalyptic horsemen who rode over Europe's battlefields had torn the dramas to shreds." Berg's second opera *Lulu* comes into such a category. At the time of his death he had completed the work except for the orchestration of a part of the last act. It was presented at Zurich in 1937.

The revoltingly disagreeable libretto was drawn from two plays by Frank Wedekind, *The Earth Spirit* and *Pandora's Box*. Lulu is the "eternal feminine manifestation of evil," a primal spirit who like a flame unwittingly attracts and destroys human moths, but in turn she is destroyed. A silent film with orchestral music serves as an *entr'acte*. The entire music is built upon a single twelve-tone row, but he used arias, duets, trios, ensembles and even sonata and rondo forms. Berg combined Sprechstimme, song, and the spoken word.

Whether this country will ever hear it is debatable. The plot would be revolting to an American audience, although Berg chose it to present a moral, not to tell an indecent story.

PAUL HINDEMITH, NEOCLASSICIST

Paul Hindemith, born at Hanau, Germany, in 1895, has the distinction of having been one of the most talented and prominent German composers of the interwar period. He had won the confidence of both conservatives and radicals. As Aaron Copland said in his book, *Our New Music,* he seemed to instill "new blood in the exhausted German musical tradition," and when he came in contact with neoclassicism, popular in twentieth-century Europe, "his own more characteristic style took shape."

In his boyhood he unconsciously laid the foundations for understanding the popular music of the country of his future adoption by having been forced to earn a living by playing in cafés, motion-picture houses, dance halls and theaters, in operetta orchestras and jazz bands. This experience is reflected in some of his early compositions.

From 1927 to 1937, Hindemith taught composition at the Berlin *Hochschule* (High School of Music). He had already been an orchestral and quartet player, had been a conductor, and had composed much serious music, ranging from "teaching pieces" for children to grand opera, with chamber music in between.

Although he met all the requirements of "Aryanism" as demanded by the Nazis, they considered his music degenerate and antagonistic to Nazi doctrine—a point in Hindemith's favor! As he had been a viola player in the Amar Quartet, a Turkish group, he was invited to Turkey to reorganize its musical life.

In 1937 the Elizabeth Sprague Coolidge Foundation of Washington, D.C., invited Hindemith to visit this country and to present some of his chamber music. He became, eventually, an American citizen, and a member of the faculty of the Yale University School of Music.

STAGE WORKS

Hindemith's dramatic works were epoch-making, not because they met with great success, but because they were "different." He was an experimenter. First he wrote *Mörder, Hoffnung der Frauen* (*Mörder, the Hope of Women*), a one-act opera on a text by Oskar Kokoschka, the painter-friend of Schoenberg; another one-acter on August Stramm's *Sancta Susanna* (*St. Susan*); *Das Nusch-Nuschi,* music for a Burmese puppet show, a gay burlesque with richly rhythmic music with text by Franz Blei; and *Der Daemon* (*The Demon*), a dance pantomime.

One of the first experimental operas in pre-Nazi Germany was *Cardillac* (1926). The libretto from a romantic story by E. T. A. Hoffmann is by Ferdinand Lyon. Hindemith turned unreservedly to neoclassicism and used forms that came directly from Bach. He probably was surprised that the public would not accept this neoclassic work, but it was too uncompromisingly severe for them to understand or to appreciate.

AN AMUSING FARCE

One of the things he wrote was for Charlot's Revue, a sketch with music, *Hin und Zurück* (*There and Back*, 1927), in which he reversed the music and the action in the second act like Schoenberg's crab-motion pieces, and it is acted and played backwards. It is very popular and is a favorite with many semiprofessional and amateur groups. Marcellus Schiffer, a writer of revues, supplied librettos for this and also for *Neues vom Tage*.

Hindemith descended somewhat in his tabloid opera, *Neues vom Tage* (*News of the Day*), a bit of flagrant twentieth-century realism in three parts. But he ascended to glorious heights in his *Mathis der Maler* (*Mathias the Painter*), an opera in seven scenes. It was written on his own libretto and was given in Zurich (1938). It is a modern nationalistic piece based on German history, art and customs. It was performed in Switzerland even while his music was being held up to shame in the Düsseldorf exhibition of *degenerate music*.

MATHIS DER MALER

Mathis was a painter who lived in the sixteenth century. The story was inspired by three panels painted by Mathis Grünewald on the Isenheim Altar exhibited in a museum in Kolmar, Alsace. They were "The Nativity," "The Entombment" and "The Temptation of St. Anthony." Hindemith has made use of modal effects, old church melodies and his own melodies in polyphonic style. In the opera libretto, he makes Mathis Grünewald the symbol of the German artist living at the time of the Reformation and during the Peasants' Wars, in Martin Luther's day. Poor Mathis was called to arms but was torn between art and his duty as a soldier. His work won out when he came to realize that the peasants were fighting not for a better life, but for revenge. His answer came to him in a dream. In the symphonic arrangement of this opera, the dream comes in the section "The Temptation of St. Anthony." Again we see "social significance" cropping up in music. We know the work in America only in the tryptich form, that is, as three movements of a symphony. It is easily one of the great orchestral works of the twentieth century.

At first, Hindemith composed along romantic lines. Then, in his first one-act stage pieces, he began using his *linear* or polyphonic kind of music. But when he came to *News of the Day,* he changed again to the friendly, dramatic, satirical. *Cardillac* was in the style of a piece for chamber orchestra in which he used polyphonic music and very little lyric melody. It is in an old style with separate songs.

THE TRUTH ABOUT GEBRAUCHSMUSIK

In the pre-Hitler days a group of young Germans and Austrians decided that "music—good as well as bad—is futile if it cannot attract an audience!" They tried to find common ground on which "producers and consumers of music," that is, composers and audiences, might meet. "In the 19th century music became a luxury but after the First World War conditions created a new audience, and a new music had to be supplied. Radio and the sound film did their share to popularize new music" (*Music Through the Ages,* Bauer and Peyser).

So Hindemith, whose name was connected with the movement, wrote music for school children, "useful music," and chamber music for amateurs, and a very good play for children, *Let's Build a City.* It was given in New York in 1931, and was enjoyed by adults as well as by children.

In the preface to his book *A Composer's World,* Hindemith objects to the term *Gebrauchsmusik,* which he finds an ugly word, "as hideous as its English equivalents workaday music, music for use, utility music, and similar verbal beauties." But the word had tagged him, and "when I first came to this country," he said, "I felt like the sorcerer's apprentice who had become the victim of his own conjurations: the slogan *Gebrauchsmusik* hit me wherever I went, it had grown to be as abundant, useless, and disturbing as thousands of dandelions in a lawn. . . ."

Hindemith is at present in Switzerland, where he is Professor of Music at the University of Zurich.

KRENEK OF VIENNA

Among the Europeans who have laid down new roots in our good earth (the United States), is Ernst Krenek (pronounced Shre'-nek), a Czech born in Vienna in 1900, who gave America a taste of German-made jazz applied to opera in his elaborate *Jonny spielt auf* (*Jonny Strikes up the Band*). It was first given in Leipzig in 1927 and was brought to New York in 1929. Although it had had sensational success in Europe, it didn't "go down" with audiences at the Metropolitan. Indeed, it floated off the American stage because it was a mixture of the "blues" and the spirituals in Teuton, not American, fashion. However, it made such a splash that it almost eclipsed everything else he did. He was adventuresome in a twentieth-century manner, and introduced into the opera a motorcar, a jazz band, a loudspeaker, and a railroad train. He uses the twelve-tone system with a startling sense of rhythm and structure.

JAZZ-BUG VS. MINSTREL

Jonny's story is a most complicated piece of realism. He is a Negro jazz-band leader, costumed so that he looks like an old-time minstrel. He steals the violin of a violinist killed under the wheels of the locomotive. With his winsome ways plus the violin, he wins the girls, outwits the law and fiddles away in the finale, when he has killed off art music. His jazz has won out, and he stands on top of a mammoth globe decorated in red, white and blue while the poor, shabby, garish world dances about him.

The scenery whets the appetite for travel. Among other scenes are the "doin's" at a Swiss hotel teetering on an Alp, a Paris hotel, a glacier, and a railway station.

Antedating *Jonny* was his *Orpheus and Eurydice* (1923), on a text by Oskar Kokoschka, the expressionist painter. The well-worn couple go through a transformation: Krenek's Eurydice becomes a modern girl who can't tolerate her husband, Orpheus. In this, Krenek brings to modern opera a new phase of romance, neoromanticism, realistic, vital, with his own gift of lyricism.

After the success of *Jonny spielt auf,* Krenek tried other operas combining jazz and twelve-tone technique with varying degrees of success. His eighth opera was *Leben des Orest* (*The Life of Orestes*), a grand opera with his own libretto on the Orestes cycle including Iphigenia. With considerable fantasy he attempted to combine many unrelated elements, Romantic, Classic, modern, jazz, ancient Greece, and the castle of a Nordic king (!) in a four-hour opera, in which the few worthy moments are lost in a welter of poor material.

He wrote a timely opera on his own libretto, *Karl V,* which told, in twelve-tone technique, of the Austro-Spanish emperor who was avid to combine many nations including Rome. It was given at Prague (1938) after Krenek had left Europe, just before experimental opera ceased to be welcome.

Krenek has written an excellent book, *Music, Here and Now* (New York, W. W. Norton and Company). He is also an authority on twelve-tone technique, although he was never a Schoenberg pupil. He is now lecturing in the U.S.A. and he once taught at Vassar College, New York.

A PRODUCT OF THE MACHINE AGE

Among other Germans, Max Brand, pupil of Krenek, is up to date, for he wrote an opera, *Machinist Hopkins* (1929), throbbing with hate and murder, in which Hopkins himself becomes an avenging machine in a machine age. It is twentieth-century and dissonant and uses the Sprechstimme, declamation (on one tone-level) and *vocalise* (sounds without words). The text is by the composer. The work goes too far for opera in its emphasis on social ills and emotional reactions to industrial conditions. It is a symptom of unrest in a restless world and twentieth-century reactions in music.

SCENE IV

Soviet Composers—
Prokofiev and Shostakovitch

OPERA AS PROPAGANDA

THE American Revolution set us free to live and, to some extent, to compose as we would, and the French Revolution freed, to a certain extent, French music. The upheaval following the Russian Revolution, however, changed the bandaged face of Russian music. Now composers must conform to the new regime presided over by politicos, not musicians. Yet the "Union of Soviet Composers" was pledged "to support the socialist program of construction with their art," which resulted in the reproduction in music of sounds of industry and of functional marches.

One of the important operas written for the Soviets was *Shah-Senem,* produced in Baku in 1934. This is by Reinhold Glière (born in 1875). It is in four acts and based on Russian, Turkish, Persian, and Arabian ideas in order to establish musical bonds with the whole Russian people. This is music used consciously as a public utility. In other times, too, operas have influenced social and political activities, as with Verdi and Auber for example.

Other Russian Soviet operas have been written, but the one that seems to fill the demands for Russian propaganda as well as for music is *The Quiet Don,* composed by Ivan Djerzhinsky, based on the masterly novel *And Quiet Flows the Don* by Mikhail Sholokhov, given in 1935 in Leningrad. It is only slightly dissonant and is replete with Russian folk melodies and rhythms. Stalin attended the première of this opera and later the composer in gratitude made an aria on one of Stalin's speeches.

SOVIETS IN COMMAND

In order to exile Western and "bourgeois" music and yet to keep foreign operas in Russia, it was ordained that the stories be changed to conform to Communist ideas.

Faust, for example, was transformed by changing Mephistofeles to an upholder of Communist theory and an enemy of established Eastern religion, morality, and ideas. So in the end, instead of Marguerite being forgiven and taken up into Heaven, Mephistofeles frees Marguerite and establishes her and her baby on a Collective Farm! (From a talk by Nicolas Slonimsky before a meeting of the American Musicological Society in New York, 1949.)

Whether the Russians, *Sovietized,* can with all their creativeness, contribute to the advance of opera, is questionable. When their composers get the freedom to write as they wish, the genius of Russia will, of course, blossom again. It is amazing what the composers have done under the present conditions. What is taking place behind the "Iron Curtain" is impossible to know.

Among other well-known writers are Dmitri Kabalevsky, and Liev Knipper.

PET HATREDS

The Soviets abhor Schoenberg, Hindemith, and Krenek. Their idols are those whom they call progressives, and include the conventional composers Tchaikovsky and Rachmaninov. How can composers in the twentieth century push back the calendar to the nineteenth? The Soviets have not only generalized as to what they want but have banned many ordinary harmonic devices such as dissonance; atonality; unresolved chords; protracted pedal point, etc. This if one were kindly is what might be called arbitrary.

SERGEI PROKOFIEV—SCHERZANDIST

Sergei Prokofiev was born in Sont Sovka in the District of Ekaterinoslav, Russia, in 1891 and died in 1953. Little Sergei was a Mozartean infant! At the age of five he composed an "Indian Gallop," which his mother, his first teacher, wrote down for him. At six, he composed some other pieces including an opera, *The Giants,* with the book by little Sergei himself! It was given in his uncle's summer home, but it has not, to our knowledge, been produced elsewhere. This is unlike Wolfgang for, discounting two previous theater pieces, his first opera,

Bastien et Bastienne, is still given. At eleven, the Russian prodigy wrote twelve piano pieces, and at twelve, he wrote an opera based on Alexander Pushkin's *Feast during the Plague.* As a man Prokofiev wrote *The Classical Symphony* to prove that he could write in the classic form, as *Mozart might have written today!*

Sergei Prokofiev, chief of the Soviet composers, a genius second only to Stravinsky among the Russians, is a master of sarcasm and the grotesque in music. He, however, doesn't like to be called sarcastic, but prefers *scherzoness,* which, he says, is made up of three words: "jest," "laughter," and "mockery."

LOVE FOR THREE ORANGES

If there ever was an opera or art work that is humorous as well as satirical, it is Prokofiev's delicious *The Love for Three Oranges* (1919), based on a work of Count Carlo Gozzi, *Fiaba dell' amore delle tre malarancie (Fable of the Love for Three Oranges).* It is told in a prologue and four fascinating acts. Prokofiev strikes out at foibles in the arts and society in a plot with fantastic, tangy, brilliant, swift, satiric music, in buffa, pageantry and magic galore. *Gianni Schicci* of Puccini is somewhat sarcastic also, but is more fun-making and parody than satire.

The most familiar pieces in *The Love for Three Oranges* are the "Royal March," the "Waltz Scherzo," and the "Laughing Song of the Prince." The opera, to quote its creator, is most "scherzandic," but we say, zany!

The Love for Three Oranges failed when first given in the Chicago Auditorium in 1921. Then it was transferred to the Manhattan Opera House in New York City and presented by the Chicago Opera Company, with the composer conducting. In 1949 it was given at the City Center in New York City in English. In the language of the theater, it was a "smash hit."

Sergei Prokofiev lived for many years in Europe and America, on our side of the "Iron Curtain." But in 1934, he went from Paris and New York to Russia, the earthly bourne, from which, for him, there was to be no return.

Prokofiev's early operas were lucid, rhythmic and melodious—for example, *Magdalene* (1911–13), and *The Gambler* (1916–27), written in Petrograd on a Dostoievsky story. He wrote a third, *The Flaming Angel,* given in Moscow in 1940. As with many other Russians, he wrote vivid ballets: *Pas d'acier (The Age of Steel,* 1927), given in

Philadelphia and New York by The League of Composers in 1930, and *L'Enfant prodigue* (*The Prodigal Son*) (1928-29), produced by Diaghilev in the last year of his most rewarding life. His *Romeo and Juliet*, on Tchaikovsky's theme, was produced in Moscow in 1936. The list of piano and orchestral works is long and just as intriguing.

After his return to Russia, Prokofiev adjusted to Soviet conditions, save once. He was reprimanded by the government for following too much in the line of Western ideas, rather than Soviet ideas. His "Symphonic Song" won him this rebuke, for which he apologized! He tried to get back into the good graces of the government with an opera about an aviator who lost his legs in the Second World War. Prokofiev's greatest crime in Soviet thinking was that he lived in the West (Paris) for fifteen years.

"Formalism" is a "crime" in Russian Soviet music. By formalism is meant Western modern techniques and methods. The Russians like marches and Prokofiev's and Shostakovitch's skill in marches have helped them.

Prokofiev's satiric music for *Lieutenant Kijé* is full of the melody, tang and rhythm we think of in connection with this original genius. His "Russian Overture" no doubt is an "overture" (a plea) for favorable Russian opinion. His theater music, *Peter and the Wolf*, is a most engaging fairy tale for children, both as a ballet and as a suite. The ballet, *Romeo and Juliet*, in which he said he had taken special pains to be simple and to touch the heart, makes us all realize that Prokofiev, whether in the East or the West, wrote music which is stimulating and effective. Here is a twentieth-century composer being original enough and daring enough to say that he wishes to touch the heart!

SCREEN MUSIC

One of the most beautiful scores that has been written for the cinema Prokofiev composed for the film *Alexander Nevsky* (1938), a Russian hero of the thirteenth century. He is celebrated by the boulevard in Moscow named after him, Nevsky Prospekt. The cinema opera tells the story of the rout of the Teutonic Knights on the icy surface of Lake Peipus in northern Estonia in 1242. Prokofiev later made a cantata of it. It is most Russian, showing as it does the influence of Mussorgsky and Borodin on orchestral coloration with Russian reed effects and the use of the maracas (a pair of gourds or calabash shells filled with dry seeds shaken with both hands).

Being none too dull and living in Soviet land, he undertook, after

Alexander Nevsky, to write an opera with a subject from the Civil War in the Ukraine—*I am the Son of the Working People,* an excellent Soviet title. Later it was changed to the shorter name of a Red warrior, *Simeon Katko.* His next was *The Duenna* based on a play by Richard Brinsley Sheridan (English dramatist, 1751–1816).

Around 1941 he started work on his opera based on the title of Tolstoy's *War and Peace,* probably the world's greatest epic novel, painting Russia under the czars and its numerous poor and easy-going, carefree nobility. Nina Mendelssohn, his wife, wrote the libretto. Prokofiev's intention in this opera was to give a picture of Russia from soul and spirit to manner and mannerisms. He seemed to have become interested in the *spirit* of man. *War and Peace* was to have been given by the Metropolitan Opera Company (1949–50 season), but it has not materialized as yet.

DMITRI SHOSTAKOVITCH

Dmitri Shostakovitch, one of the younger men of music, was born in St. Petersburg, now Leningrad, in 1906. He is a child of the Soviet and his music is of new Russia. It has *cool* power, not warm like a Wagner or a Puccini. It has stark color, noise, which harks back to tradition, yet is bound with Soviet restrictions. In it can be heard the Russian church, the folk, the military with its rhythms, strenuous dances and muscular marches. It often has humor, bitter satire and twentieth-century dissonance when anchored to classic forms, or even vulgar tunes. His power of satire can be seen in the delightful polka, "The Age of Gold," a criticism of the capitalistic system which amuses the most ardent capitalist. It was written for a convention at Geneva, during the Second World War.

Shostakovitch wrote the opera *The Nose.* He opens "operations" at a barber shop, not with our traditional "barber shop chords," but with a sneeze sounded in a series of dissonant chords. Even the swish of the razor is heard!

His reputation in the West was first based on his symphonies. He has written ten. The seventh was composed while he was a fire warden during the Siege of Leningrad. All have excellent and exciting features as well as banalities and prolixities. His earlier symphonies, particularly the first, second and fifth, are human and interesting.

LADY . MACBETH

What interests us most is the opera *Lady Macbeth of Mzensk,* an opera of blood and hate. It is expressionism in story and music with no regard for good taste or human feeling. It makes the Italian verismo sound like baby-play. It is a sample of what others do in better taste. It is the twentieth century in opera.

Lady Macbeth of Mzensk tells the story of a married woman with a lover who is thrashed by her father-in-law. He is killed by her, who with her lover kills her husband. The woman and her lover are sent off to Siberia. She is jilted by her lover who falls in love with another on the way to exile; she throws her off a bridge into a river and follows her, to the audience's keen delight . . . for both drown!

The scenes are lurid, made more vivid by the dissonant music . . . brutal music. In Act II, where Katerina's old father-in-law beats the lover, you can actually hear the whip lashes in the raucous music.

Lady Katerina's is no sad "blues" song, no romantic love song . . . it is an agonizing wail. Expressionism to the nth plus degree but with an occasional intimation of earlier operatic fashions. With a violin solo, Shostakovitch gives most amazingly well the stillness of a summer morning. The opera is skillful but unpleasant. It leaves a bad taste in the ears if that be possible! It is acrid and often mounts from pianissimo to thunderous climaxes, and travels with abandon from key to key. Power, energy, clash, impersonal nervous vigor is the composer's, but not his characters'. Drive and theatricality are the core of this opera and much of his music. Unfortunately the hand of this master is often wasted on dross and sheer repulsiveness. Of course, the brutal tale needs brutal music, but in any art there must be control of the materials.

This Lady Macbeth is no relation to Shakespeare's Scottish lady. Lady Macbeth of Glamis was unscrupulous and ambitious, and her deeds unseated her mind; Katerina of Mzensk is a fiend.

It was first performed in Moscow in 1934. America saw it first in Severance Hall, Cleveland, Ohio, 1935; then in a New York performance under the banners of The League of Composers, in the Metropolitan Opera House in the same year, conducted by Artur Rodzinski.

PRAVDA REBELS

Pravda, the government-controlled newspaper, called it "a leftist mess instead of human" and went on to say that it was "fidgety, screaming and neurasthenic." So startling in innovations was this music of Dmitri Shostakovitch that the Russian government called him to account with Prokofiev and other Russians of art and science. Their abject written repentences have permitted them, to the good of the world, to continue to compose, but in Russia.

In 1949, Shostakovitch came to New York City to a peace rally. He didn't like "capitalistic" musical manners and criticized petty things about the audiences.

It is not safe to prophesy how long the works of modern Russians will continue. It depends on whether the deadening hand of *government* which killed Chinese and Egyptian music in ancient times is laid upon its mind and throttles inspiration.

As an expressionist, Shostakovitch has carried opera to a point where it will either use some of his freedoms, or revolt and go back again to some romantic and less dissonant and vulgar resting place. Who can tell?

SCENE V

Modern Italians and British

ITALY IN THE TWENTIETH CENTURY

In Italy several composers, although belonging to the early twentieth century, like Alfano (1876-1954), Pizzetti, Respighi, Casella and Vittorio Rieti (1898-), who is now an American citizen, contributed little to the advance of contemporary opera, for all are nearer to the nineteenth-century fashion.

MALIPIERO

But Gian Francesco Malipiero, born in Venice in 1882 of a noble Venetian family, comes nearer to being of this century than any other of his contemporaries. He writes in his own way and in all musical forms. He dislikes conventional Italian opera, but adores his mellow language and its old classic poetry on which he bases most of his librettos. In a one-act opera (comedy) by Goldoni (1707-1793), *Le baruffe chiozzotte* (*The Row at Chioggia*), he condenses dialogue to swift, short exclamatory sentences, in his *recitativo parlando,* to correspond to the speaking voice, and makes use of the ancient in a modern fashion (synthetic opera).

SETTE CANZONI

Malipiero's opera is continuous music, with a special use of motifs. It is terse and excellently adapted to such a speech as Antony makes in his *Giulio Cesare* (*Julius Caesar,* 1936), which Malipiero wrote for Mussolini's favor! This was one of a trilogy of short operas, *Antonio e Cleopatra* and *Ecuba* (from Euripides) being the other two. He did an amusing thing in his *Sette canzoni.* In a prologue called *"La morte delle maschere"* ("The Death of the Masques"), Orpheus, the Greek god of music and our old friend, is made to look up all the stock figures of Italian commedia dell' arte. Orpheus, as impresario, insists that the characters sing ancient and real songs to old poetic texts, *not* stage people's songs. These scenes are connected by *intermezzi*—another old idea brought up to date. The League of Composers presented the *Sette canzoni* in its early days.

In Malipiero's trilogy about the city of Venice, *Il Mistero di Venezia* (*The Magic of Venice*), he first tells a legend of the founding of Venice, *Le aquila d'Aquileia* (*The Eagle of Aquilla*); then he goes back to the commedia dell' arte for *Il finto Arlecchino* (*The False Harlequin*); and in *I corvi di San Marco* (*The Ravens of St. Mark's*) he shows present-day Venice, in which the spirit of the beautiful past has been forgotten among the modern jazz lovers, pseudo-artists and antique dealers. It is a melodrama—to be danced. Again the new goes back to the old.

Malipiero's system is so new that it is old. He re-created, not just annexed, old forms. He has revived classic subjects in eighteenth-century opera buffa style. He can put different elements together (syntheses) that act and stir the imagination. He is different and has made somewhat of a break with Italian traditional music. He has written fifteen operas (nine of which are included in three trilogies).

TWELVE-TONE AND OPERA

One would hardly associate the twelve-tone technique of Schoenberg with Italy and opera, but all these and fame, too, exist in the career of Luigi Dallapiccola, the most highly regarded of the twentieth-century composers of Italy. He is known for a remarkable opera, *Il prigioniero* (*The Prisoner*) on which he had worked from 1944 to 1948. Before that he had completed *Canti di prigionia* (*Songs of Prison*).

Luigi Dallapiccola (1904) was the son of a professor of classical languages in the only school in Istria where the Austro-Hungarian government permitted Italian to be taught. When World War I broke, the family was sent to Graz in Styria, and the father was deprived of his teaching position. The only bright spot in this dreary concentration-camp period of twenty months was the opera house at Graz where Luigi, by the time he was fourteen, had acquired a deep understanding of, and love for, opera. The first time he heard *The Flying Dutchman* he determined to make opera his life work.

Psychologically, the workings of the young boy's mind led to his making studies of tyranny and imprisonment, resulting in an almost unconscious fixation that expressed itself in the opera and the songs. His mental anguish during the internment at Graz was greatly deepened when he learned in 1938 that the Italian Fascist government had officially announced a "race manifesto" to which, fortunately, the Italians were hostile. It was only through his music that Dallapiccola could express indignation. He did not know that other composers were writing what would be regarded as "protest music," as for example, Schoenberg's "Ode to Napoleon Bonaparte." The work *Preghiera di Maria Stuarda (Prayer of Mary Stuart)* came out of this anguish. The occasion of its performance over the Flemish radio at Brussels, in 1940, came only a month before the Nazi invasion of the Low Countries. This prayer was a part of the *Canti di prigionia* which had one performance in Rome in 1941, and was lost to the world until it was "rediscovered" by the I.S.C.M. (International Society for Contemporary Music) and presented in its London Festival in 1946.

In 1940, Dallapiccola's opera *Volo di notte (Night Flight)* was performed, and at that time he made up his mind to write his own libretto for another opera, basing it on Villiers de l'Isle-Adam's story, *La torture par l'espérance (Suffering through Hope)*. For this he drew also on a Flemish epic by Charles de Caster. He wanted to write "a work that would portray the tragedy of our times and the tragedy of persecution..." (in an article in the *Musical Quarterly,* July, 1953, on "The Genesis of the *Canti di prigionia* and *Il prigioniero*").

The scene is set in the sixteenth century, during the Inquisition. The depressing story concerns the prisoner's attempt to escape, lured on by promises of the guard, who proves to be the Grand Inquisitor. The one feminine role is the prisoner's mother who appears only in the prologue. A chorus of monks plays an important part in the final scene and in two interludes. The music is twentieth-century in effect, dissonant and severe. It is written in twelve-tone technique, showing how surprisingly expressive the system can be when handled by a sensitive composer.

The Prisoner had four performances by the Opera Theatre of the Juilliard School of Music, New York, in March, 1951, in an English translation by Harold Heiberg.

A MODERN SACRA RAPPRESENTAZIONE

A work that has not yet been heard in America is Dallapiccola's *Job* (1950) for which he uses a sixteenth-century term—"sacred representation." It could be performed in the open air, in the cathedral square as of old, or on the radio. The score calls for a narrator, a singing chorus, two speaking Sprechstimme choruses, soloists for the roles of Job and seven others, an orchestra with much percussion and an organ. *Job* is in seven sections and is written on a twelve-tone row, treated contrapuntally.

Mr. Skulsky, in the article "Opera 1954" in the *Winter Juilliard Review,* calls the work "Dallapiccola's greatest achievement to date, for the composer proves here unmistakably that this system (the twelve-tone), if not used as a means in itself, but as a natural way of thinking, can bring forth the greatest variety in expression and the most intense dramatic strength."

TWO YOUNG ITALIANS

Geoffredo Petrassi and Vieri Tosatti are the gifted composers of the younger generation in Italy. Petrassi wrote significant vocal music in several cantatas, the most important of which is *Noche oscura (Dark Night,* 1950–51), in which a mystical experience is described. His early stage works include a ballet *La follia di Orlando (The Folly of Orlando,* 1942–43), and a one-act opera *Il Cordovano (The Man from Cordova,* 1944–48).

In his opera *Morte dell' aria (Death in the Air,* 1949-50), "he sought to integrate human conduct and moral responsibility, and arrived subsequently at the conclusion that the fundamental problem of individual existence, *la condition humaine* (the condition of man), is primarily a spiritual problem which depends on faith,"—so writes John S. Weissmann in the *Musical Quarterly (Current Chronicle),* April, 1953.

Vieri Tosatti, a Roman born in 1920, was first a pupil of Petrassi and later of Pizzetti. He seems to be an "eccentric" who loves to play bizarre jokes. One of his recent compositions, a cantata for soloists, chorus, orchestra, and reciting voice is concerned with "a three-round boxing match."

A comic opera, *Il sistema della dolcezza (The System of Sweetness),* was composed in 1947–48 and has had several performances in Bergamo and Genoa with others in view. The subtitle is "absurd musical drama in two tableaux" and it is based on a tale by Edgar Allan Poe, "The System of Dr. Tarr and Dr. Fether." The action takes place in an insane asylum where the patients take over doctors and nurses and tar and feather them! Evidently opera, even in the country which took it most seriously, is elastic enough to stretch to all kinds of literary and musical aberrations.

BRITTEN OF BRITAIN

Benjamin Britten, today, is the most notable opera maker in England. He was born in Lowestoft, Suffolk, in 1913, a year before the First World War.

Britten was something of a child prodigy in composition, and was taught early to play the piano and the viola. He studied with the composers: Frank Bridge, John Ireland, and Arthur Benjamin.

Having to earn his living, he wrote music for documentary films and quickly won a reputation. It was in the film studio that he met the English poet W. H. Auden. They collaborated as early as 1935 on a work of which it was said that the audience did not know whether to consider Britten's "daring style as the outcome of courage or of foolhardiness"! (*Benjamin Britten*, by Scott Goddard from *British Music of Our Time*. Pelican Books.)

From 1939 to 1942, Britten lived happily in Amityville, Long Island, and for a short while was a member of an artists' colony in Brooklyn headed by Auden. He was well known among the American composers and counted among his friends Aaron Copland, Paul Bowles, and others. He also made a visit to California, saw much of the United States, and inhaled its legends. The outcome was an opera about the legendary Paul Bunyan who was supposed to be so gigantic that when he walked through the forests he trampled down the great trees as if they were blades of grass.

Auden wrote the libretto for this "choral operetta" which was presented in 1941 by the Opera Workshop of Columbia University in New York City. The score has never been published and Britten said of it, "The critics damned it unmercifully but the public seemed to find something enjoyable. . . ."

PETER GRIMES

While in California he read George Crabbe's poem "The Borough," and it so excited him that he decided to write an opera based on it, with scenery of the coast of England where he was born, near the Borough, and where he now lives. No sooner thought of, than started! Dr. Serge Koussevitzky commissioned the work and gave Britten funds to write the three-act opera which became *Peter Grimes*. It tells a heartbreaking, stark story of seacoast life that could just as well be set in Gloucester, Massachusetts, or any other northern fishing town. The music is tangy, salty, powerful, modern, but not too difficult to understand. The choral settings are beautiful. The story is sincere, exciting and tragic. The librettist is Montagu Slater. You can hear the fog horn, "smell" the salt air and see the fishermen and townsfolk. Although contemporary, the music makes use of five distinct arias in eighteenth-century form, and he uses the leitmotif in his own way.

It was significant that the world première of a new English opera opened Sadler's Wells after the war. Eric Walter White in his *Benjamin Britten: A Sketch of His Life and Works* (Boosey and Hawkes) says ". . . *Peter Grimes,* as well as being a masterpiece of its kind, marked the beginning of an operatic career of great promise and perhaps also the dawn of a period when English opera would flourish in its own right." *Peter Grimes* was first given at the Sadler's Wells Theatre in 1945, a month after the Germans ended the bombing of England.

Its first American performance was in the Berkshire Music Center at Tanglewood, Massachusetts, in 1946 where it was conducted by Leonard Bernstein. The Metropolitan première was conducted by Emil Cooper in 1948. It has been translated into German, French, Flemish and Italian and has been sung in many foreign countries.

The music has rhythm and melody and a translucent orchestra for which Britten is noted. It should have an influence on Anglo-Saxon drama with music.

POOR LUCRETIA

Britten's *Rape of Lucretia,* built on the ancient Sabine story, opened at the Edinburgh Festival, Scotland, in 1946. It was given in New York in the season of 1948–49 at the Ziegfeld Theatre where it had twenty-three performances. The virtuous wife of a Roman noble is dishonored by a warrior friend of her absent husband, after which, rather than live, she takes her own life. William Shakespeare's "Rape of Lucrece" has more power and drive than the libretto by Ronald Duncan, which was based on a play written by André Obey for the French producer and actor Jacques Copeau in 1931. While Duncan followed the French play, he went to Ovid and Livy for the sources of this story of Etruscan treachery. Obey's play leaned heavily on Shakespeare.

The composer went far back for models. It is a cross between an opera, a Greek drama with a chorus and a modern play with music. He uses a chorus to explain the story, but instead of a group of people, he has a man for one chorus, and a woman for the other, stationed at left and right of the stage, who read out of large books. In the American production, part of the action was directed by the skilled and inspired choreographer, Agnes de Mille.

The music, both sung and declaimed, much of which might better have been spoken, accompanies a pompous and verbose text. The opera was revised more than once as composer and librettist worked together.

Britten used an orchestra of chamber-music size of about a dozen players. The recitative was accompanied by piano in a manner comparable to the use of the harpsichord in the early days of opera.

The scenery is not as intriguing to the eye as in many operas, but its sparseness seems to be a part of an experiment the composer and librettist were trying, an experiment to mitigate the high cost of opera. The economic problem also involved the number of singers and instrumentalists. Chamber opera makes special demands on its audience as well as its performers. And as Eric Walter White points out, with reason, in *Benjamin Britten: A Sketch of His Life and Works,* "The equipoise between voices and instruments is too precarious for the listener ever to be lulled into a sense of complete relaxation and security; and many listeners—particularly those reared on a rich diet of lush orchestral fare—are apt to resent the necessity of making this special effort. This is one of the problems that Britten and his collaborators have had to face when producing *The Rape of Lucretia, Albert Herring* and his version of *The Beggar's Opera.* There is one remarkable spot: the interlude of the ride of Tarquinius, which paints a realistic picture in the breathtaking pace of both the horse and the man's mind.

Britten is a modern master of trenchant, elevated, lyric song as may be proven by *The Holy Sonnets of John Donne* (1945) and the supremely touching and spiritual Canticle I ("My Beloved is Mine and I am His"). This "songsmith" has a theater sense, too.

CHAMBER OPERA

Albert Herring was given for the first time in America at the Berkshire Music Festival on August 8, 1949. It uses a story by Guy de Maupassant, made into a book by Eric Crozier. It calls for a cast of thirteen, and an orchestra of twelve, without chorus. It is a chamber opera, inexpensive to produce, intended as a companion piece and a contrast to *Lucretia.* Although called a play set to music, it is a comic opera in three acts. It was staged by Boris Goldovsky and Sarah Caldwell, with settings by Charles Elson. One New York paper said that it was a magnificent comic opera, strong words for anything less than *Die Meistersinger* or *The Marriage of Figaro.* Others said that it was rambling and inconsequential.

As early as 1938, an English critic, Henry Boys, wrote that Britten "could undoubtedly become the most original and probably the most successful maker of light music in England since Sullivan." High praise! But there is no doubt Britten has caught the spirit of satire and sentiment that he has blended with British skill.

The story of *Albert Herring* is of a young man of twenty-two, who was tied to his mother's apron strings and was a model of virtue. He breaks loose after being given lemonade loaded with rum, and the comedy stems from the funny things he does as a lately freed man "on a drunk." Fantasy and cockeyed reality are mixed. The music has some sustained melody, with the delightful song for children and a chorale for the May Day, which Britten combines with contrapuntal forms, used humorously and, of course, with plenty of dissonance. We must wait to decide which of his operas have the divine breath that insures immortality.

Britten was probably led to write chamber operas because he had been giving stage works with small casts and few instruments—all over the British Isles and on the Continent.

THE BEGGAR'S OPERA AGAIN

Cleverly indeed Britten revamped *The Beggar's Opera,* which is said to have made the producer, Rich, gay, and the author, Gay, rich, after it had a sixty-two-night-run in London (1728). Britten uses his twelve-piece orchestra and has preserved with his own up-to-date setting of the music the original transparency and blitheness of the satire on eighteenth-century morality and politics. Happily, it seems as timely and as winning as ever, in spite of its ancient settings, costumes of beggars and "shabby-genteels" and cockney "lingo."

Tyrone Guthrie was Britten's collaborator and they both had the desire to restore the original closely. Britten said that "The tunes to which John Gay wrote his apt and witty lyrics are among our finest national songs." He sees in them a strong Handel and Purcell influence that may have been cause or effect in these seventeenth- and eighteenth-century "traditional tunes." "They have strong, leaping intervals, sometimes in peculiar modes, and are often strange and severe in mood." For his arrangements Britten went back to the original edition as arranged by Dr. Pepusch. He used 66 out of the 69 original airs.

THE TRAGIC BILLY BUDD

Herman Melville's novel *Billy Budd, Foretopman* gave Benjamin Britten the inspiration for his next full-length opera. He asked the British writer E. M. Forster to collaborate with him. In spite of being over seventy and never having written a libretto before, Forster agreed. Eric Crozier shared the work of writing the book, which consists of a prologue, four acts and an epilogue. The libretto tells Melville's grim story of a handsome and much-liked young boy, foretopman on H.M.S. *Indomitable,* who was wrongly accused of mutiny by an evil master-at-arms. Billy Budd had a speech defect—he stammered. At the moment the malevolent John Claggart made the accusation to the captain, Budd's fists worked more rapidly than his tongue. Claggart was accidentally killed, and Budd had to hang for killing a superior officer.

Most of the libretto is in prose and is handled in a style approaching declamation. The sea chanteys are in verse and other sections are in free verse or, at least, sound metrical.

Britten successfully met the difficulty of writing an entire, four-act opera for male voices. The problem was helped along by the transparency and wide range of his orchestra, and by a children's chorus.

"The music of *Billy Budd* is highly integrated," Erwin Stein writes, in the book *Benjamin Britten,* a commentary on his works by a group of specialists, edited by Donald Mitchell and Hans Keller (Philosophical Library). "Certain themes, motifs, chords and rhythms recur as part and parcel of the opera's musical idiom. They are characteristic of certain persons or situations, principles or ideas, and are at the same time the material for the opera's architecture."

Again Stein states: "Though limited by cast and setting, the operatic scope of *Billy Budd* is amazingly wide. It includes features that are usually to be found only in the spoken drama . . . I believe, new in opera . . . That music and words do not trespass upon each other's domain is ensured by the soberness of Britten's music and by his realistic attitude towards the words. They are always composed so as to be to the point, and always audible, when they need to be understood . . ."

The première took place at Covent Garden, London, in December, 1951. In November, 1952, *Billy Budd* was given by the National Broadcasting Company in its TV Opera Workshop, and less than three weeks later it was presented by the Indiana University at Bloomington.

LET'S MAKE AN OPERA

"The Little Sweep" is the opera part of an entertainment for young people, for which Eric Crozier wrote the book, called *Let's Make an Opera*. The story is based on "The Chimney Sweep," from William Blake's *Songs of Innocence*.

The first two acts of *Let's Make an Opera* illustrate the rehearsal and preparation of "The Little Sweep," and the third act is the performance itself of the forty-minute opera. The cast includes six adults, six children and the conductor who rehearses the "Audience Songs" with the audience. A string quartet, piano duo and percussion constitute the orchestra. Spoken dialogue is used between the musical numbers.

The première took place at Aldeburgh, England, in 1949, and the opera was taken on tour throughout the country by the English Opera Group. It has had numerous performances in the United States and Australia, and has been translated into the German and French with performances in Europe, in Israel and the Philippines.

A CORONATION OPERA

When Queen Elizabeth II was crowned, the unprecedented honor of writing a coronation opera fell to Benjamin Britten. The theme was Queen Elizabeth I and Essex. The present young Queen accepted the dedication and attended the gala performance on June 8, 1953, at Covent Garden.

William Plomer found the background for the libretto in Lytton Strachey's *Elizabeth and Essex,* and the opera was named *Gloriana*. Both librettist and composer have centered their attention on Elizabeth, "to place in relief her character as a Queen, who, though ageing, is still at the height of her powers." Eric Walter White writes "... and it is here that Britten and Plomer have scored their most incontrovertible success." In the general criticisms, however, *Gloriana* was not considered up to the standard of Britten's earlier operas.

Britten made use of dances—pavane, galliard, lavolta, march and coranto (courante)—in which it is said that he "captured the genuine Elizabethan idiom."

A new problem opera, *The Turn of the Screw,* a setting of Henry James's story, presented at Venice in September, 1954, created a favorable impression, but neither *Gloriana* nor *The Turn of the Screw* has been heard in this country.

FIRST OPERA VENTURE A SUCCESS

One of Great Britain's foremost composers, Sir William Walton, waited until he was fifty-two to write his first opera, *Troilus and Cressida.* The book, by Christopher Hassell, was drawn from Chaucer and Boccaccio rather than from Shakespeare.

Sir William Walton has done much serious composing including chamber music, symphonies, and an oratorio, *Belshazzar's Feast,* built on gigantic choral and orchestral lines. So he came to operatic problems well prepared from a mighty task.

In the New York *Herald Tribune* of December 26, 1954, Cecil Smith, an American who is critic of the London *Daily Express,* wrote, ". . . even his staunchest admirers had hardly dared to expect that his very first opera could turn out to be such an exceedingly good one."

The soundness of Walton's composing technique has been compared to that of Vaughan Williams. "His language, which combines conservative elements with contemporary harmonic dissonant materials and rhythmic patterns of the early Stravinsky, is romantic in expression," Abraham Skulsky writes (*Juilliard Review,* Winter, 1955). "He too approaches the field of opera in a grand style, with the chorus playing an important part in the opera. The vocal parts are extremely well written and one of the most interesting aspects of this opera is the role of Pandarus, which is sung by a tenor buffo."

The action takes place in Troy and in a Greek military encampment.

English composers are venturing into the opera field with new enthusiasm. In addition to *Troilus and Cressida* and *The Turn of the Screw,* Lennox Berkeley's opera *Nelson* and his one-act farce, *A Dinner Engagement* and Michael Tippett's *The Midsummer Marriage,* for which he wrote his own libretto, were performed in London during the 1954-55 season.

SCENE VI

Opera Composers in New Germany and Austria

FIVE or six composers in the Germany of today are regarded as its leading composers: Werner Egk, Carl Orff, Boris Blacher, Wolfgang Fortner, Karl Amadeus Hartmann and Gottfried von Einem. They do not form a group, neither does any one composer dominate. "In Germany it is more a case of each man for himself, and the musical attitudes, characteristics and styles of the composers named display a wide variety," an American composer, Everett Helm, who recently spent several years in Germany, wrote in the *Musical Quarterly*'s *"Current Chronicle"* of October, 1950.

Mr. Helm describes Egk's style as "neither very progressive nor unduly conservative" and "based squarely on firm tonality." Egk wrote a ballet *Abraxas* on a Heine poem that was banned as immoral by Munich but was produced in Berlin.

CARMINA BURANA

Carl Orff (1895–), one of the most important of the contemporary German composers, became known to the New York public in 1954 through an exciting performance, by the chorus and orchestra of Boston University under the direction of Leopold Stokowski, of *Carmina Burana* (1937), sometimes described as a "scenic cantata." It is a setting of thirteenth-century manuscripts discovered in 1803 in the Benedict-Beuren monastery in Bavaria, anonymous poems written by wandering minstrels, or *goliards,* who were important in the cultural life of that period. They were young ecclesiastics who had left their orders and had become "the bohemians of the Middle Ages." Orff chose poems, some in vulgar Latin and some in old German, which he has set in a fascinating musical style deliberately simple, non-contrapuntal, modal, creating an effect of primitivism—or even neoprimitivism.

Orff has been specially interested in music for the stage. According to Mr. Helm, "he feels that the forms and traditions of occidental music have run their course and are no longer valid . . . Only music that accompanies the spoken (or sung) word seems to him to offer any possibilities to a contemporary composer." Of the same type, in fact a companion piece to *Carmina Burana,* is *Catulli Carmina* (1943), songs on texts by Catullus, called *Ludi scaenici. Trionfo di Aphrodite* has been combined with the other two to form a "scenic triptych" for stage performance.

Among Orff's operas are *Der Mond* (*The Moon*), *Die Kluge* (*The Clever Wife*), *Die Bernauerin* (*The Woman from Bernau*) and *Antigone.*

In 1949, Carl Orff's setting of Sophocles' Greek tragedy *Antigone* was given at the Salzburg (Austria) Festival, for which he used a translation by the German poet Friedrich Hölderlin, dating from 1803. Milos O. Ptak describes the Salzburg performance in the *Current Chronicle* of the *Musical Quarterly* of January, 1950. He tells of the unconventional orchestration, consisting of four pianos, six each of double basses, oboes, and trumpets, four flutes, three harps and an assortment of xylophones, stone pianos (?), cymbals and castanets requiring fifteen players. Mr. Ptak ventures the criticism that the work "has a paucity of orchestral effects," in which "the meagerness of melody and the absence of harmony leave the sparingly used orchestral color and the power of the story as life-giving elements."

Abraham Skulsky offers the criticism: "Another reaction took place in Germany, where Carl Orff went back to a primitive conception of musical drama. A musical language of the utmost simplicity, rhythmical obsession and the strongest sense of sound *per se* are the principal factors in this composer's music."

ANTI-ROMANTIC OPERA

A German composer born in 1903, in China, Boris Blacher, has developed in his instrumental works an original rhythmic pattern, and an anti-Romantic bent that amounts almost to an obsession. He believes in absolute music, even though he has made a setting of *Romeo and Juliet,* concerning which he stated that this composition for soli, chorus and orchestra could be performed as a chamber opera, as a cantata, or as a ballet. This sounds as though Blacher had attempted to "denature" opera in his effort to write objectively and not with the subjective treatment that opera demands. *Romeo and Juliet* was presented at the Salzburg Festival, 1950.

The Berlin Städtische Oper (City Opera) produced in 1949 Blacher's ballet *Chiarina,* that takes place in a fashionable spa in the 1890's, and is written in a light, half-satirical vein for entertainment. Everett Helm says: "To this story Blacher has written an unpretentious, at times ribald, at times bantering score that is more remarkable for its instrumental color than for the musical ideas therein contained."

VON EINEM'S THE TRIAL

The only one of the operas by contemporary Germans that has been heard in New York is Gottfried von Einem's setting of the Kafka psychological drama *The Trial,* which was presented at the City Center in 1953. Although it was not considered a success, it illuminated the enigmatical play and had much to interest the listener with a curiosity about new opera and especially about the work that is coming out of Germany today. Von Einem wrote an earlier somewhat conservative opera, *Danton's Tod (Danton's Death).* He is a pupil of Boris Blacher and some of the critics think that in spite of his undoubted talent he has not yet established his own style. He combines chromaticism and certain Stravinsky rhythmic formulas with yesterday's realistic melody-line and stark harmonies.

A TEACHER OF YOUNG GERMANS

Wolfgang Fortner, although he has added nothing to the opera repertory, has been the teacher of several of the younger Germans, such as Hans Werner Henze, who is named by Everett Helm as "the most successful and best known of young German composers." He works in the twelve-tone system, although his teacher Fortner does so only occasionally, as in a recent cantata, *The Sacrifice of Isaac.*

Henze is the composer of a one-act opera, *Das Wundertheater* (The Magic Theater), produced in 1949 as a running-mate with Blacher's ballet *Chiarina.* The story, based on Cervantes, satirizes the itinerant theater of the Spanish writer's day. The players speak to orchestral accompaniment and the effect of the work is highly humorous.

Karl Amadeus Hartmann wrote a fresh opera score, *Die Simplicius Simplicissimus Jugend* (The Simplest of Simple Youth) which was performed in Cologne in 1948.

Both Germany and Austria reflect the aftermath of World War II, which fatally interrupted the studies of the younger generation. Not only did many men of promising talent lose their lives, but from the time party politics entered the classroom, musical instruction deteriorated. Opera houses were destroyed and many institutions ceased to exist. Therefore there are few well-instructed or talented Germans writing opera.

YOUNG VIENNA

For many years Vienna had functioned as one of the musical capitals of the world. There in the early part of the twentieth century the bold experiments of the Schoenbergian school were pitted against the output of those who clung to tradition. The short realistic opera and an up-to-date buffa were crowding the last gasps of a post-Wagnerianism off the boards. Vienna still has her Opera and her Philharmonic, but creatively she has lagged behind.

Theodor Berger (born in 1905) won the Music Prize of Vienna in 1949 for a descriptive orchestral work, *Ballade*. Friedrich Wildgans (1913) has written orchestral scores and an opera; and the Hungarian Karl Shiske (1916) has won acclaim for an oratorio.

Kurt Blaukopf, Viennese critic, writes in *Current Chronicle* of the *Musical Quarterly,* January, 1950: "The features these three composers have in common are a direct appeal to the visitor . . . the preservation of the elementary principles of tonality; a desire to overcome the *clichés* of academicism; and finally the ability to absorb the most divergent stylistic influences of foreign contemporaries, without losing their own personal and national characteristics."

It would be hard to find a better statement of aims for the composer of today.

A YOUNG SWISS COMPOSER

In the Salzburg Festival of 1954, an opera, *Penelope,* by Rolf Liebermann, a Swiss composer and pupil of Wladimir Vogel, was presented. The librettist of this and of a previous opera, *Leonore 40–45,* is Heinrich Strobel, chief of the music department of one of Germany's leading radio stations. Liebermann occupies a similar position in Zurich.

According to Abraham Skulsky ("Opera, 1954," *Juilliard Review*), "It is a modern tragedy projected in antiquity and takes place constantly on two different planes: the ancient one, which presents a sort of external picturesque frame and is colorful, refined and satiric in character, and the modern one where the real drama of the homecoming takes place and which has the character of *opera seria*." The opera deals with the problem of the returning prisoner of war. "One of the most skillful among the younger generation of composers," Mr. Skulsky calls him.

"He dominates in a rare way all the resources of contemporary materials, from the twelve-tone system to rhythmic and sonorous elements derived from Stravinsky." In one intermezzo he combines pure romantic song with background music of a jazz band playing boogie-woogie!

Liebermann and Strobel worked with a definite aim: modern opera must deal with contemporary conditions and must avoid the trimmings that characterized nineteenth-century opera. It must also avoid the pitfalls of film-realism. And yet opera composers have never before had as wide a range of subjects, styles, size and length as they have today from which to choose. Their stories may be mythological, historical, from contemporary life, from the countryside, the city, realistic, symbolic; the works may be long or short, chamber music or symphonic, soloistic or choral, with music throughout or with spoken word. A palette of many hues.

ACT IX. Opera in America from Revolutionary Days to Television

PRELUDE

The Pioneer Era

PILGRIMS AND CAVALIERS

OPERA and all music in America had a different road to travel from that of any of the countries in Europe. When the Pilgrims landed "on the stern and rock-bound coast" in 1620, music was the last thing in the world that they would have thought of, nor were they to have any opportunity for years to come to write it.

While Bach and Handel were writing superb music in Europe, and opera singers in Handel's day had reached the height of the art of song, and instruments were being brought to their glory, the people on the American continent, still hugging the eastern seashore, were just beginning to make baby attempts to express themselves in music.

NO MUSICAL FREEDOM

The first settlers came to the New World in search of religious freedom. Yet, the ones that risked life and fortune to worship God as they wished ruled out everything but psalm singing until one hundred years after the landing at Plymouth Rock. It cannot be denied that the Dutch in what later became New York State, the Germans and Swedes in Pennsylvania, and the Scotch and English settlers in most of the other colonies, sang secular songs while working in the fields, the forests, on the streams and at home. The women undoubtedly sang while spinning, weaving, sewing, cooking, washing and lulling their children to sleep. Thus some music was kept alive, despite the prohibitions of the churches. In addition, the settlers clung to the old familiar songs. They used only the simple tunes brought from the various parts of Europe from which they had come. This is proved, for example, in the versions of Anglo-Saxon folk songs still sung in the mountains of North Carolina, Kentucky, and West Virginia.

The early settlers in New England began by rhyming the psalms and singing them by heart. Music, they said, was made by God, and to make it with instruments was "artificial" and against their religion. Not using instruments, of course, held back the composing of instrumental music. A prosperous citizen, horrified at the thought of installing an organ bought for a church in Boston, offered to pay for it, "if you let me dump it into Boston Harbor." This was when Europe was already enjoying the music of Lully, Rameau and Alessandro Scarlatti.

A European dancing-master in the New World was forbidden to teach dancing! But think of the beautiful ballets being given in Europe at this time. In 1675, five years after the chartering of the Hudson's Bay Company, there was a law that forbade the playing of any kind of instrument except the drum, the trumpet and the Jew's harp. No one knows, to this day, why those three instruments escaped censorship.

Nobody was allowed to compose new songs because new songs were thought to be confusing and to make the composer vain. The Pilgrims loved to sing in church but not from notes. Notes were considered to be as sacrilegious as were instruments. You *must* know the music by heart. That only was holy.

It is easily seen that opera, which was play-acting with music, telling the stories of love and adventure, was considered a creation of the Devil. Fortunately, after 1720, two years after New Orleans was settled by the French, immigrants from the mainland of Europe, particularly Germans, came over and tried to teach music. In spite of all restrictions, people had begun to miss and yearn for making music. And soon singing schools were founded and music engravers and publishers reaped new harvests. Music in America was started on its way with the advent of these teachers, publishers and engravers.

MUSIC OF THE CAVALIERS

While the severe Puritans in the North were permitting only the singing of psalms and hymns, the Cavaliers in Virginia were more friendly toward music, and in Charleston public concerts were encouraged and a music society, the St. Cecilia, was founded in 1720. Charleston, South Carolina, has the honor of having presented the first stage work in America in 1735, a ballad-opera *Flora or Hob in the Wall*. After 1754 the theater regularly housed plays and operas.

Picturesque Williamsburg, possibly as early as 1722, had the first theater in this country. John Tasker Howard tells us (*Our American Music*) that George Washington, "ever a lover of the theatre, saw his first play on Virginia soil."

SCENE I

Opera's First Steps Lead to the Metropolitan

THE IMITATIVE ERA

IN THE 1700's the operas or operettas in America were much like Gay's *The Beggar's Opera* with the difference that they used American songs, characters, jokes, topics and speed. In fact they were much like the old Singspiel. This was of course the imitative era when European plays and operas were used as examples.

New York City, the port of importance on the Hudson, had ballad-operas as early as 1732. *The Conscious Lovers* was shown, probably in the new Nassau Street Theatre, about 1750. This ballad opera had dances and songs which took the place of the European interludes and preludes. But finally the people turned against the play-givers because of some petty thieving in the theater, which was blamed on the actors, and a mob destroyed the building.

From 1773, however, until after the Revolution, the Continental Congress banned horse-racing, "gaming, cock-fighting, exhibition of shows, plays and other expensive diversions and entertainments" (Howard). So whereas opera was a part of the European's make-up, in the New World it had a hard time.

Francis Hopkinson's *Temple of Minerva,* the nearest thing to opera in those days, was in reality a political oratorio. In this form, of course, it was more acceptable to the religious settlers than if it had been called an *opera,* a work for the "abhorrent theatre." It used a Greek story for its plot and praised the alliance of America with France. Today, it would be called propaganda. It had arias, ensembles and choruses, and began with an overture. In 1781 it was given with George Washington in the audience.

Hopkinson (1737-91) was an intimate friend of Franklin, Washington and Jefferson. His works have charm and quaintness. He is the first American-born composer of opera and must have seen *The Beggar's Opera* in New York (1750).

Then there was James Hewitt's *Tammany* (1794). This opera was about Chief Tammany, an Indian, after whom New York City's Society of Tammany Hall was named. This also was a political opera, in which the anti-Federalists and the Federalists had a field-day.

FRENCH OPERA IN NEW ORLEANS

A couple of years before the War of 1812, New Orleans gave a series of French operas. Louisiana because of her French and Spanish population was fond of opera and European music. Very early in the 1800's, traveling companies made short trips to the musical South and even to the North. They avoided Boston, however, because Bostonians wanted only oratorios by Handel and Haydn—nothing as exciting as love stories in music!

AN ORCHESTRAL ACCOMPANIMENT

Imagine!—in the 1750's, no orchestra had as yet been used with an opera in America. Think of the skilled orchestras, ballets and singers of Europe at this time, and how the violin had become king of music-makers. Yet not until 1752 was an orchestra used with *The Beggar's Opera* and this in a new theater in Upper Marlborough, Maryland. Again the South was ahead.

AN EARLY OPERA IN NEW YORK

It has been said, although history contradicts it, that the first American opera ever given in New York City was *The Archers of Switzerland* in 1796, by the many-sided musician, Benjamin Carr (1768–1831), English-born composer, singer, organist, publisher and dealer. This work in ballad-opera style relates the William Tell story twenty-three years before Rossini told his version. Carr, with Hewitt and others, was a connecting link between the no-music era and the budding music period in America. He was one of the founders of the famous old Musical Fund Society, established in 1820 in his home town, Philadelphia.

During the last part of the eighteenth century, New York and Philadelphia imported opera. New York was fortunate in not having many Quakers or too many Puritans, so she could welcome *The Beggar's Opera*. English comic operas were also given throughout the young states and even French opéra comique was well attended. Among some of these were the operas of André Grétry.

Philadelphia gave the first original ballad opera in 1754, but the season was a failure. Then she tried again, and in 1759 was permitted to build a playhouse and had a good season of seven months. But the straitlaced people of the colony conspired against the music lovers and the government banned opera in Pennsylvania until some seven years later.

Although Moravians in Pennsylvania had always been musical, they had little effect, at first, on American music, because they kept to themselves. Later, however, they contributed, in their still continuing Bach festivals, to American appreciation of music.

"HOME, SWEET HOME"

In 1823, an English comic opera, *Clari, the Maid of Milan,* was given in New York City. In this was heard, for the first time, "Home, Sweet Home." The opera score was by Sir Henry Rowley Bishop, with words by John Howard Payne. Bishop also wrote the much-used coloratura song, "Lo, Hear the Gentle Lark."

GRAND OPERA—A "FIRST"

The first grand opera heard in New York was Carl Maria von Weber's *Der Freischütz.* It was given in 1825 in English at the Park Theatre. Had the custom of giving opera in English been continued, it might have had an easier road in America. Opera was never popular for long, in the early days, probably because people couldn't understand it. Another reason might have been that theaters did not have the equipment to produce adequate scenic effects. Strange that the elaborate *Der Freischütz* was attempted, and too, Louis Antoine Jullien's *Fireman's Quadrille* (about 1850), with flames flashing from the ceiling, fire bells clanging, fire hoses spouting water, and glass crashing!

MANUEL GARCÍA

But soon New York had her first season of Italian opera. In 1825 Manuel García, a Spanish tenor and composer, brought his family to New York. The people of the city called him the "Musical Columbus," because he discovered opera for them. He also gave New Yorkers the first taste of Rossini's *The Barber of Seville.*

His daughter, Maria García Malibran, became the most famous

singer of her time. So celebrated was she that as late as 1935 the opera *Maria Malibran* by Robert Russell Bennett, with book by Robert A. Simon, was written in tribute to her. It was produced at the Juilliard School of Music in New York.

From Manuel García's time to our own, American opera as well as American music has had a hard time. For many years, only European composers could get their operas produced.

WILLIAM FRY

William H. Fry (1803–64) an American writer of symphonies, lecturer and critic, who lived through some of our Civil War, breathed fire and brimstone against European composers. He was the first native-born American to write a grand opera—*Leonora* (produced in 1845). Yet during its second run, this rabid fulminator against foreign influences, in order to have it produced again, allowed it to be translated into Italian! It was heard at the old Academy of Music in New York on 14th Street in 1858. *Leonora* was based by the composer's brother, Joseph R. Fry, on the play *The Lady of Lyons* by Lord Bulwer-Lytton, author of *The Last Days of Pompeii* and of *Rienzi,* which Wagner used for his opera.

To be sure, *Leonora* was not American opera. America was too young in music to create so highly complex a form as opera. It was in the style of the light operas of Donizetti and Balfe. From newspaper accounts it was considered very pleasant. Eighty-five years later a concert performance was given in the New York Public Library. His next opera was on a French theme, *Notre Dame de Paris* (*Our Lady of Paris*) and was given in Philadelphia.

JENNY LIND

One of the influences that might have stimulated opera was the coming of the "Swedish Nightingale," Jenny Lind, under the auspices of P. T. Barnum, circus and entertainment proprietor extraordinary. He used as much ballyhoo for the singer as was given to his other features, Tom Thumb and Jumbo, the elephant.

Another important influence intended to stimulate opera was the taking over of the Academy of Music by Ole Bull (1810–80), the Norwegian violinist. He was a friend of Wagner and of Grieg, and was worshiped by Americans, but his sally into opera was unsuccessful.

RIP VAN WINKLE

In the era of the songs of Stephen Foster, we began to use our own American legends for opera. We were building our national music by degrees. George Bristow (1825-98) composed the second American opera, *Rip van Winkle*. It was given at Niblo's Garden in New York City in 1855 and ran for a month. The story is based on Washington Irving's "Rip van Winkle" who was supposed to have gone to sleep in the Kaaterskill Mountains (now Catskills) for twenty years. It is a light opera with spoken dialogue, music of no special quality, and the libretto uses love scenes and episodes absent in the original Irving story.

BRISTOW AND FRY VS. GERMAN MUSICIANS

Bristow and Fry began a crusade against the German musicians lest they blow out the new and tender fires of American composition. Considering what the aliens had done for American music, it seems a bit ungrateful. But it is understandable and important. Not, however, until deep in the heart of the nineteenth century, in spite of Mr. Fry and Mr. Bristow, did a few American names appear among the writers and singers of opera.

ORCHESTRAS MAKE THEIR APPEARANCE

In the year 1810, Gottlieb Graupner, a man of Germany, who had played oboe in an orchestra directed by "Papa" Haydn in London, started the first orchestra in the United States, the Philharmonic Society in Boston. America was now started on her march of music. Then came the New York Philharmonic under Ureli Hill in 1842, and the Theodore Thomas Orchestra in New York and eventually Chicago. From then on, slowly but surely, orchestras were founded in many parts of the country. Some fell by the wayside, some persisted, but all had a definite influence and stimulated music.

A MODERN PIONEER—WALTER DAMROSCH

About forty-one years passed between *Rip van Winkle* and the year 1896, when another opera on an American subject was written and produced. It was Walter Damrosch's *The Scarlet Letter,* based on Nathaniel Hawthorne's tragic novel about the unfortunate Hestor Prynne.

Walter Damrosch (born in Breslau, Germany in 1862, died in New York, 1950) presided long over American music. He was the first to

use radio to teach music appreciation. He was the first to take opera
companies on the road. He brought the first German opera singers to
America. He conducted orchestra and oratorio, and did many other
good deeds for music. He made *The Scarlet Letter* known by taking
it on tour. It was not particularly American music, for it follows the
German romantic style, so Wagnerian that it has been called the
"Nibelungenlied of New England"! It was sung by a German cast in
English—or *near-English,* for Johanna Gadski, who never spoke even
fair English, headed the cast. It was given first in Boston and later at
the Metropolitan, with the composer conducting.

Walter Damrosch's second opera was on a French theme, based on
Edmond Rostand's *Cyrano de Bergerac.* The opera was first given at
the Metropolitan Opera House in 1913. Its book was by the eminent
music critic, W. J. Henderson, of the New York *Sun.* It lived for only
five performances.

Twenty years later Damrosch wrote another opera, with verses by
Arthur Guiterman, based on the tragic story by Edward Everett Hale,
The Man Without a Country. This story, on an American theme, is
about a naval officer Nolan, who when being tried for treason, said
"Damn the United States...I never want to hear the cursed name
again." Hale communicated the color, excitement and tragedy of
Nolan's punishment which the music unfortunately doesn't match. It
was first produced in 1937 at the Metropolitan Opera House with
Damrosch conducting. Arthur Carron was Nolan and Helen Traubel,
appearing for the first time at the Metropolitan, was Mary.

Walter Damrosch, his father, Leopold, and his brother, Frank, were
influential for what they did for music in America. He and his father,
who was a conductor, made it possible for the Metropolitan Opera
House to have Wagnerian opera. Walter conducted German opera
after his father's death when he was but twenty-one years old! He advanced opera by encouraging it, conducting and teaching, more than
by writing it.

THE U.S. IN MUSIC

America is fortunate in having its own Negro, cowboy, Indian,
pioneer, and other music on which to base opera. In the nineteenth century composers began to realize the beauty of Negro and Indian tunes
and gave American citizenship to their tangy music.

Charles Wakefield Cadman (1881–1946) delighted everyone with his
songs from the land of the sky-blue waters. His Indian opera in two

acts, *Shanewis* (*The Robin Woman*), with a libretto by Nell R. Eberhardt, was given at the Metropolitan in 1918. It is a love story between an Indian and a white. Cadman was interested in authentic Indian melodies and the opera is tuneful.

His second opera, *The Witch of Salem,* with text by Mrs. Eberhardt (1926), ran for two performances in Chicago, but on many other American stages. Cadman, like many composers, wrote beautiful songs and yet had not the developed sense of theater to make an opera *act*. That he was a popular song-writer is evidenced by "The Land of the Sky-blue Water," "At Dawning," and a long list of others. Cadman was a specialist in Indian music.

Arthur Nevin (1871–1943), brother of the more famous Ethelbert Nevin, wrote an opera, *Poia,* based on the legends of the Blackfeet Indians, with text by Randolph Hartley, that had its première in Berlin, Germany, in 1910. It was given by the Chicago Opera Company in 1918.

Henry F. B. Gilbert (1868–1928) did valuable research in Indian and Negro folk music. The Negro studies resulted in *The Dance in Place Congo,* a symphonic poem which was mounted as a ballet at the Metropolitan Opera House in 1918. It is based on five songs of Louisiana Creole Negroes.

PRIZE-WINNER

Henry K. Hadley (1871–1937), composer and conductor, won more prizes than almost any other modern composer. His name has been further honored because of the Henry Hadley Foundation, organized as the National Association of American Composers and Conductors to further the cause of American music and musicians.

Hadley's best-known opera is *Cleopatra's Night,* an Oriental tragedy in two acts, set in Egypt, based on a story by Théophile Gautier, made into a libretto by Alice Leal Pollock. It was given at the Metropolitan in 1920, with Frances Alda and Orville Harrold in the leading roles. Another of his operas, *Azora, Daughter of Montezuma,* from a *Legend of Mexico,* was given in 1925, by the Chicago Opera. Although these operas did not hold the stage, his chamber works and his rhapsody for orchestra, "The Culprit Fay," a prize-winner, are still heard.

Another prize-winner was *Bianca* (1916), an opera on a libretto adapted from Goldoni's comedy *The Mistress of the Inn,* produced at the Park Theatre, New York.

PARKER WINS PRIZES TOO

Horatio Parker (1863–1919), one of our important composers, wrote fine choral works, a well-known oratorio *Hora Novissima,* and two operas, *Mona* and *Fairyland,* both of which won $10,000 prizes. When the directors of the Metropolitan Opera House offered a prize for an American opera with an English text, Parker asked Brian Hooker, a faculty colleague at Yale University in New Haven, Connecticut, to write a libretto. This collaboration resulted in *Mona,* the story of a Druid princess, in love with the Roman governor's son, yet hating the Romans who had conquered Britain. In spite of seeming success with the public, the opera did not outlive its first season, 1912.

In 1913 the National Federation of Music Clubs offered a prize for an opera to be performed at the 1915 biennial in Los Angeles, California. Again Parker and Hooker collaborated and received the award. *Fairyland* had six performances at the biennial, and, sad to say, has never been heard again.

THE OPERA AND BROWNING

Richard Hageman, born in 1882 in Holland, known for some beautiful songs, wrote the opera *Caponsacchi* (1931), presented at the Metropolitan in 1937, five years after it had been given in Freiburg, Germany. It has three acts, with an excellent libretto by Arthur Goodrich based on Robert Browning's poem *The Ring and the Book.* It has a thoroughly European plot, with music less original than pleasing.

TAYLOR-MADE OPERA

A conservative in music, Deems Taylor, born in Brooklyn, New York (1885), held all sorts of jobs from carpentry to music critic for the New York *World.* His orchestral suite, *Through the Looking Glass,* put him on the so-called "classical" musical map.

His operas are somewhat conservative and have received the most performances of American grand operas ever given at the Metropolitan. *The King's Henchman* held the stage for three seasons, with fourteen performances; and *Peter Ibbetson* beat the *Henchman* with sixteen performances in four seasons. Most American operas have had two or three performances in a season, with perhaps a second season, and then have vanished. Both operas show their roots, particularly *Peter Ibbetson,* in impressionistic and romantic music. In 1927 *The King's Henchman* appeared with its story set in tenth-century England, and its attractive book by Edna St. Vincent Millay. It is a tragic *Tristan und Isolde* tale of love and death. The cast was superb, with Edward Johnson, Florence Easton and the valorous Lawrence Tibbett.

THE DREAM WORLD

For his *Peter Ibbetson* Taylor chose the exquisite and diaphanous story, adapted by Constance Collier from George Du Maurier's fantasy, *Peter Ibbetson*. Charm is added to the music by the singing of the whole first act in French, and by the insertions of French folk music, dream scenes and exciting dramatic material with straight lyric parts. The story takes place in England and France. The music is serious and dignified, sired by Wagner, Debussy and Massenet. It is, however, diverting, beautiful, but unhappily has been too easily neglected by the lyric stage.

WHAT AMERICAN COMPOSERS DID

While the foregoing, from Cadman through Taylor, advanced opera little, they did show the world that American opera was a reality and therefore they became a spur to composers.

SCENE II

Touching on Light Opera

LIGHT OPERA, or musical comedy, beloved of all peoples, will be only lightly touched upon, for there is not space enough to record the thousands of operettas so skillfully made. They become ever richer in the type of songs and ballets because of their freedom from shackling tradition and lack of fear of humable tunes.

All light opera up to the year 1923, after World War I, was rich in dances, choruses, topical songs and finales at the close of the acts, in which all hands and voices helped to end the operetta with gusto. They have more or less of an overture. Besides, they have spoken words during the acts to tie the action together; some songs which are a part of the action, and others to relate the character's feeling and the foibles of the era. But there is no very conscious tying together of the music with any symphonic order. Instead of unity, as in grand opera, the comic opera, or operetta, is really a string of songs connected by speech, occasional recitative, or dances. You can see by referring to the old German Singspiel and English ballad opera how nearly the light opera approaches them. Besides, there is a decided leaning to ballet and ballet forms in American light opera which is also a throwback to the origins of French opera. It goes in circles. The only reason for inclusion here of light opera in America is that it is showing new methods and ideas which may affect opera, cinema opera and television opera.

Light opera in every country has had an easier road to travel than grand opera, or opera seria. First of all, light opera can be less expensively produced; secondly, light opera is given on successive days and not forced, however good it may be, to make room for another opera the next night or the next week as in America. This self-sacrifice, or the constant making room for another opera so soon, is called the "repertory system." Producing opera is far more costly even than it used to be, partly because of the increased demands of unions, actors, stage hands, etc. With the extra rehearsals needed for the different operas, these charges reach astronomical costs, while the admission prices have to be held in check. Composers who must eat don't want to write works which have a slim chance to run but two or three nights the first season, and probably never again, depending on the substitution of the "old familiars," which the audiences demand.

Grand opera to develop in America should be subsidized. The growing audience for opera will probably accomplish this need. Imagine the difference between the run of an *Oklahoma!* in New York City, with its 2,248 performances, and the two champion runs of Deems Taylor's operas (see page 432). Yet had *Peter Ibbetson* or *Emperor Jones,* with their Tibbett and Lucrezia Bori, been given with essential ballyhoo on successive nights, as are operettas, they, too, might have achieved a success approaching that of the Rodgers and Hammerstein *South Pacific,* with Ezio Pinza and Mary Martin.

It is easy to see why composers give their attention to light opera. First, it appeals to more people, and does not have to abide by the rules, ceremonials and traditions that still plague most writers of grand opera, and there is always the beguiling chance of a long run.

THE METROPOLITAN VS. THEATER BUILDINGS

One of the most fortunate things in New York City about light operas is that they do not have to wait to be accepted by the Metropolitan. No, these lighter dramas with music, ballet and scenery fit into a theater, and so in New York a dozen such lyric dramas might be seen and heard during a season to the delight of audiences and to the advancement of musical art. Should these operettas or musical comedies add to the development of grand opera and more opera houses—and they *could*—they will have served as great a purpose as the German Singspiel for Germany and the vaudevilles and ballets for France.

THE FIRST KING OF LIGHT OPERA—VICTOR HERBERT

Victor Herbert, a relative of Samuel Lover, the author of *Handy Andy,* first saw the world as an Irishman in 1859 and left it as an American citizen in 1924. His operettas, each more beautiful than the other, were most of them written before his Indian grand opera, *Natoma,* given by the Chicago Opera Company at the Metropolitan in New York in 1911, a few days after its première in Philadelphia.

It had the same eminent cast (Chicago Opera Company) in both performances: Mary Garden and John McCormack and other competent singers. *Madeleine,* in one act, set in France, was given by the Metropolitan Opera Company in 1914. With all the fine casts, these two operas died an untimely death in comparison with his light operas, *Serenade, The Fortune Teller, Babes in Toyland, The Red Mill, Sweethearts, Naughty Marietta, Mlle. Modiste, Eileen* and others, which are still sung and produced.

Although Victor Herbert wrote one of the first dagger dances in America in his *Natoma,* who remembers it? But how many *do* remember "March of the Toys" from *Babes in Toyland,* "Ah, Sweet Mystery of Life" from *Naughty Marietta,* "Kiss Me Again" from *Mlle. Modiste,* and so on. Had Victor Herbert had librettists as good as Sullivan's, Richard Rodgers' or Oskar Straus's, he would today live more securely in the history of music and might have been even more of an influence on opera itself.

ROBIN HOOD

Reginald De Koven (1861–1920) is famous primarily for his *Robin Hood,* a light and lilting opera about the noble gallant of Sherwood Forest in England. It was first given in 1890 in Chicago, with a book by Harry B. Smith. It toured for twenty years with the Bostonians, an enticing singing and acting company, which gave it one thousand performances. *Robin Hood* of old, always a gatherer of treasure, was a gold mine. It is a robust little opera, with songs such as "Nut Brown Maiden" and "Oh, Promise Me."

De Koven wrote two grand operas, *The Canterbury Pilgrims* (1917) and *Rip Van Winkle* (1920), neither of which was successful. This author of many songs and always tuneful music has had no influence on opera—even though his "Oh, Promise Me" seems to be an immortal song.

SHOW BOAT

One of the writers of popular song-hits was Jerome Kern (1885–1945) whose best-known musical comedy *Show Boat* won the praise from Cecil Michener Smith in his book *Musical Comedy in America* that; "No other American piece of its vintage [December 27, 1927] left so large a permanent musical legacy, and certainly no other surpassed it in quality." Kern wrote it on commission from F. Ziegfeld to Oscar Hammerstein's libretto on Edna Ferber's novel. It held the boards for years, and was made into movies more than once. "Ol' Man River" has become a classic. Kern wrote many other musical comedies, or operettas, among them: *Very Good Eddie, The Cat and the Fiddle,* and *Roberta.*

FRIML AND ROMBERG

Following in the footsteps of the Viennese operetta school of Franz Lehar, Leo Fall and Oskar Straus, were two Austrian-Americans, Rudolf Friml (1884?), and Sigmund Romberg (1887–1951).

Lehar's *The Merry Widow* (1905) aroused interest throughout this country in the early part of the twentieth century. A close rival was Oskar Straus's *A Waltz Dream* (1907). It might interest opera "fans" that a famous figure in the history of the Metropolitan, Edward Johnson, made his American debut in this Viennese operetta. The young Canadian tenor Johnson made an enviable career, especially in such operas as *L'Amore dei tre re,* in which he made his first Metropolitan appearance, November 16, 1922, *Pelléas et Mélisande, Peter Ibbetson,* and many others in which he sang major roles. He followed his career as a singer with that of General Manager of the Metropolitan Opera Company.

After this important detour, we come back to Oskar Straus and his next success, *The Chocolate Soldier* (1908), based on George Bernard Shaw's *Arms and the Man.* Straus came to America as a refugee and died here in 1952.

Leo Fall (1873–1925) as conductor of grand opera in Vienna, was best-known for *The Dollar Princess* (1907).

Rudolf Friml, concert pianist, who came to this country as accompanist to Jan Kubelik, violinist, turned to musical comedy with much success. His first score was *The Firefly.* Friml worked with Otto Harbach as his librettist in a series of comic operas that included *Katinka, The Vagabond King* and *Rose Marie.*

Sigmund Romberg, of Hungarian birth and American citizenship, dropped his profession as an engineer after he came to this country and began writing popular music. He wrote seventy or more musical revues and operettas. In *Blossom Time* the popular waltz was based on a theme from Schubert's *Unfinished Symphony.* Among his best-known works are *The Student Prince, The Desert Song,* and *Maytime.*

VINCENT YOUMANS

Vincent Youmans (1898–1946) is another writer of musical comedy who made his mark with *No, No, Nanette,* from which comes one of the most popular of popular songs, "Tea for Two." He also wrote *Hit the Deck, Bambolina, Wildflower,* etc. His career was cut off early by illness.

GERSHWIN'S MUSICAL-COMEDY CAREER

Of all the American composers who have held the public interest, George Gershwin (1898–1937) comes first. A Gershwin program assures "standing room only" at the Stadium Concerts in New York City, at Carnegie Hall or anywhere else. His folk opera *Porgy and Bess* was revived with acclaim in America and made an almost hysterical success in Europe (1954–55). He is far-famed for his "Rhapsody in Blue," which he played with Paul Whiteman in the memorable concert of "Classical Jazz" in old Aeolian Hall, on February 12, 1924. Instead of being trained as a "highbrow" musician as were Victor Herbert and Rudolf Friml, he did it the other way around. He started as a "song-plugger" in Tin Pan Alley, and made a popular success in the musical-comedy field with *Lady, Be Good, Strike Up the Band, Funny Face, Girl Crazy,* and many others.

For the first time a Pulitzer Prize was awarded to a musical play, *Of Thee I Sing,* by George S. Kaufman and Morrie Ryskind with lyrics by Ira Gershwin. It was set to music by George Gershwin. For the first time politics had figured in an American musical comedy. It was in 1931, two years after the depression, and the authors discussed serious conditions through the medium of a satirical but fun-poking plot. Book, lyrics and music were well mated. Cecil Smith says that "In its loud and raw way, 'Of Thee I Sing' was a genuine music drama." Except for a less successful work, this was his last musical comedy. Gershwin had turned his face *Porgy-and-Bess*wards.

IRVING BERLIN DIPS INTO POLITICS

In spite of his "Alexander's Ragtime Band," one of the first songs that brought Irving Berlin fame, he was not a composer of jazz but of sentimental songs—hundreds of them. Of Russian birth (1888) he was brought to America as a baby. With Moss Hart, Berlin wrote *Face the Music,* a satire on conditions in the police force. Next came a revue, *As Thousands Cheer,* which received greater acclaim than any other satire in its class except Arthur Schwartz's *The Band Wagon.*

The two world wars brought scores from Berlin's pen: *Yip, Yip, Yaphank* which included "Oh! How I Hate to Get Up in the Morning," written when he was a private at Camp Upton; and in World War II the revue *This Is the Army* produced and sung by soldiers. "God Bless America" was brought out of his "rag bag" and sung by Kate Smith just before World War II. John Tasker Howard says it became almost an unofficial national anthem.

COLE PORTER

Another musician trained for "highbrow stuff" was Cole Porter (1892–) from Indiana, who studied in Paris at the Schola Cantorum, although he began writing light opera when he was only eighteen. As he developed he wrote his own lyrics too. His best-known song, "Begin the Beguine," comes from *Jubilee,* which Porter wrote with Moss Hart. Several Broadway successes preceded his greatest hit, *Kiss Me, Kate,* for which Bella and Samuel Spewack wrote the book, a play (Shakespeare's *The Taming of the Shrew*) within a play.

FOR THE PEOPLE

Kurt Weill, born in Germany (1900), uprooted there, during Hitlerdom, later going to France and still later becoming an American citizen, died at the age of fifty (1950). In all three "fatherlands," he studied the likes, dislikes and "like-to-likes" of the people. A pupil of the progressive Busoni and the able Humperdinck, he branched out for himself in making opera refreshingly appealing in twentieth-century fashion and was able to please both "the people" and the pedants.

When Weill came to America in 1933, he started out consciously to create a new and modern kind of music play, using modern harmonies, startling dissonances, jazz melodies and rhythms. In Europe and in America, he studied classical and popular fancies. He studied our folk song and jazz; he studied our habits and peculiarities as well as our needs. He succeeded vastly and died far too soon. Nevertheless, his seventeen years in America made an imprint, for with Menotti and Blitzstein, he gave America a new feeling for theater and opera music from which countless may profit.

In Europe, Weill's *Dreigroschenoper* (*Three-Penny Opera*), in 1928, had been very successful. It was given two thousand times and was based on the plan of *The Beggar's Opera.* He gave one operetta the unusual name, *A Kingdom for a Cow!* Including the audience in the structure was a stunt he used in one opera. His last, *Down in the Valley,* an American chamber opera, based on the familiar folk song, is given repeatedly all over the U.S.A. It is exciting and melodious. It is singable by amateurs.

Weill wrote an interesting folk play score (1949) in the operetta *Lost in the Stars,* given in New York with success. The words were by Maxwell Anderson, based on the poetic prose tragedy *Cry, the Beloved Country,* by Alan Paton. It would have taken a greater man than Weill to approach, however, the superb poetic quality of the book.

AMERICAN TRENDS IN AMERICAN PLAYS

Weill's score for *Street Scene,* a play by Elmer Rice, unbelievably glorified the play and made it more powerful. He wrote excellently for films. And his incidental music to Paul Green's *Johnny Johnson* and to *Lady in the Dark* added to his stature.

Opera with the new American brands now becomes the voice of the people as well as entertainment. Song is again reinstated as a medium of expression. The voice becomes another instrument with the orchestra, whether in a song, ballet or just *vocalise.* America is forging a new kind of dramma per musica—call it what you like. Gershwin made a beginning; Gruenberg, Blitzstein, Menotti and Weill went on with the march of opera in America, as Britten is doing in England.

THE NEW MUSICAL PLAY

Among the many new lighter kind of opera or musical plays, which show the American skills in story and music, that have affected the future of drama with music are the works of Richard Rodgers and Oscar Hammerstein II. If ever there were well-matched composer and lyric writer, it is here. Gilbert and Sullivan were fortunate to have had each other, and so has been Rodgers with Hammerstein, and before Hammerstein, Lorenz Hart.

These new forms of singing or lyric drama have their story and their music. The play's action is fitted to music and lyrics; and scenery and ballet are stripped of expected and traditional treatment, tricks, and old formalities. Instead, they have most singable and enchanting music with constant movement of story. So is born a new form of operetta which is neither musical comedy nor comic opera. It has none of the old-fashioned ensembles and artificial things which had grown up through the ages. It is not in the least like grand opera or opéra comique, for it has none of their pomp, serious or tragic librettos, massiveness, or orchestral continuity. It is elaborate, but often it doesn't seem so.

Oklahoma! is simple, sun-drenched. *Carousel,* based on Ferenc Molnar's *Liliom,* is direct and moving, with ballet so poignant that it can never be forgotten. "This is a new form, romantic, fresh, vigorous, rhythmic, enthralling in its music and lyrics" (*Music Through the Ages*). *Allegro,* with its ballets, many scenes and motion picture film, light and sound innovations, is too elaborate and elongated. These musical plays are intensely, innovatingly, youthfully American. Agnes de Mille, as choreographer, had her real opportunity to show unique genius in the ballets of these three works.

Richard Rodgers (1902-), when teamed with Lorenz Hart, wrote *A Connecticut Yankee* and other musical comedies in somewhat the old way. Before *Oklahoma!,* their "shows" were along usual lines.

From *Oklahoma!* every song and lyric is worth listening to, but there isn't space, so let's be satisfied with "Oh, What a Beautiful Mornin'," "The Surrey with the Fringe on Top," "People Will Say We're in Love."

Allegro seems to take a more serious view of lyric drama and points a moral, that only worthwhile things are worthwhile! Yet the work, complicated, inventive in scene and action as it is, has a gray tinge, while their *South Pacific* (1949) glows again. It took the Pulitzer prize in 1950. This illustrated the usual skill in translating an atmosphere, to an audience, of a region that wasn't even known to the makers of the opera. It has enchanted and captivated everyone—musically, vocally and scenically. Some of its hits are "I'm Gonna Wash That Man Right Outa My Hair," sung by Mary Martin; "Some Enchanted Evening," sung by Ezio Pinza; and "Bali Ha'i" sung by Juanita Hall. Rodgers and Hammerstein had the courage to give a basso, not a tenor, the role of hero, and one "on in years" as well!

THE KING AND I

This is a musical play based on the novel *Anna and the King of Siam* by Margaret Dorothea Landon (John Day). Although for its success it did not need a fascinating actress, it had, to the glory of the composer and lyric writer and the public, the entrancing Gertrude Lawrence for the first few months until her untimely death. Yul Brynner was the King of Siam. The play made the audience feel that they were in Siam although no tinkling bells or other Siamese instruments were used to carry out the picture. Somehow this story of frustrated love between the Anglo-Saxon governess and the Eastern king was told in music, beautiful color and restrained scenery in a way to make the audience feel it was actually Siamese. When the composer and librettist were asked whether they had ever been in Siam they replied in their own cogent words that they'd never seen Oklahoma when they wrote the play, nor was it necessary for Puccini to be a Japanese in order to write *Madame Butterfly*. So they turned out "Broadway music" from which alluring songs are still ringing in our ears.

Here was a musical play dealing with Freedom versus Tyranny ending in a death, and unrequited love, which was probably one of the great successes of Broadway. The fact that Oscar Hammerstein is a poet and not a mere hack and is teamed up with a composer of Rodgers' caliber accounts for this incredible feat.

That *The King and I* raised the standard of this type of lyric drama, even above their own superlative output, is undebatable.

ME AND JULIET

Although a very ungrammatic title this entertaining manufacture by these two accomplished writers is their first work that they called a musical comedy. When asked why they abandoned the musical play and adopted musical comedy Rodgers said that they wanted a "change of pace." That's what they accomplished. In this musical confection they wrote a delicious piece about life backstage, a joy to the audiences, but a bane to the critics. The critics were not too good to this when the comedy appeared but it ran on Broadway for more than a year. The fact is that critics are surfeited with the theater and know its secrets and do not find it too entertaining any more, while the audience unaccustomed to theater is thrilled to be taken behind the scenes, even, as in this play, to the electricians' bridge backstage! It is interesting to realize that just a change of pace (swifter) constitutes a change from a musical play to a musical comedy.

Among the other fascinating work of Richard Rodgers is *State Fair*. "Clang, Clang, Clang Goes the Trolley," and "It Might As Well Be Spring," are two of its unforgettable songs.

LEONARD BERNSTEIN, THE VERSATILE

Leonard Bernstein has written two musical comedies: *On the Town,* and *Wonderful Town!* The first opened in 1944 in Boston. The book and lyrics are by Betty Comden and Adolph Green with additional lyrics by Bernstein. It had a two-year run in New York City. The second musical comedy was based on the Joseph Fields–Jerome Chodorov comedy *My Sister Eileen,* from the Ruth McKenny stories. The book is by Messrs. Fields and Chodorov; lyrics are by Betty Comden and Adolph Green.

Bernstein's only opera to date is *Trouble in Tahiti,* which runs for scarcely an hour. It shows his genius for character probing, is graceful and in good taste. This is what the *New York Times* said after its first New York City performance April 19, 1955: "Mr. Bernstein's miniature opera looks under the immaculate surface of life in the suburbs. To set the popular cultural standard, he begins with some radio crooning that expresses banal advertising slogans about happiness, health and success. The main sequences of the opera, however, make a serious attempt to explore the minds of a young husband and a young wife whose lives have become empty. In the space of a half hour, Mr. Bernstein cannot exhaust the subject. But musically, as well as intellectually, *Trouble in Tahiti* is a sober, thoughtful look into life that is sleek only on the surface."

Trouble in Tahiti, written for small orchestra, was given its first performance at the Creative Arts Festival at Brandeis University (Waltham, Massachusetts), June 12, 1952. It has had dozens of performances across the continent and in New York City, as well. Its first professional production by David Brooks was received with critical "raves" from every New York newspaper. There are but three "acting characters." Its simplicity of structure and delightful music was the chief cause for its widespread popularity even before it reached Broadway. At the opening the excellent actress Maureen Stapleton played the "sloppy-witted" suburban wife, Flora Meighan, revealing her as a tragic being to superb effect.

Musically Bernstein is a realist with a genius for tempering the harsh winds of modernity to the precise demands of his characters and plot. He can turn a lovely air with just enough "new thought" to make it palatable to both so-called modernists and traditionalists. He can thunder, too, as he heightened the terrors in the cinema *On the Waterfront* which won eight awards known as "Oscars" from the motion picture arts association.

SCENE III

American Innovators

AMERICA has developed a new category of opera, which is neither seria nor buffa. These works are better adapted to small theaters than to grand-opera houses, and are the product of the American ability to treat serious subjects with a light touch, as for example, *The King and I* and *Porgy and Bess*. They are more important than comic opera or operetta and happily are less hampered by tradition than so-called grand opera. To this end a movement towards the establishment of a lyric theater in America has given impetus consciously or unconsciously to many of the composers who appear in this scene.

No doubt if this category had been established earlier, many estimable works which did not meet with success would have found a niche.

GEORGE ANTHEIL

The opera *Transatlantique* of George Antheil, (1900–), given in Frankfurt, Germany, 1930, was hardly successful, except for showing a new trend in the writing of light opera. In this, he was brave enough to use jazz tunes and any kind of noise-maker in order that the opera should seem modern. Hot jazz dominates. It is crude but daring, but unfortunately did not have the qualities to make it a permanent part of the operatic repertory. The story wasn't very much, but it *was* up-to-date. It was about an oil magnate and a beautiful woman. Antheil used modern night clubs and ocean liners and Brooklyn Bridge instead of a baronial castle or a draw-bridge. He called it the first modern political opera. In it, he wanted to satirize the "wicked" capitalistic system. *Helen Retires,* on a libretto by John Erskine, produced at the Juilliard Opera School, and his other stage works were not specially important.

GEORGE GERSHWIN

What is considered to be an object lesson to composers, or would-be composers of opera, is George Gershwin's folk opera, *Porgy and Bess.* It has an excellent book by Dorothy and DuBose Heyward, on a story of the South (Catfish Row, Charleston, North Carolina). The music is of rare excellence. When presented in New York City, at the Alvin Theatre in 1935, it had an all-Negro cast of highest caliber with Todd Duncan and Anne Brown in the title roles. When the opera toured Europe on a "good will" journey, it opened with William Warfield and Leontyne Price as Porgy and Bess.

For a light opera, its continuity is exceptional, and presages new developments in which folk and art elements are blended. The music is tangy, sentimental, vigorous, melodious, Negroid without being overdone. No one has as yet followed Gershwin, but he certainly has given other men courage to tell stories in new kinds of musical set-ups.

Born in Brooklyn in 1898, Gershwin died in Hollywood in 1937, ever to be missed, for he might have gone on with a new kind of grand opera, frothy, "blue"-ish, American and solid—four difficult ingredients.

AARON COPLAND

Aaron Copland (1900–), known best for his "Music for the Theatre" and his instrumental "El Salon Mexico," has written with skill for the theater in ballet, film music, and play. A theater piece, *The Second Hurricane,* in two acts with Edwin Denby's libretto, was written with rare insight for young people. It was given at the Neighborhood Playhouse in New York City in 1937, directed by Orson Welles and Lehman Engel. This was long enough for a whole evening but not verbose or *note-ose!* Like most of his work, it is sensitive, resourceful twentieth-century, with excellent choral and orchestral writing.

After eighteen years Copland wrote another opera. Although very successful with ballet, this opera, *The Tender Land,* did not prove to be a success with critics and was given only twice at the New York City Center Theatre in New York City.

In a revised version *The Tender Land* was given at Tanglewood in the Berkshires. The play was better suited to the smaller house and it should be welcomed throughout this country by the "little opera" companies.

The opera was inspired by a picture the composer saw which touched him deeply. Though endowed with the ever fresh and delightful music of Copland, it didn't have the dramatic quality needed and so often lacking in American opera. The libretto was written by Horace Everett, an alias for the name of an artist who didn't want his professional name known. *The Tender Land* through the generosity of Rodgers and Hammerstein was commissioned by the League of Composers, which with the rest of Aaron Copland's compatriots should be proud of an excellently composed operatic score.

His rhythmic power is always in evidence and no better than in his ballets, *Billy the Kid* (1938), *Rodeo* (1942), the engaging *Appalachian Spring* (1943-44), and others. Pure Americana!

Copland's music always has distinction. In 1950 he received a second "Oscar" for the best film music of the year 1949, written for the excellent motion picture *The Heiress,* based on Henry James's *Washington Square.*

DOUGLAS MOORE

Among other American operas is *The Devil and Daniel Webster* by Douglas Moore (1893-), with a text of quality by Stephen Vincent Benét. It opened the Brander Matthews opera productions at Columbia University Opera Workshop (1939). Dr. Moore also wrote *Giants in the Earth,* in three acts, given, too, at Columbia's Brander Matthews Theatre under the same aegis March 28, 1951. The libretto was written by Arnold Sundgaard on the story of the same name by O. E. Rolvaag. It tells of the hardships met in the 1870's by the Norwegian immigrants to the Dakota territory. The librettist did not do as good a job as the composer. The music has a lyric and dramatic line and heightens the picturesque and tragic quality of the story. *Giants in the Earth* won a Pulitzer award.

A SENSITIZED MODERN INNOVATOR

It is only natural that Americans should be innovators, even in so well established a medium as opera. Louis Gruenberg and George Antheil, up to this point, had the courage to depart from prevailing styles and make their own. Now comes Virgil Thomson, born in 1896. His skill lies in writing suggestive, delicate, limpid, American-flavored twentieth-century music.

Here we are concerned with opera. In his *Four Saints in Three Acts* (stage première in 1934) with libretto by Gertrude Stein, he mated her unusual words to unusual music and gave them meanings no one but she or one blessed with the powers of divination can understand. All the characters were beautifully voiced Negroes in translucent plastic garments, who sang, sometimes in chantlike dialogue, or continuous music, with occasional definite breaks in song-speech—"Pigeons on the Grass, Alas." Could it have been a parody of Handel and older cantatas? Although no one knew what any of it meant, it still stays with those of us who saw and heard it. If this isn't a phenomenon, *we* don't know what is! The music is continuous, even though it is punctuated by group singing of unusual beauty. This seems to prove that it is the music and not the story that carries opera.

Thomson's most recent opera is *The Mother of Us All,* also written with Gertrude Stein. Here is another proof of how twentieth-century music, used with discretion and good sense, can make an opera "go" despite its vast improbabilities, other things, such as action, being taken into consideration. This story uses actual characters past and contemporary with the heroine, like Susan Anthony of bygone years, linked with characters who lived after her day, as well as those in her own. They, being of all centuries and for all centuries, make it a most amusing and enticing thing. The music is tender, warm, lilting, with a fine use of American folk tunes, Thomson's bent, and of course is composed with his usual sensitivity and skill. These operas, with books by the amazing Gertrude Stein, say things that are not only Stein-ish, but Alice in Wonderland-ish. But they turn out to be "important—unimportant—important—" one really can't tell. Let them penetrate the mind and heart—unforgettable and poignant. Watch for Thomson's music in revivals of the films, *The Plough That Broke the Plains, The River,* and *Louisiana Story.* In these you will hear his excellent use of old, original and never stilted music. He is the composer of the ballet *Filling Station* and others.

Virgil Thomson's music always seems simple and transparent, yet it is twentieth-century with delicacy and without the hauled-in clangor, fuss or self-consciousness of many modern composers. He was music critic for the New York *Herald Tribune* from 1940 until 1954.

ANOTHER AMERICAN INNOVATOR—BLITZSTEIN

A new kind of American singing-acting operetta seems to be developing to form a new kind of music drama, as heard in the works of Marc Blitzstein (1905–), who was called America's *"enfant terrible,"* before he wrote *Regina.* Aaron Copland says "he has invented something of a cross between social drama, music revue and opera." His operettas, *The Cradle Will Rock* (1937), and *No for an Answer* (1941), are so old, in their way, that they are new. The singing-speech is almost as old as the beginning of opera in the seventeenth century, or maybe even in the festivals in ancient Greece. The speech is expressive of the idea of the characters. When it is not, their speech becomes more important or more amusing, because of the contrast between the idea and the music. In Blitzstein's operas or singing plays, the actors are not trained singers, or singer-actors, but actor-singers. Their speech follows along with the melody, which is simple, with a rather complicated accompaniment. *The Cradle Will Rock* has polished jazz songs, spoken dialogue and recitative, the tools of opera. It also proved to have "social significance," and Blitzstein has the genius to make it exciting and interesting. His *No for an Answer* is based on popular songs, chorales, and is a bit more operatic in feeling than *The Cradle Will Rock*.

During the Second World War, Blitzstein was a private in the Eighth Air Force. He worked on radio and films when stationed in London. His cantata *Airborne* (1948) is a moving musical experience as well as a social commentary. Blitzstein's radio opera *I've Got the Tune,* is a bitter anti-Nazi drama.

The Cradle Will Rock was intended for Orson Welles' Mercury Theatre in New York, but its leftist ideas caused trouble with the unions and its first appearance was given under strange conditions. The actors wore their street clothes, there was no scenery, and instead of being on the stage, they were in the audience. The composer sat at an upright piano from which he gave a resumé of the doings in the play, as well as playing the musical accompaniment.

Blitzstein, owing to his social viewpoint, writes his own dramas with punch and poignancy. Probably the reason why most operas do not "act" is because the composers are not fired by their material and their material is not of their own time.

Marc Blitzstein, pioneering, unassuming and able, may make a mark on opera. Who knows?

The last drama with music of Blitzstein's, *Regina,* in the opinion of these writers, is the best thing that has been done in story with music by an American. He has written his own book as well as the music and based it on Lillian Hellman's acrid and brilliant story of greed, *The Little Foxes.* The musical drama far outweighs the play in power and tragedy. The lines are spoken or sung, making practically a continued musical background, and the music and declamation hark back and forward as he uses all the ancient and new "bests."

There is good dancing, but not of the ballet type. Like Mozart, he has a band of his own on the stage, the "Angel Band." The piece is staged stylistically enough to give it a tang.

If there was ever a more tragic song than that which Birdie sings about her former home, Lionnet, we haven't heard it. Its indigo pales the "blues." He has made the characters live in astringent or mouth-puckering music and has written for the pathetic and raucous equally well. *Regina* has two acts of excitement, pep, pathos and beautiful music, song and dance and jazz band. This seems to presage a bright future for American opera—an opera which depicts character, manners and psychological relationships, as well as giving entertainment. Why it failed to remain on the boards more than a few weeks in New York City is beyond explanation. Some say it was because it had been called "opera" and not a "show"!

OPERA IN MANY VEINS

Gian-Carlo Menotti (1911–) is an Italian with a hardy sense of good theater. He was born in Italy, studied at the Curtis Institute of Music and lives in America. *Amelia Goes to the Ball* "went to bat" for him, for she led him into the Metropolitan Opera House in 1938, with a libretto of his own making. This is a delightful opera buffa. It straddles the continuous style with the old-fashioned spirit, dissonance, consonance, excitement, wit and speed. He was commissioned by the National Broadcasting Company to write a radio opera, and this he did, again to his own libretto, in another amusing opera buffa, *The Old Maid and the Thief* (1939). His *Island God* was given at the Metropolitan Opera House in 1942—without too much success. Another in comic vein, *The Telephone* (1948) a one-act operetta, is of lightest texture, swift, and amusing.

The Medium (1948) is a tragic, dour, fantastic, gripping drama, setting forth in music, with an excellent libretto which Menotti wrote himself, the power of a spiritualistic medium who fools herself as well as her clients. It embraces a superb sense of the macabre and mystic. It was carried into being magnificently by Marie Powers, probably one of the most forceful and splendid singing actresses of our stage. *The Medium* has had over 600 performances throughout America, not counting radio and television.

THE CONSUL—AND ANGUISH

Menotti's *The Consul* had its first season (1950) in New York City at the Ethel Barrymore Theatre. Whether it is called a play with music or music with a play or some kind of opera, makes little difference. It strikes with tremendous power and seems to illustrate, for all time, the undivorceable marriage of text and music. Neither text nor music could stand alone. His libretto fulfills and gives the tragic story and the music aids it. It is a grim account of grim times in a grim flat somewhere behind the "Iron Curtain." A drab little family —a dreary about-to-die baby, grandmother, mother and father—are a group hounded by the secret police. The husband has to flee. The wife, Magda, attempts to get succor from the Consul. Day after day she, with others, attempt to see him. Never does she get beyond the harassed secretary. The scenes in the Consul's antechamber are heartbreaking and one of two or three songs that may be called arias was sung here by a remarkable singing actress, Patricia Neway, "Papers, Papers, Papers," which have to be filled out, over and over and over again to no avail. In the first act, the grandmother acts as well as sings a lullaby to the dreary baby, to make it smile and rest. So poignantly does she sing that the scene is unforgettable. The drama ends in frustration and suicide—the entrée and dessert of too many European postwar families.

The music is in the twentieth-century vein, with occasional reminiscence of the more melodic writers of the nineteenth century—unforgettable, yet unhumable.

Menotti has reverted to repetition, the bugbear of Wagnerites and post-Wagner composers. But—repetition is to italicize in the songs, not just to fulfill rhythm or prolong a song. Over and over again, Magda sings, "I must see the Consul." Over and over again, the Secretary says, "Sign on the dotted line"—"The Consul is too busy"— until the people of the audience suffer exhaustion and frustration along with Magda and applaud as an outlet during Act Two to relieve themselves from emotional strain. It is a tremendous accomplishment in drabness and anguish with but a few moments of comic relief. Menotti uses the macabre, visions, hallucinations, to help the plot.

THE SAINT OF BLEECKER STREET

"Mr. Menotti", said Brooks Atkinson in the *New York Times* for December 28, 1955, the day after the opening of *The Saint of Bleecker*

Street, "has provided us with a magnificent theatrical experience. *The Saint of Bleecker Street* is the most powerful drama of the season." That from the drama critic of the *New York Times* about an opera, quite out of his realm, save for its intense theater elements! "It is a modern *Verismo* opera" says Olin Downes, music critic of the *Times,* "with a dash of modern psychology to it, with a technique of the musical theater of which Mr. Menotti is the unique master."

This opera, the form of which is his own, cut out by the drive of the characters themselves, as were *The Consul* and *The Medium,* shows vividly Mr. Menotti's genius in being able, not only to appreciate the troubles of today, but also to "operatize" them, giving them drama and drive, beauty or ugliness as the theme demands.

The story of *The Saint of Bleecker Street* is one of Italian America in the Bleecker Street section of New York City. It is an amazing handling of morality, the Roman Catholic ritual and incestuous implication—a tremendously dramatic opportunity which Menotti has expertly seized. There is an occasional bit of wit of no high order, and sometimes an intrusion, but there is always color and drive. "The choral writing in the final scene is very skillful," says Olin Downes. The story is not great literature nor winged English; what there is of plot, as Atkinson said, is "trivial"; but the genius of Menotti is not the story, but that the story *acts.*

The presentation of the opera was first-class. The music suited the incidents as they unrolled. The singing of principals and Italian-American choruses couldn't have been much better.

Menotti may have been upbraided for remembering Puccini, Wagner and others too accurately. But how well he employs them! How well he succeeds! And how much of his own he has added!

Lincoln Kirstein supervised the production; the librettist and stage manager was Gian-Carlo Menotti. The cast of singers was excellently chosen. Virginia Copeland's Annina, the Saint, was tense and intense; David Poleri was Michele, the brother of the Saint; Desideria was sung by Gloria Lane, and others of fitting caliber completed the cast.

"The second act," says Olin Downes is "by far the strongest, and the one in which Menotti writes with the most brilliant versatility and the most convincingly warm and sensuous feeling. The opening of this act, with the wedding festival, the photographer's flashlight that sets the scene going, the dance to the juke box, and the attendant antics, is in itself an inspiration. One of the happiest ideas of this act is the three wedding songs in the Neapolitan manner, sung by as many of the wedding guests, in Italian. Each of these joyous, florid songs is a variant of the first and they have delightful color, humor and feeling. The solo of Desideria is one of the two numbers, magnificently sung by Gloria Lane, with her rich and sensuous voice, which held up the show. The other was the big aria by Michele in which Mr. Poleri was as dramatic in diction as he was in song. They were minutes applauding him." (The *New York Times,* December 28, 1955.)

This opera is an intriguing one and ran for four months or more.

Take any nine or ten operas of America and study them in juxtaposition to one of the Menotti operas and it will be readily seen what the usual American opera (grand opera or approaching–grand opera) lacks . . . actability and inevitability of plot. Aaron Copland, indeed, was aware of this. For this reason, not able to get the libretto he wanted, he held off from opera writing for eighteen years!

A CHRISTMAS OPERA

Amahl and the Night Visitors is like a Christmas card come to life, set to music, with the wonder, pathos, color and quality of Heavenly grace, hope and blessing. It was one of the operas commissioned for television by the National Broadcasting Company, which if it has done nothing else deserves its place in the sun for inspiring this lovely work —somewhat in the key of Massenet's *Jongleur de Notre Dame* in its religious fervor.

SCENE IV

Opera Moves Across the Continent

WHILE WE have not been an opera-writing nation and have not been in competition with Italy, France, Germany and other European countries, and although we have had but one (sometimes two or three) principal opera houses devoted to European opera, we have been developing our own kinds of opera outside of the traditional paths.

There are, however, and always have been some centers in the United States for the incubation of opera such as: New Orleans, which from earliest music history in America has had its own opera house; San Francisco, with many experiments and successes and from time to time good working opera companies; New York, with its Metropolitan Opera and many more or less important professional and semi-professional groups; Boston, always in the cultural belt with its past opera company and reception of visiting troupes, particularly its pioneering New England Conservatory of Music; Tanglewood in relation to the Berkshire Music Festival; in Ohio the opera at Cincinnati Zoo with its traditional repertory which has stimulated the love of this form of music and its very active Music Drama Guild, to say nothing of its excellent Karamu in Cleveland. (See below for further discussion.) Chicago also has been an active center with a splendid opera house, and it continues to stimulate musical movements with its excellent facilities; in addition, Philadelphia has been an active member of opera-giving centers with an opera house which has seen many noble productions.

We set below, to confound those who say that America takes little interest in opera, that there were:

> 1,250 performances of opera given across the nation from October 1953 to October 1954, in
> 45 states, by
> 444 companies;
> 70 companies gave performances in the original tongue,

374 in English, particularly contemporaneous opera;
⅔ of the 1,250 performances were in English,
⅓ in the original tongue;
⅓ of all the performances across the continent were given by four New York Opera companies: the Metropolitan, City Center, Amato and Puma (according to Frank Merkling, one of the editors of the excelling Metropolitan Opera Guild's *Opera News,* writing in the February, 1955 number of *Musical America*).

The following states have opera companies or producing centers (from one to thirty-three): Alabama, Arizona, Arkansas, California, Colorado, Connecticut, Delaware, District of Columbia, Florida, Illinois, Indiana, Iowa, Kansas, Kentucky, Louisiana, Maine, Maryland, Massachusetts, Michigan, Minnesota, Mississippi, Missouri, Montana, Nebraska, New Jersey, New Mexico, New York.

A pioneering company has been Fortune Gallo's La Scala that for years has made transcontinental tours, bringing opera to new audiences and being a training school for young artists.

Each time a good performance is witnessed anywhere, the seeds are sown for the possible flowering of new local companies. Of the 1,250 performances in towns, cities, villages and hamlets, 262 were given in educational institutions such as: universities, schools, conservatories, colleges and school camps. The rest were given in churches, museums, hospitals, clubs, in groups of all kinds, town halls, festivals, carnivals, meetings of lodges, unions, and settlements.

The above data proves that interest in opera has never been greater in America and by the fact that from the season 1953 to 1954 the number of performances of opera in the U. S. A. grew from 400 to 1,250. In the case of the season 1952 to 1953 only one state of the U. S. A. was without operatic performance of its own. Indeed the wide swathe that opera, traditional and contemporaneous, is cutting across the country augurs hopefully for the composers in our land.

In *Opera News* for October 27, 1952 is recorded "In addition to the eighteen standard operas by Mozart, Verdi, Puccini, etc., Americans .... heard seventy-eight other works by composers of the past. Of these *Die Fledermaus* takes the lead with 253 performances by professional companies, 20 by educational institutions. *Carmen* follows with 158 performances tying with *La Traviata*." Schools and colleges prefer *Figaro*. (Quotations from *Opera News,* by permission of Metropolitan Opera Guild, Publisher.)

That there is an aroused interest across the continent for opera is beyond a doubt and that the Metropolitan Opera Saturday afternoon broadcasts have been a mighty stimulus is evident. Furthermore, from Radio Station WNYC in New York "Mr. and Mrs. Opera" with Ruby Mercer as the mistress of ceremonies and T. Cowan's "Velvet and Gold Opera House," both weekly programs, reach millions of listeners every year.

Among the many institutions giving opera, from one to thirty-two a year have been produced, ranging in type from Bach's *Coffee Cantata* in opera form to Stravinsky's *Mavra,* or *Parsifal,* and from Converse's *The Pipe of Desire* to Bernstein's *Trouble in Tahiti.*

Arnold Gamson has been specializing in revivals of early operas in concert form with the American Opera Company in New York City.

The United States is supplied with opera! All it needs, and it needs it badly, is well-established opera houses suitably equipped; repertory and adequate scenery to satisfy the workers, the local audience, the visitors, and to inspire the young musician to work in one or more of the operatic arts. Here is where America is behind the other countries: in the lack of a public or national subsidy or subsidies which will make the opera-producing company independent of box-office receipts. This is what all European cities small and large have, and what makes it possible for people to attend opera at prices lower than our moving pictures.

Apart from the standard operas, among the favorite contemporaneous and American productions throughout the land were *Amahl and the Night Visitors, The Telephone,* and *The Medium,* by Gian-Carlo Menotti; *Down in the Valley,* by Kurt Weill; *The Lowland Sea,* by Alex Wilder; *The Jumping Frog of Calaveras County,* by Lucas Foss; *The Devil and Daniel Webster,* by Douglas Moore.

Less popular but given very often were: *The Beggar's Opera,* by John Gay; *Let's Make an Opera,* by Benjamin Britten; *Riders to the Sea,* by Lord Dunsany; *Comedy of the Bridge,* by Bohuslav Martinu; and *Trouble in Tahiti* by Leonard Bernstein.

Among the hundreds of institutions delivering opera to the United States a few are pre-eminent.

The Juilliard School, New York City, has been giving old and new and even premières of traditional operas since 1931 or thereabouts. Among them: Louis Gruenberg's *Jack and the Beanstalk,* George Antheil's *Helen Retires;* Albert Stoessel's *Garick;* Beryl Rubinstein's *The Sleeping Princess;* Robert Russell Bennett's *Maria Malibran;*

Joseph Wood's *The Mother;* Randall Thompson's *Solomon and Balkis.* Besides this, Luigi Dallapiccola's *The Prisoner* (in English); the first showing in America of Richard Strauss's *Capriccio;* Mozart operas seldom if ever given, such as *Idomeneo,* and Handel's *Serses (Xerxes);* Darius Milhaud's arrangement of *Le jeu de Robin et Marion (The Play of Robin and Marion)* by Adam de la Hale (c.1240–88).

Columbia University Opera Workshop has pioneered with opera. Among the many new and old works given there have been: *The Devil and Daniel Webster,* and *Giants of the Earth* by Douglas Moore; Ernst Bacon's *The Tree on the Plain;* Bernard Wagenaar's *Pieces of Eight;* Norman Lockwood's *The Scarecrow;* Benjamin Britten's *Paul Bunyan;* Gian-Carlo Menotti's *The Medium; The Mother of Us All* by Virgil Thomson; Otto Luening's *Evangeline;* and Jan Meyrowitz's *The Barrier.*

Very active too has been The Chautauqua Opera Association, catering to audiences gathered from almost all corners of the world to hear the best in music. All the operas are in English, and from traditional sources with the exception of Albert Stoessel's *Garrick,* Douglas Moore's *The Devil and Daniel Webster,* Lucas Foss's *Jumping Frog of Calaveras County,* and *Amahl and the Night Visitors,* by Gian-Carlo Menotti.

The University of Indiana has been in the forefront of universities giving opera. Indeed, the town of Bloomington has become a vital opera center. It has the courage to give *Parsifal* annually with its own students and is interested in both contemporaneous and traditional opera.

Ohio is advanced and has long been giving opera at the Cincinnati Zoo. To be sure it is traditional opera. Cleveland is famous for the Lyric Theatre at Karamu House. It gave fifty performances of a new opera by Carl Orff, a hundred performances of Kurt Weill's *Lost in the Stars,* and many performances of Stravinsky's *L'Histoire du soldat (Story of a Soldier).* Local people, amateurs, appeared in these operas. One housewife who took part as Madame Flora in *The Medium* was brought to New York for the same part. It is a satisfaction to realize that this is an interracial theater, mainly manned and "womaned" by Negroes. The Karamu Quartet has performed well over the radio. The movement was started and maintained by Mrs. Rowena Woodham Jeliffe.

Ann Arbor, or the University of Michigan, and the Interlochen National Music Camp have brought up this state's opera average to high altitudes, while Massachusetts with opera at Tanglewood near Lenox, the New England Conservatory of Music in Boston, Harvard University, Brandeis University, and her many festivals and colleges help New England to a high score. Boris Goldovski, at the Conservatory of Music in Boston, had the courage to give for the first time in America a cut version of the over-long *Les Troyens* (*The Trojans*) of Hector Berlioz. Worcester, too, and many other New England towns are deep in their interest of opera, while Hartford, Connecticut, with its orchestra and general musical atmosphere has been for a long time opera-minded. The Julius Hartt Foundation there has encouraged opera. Hartford and other cities have many new productions to their credit: *The Bridge,* by B. Martinu; *Macbeth* by Verdi, *Dido and Aeneas* by Purcell, and old standbys as well. In 1934 it gave Virgil Thomson's *Four Saints in Three Acts* produced by the Society of Friends and Enemies of Modern Music.

South Carolina is well appreciated for its Lyric Opera Company under the guidance of the School of Music of Converse College in Spartanburg.

Colorado is distinguished for its Denver Opera Company and has received no little praise for its renovation of the Tivoli Opera House in the old boom town of Central City. Colorado is well on the path to many more performances.

In the very far west on the Pacific coast, Seattle with her University of Washington Opera Workshop has been in the vanguard of service.

The Eastman School in Rochester, New York, has stimulated the production of opera. The director, Howard Hanson, wrote *Merry Mount* which was given at The Metropolitan Opera House, and presented at Eastman in May, 1955.

Kentucky too is established on the list of opera performances. We happened to be in Lexington at the time of her annual opera season at the University of Kentucky, and heard a very interesting *Marriage of Figaro* in English.

The cultivation of children's taste for opera has been the aim of many groups, among them the New York Youth Opera Association. In April, 1955, it gave *The Magic Mirror,* on the well-known fairy tale *Snow White and the Seven Dwarfs* with libretto by Constance McKay and music by Wheeler Beckett, at the Mosque Theatre (capacity 3,000!) in Newark, New Jersey, another state which has been receptive to opera. A full orchestra was used as well as professional singers. Some years ago, at the Heckscher Theatre in New York, opera for children was regularly relayed delightfully.

A recent opera for children, *Babar,* by Nicolai Berezowsky (1900–1954) was introduced by Thomas Scherman and the Little Orchestra Society at Hunter College Auditorium, New York City. Scherman also presented, in concert form, the radio opera, *Archie and Mehitabel,* by George Kleinsinger, on a libretto drawn from the stories of the philosophical cockroach by Don Marquis. The composer is preparing the score for a full-length opera.

Julia Smith, a Texas-born composer living in New York, wrote two full-length operas, *Cynthia Parker* (1939) and *Stranger of Manzona* (1941), both of which have had two performances. She has also written two operas for children: *The Gooseherd and the Goblin* (1949) which has had twenty-five performances, and *Cockcrow Six Times* (1954).

The Henry Street Settlement gave the first performance of Aaron Copland's *The Second Hurricane* in 1947. The Greenwich House Music School give standard operas (*Faust,* etc.) and some American novelties.

In addition to the few centers of opera given above, such agencies as the following encourage opera:

1. The New York Federation of Music Clubs promotes the formation of "grass-roots" opera. These are groups after the model established by A. J. Fletcher in North Carolina, the North Carolina Grass-Roots Opera. Numerous organizations far from the route of traveling opera companies have begun to produce "grass-roots" opera which absorbs local talent, and is planned with skill, to meet the exigencies of slender purses and facilities.

2. A typical opera group encouraged by the National Federation of Music Clubs is the Community Opera, Inc., which gives productions in any institution summoning it. It is of value even to New York City, which is overstocked with singers. It has given a hundred performances, and eighteen different operas, both old and new, in its first two seasons. Gladys Mathew is the director.

3. Another venture taking in continental sweep has been the National Opera Association under the guidance of the National Music Council.

4. Invaluable assistance has been given to composers through organizations commissioning operas. Among them are: The former League of Composers (now merged with the International Society for

Contemporary Music [U. S. Section]); the Julius Hartt Foundation; The Juilliard School of Music; and others.

The spread of little-opera performances in schools, universities, colleges, churches, opera clubs, special foundations, women's clubs, men's clubs, choral clubs and other social associations will without a doubt encourage the writing of opera among the American people and finally develop a sense of good theater or a sense of what will act well, the handmaiden of the art of opera composition.

Among other New York City unique opera companies is the Lemonade—presenting operas in the crypt of a church!

ADDENDA

Opera has so sprung up all over the world, in the last ten years particularly, that in a book of these dimensions many cannot even be listed. Below, however, we are naming a few. All styles and combinations of styles are severally used in these operas.

The Veil (U.S.A.)	Bernard Rogers
The Triumph of Joan (U.S.A.)	Norman Dello Joio
Volpone (U.S.A.)	George Antheil
The Taming of the Shrew (U.S.A.)	Vittorio Giannini
The Marriage (Czech)	Bohuslav Martinu
Babar (U.S.A.)	Nicolai Berezowski
The Mighty Casey (U.S.A.)	William Schuman
Die Liebe Des Dänae (German)	Richard Strauss (posthumous)
The Trial (German)	Gottfried von Einem
Danton's Tod (German)	Gottfried von Einem
The Bridge of San Luis Rey (German)	Herman Reutter
A Dinner Engagement (British)	Lennox Berkeley
Nelson (British)	Lennox Berkeley
Pilgrim's Progress (British)	R. V. Williams
Trial of Lucullus (U.S.A.)	Roger Sessions
The Dybbuk (on a Hebrew story) (U.S.A.)	David Tamkin
Family of Taras (Soviet)	Dimitri Kabalevsky
Ivan Bolotnikov (Soviet)	Leonid Stepanov
From My Heart (Ukranian)	Herman Zhukowsky
Penelope (Swiss)	Rolf Lieberman

The Ruby (U.S.A.)	Norman Dello Joio
Troilus and Cressida (British)	William Walton
Six Characters in Search of an Author (U.S.A.)	Hugo Weisgall
Don't We All (U.S.A.)	Burrill Phillips
The Nightingale (U.S.A.)	Bernard Rogers
A Childhood Miracle (U.S.A.)	Ned Rorem
Transposed Heads (U.S.A.)	Peggy Granville–Hicks

NOTE: For the hundreds of other performances of opera in dozens of other cities of the United States, we, with pleasure, refer you to the outline in *Opera News* published by the Metropolitan Opera Guild at the end of each New York opera season.

SCENE V

Film and Television Opera

Two media have raised their heads and are now stretching their resources toward discovering the correct procedures for transmitting operatic performance. The directors of the cinema and television companies realize the definitely growing public for opera.

That the perfecting of these means of giving opera is going on apace cannot be gainsaid. Not only will it stimulate the people's love for music, but as these companies commission operas, composers will be in demand and receive compensation.

The composer who writes for the film story today usually either supplies the music as the film develops, or after the film is completed. It is music, usually, after the barn door is closed. This is not so with the composer of opera who has it all his own way, except for certain adjustments to the mechanical needs. The composer for the cinema cannot therefore be concerned with the inner drama of the plot, as much as with the outer; meeting footage of the film and time scheme, etc. The music is more commotional, therefore, than emotional. It heightens or lessens dramatic effect of action on the outside rather than being a part of the motivation of the character. Film music must intensify exterior action, create a certain amount of continuity, and do all this without showing through the story too much, unless it is an incidental song or march. In short, film music must be background music.

So far, some of the best composers have been writing excellent background music for the films: Georges Auric, Aaron Copland, Louis Gruenberg, Virgil Thomson, George Antheil, Kurt Weill, Eric Korngold, and Leonard Bernstein. A formidable lineup but, eminent as they are, they must follow the director's commands. The technique of writing for the film is difficult, often irritating.

On the other hand, the motion pictures have been instrumental in giving screen versions of old and new operas, not always too suc-

461

cessful, for they have taken liberties with the stories and injected, very often, new scenes which are disconcerting to those who know the originals. There are, however, some very good film versions, such as: *Aïda; The Beggar's Opera; Il Trovatore; The Elixir of Love; La Traviata; Manon Lescaut; Casta Diva (Norma)*; *The Barber of Seville; The Marriage of Figaro; Rigoletto; Pagliacci; Louise;* etc.

There have been numerous light operas, musical comedies, and musical plays transferred to film. *Interrupted Melody,* the life of Marjorie Lawrence, has just appeared in moving picture theaters. It consists of scenes from many operas in which Marjorie Lawrence performed. Many of the Metropolitan directors assisted in the filming.

Walt Disney first gave many persons an idea of the limitless resources of the cinema. His *Fantasia* was an object lesson in the use of music and screen drama.

Should the filming not become a perfect method for reproducing opera, it has given us the advantage of the "dubbing in" system. Now, on both screen and video, a fine actor who cannot sing can be used with the voice of a great singer "dubbed in" from behind the scenes. This offers exceptionally good acting in opera as well as great voices; an advantage indeed. This device, however, must be handled with the most microscopic care, to keep the illusion.

At first there were few directors who knew the techniques of opera, cinema, and television. Today these three classes of producers know enough to supplement themselves with the proper assistants.

Formerly the cinema producers would have atrocious close-ups making the opera oversensational and interrupting with pictorial emphasis which threw the story and music out of gear. As time goes on, these faults and others are being eradicated.

One of the problems of televised opera or screen plays is the mercilessness of the camera on the insincere actor. There has to be an end to the meaningless gesture and some of the pomposity of the lyric stage—not all the pomp, for pomp is cousin to glamour and glamour must be saved if opera isn't to lose its charm. Glamour is the rose spectacles through which the ineptitudes of the usual silly opera story is seen. Opera is a means of saying the impossible and making it believable. Therefore, the production of opera is a difficult job at best.

At the ordinary play or opera, the people seated near the stage are the only ones who have much idea of the artifice (grease-paint, etc.) of playacting, so those that can't afford seats near the stage are fortunate. In the cinema or video-opera, every detail is visible to millions.

Everyone has a front seat. "Familiarity breeds contempt" was said long before electronics was rampant. These millions now can make an actor, or break him by not tuning in on his performance, even if the only thing they find to criticize is the way he wears his necktie. Such things as this flare up to discourage the producers. Not only the singers, but the orchestra and conductors, formerly lodged in darkened orchestra pits, now come out in daylight and are subject to minute examination. The true light of the screen shows the conductor, back, front, sideways, angry, smiling, exuberant, or bored. The close-up, or the technician's delight, will make or break screened opera (cinema or video). A close-up of a player blowing the saxophone or French horn is silly enough. How do close-ups of kissing couples, screaming coloratura into the ears of the beloved, impress audiences in the "first row"?

All transmitted opera must leave certain areas to the imagination of the audience. It cannot hope to fill in all the gaps any more than traditional opera fills up its scenes with unnecessary close-ups and unnecessary details. The screen has been so marvelous technically that it is tempted to run away with its own great skills. For example, in the opera *Tosca* we learn in the scene during which Tosca murders Scarpia that a dance is being given in the ballroom below. This we know only by the music that rises toward the room when the window is opened. The contrast with the scene in which Tosca is acting is tremendous. Here there are no whirling ballroom couples shown to announce the ball, nor any other material device, save the music coming from the ballroom. This sort of thing is what the screen must learn—leave something to the imagination.

The screen has conquered many difficulties even though it has many still to conquer. Filmed plays have attracted the services of eminent composers who have written excellent background music. Among the many can be listed: *Our Town,* with music by Aaron Copland; *Louisiana Story* (Virgil Thomson), *A Fight for Life* (Louis Gruenberg), *Henry IV* (Sir William Walton), *On the Waterfront* (Leonard Bernstein), and countless others.

The film, as well as TV, is developing composers, librettists and directors who will give us opera of the future.

TELEVISION OPERA ADVANCING

From 1950, TV opera has become a reality with high hopes of its being a permanent and beautiful addition to life.

To this end, some of the broadcasting stations which have given tabloid or shortened editions of the operas can be thanked; but above all the National Broadcasting Company Opera Theatre deserves the palm. This company, jointly headed by Samuel Chotzinoff as producer and Peter Herman Adler as music and art director, and with David Sarnoff as inspirer and chairman of the board, have been giving complete operas, traditional and contemporaneous, in a most acceptable manner. They have dropped all the extra scenic excursions and give the opera at it was originally planned by the composer. Furthermore, they have commissioned new scores, a mighty stimulant to the composers. Among these commissioned works is Menotti's *Amahl and the Night Visitors*. Besides, N.B.C. gave the first performances in America of Benjamin Britten's *Billy Budd*, Leonard Bernstein's *Trouble in Tahiti*, the world première of Bohuslav Martinu's *The Marriage*, and Vittorio Giannini's *The Taming of the Shrew*. Among their interesting revivals, practically never seen in our theaters, have been Verdi's *Macbeth*; Tchaikovsky's *Pique Dame* (*The Queen of Spades*); Puccini's *The Cloak, Sister Angelica* and *Gianni Schicchi* (three one-act operas); and Offenbach's quite recondite *R.S.V.P.* Below we list the other operas given by the National Broadcasting Company to impress upon our readers the opportunities for hearing opera very well produced with a front seat and at no extra expense.

From 1950 to 1955 this is the list of operas given by the National Broadcasting Company alone, to say nothing of the tabloid operas by other well-intentioned opera producers on screen and video.

The Barber of Seville	— Rossini
Der Rosenkavalier (in two sessions)	— Strauss
Carmen	— Bizet
The Marriage of Figaro	— Mozart
Pelléas and Mélisande	— Debussy (Probably one of the loveliest performances ever given.)
Salome	— Strauss (Most comprehensive and delightful.)
The Abduction from the Seraglio (in color)	— Mozart
Tosca (in color)	— Puccini (Probably one of the finest performances of Tosca on any stage was given by Leontyne Price.)
The Saint of Bleecker Street	— Menotti (A shortened version.)

Griffelkin by Lucas Foss, commissioned by the N.B.C., is scheduled for 1955–1956.

As time goes on, other companies will find it imperative to give performances of opera, old and new, to satisfy the growing interest in the New World.

There are certain devices possible to use in the broadcasting of operas which can cover deficiencies and enhance beauties both in orchestral and vocal media. When used well these devices will increase opera interest; when used badly or even poorly they will do much to lessen opera interest.

CURTAIN

The Magic Circle

IN THE beginning, American music was imported. If it wasn't imported in music books, it was brought over from Europe by such men as Graupner. Recently, owing to wars and economic conditions in Europe, Asia, Africa and points north, east, south and west, foreign-born composers, who become excellent Americans, have been bringing us music, not to stifle ours, but to enrich it. So after nearly three hundred years, America, on a sure foundation of her own folk and popular music, is welcoming and absorbing again the best of alien contributions.

REPERTORY

Serious opera, in Europe's early centuries, was an occasional entertainment, a ceremonial to celebrate a particular event such as a coronation, a birthday, a marriage, or a saint's day. For many years it was the food of kings.

The language for opera was Italian, unless it were given in France. Opera was an industry in Italy until well into the twentieth century. A singer thought himself untrained unless he had studied in Italy or France.

Opera, as we have it now, started in the early part of the nineteenth century, when Napoleon was on the rampage in Europe. In the eighteenth century, an opera might be given in a few cities, but it was never taken up and regiven year after year—as was *Faust,* or *Carmen,* or others, in the nineteenth century. People then wanted new operas continually as we demand new movies and plays, with revivals few and far between. There were so many nineteenth-century operas (25,000 and mostly Italian!) that it was imperative not to "repeat." What a quiz question—"Name 1,000 operas written up to 1800" would be! But, when an opera in Europe in the eighteenth and nineteenth century made a hit, 40 or more consecutive performances were sometimes given! For example, Rossini's *Barber of Seville,* after it "caught on," received 47 performances. We also, fortunately, go on manu-facturing own own American idioms like new folk tunes, boogie-woogie, bebop and "suchlike," and influencing with this our own music and foreign composers. Kurt Weill, Korngold, Krenek, even Stravinsky, as well as many others, have drunk from the American fountain of folk song, jazz and near-jazz. So the circle is completed and joined. The New World holds a key to the stage of dramma per musica.

The future of opera in the New World is more promising than ever in its history. Nine million people listen to opera every week (Metropolitan Opera broadcast) in America! Has any other country in the heyday of opera ever mustered such an audience?

Today, in America, we see a flashback to older times, for operas like Menotti's *The Consul,* and *The Saint of Bleecker Street* and Blitzstein's *Regina* were given runs in theaters (not opera houses) as if they were plays. We see too the flashback plainly in the uses and developments of ballet.

The small orchestra and the small cast are combining now to make possible the giving of opera more frequently and so remove the "scare" from the sound of the word "opera" among the people.

We have seen the composers, librettists, singers and instrumentalists play their parts. We have seen opera travel through bad eras and good ones. We have seen it improve and decline, develop new good or bad traits, fall into ruts and be pulled out by some genius. The road has proceeded from Ancient Greece, where everything started, down to America getting a foothold in opera seria. The outlook seems promis-ing but this book, dealing not in prophecy, must draw the

CURTAIN

BIBLIOGRAPHY

I

General Information on Operas and Opera Writers

Bauer, Marion, *Twentieth Century Music*. New York: G. P. Putnam's Sons, 1947.

Bauer, Marion, and Peyser, Ethel, *How Music Grew*. New York: G. P. Putnam's Sons, 1939.

—— *Music Through the Ages*. New York: G. P. Putnam's Sons, 1946.

Brockway, Wallace, and Weinstock, Herbert, *The Opera: A History of Its Creation and Performance, 1600–1941*. New York: Simon and Schuster, 1941.

Chase, Gilbert, *The Music of Spain*. New York: W. W. Norton & Co., Inc., 1941.

Chorley, Henry F., *Thirty Years' Musical Recollections*. New York: Alfred A. Knopf, Inc., 1926.

Dent, Edward J., *Foundations of English Opera*. New York: Cambridge University Press, 1928.

—— *Opera*. Baltimore: Penguin Books, Inc., 1940.

Einstein, Alfred, *Music in the Romantic Era*. New York: W. W. Norton & Co., Inc., 1947.

—— *A Short History of Music*. New York: Vintage Books, Inc., 1954.

Graf, Max, *Modern Music*. New York: Philosophical Library, 1946.

Hanslick, Eduard, *Vienna's Golden Years of Music*. New York: Simon and Schuster, Inc., 1950.

Heinsheimer, H. W., *Menagerie in F Sharp*. New York: Doubleday & Co., Inc., 1947.

Henderson, W. J., *Some Forerunners of Italian Opera*. New York: Henry Holt & Co., Inc., 1941.

Hoover, Kathleen O'Donnell, *Makers of Opera* (intro. Carleton Sprague Smith). New York: H. Bittner & Co., 1948.

Howard, John Tasker, *Our American Music*. New York: Thomas Y. Crowell Company, 1941.

Lang, Paul Henry, *Music in Western Civilization*. New York: W. W. Norton & Co., Inc., 1941.

Loewenberg, Alfred, *Annals of Opera, 1597–1940* (compiled from the original sources). Cambridge, England: W. Heffer & Sons, Ltd., 1943.

Pratt, Waldo Seldon, *The History of Music*. New York: Carl Schirmer, 1908.

Rolland, Romain, *Some Musicians of Former Days* (trans. Mary Blaiklock). New York: Henry Holt & Co., Inc., 1915.

Schoenberg, Arnold, *Style and Idea*. New York: Philosophical Library, 1950.

Schumann, Robert, *On Music and Musicians:* New York: Pantheon Books, 1946.

Slonimsky, Nicolas, *Music Since 1900: An Encyclopedic Survey of Modern Music, 1900–1948*. New York: Coleman-Ross Co., Inc., 1949.

Smith, Cecil, *Musical Comedy in America*. New York: Theatre Arts Books, 1950.

Strunk, Oliver (ed.), *Source Readings in Music History*. New York: W. W. Norton & Co., Inc., 1950.

Taubman, Howard H., *Opera Front and Back*. New York: Charles Scribner's Sons, 1938.

—— *How to Build a Record Library*. Garden City, N. Y.: Hanover House, 1953.

II

Information on Composers of Operas

Hipsher, Edward, *American Opera and Its Composers*. Philadelphia: Theodore Pressner Co., 1927.

Barzun, Jacques, *Berlioz and the Romantic Century*. Boston: Atlantic Monthly Press Book, Little, Brown & Co., 1950.

Peyser, Herbert F., *Hector Berlioz: A Romantic Tragedy*. New York: Philharmonic Symphony Society, 1949.

Memoirs of Hector Berlioz (trans. revised by Ernest Newman). New York: Tudor Publishing Co., 1935.

Berlioz, Hector, *Evenings in the Orchestra* (trans. C. E. Roche, intro. Ernest Newman). New York: Alfred A. Knopf, Inc., 1929.

Curtiss, Minna, *Bizet, Offenbach and Rossini. Musical Quarterly,* Vol. XL, No. 3, pages 350-359, 1954.

Goss, Madeleine B., *Bolero: A Life of Maurice Ravel*. New York: Henry Holt & Co., Inc., 1940.

White, Eric Walter, *Benjamin Britten: A Sketch of His Life and Works*. London: Boosey and Hawkes, 1954.

Benjamin Britten: A Commentary on His Works from a Group of Specialists (ed. Donald Mitchell and Hans Keller). New York: Philosophical Library, 1953.

Helm, Everett, *Contemporary Germans* (Egk, Orff, Blacher, Fortner, Hartmann, von Einem). New York: *Musical Quarterly,* Vol. XXXVI, No. 4, pages 600-602, 1950.

Dallopiccola, Luigi, *The Genesis of the Canti di Prigionia and Il Prigionero: An Autobiographical Fragment.* New York: *Musical Quarterly,* Vol. XXXIX, No. 3, pages 355-372, 1953.

Thompson, Oscar, *Debussy.* New York: Dodd, Mead & Co., 1937.

Einstein, Alfred, *Gluck.* New York: E. P. Dutton & Co., Inc., 1936.

Peyser, Herbert F., *George Frideric Handel.* New York: Philharmonic Symphony Society, 1951.

Peyser, Herbert F., *Joseph Haydn: Servant and Master.* New York: Philharmonic Symphony Society, 1950.

Curjel, Hans, "Rolf Liebermann." New York: *Musical Quarterly,* Vol. XXXIX, No. 2, pages 267-275, 1953.

Finck, Henry T., *Massenet and His Operas.* New York and London: John Lane, 1910.

Davenport, Marcia, *Mozart.* New York: Charles Scribner's Sons, 1932.

Dent, Edward J., *Mozart's Operas: A Critical Study.* New York: McBride, Nast, 1913.

Einstein, Alfred, *Mozart: His Character, His Works.* London, New York, Toronto: Oxford University Press, 1945.

Peyser, Herbert F., *Mozart and Some Masterpieces.* New York: Philharmonic Symphony Society, 1941.

Wörner, Karl H., *Carl Orff.* New York: *Musical Quarterly,* Vol. XXXIX, No. 3, pages 435-437, 1953.

Weissmann, John S., *Goffredo Petrassi.* New York: *Musical Quarterly,* Vol. XXXIX, No. 2, pages 260-267, 1953.

Fiorentino, Dante del, *Puccini, Immortal Bohemian: An Intimate Memoir of Giacomo.* New York: Prentice-Hall, 1952.

Dent, Edward J., *Allessandro Scarlatti, His Life and Works.* London: E. Arnold, 1905.

Jacob, H. E., *Strauss (Johann) Father and Son: A Century of Light Music* (trans. Marguerite Wolfe). New York: Greystone Press, 1940.

Peyser, Herbert F., *Richard Strauss.* New York: Philharmonic Symphony Society, 1952.

Richard Strauss: Recollections and Reflections (ed. Willi Schuh, trans. L. J. Lawrence). London: Boosey and Hawkes, 1953.

Tansman, Alexandre, *Igor Stravinsky: The Man and His Music* (trans. Thérèse and Charles Bleefield). New York: G. P. Putnam's Sons, 1949.

Lederman, Minna, *Stravinsky in the Theatre* (edited, with an introduction). New York: Pellegrini and Cudahy, 1949.

The Diaries of Tchaikovsky (trans. Wladimir Lakond). New York: W. W. Norton & Co., Inc., 1945.

d'Amico, Fidele, *Vieri Tosatti*. New York: *Musical Quarterly*, Vol. XXXIX, No. 3, pages 439-441, 1953.

Gatti, Carlo, *Verdi: The Man and His Music* (trans. Elizabeth Abbott). New York, G. P. Putnam's Sons, 1955.

Toye, Francis, *Giuseppe Verdi: His Life and Works*. New York: Alfred A. Knopf, Inc., 1946.

Verdi: The Man in His Letters (ed. Franz Werfel and Paul Stefan). New York: L. B. Fischer Publishing Corporation, 1942.

Newman, Ernest, *The Wagner Operas*. New York: Alfred A. Knopf, Inc., 1949.

—— *The Life of Richard Wagner* (four volumes). New York: Alfred A. Knopf, Inc., 1933-1946.

—— *Wagner as Man and Artist*. New York: Alfred A. Knopf, Inc., 1924.

Burch, Gladys, *Richard Wagner: The Man Who Followed a Star*. New York: Henry Holt & Co., Inc., 1941.

Lavignac, Albert, *Music Dramas of Richard Wagner*. New York: Dodd, Mead & Co., 1942.

Wagner, Richard, *My Life*. New York: Tudor Publishing Co., revised edition, 1936.

Poate Stebbins, Lucy and Richard, *Enchanted Wanderer: The Life of Carl Maria von Weber*. New York: G. P. Putnam's Sons, 1940.

III

Information on Operas and Their Plots

Annesley, Charles, *Standard Opera Glass: Plots and Critical Remarks* (rev. ed.). New York: Tudor Publishing Co., 1934.

Biancolli, Louis, ed., *The Opera Reader*. New York: McGraw Hill Book Co., Inc., 1953.

Blankopf, Kurt, "Romeo and Juliet" (Blacher). *Musical Quarterly*, Vol. XXXVII, No. 1 (1951), pp. 92-94.

Blum, Daniel, *Opera World: Seasons 1952-53, 1953-54.* New York: G. P. Putnam's Sons, 1955.

Downes, Olin, *Ten Operatic Masterpieces.* New York: Charles Scribner's Sons, 1952.

Goldovsky, Boris, and Peltz, Mary Ellis, *Accents on Opera.* New York: Farrar, Straus & Cudahy, Inc., 1953.

Gorffi, Guido M., "The Rake's Progress" (Stravinsky). *Musical Quarterly,* Vol. XXXVIII, No. 1 (1952), pp. 145-152.

Grabbe, Paul, *Minute Stories of the Opera.* New York: Grossett & Dunlap, 1932.

Helm, Everett, "Penelope" (Rolf Liebermann). *Musical Quarterly,* Vol. XLI, No. 1 (1955), pp. 89-93.

Krehbiel, Henry Edward, *A Book of Operas: Their Histories, Their Plots, and Their Music.* New York: The Macmillan Co. (reissue, 1936).

Lawrence, Robert, and Peltz, Mary Ellis, *The Metropolitan Opera Guide.* New York: Modern Library, Random House, 1939.

Lessing, Gotth. E., ed., *Handbuch des Opern-Repertoires* (Handbook to the Opera Repertoire). London: Boosey and Hawkes, 1952.

Lindlar, Heinrich, ed., *Musik der Zeit: Eine Schriftenreihe zur Zeitgenossischen Musik* (Music of our Time: A Catalogue of Contemporary Music). London: Boosey and Hawkes, 1954.

McSpadden, J. Walker, *Light Opera and Musical Comedy.* New York: Thomas Y. Crowell Co., 1936.

Newman, Ernest, *Stories of the Great Operas* (three volumes). New York: Alfred A. Knopf, Inc., 1929-31.

Operas and Ballets (Illustrated Catalogue). London: Boosey and Hawkes, 1954.

Ptak, Milos O., "Antigone" (Orff). *Musical Quarterly,* Vol. XXXVI, No. 1 (1950), pp. 106-109.

Sanborn, Pitts, *The Metropolitan Book of the Opera: Synopses of the Operas.* Garden City, N. Y.: Garden City Publishing Co., 1942.

Seltsam, William H., *Metropolitan Opera Annals: A Chronicle of Artists and Performances.* New York: H. W. Wilson Co., with The Metropolitan Opera Guild, 1947.

Thompson, Oscar, *Plots of the Operas,* as compiled for *The International Cyclopedia of Music and Musicians.* New York: Dodd, Mead & Co., 1940.

Upton, George Putnam, *The Standard Operas.* Chicago: A. C. McClurg & Co., 1928.

Upton, George Putnam, *The Standard Light Operas*. Chicago: A. C. McClurg & Co., 1902.
—— *The Standard Oratorios*. Chicago: A. C. McClurg & Co., 1909.
Weissmann, John S., "The Turn of the Screw" (Britten). *Musical Quarterly,* Vol. XII, No. 1 (1955), pp. 95–99.
Wörner, Karl H., "Moses and Aaron" (Schoenberg). *Musical Quarterly,* Vol. XI, No. 3 (1954), pp. 403–412.

IV

Miscellaneous Information on Subjects Relating to Opera

Bekker, Paul, *The Story of the Orchestra*. New York: W. W. Norton & Co., Inc., 1936.
Copland, Aaron, *Our New Music*. New York: Whittlesey House (McGraw-Hill Book Co., Inc.), 1941.
Chujoy, Anatole, *The Dance Encyclopedia* (intro. Anton Dolin, Foreword by Lincoln Kirstein). New York: A. S. Barnes & Co., 1949.
Cushing, Mary Watkins, *The Rainbow Bridge* (Story of Olive Fremstad). New York: G. P. Putnam's Sons, 1954.
Darnton, Christian, *You and Music*. Baltimore: Penguin Books, Inc., 1946. (Out of print.)
Debussy, Claude, *Monsieur Croche: The Dilettante Hater*. New York: Lear Publishers, 1948.
Einstein, Alfred, *Schubert: A Musical Portrait*. London, New York, Toronto: Oxford University Press, 1951.
Fokine, Michel, *Book of the Dance*. New York: G. P. Putnam's Sons, 1934.
Haigh, A. E., *The Attic Theatre*. Oxford: Clarendon Press, 1907.
Hale, Philip, Boston Symphony Programme Notes (ed. John N. Burk). Garden City, N. Y.: Doubleday Doran & Co., 1935.
Hanslick, Eduard, *The Beautiful in Music* (Seventh Edition). New York: Novello, Ewer & Co., 1891.
Henderson, W. J., *The Art of the Singer*. New York: Charles Scribner's Sons, 1906.
Hindemith, Paul, *A Composer's World*. Cambridge: Harvard Univ. Press, 1952.
Kirstein, Lincoln, *Ballet Alphabet*. New York: Kamin Publishers, 1939.
Leiser, Clara, *Jean de Reszke and the Great Days of Opera*. London: G. Howe, Ltd., 1933.

Marek, George R., *A Front Seat at the Opera*. New York: Allen, Towne & Heath, 1948.

Melba, Nellie, *Melodies and Memories*. New York: Geo. H. Doran, 1926.

Peyser, Ethel, *The House that Music Built*. New York: Robert M. McBride, 1936.

—— *How to Enjoy Music*. New York: G. P. Putnam's Sons, 1933.

Peyser, Herbert F., "Some Observations on Translation." *Musical Quarterly*, Vol. VIII, No. 3 (1922), pp. 358-371.

Reese, Gustave, *Music of the Middle Ages*. New York: W. W. Norton & Co., Inc., 1940.

—— *Music of the Renaissance*. New York: W. W. Norton & Co., Inc., 1940.

Index

477